£3
American
Politics
(32)

#WeToo

IN THE

WHITE HOUSE

LOVE, SCANDALS
AND POWER

NIGEL
CAWTHORNE

GIBSON SQUARE

Also by Nigel Cawthorne:

Outraged of Tunbridge Wells; Original Complaints
I Don't Believe It: Original Complaints
I Know I am Rude: Prince Philip on Prince Philip
Call me Diana, the Princess of Wales on the Princes of Wales

This edition published for the first time by Gibson Square in 2018

UK   Tel: +44 (0)20 7096 1100
US   Tel: +1 646 216 9488

     rights@gibsonsquare.com
     www.gibsonsquare.com

     ISBN 9781783341474

Printed and bound in Great Britain by Clays Ltd, Elcograf S.p.A.

Contents

I

Donald Trump, #45

You cannot rape your spouse

Donald Trump has always prided himself on being a lady-killer. As the acknowledged master of fake news and alternative facts, what does he actually mean by that?

Well, for one, big and brash and loaded with cash, it means that he was the self-advertised leading light of the Manhattan singles scene of the late twentieth century. He's had not one but three – by his own account 'trophy' – wives and numerous blonde girlfriends, often culled from his own modelling agency, as well as tried his luck with many a blonde film star and other celebrities, including Diana, Princess of Wales. He tried it on aggressively. According to at least twenty two accusers Donald knew no bounds as a 'lady-killer' and sexually harassed them by groping their crotch and kissing them. Then, of course, there is also the rich and pliable supply of blonde female sex workers.

The Donald always knew the right way to approach the women he was attracted to. According to the embarrassing *Access Hollywood* tape that came out just before the 2016 election, it was 'grab them by the pussy', in his own words. It has stuck in the imagination around the world, and Michael Wolff, author of *Fire and Fury* described Trump as 'possibly the world's most famous masher' – urban idiom for a man who makes unwelcome sexual advances, often in public places and typically to women he does not know.

The Donald started early. In second grade at Kew-Forest School in Forest Hills, he pulled Sharon Mazzarella's pigtails. She, however, did not appreciate this attack and bashed him over the head with her metal lunchbox. By way of contrast, he also said he beat up other boys and boasted that he had punched a music teacher, though none of his contemporaries remembered the incident or indeed him mentioning him taking on someone bigger than himself.

As a teenager from one of the boring New York City boroughs, Queens, Trump was eager for sex. He and a friend used to jump on the subway and make an escape for the excitement of Manhattan's Times Square, which was then full of go-go bars, sex shops, peep shows and adult theatres – not to mention streetwalkers and other hustlers. When his father found out, young Donald was sent away to the New York Military Academy. It was a boys-only establishment where inmates slept in barracks and took communal showers. He took an early beating by a drill sergeant whom he described as 'fucking prick'. You could be expelled for the possession of pornography, and nudity in the barracks was forbidden – outside the showers, presumably.

Women were not admitted to the academy for another decade. Students were allowed female visitors, but they would be punished for holding hands. But then it seems young Donald was not interested in holding hands exactly in any case. Movies were shown the chapel and wolf-whistles at Hollywood starlets invited a punishment drill. Hazing included kissing the school's donkey mascot on the ass. The only other entertainment was the all-male theatre group, so there were plenty of opportunities to dress up in drag, a precursor perhaps to his scene with his personal lawyer Rudy Giuliani in drag whose fake breasts he grabbed. Always conscious of his appearance, Donald attempted to get a tan by putting a UV bulb in the overhead light fitting in the dorm. Like Ronald Reagan, he was prematurely orange.

By the time he was a senior, Trump was showing good-looking young women around the campus.

'They were beautiful, gorgeous women, dressed out of Saks Fifth Avenue,' said one classmate.

Other cadets' dates were dismissed as 'dogs'.

It paid off. In the senior yearbook of his class, Trump was identified as a 'ladies man' and pictured with one of the academy's secretaries.

Trump was captain of the baseball team; in football, he was a tight end. He was also promoted captain of A Company, but relieved of duty after one of his sergeants caused an incident and Trump was criticised in an early incident of his laissez-faire approach to discipline. True to form Trump himself claimed that his re-assignment to a desk job was in actual fact a promotion.

All at the same time, the Vietnam war was raging far away and in the headlines. Yet, despite his military training that finished in 1964, he avoided the draft by going to college. After a series of academic deferments, he eventually secured a medical one which declared him unfit for military service as the war was reaching its climax. This was an easy option for any rich man's son and Trump's father was a millionaire property developer in Queens and Brooklyn. The family's fortune had been established by his German-born grandfather who ran brothels in the Klondike during the Gold Rush. He later returned to Germany and had to leave again after being labelled a draft dodger – an epithet his grandson he shared with his grandson.

The young Donald side-stepped the jungles of Southeast Asia for the Wharton School of Business at the University of Pennsylvania – he transferred to the school after two years at Fordham University in Manhattan.

But don't think that meant he was afraid of putting himself in the way of danger or that, in his own mind at any rate, he had been fighting an epic battle. Boasting of sleeping around during the AIDS epidemic of the 1980s, he told Howard Stern in a live interview: 'I've been so lucky in terms of that whole world. It is a dangerous world out there – it's scary, like Vietnam. Sort of like the Vietnam era. It is my personal Vietnam. I feel like a great and very brave soldier.' The Donald happily twisted around the 1960s' famous dictum – 'Make love not war'. He had apparently been a hero after all, and during his Presidential campaign he would dismiss Senator John McCain, shot down over Hanoi in 1967 and imprisoned and tortured by the Vietnamese for five-and-a-half years, as a 'non-hero'.

'Every time I saw him he had a pretty girl on his arm,' said a classmate.

The Donald even pulled a blind date with the aspiring actress and model Candice Bergen. It was not a memorable evening.

'I have no memory of it,' she told *People* magazine fifty years later. 'I just remember that he was wearing a three-piece burgundy suit, and burgundy boots and a burgundy limousine. He was very co-ordinated.' It was, she added, 'a very short evening.'

Naturally, The Donald had his own version. He told the *Boston Globe*: 'She was so beautiful. She was dating guys from Paris, France, who were thirty five years old, the whole thing. I did make the move. And I must say she had the good sense to say, "Absolutely not".'

Otherwise, The Donald said did very well at Wharton, a good college but, at that time not the leading business school it is today. It was, he said, 'the hardest school to get in… the best school. It's like super genius stuff'.

On the TV talk show *The View* in 2011, he said: 'I was a really good student at the best school. I'm like a smart guy, OK.'

Typically, some in the press pooh-poohed this. *The New York Times* questioned whether he even graduated. Nobody has seen the records.

After graduating – or not – The Donald returned to New York, where he found he was supremely qualified to go to work for his father. But he soon found that Queens no longer suited his glitzy style and moved across the East River to an apartment in Manhattan.

'One of the first things I did was join Le Club, which at the time was the hottest club in the city and perhaps the most exclusive – like Studio 54 at its height,' he said.

It was swanky, boasting as members two dukes, four barons, thirteen counts, thirteen princes and three princesses.

That is not, however, the vibe that stuck in Donald's mind. He saw his future self: 'It was the sort of place where you were likely to see a wealthy seventy-five-year-old guy walk in with three blondes from Sweden'.

Despite ostensibly having all the right credentials, when Trump applied for membership, he was blackballed. This was, he said, 'because I was young and good-looking'. He was eventually allowed to become a member if he promised not to approach married women – Le Club was, in his retelling, a no-holds barred battle ground for family values as well as deeply involved with showcasing multiple Swedish blondes with solitary elderly millionaires.

'I met a lot of beautiful young single women, and I went out almost every night,' he said. 'Actually, I never got involved with any of them very seriously.'

In fact, the blondes who circulated Le Club in search for millionaire defenders of family values proved a disappointment. 'These were beautiful women, but many of them couldn't carry on a normal conversation. Some were vain, some were crazy, some were wild, and many of them were phonies.' How would he be able to find his match in such an environment?

'Good looks had been my top – and sometimes, to be honest, my only – priority in my man-about-town days,' he said.

In truth, he wasn't an unmitigated success with these women either. They had a very precise idea of what they wanted.

It boiled down to the fact that his Queens bling failed to dent the morals of Manhattan girls. 'I quickly found out that I couldn't take these girls back to my apartment,' he said, 'because by their standards, what I had was a disaster, and in their world appearances were everything.'

These girls were so superficial and not for him. It would be some years before they could enjoy ostentatious splendour of Trump Tower, nonetheless. Meanwhile, he no longer aimed at these dull club bimbos. He shimmied up the social ladder and adjusted his sights to women who had places of their own.

'Often times when I was sleeping with one of the top women in the world I would say to myself, thinking about me as a boy from Queens, "Can you believe what I am getting"?' he said fluffing himself.

He also declared war on his former image and started attending glitzy parties accompanied by glamorous women. These he got by calling modelling agencies and asking for help to fill out the guest list. He also became a regular at fashion shows to get photographed alongside supermodels. For years, he would finesse his self-publicity campaign and call columnists to ask them to rate his latest piece of arm candy on a scale of one to ten.

In his 1990 book *Trump: Surviving at the Top*, Donald recalled his relationship with celebrity hotelier, the 'Queen of Mean' Leona Helmsley, who was jailed in 1989 for tax evasion after boasting to her housekeeper: 'We don't pay taxes; only little people pay taxes.'

Leona took up the dashing young Donald when he was just starting out in the real estate business, while her husband – worth $6 billion and owner of the Empire State Building – was already in his mid-sixties.

The Donald could not understand her infatuation with him as he was not tremendously successful at that time. But Leona always liked having him around. At the 'I'm Just Wild About Harry' parties she gave for her husband, Donald was always given a great seat, usually right next her, and, he said: 'She went around telling everybody that "this young man will be the next Harry Helmsley", that I was the smartest of the smart, and that there was nobody to compete with me. I was very flattered.'

His and Leona's was not a match made in heaven, however. Donald found himself on the wrong end of a jealous outburst when he turned up at one of her parties with 'a young and very attractive fashion model' as his date.

'As soon as Leona saw who was with me, she became incensed. "How dare you bring that tramp to one of my parties?" she screamed, looking the girl directly in the eyes....'

The next day, she called him at his office and said, 'you [expletive] son-of-a-bitch. I watched you politicking the room and all of my guests in order to get your convention centre passed.'

Once again Donald had completely misunderstood what a woman wanted him to do. 'She also asked that I not bring to her parties "pretty girls" that would make other women in the room look bad.'

He was not best pleased with Leona Helmsley tough words. 'The real estate business, especially in New York, is full of bullies,' he said knowingly.

The publicity war was won though. By 1976, *The New York Times* were smitten with Trump: 'He is tall, lean and blond, with dazzling white teeth, and he looks ever so much like Robert Redford. He rides around town in a chauffeured silver Cadillac with his initials, DJT [Donald John Trump], on the plates. He dates slinky fashion models, belongs to the most elegant clubs and, at only thirty years of age, estimates that he is worth "more than $200 million".' That figure was called into question, though DJT stoutly defended it – more on this below.

Trump's first major real estate deal in Manhattan was the redevelopment the rundown Commodore Hotel on forty-second Street and Lexington Avenue next to Grand Central Station, transforming it into the Grand Hyatt New York. When he took over, the ground floor was occupied by dingy storefronts, one of which was a massage parlour called Relaxation Plus.

'But nobody ever got into what the Plus meant,' said Trump – except of course he himself as he is 'super smart'. He referred to the establishment coyly as a 'spa'.

Finally his long campaign in the battle of the sexes paid off. Trump could put a picture of a trophy girlfriend on his desk. This was Ivana Winklmayr. Trump said that he had met her in 1972 when she had been part of the Czech Olympic ski team in Sapporo, Japan. However, when *Spy* magazine contacted the secretary general of the Czech Olympic Committee, they said: 'Who is this Ivana woman, and why do people keep calling us about her? We have searched so many times and have consulted many, many people, and there is no such girl in our records.'

Born in Moravia in 1949, Ivana Marie Zelníčková was two-and-half years Donald's junior. In 1971, she married sky instructor Alfred Winklmayr. They divorced two years later. Curiously, this marriage has been expunged from the official narrative and the divorce was overlooked in her 1995 memoir on that very subject *The Best Is Yet to Come: Coping With Divorce and Enjoying Life Again.*

She emigrated to Canada, living in Montreal with an old boyfriend named George Syrovatka who was running a ski shop there. Ivana then bleached her brown hair, piled on the make-up and became a model. Then in the summer of 1976, a modelling assignment took her to New York.

Ivana and three other Montreal models were on line for a table at Maxwell's Plum, a restaurant and bar which *The New York Times* called 'a favorite watering hole for the 'swinging singles' set'. There was a tap on the shoulder by a businessman who introduced himself as 'Donald' and said he was a friend of the owner. He used his pull to get them a table, then invited himself to join them.

Naturally he picked up the tab. Afterwards he drove them to the Americana Hotel where they were staying and got their phone numbers. The next day Ivana was sent three-dozen red roses.

When she returned to Montreal, Donald began phoning, sometimes several times a day. Then when she was doing a catwalk show at the Ritz-Carlton, he flew up to Canada, said hello, then flew straight back to New York.

'Why does he do these things?' she asked.

He told everyone that she was 'one of the top models in Canada', of course. Nothing less would do. 'She was also the "greatest skier in the world".'

'Have you ever seen anybody that's so beautiful and so smart?' he crowed. She could speak French, Czech and Russian – and her English was coming along.

It was Ivana who dubbed him The Donald. 'As most people know, English isn't my first language, in fact it's my fourth,' she told the *Washington Post* in 2015. 'When I came to live in New York, I really had to learn the language from the beginning almost. Some things come easily, some things don't. And for whatever reason, probably because I was going at my usual turbo speed, I started putting "The" in front of most people's names. Yes, you know the outcome – "The Donald" just slipped off the tongue, and now it seems to be making its ways to the political history books.'

He complained, but said he had 'no choice' but to accept the nickname. In fact, 'I don't mind that it stuck,' he said. 'I think it's an endearment.'

Soon he started using it to his own ends. The opening sentence of his 1997 book *The Art of the Comeback* read: 'It's usually fun being "The Donald".'

However, in the article in *Spy* magazine in 1989 that first made reference to her habit of putting 'the' in front of people's names, Ivana actually called her husband 'The Don' – more like *The Godfather*.

When he first met Ivana, Trump told anyone who would listen: 'I found the combination of beauty and brains almost unbelievable. Like a lot of men, I had been taught by Hollywood that one woman couldn't have both.'

Ivana was initially not overly impressed with The Donald. She said he was 'just a nice all-American kid, tall and smart, lots of energy: very bright and very good-looking'. And she was not after him for his fame and money. Like the girls in Le Club, she was not deceived – he 'wasn't famous' and he 'wasn't fabulously wealthy'.

Although Ivana told Trump that she was living with her boyfriend and they planned to get married, Donald pestered her for a date. Eventually, she agreed to fly down to New York. He'd pay the fare. Then began a whirlwind affair where The Donald even hired her a bodyguard.

Addressing her as 'Sweetie Pie', he wrote a letter begging her to move to New York and live with him.

'I love you. I want to be with you. I think you are fabulous,' he wrote. Promising that she would never regret her decision, he went on to promise: 'I will always love and protect you.'

At the age of thirty, Trump was ready to put down roots and envisioned a marriage like that of his parents.

'For a man to be successful, he needs support at home, just like my father and mother, not someone who's griping and bitching,' he said. And Ivana, like his Scottish mother, was an immigrant. But a husband can of course do the griping and bitching himself. In September 2015, he tweeted: 'My grandparents didn't come to America all the way from Germany to see it get taken over by immigrants.' By then, he had been sacked from *The Apprentice* 'due to the recent derogatory statements by Donald Trump regarding immigrants'.

After he took Ivana to meet his folks in Queens, she invited him to Montreal to meet her boyfriend. As it was, they got on quite well, under the circumstances.

Undaunted, The Donald continued pursue his quarry with the zeal he employed in his business deals. One of his tried and tested tactics was to inflate his worth. While telling *The New York Times* he was worth 'more than $200 million', his tax return showed an income of just $24,594 that year, though there were also payments from family trusts and other assets. Two years later he made a thumping loss of over $3.4 million.

Possibly penniless, Trump nonetheless told Ivana's friend and fellow model Yolande Cardinal: 'I'm never going to marry a girl from New York. They're only after money.'

He bearded Ivana again during a Christmas skiing trip to Aspen. Although she bested him on the slopes, on New Year's Eve he presented her with a three-carat diamond ring from Tiffany's and asked her to marry him. Then he set Rottweiler attorney Roy Cohn – who had sent Julius and Ethel Rosenberg to the electric chair and worked as Senator Joe McCarthy's chief counsel during his anti-Communist 'witch hunts', as well as represented Mafiosi Tony Salerno, Carmine Galante and John Gotti – to drawing up ever more stringent prenups.

Meanwhile Ivana's Canadian beau George Syrovatka also popped the question. To escape her two suitors, Ivana flew off on a modelling assignment in Tahiti where she could not be reached by phone. The Donald resorted to sending telegrams insisting that she return. Ivana did not reply. Eventually, after she had returned to Montreal in February, she agreed to become the first Mrs Trump, leaving Syrovatka suicidal.

With the wedding set for April 1977, Ivana was provided with a lawyer recommended by Roy Cohn, but at the last minute she balked at a prenup clause demanding the return of any clothes and gifts in the event of a divorce. She and Donald also argued over money. Ivana insisted on a $100,000 'rainy day' fund if things did not work out. After all she was giving up her modelling career and moving to New York.

After they had kissed and made up their lover's financial tiff, Donald took her to the opening of Studio 54. It left Le Club in the dust. He saw 'things happening there that to this day I have never seen again. I would watch supermodels getting screwed… well-known supermodels getting screwed on a bench in the middle of the room. There were seven of them and each one was getting screwed by a different guy. This was in the middle of the room.' He instantly became a Studio 54 regular.

The wedding at the Marble Collegiate Church on Fifth avenue was conducted by the Trump family cleric, the Reverend Dr Norman Vincent Peale, author of the motivational bestseller *The Art of Positive Thinking*. The reception was at the 21 Club, whose floorshow was more restrained than Studio 54, and the honeymoon was in Acapulco. He said he wanted to have five children, as his parents had, so he could be sure that 'at least one of them will turn out to be like me'. Ivana said she wanted to stop after two or three, increasing the odds that one of them wouldn't.

They holidayed that summer in the Hamptons on Long Island. The couple who rented them the cottage spotted them kissing on the dunes and noted: 'They're so in love.'

Back in New York, the pregnant Ivana was left alone in a Spartan two-bedroom apartment while Trump went out hustling and socializing. The flat had a prestigious address though. It was in Olympic Tower, which had been developed by shipping magnate Aristotle Onassis and was home to billionaire Saudi arms dealer Adnan Khashoggi. Soon after Donald J. Trump Jr was born that December, Donald and Ivana moved to an eight-bedroom apartment at 800 Fifth Avenue.

As well as attending to child-rearing, Ivana was made vice president overseeing interior design at the Commodore Hotel.

Rich men did not hire their wives for such tasks at the time. But executive vice president of The Trump Organization Louise Sunshine was not surprised, insisting that Ivana and Donald were cut from the same cloth. They could have 'come from the same sperm,' she observed diplomatically. (The workers then decorated the building site with crude nude drawings of Ivana and assistant project manager Barbara Res, who The Donald dubbed 'Donna Trump'.)

With the transformation of the Commodore Hotel into the Grand Hyatt complete, The Donald bought the old Bonwit Teller department store on Fifth Avenue, tearing it down to build Trump Tower on the site. The art deco storefront boasted two fifteen-foot-tall, bas-relief near-naked goddesses dancing high above the sidewalk. Penelope Hunter-Stiebel, curator of the Metropolitan Museum of Art, rushed downtown to save them, but a workman wielding a jackhammer said: 'Young Donald said there's a stupid woman uptown at a museum who wants them and we have to destroy them.'

When *The New York Times* complained about this vandalism, a spokesman for The Trump Organisation calling himself John Barron phoned to explained that they were 'without artistic merit'. John Barron turned out to be Trump himself. Later concerning an action over the employment of illegal immigrants from Poland on the project, he used the pseudonym again. Admitting as much to a reporter, he offered the comeback: 'Lots of people use pen names. Ernest Hemingway used one.'

Women were always part of his narrow escapes. In 1982, strikes halted developments across the city, but work on Trump Tower continued after Donald assigned three large duplexes on the sixty-fourth and sixty-fifth floors to Verina Hixon, the girlfriend of Teamsters' union boss John Cody. The House Subcommittee on Criminal Justice called attention to another aspect of Cody and christened him 'the most significant labour racketeer preying on the construction industry in New York'.

Hixon insisted on having an indoor swimming pool, the only one in the building. For six months she had between thirty and fifty workmen at work on her apartment alone, installing mirrors, closets and a sauna. Every time Trump cavilled, Hixon called Cody and deliveries of building materials stopped until she got her way.

However, when mobster Cody was jailed for racketeering, Trump dropped the charm and took Hixon to court for non-payment of maintenance charges. She had also defaulted on a $3-million loan and explained that she had never worked and only had $2 in the bank. She was supported, she said, by her ex-husband's alimony payments. When she went bankrupt, her apartment was seized.

Subpoenaed by federal investigators in 1980, Trump flatly denied giving Hixon the apartment to facilitate the completion of Trump Tower. Nevertheless, Cody said he knew Trump quite well, though Donald liked to keep him at arm's length by dealing with him through Roy Cohn. Cody pulled a second sentence for plotting to assassinate his successor in the union. After he died in 2001, Donald called him 'one psychopathic crazy bastard' and 'real scum' – clearly not something you would say of a Mafia boss when they were still alive.

In Trump Tower, The Donald retained a $10-million fifty-room apartment on the sixty-sixth, sixty-seventh and sixty-eighth floors. The building only had fifty-eight floors, but he skipped some floor numbers to give occupants of the upper floors – including, presumably, himself – a psychological boost by making the erection seem taller than it was. Also Trump took no chances. As the building went up, he asked the architect to plan a second apartment in case his marriage broke up.

Following the building's opening in November 1983, Trump was given a profile in *GQ*, which first drew attention to the size of his hands, saying they were 'small and neatly groomed'. Soon *Spy* magazine echoed the cry, calling Trump a 'short-fingered vulgarian'.

When the Trump issue of *GQ* sold well, The Donald was persuaded to write his first book. This was *Trump: The Art of the Deal* and largely ghosted by Tony Schwartz. Publicity for its publication involved handing out 'I ☉ DONALD TRUMP' bumper stickers. Trump also sent a copy of the book to *Spy* with the fingers on his picture on the front cover ringed with gold marker. After *Spy* folded, co-founder Graydon Carter, who went on to edit *Vanity Fair*, continued to receive pictures of Trump torn from magazines and newspapers with the fingers circled in gold. In April 2015, Trump attached a note saying: 'See, not so short!' Carter replied: 'Actually, quite short.'

In 1984, Cohn was diagnosed with AIDS. He had long hidden his homosexuality, even instigating the 1950s' 'lavender scare' where he and Joe McCarthy extended their 'red scare' witch-hunt to homosexuals. Before Cohn died, Donald blithely let the cat out of the bag.

In *Trump: The Art of the Deal*, he said of his mentor: '... all Roy's friends knew he was gay, and if you saw him socially, he was invariably with some good-looking young man. But Roy never talked about it. He just didn't like the image. He felt that, to the average person, being gay was almost synonymous with being a wimp. That was the last thing he wanted to project, so he almost went overboard to avoid it. If the subject of gay rights came up, Roy was always the first one to speak out against them.'

The dying Cohn said: 'I can't believe he is doing this to me. Donald pisses ice-water.' Cohn died penniless in 1986, denying to the very end that he had AIDS.

Around this time, Ivana was beginning to discover Trump's cold side too. After renovating the Wollman Rink in Central Park, rumours circulated that he was having an affair with shapely brunette figure-skater Peggy Fleming.

Trump decided to save their marriage and proposed magnanimously to Ivana that they have an 'open marriage'. Ivana responded with what she felt was the best way of dealing with it and said, 'If I ever catch you being unfaithful, I'll kill you'. Donald heard Ivana and soon despatched her to manage the renovation of the Trump Castle Hotel Casino in Atlantic City, where she would be out of the way.

In his next book *Trump: Surviving at the Top*, published in the year of his bitter divorce from Ivana, Donald now outed married father-of-two Malcolm Forbes as gay, after *Forbes* magazine ousted him from its' famous rich list, the Forbes 400, by slashing Trump's estimated worth from $1.7 billion to $500 million. According to Donald, the reason for Forbes' attack was 'yacht envy'. The Trump Princess measured 282 feet, while Forbes' boat was a relatively paltry 150 feet. Also there was an incident at the Oak Room Bar in Trump's Plaza Hotel when Forbes' two underage male guests were refused a seat by the management. Donald told *Vanity Fair*: 'You know the story about me and Malcolm Forbes, when I kicked him out of the Plaza hotel? No? Well, I did. You'll read all about it in my new book.'

Later, in 2009, the emails between The Donald and porn star Stormy Daniels where she revealed that her sex play included an unusual act – spanking him with a copy of *Forbes* magazine added a new dimension to their spat.

In an effort to buff up his tarnished image as a billionaire, Trump bought the Palm Beach estate Mar-a-Lago in Florida, which was so opulent that the U.S. National Park Service could not afford to maintain it. He turned it into a private club. Many of the guests at pool parties there were models from Miami and Trump insisted on a sex ratio of at least three women to every two men, or close to what he had seen at Le Club all those years ago was the appropriate number for over-aged millionaires.

On special occasions though, that ratio soared even higher. 'There's a hundred beautiful women and ten guys,' said veteran adviser Roger Stone. 'How cool are we?'

More pictures of Trump with beauties resulted from his visit to Hugh Hefner's *Playboy* mansion. Naturally, Donald himself went out with a Playmate or two. One was Anna Nicole Smith, Playmate of the Year 1993.

'I saw Anna Nicole Smith the first day or week that she was in New York,' said Trump. 'She was six feet tall, she had the best body, she had the best face. She had the best hair I've ever seen. Hair is my thing. I'm really into hair, OK? [We got that Donald] And she had the most beautiful. Now, when she opened her mouth, it was different. Let's face it.'

They were frequently seen out together. The twenty-six-year-old Smith found fame when she married eighty-nine-year-old billionaire oil tycoon J. Howard Marshall, who she had met while performing at a strip club in Houston. He died after a year of marriage.

There was also Donald's venture into the world of beauty pageants. This was a natural move as Atlantic City, where he was busy building hotels and casinos, was home to the first Miss America contest in 1921. He began by investing in the American Dream Calendar Girl Model Search contest in 1992.

The Donald was perfectly forthright about why he went into the beauty pageant business after a series of casino and hotel bankruptcies in the early 1990s.

'I was a great genius in the eighties,' he told the Associated Press in 1999. 'Then I was a great moron in the early nineties. That's probably why I bought this pageant – so I could get a date. Now they call me a genius again. It's great.'

The pageant was owned by George Houraney and Jill Harth. At their first meeting, Trump allegedly asked Houraney: 'Are you sleeping with her?' The couple pointed out that they were married.

But Trump was soon introducing Harth as his 'new girlfriend'. According to Harth, Trump banned black women from the contest, as well as from his pool parties at Mar-a-Lago.

The following year, Harth and he were at Mar-a-Largo. 'When we got to the dinner table,' Harth said, 'Donald started right in on groping under the table.'

Later he took her to a bedroom belonging to his eleven-year-old daughter Ivanka. According to Harth's attorney Lisa Bloom: 'He forced her into this private bedroom – a children's bedroom – closed the door, and forced her up against the wall. He was much bigger and stronger than she was. She said he reached his hand up her skirt and touched her private parts and she said, 'Stop it, stop it,' and pushed him off of her and ran off.'

Trump denied this ever happened, telling the *National Enquirer* owned by his friend and billionaire fixer David Pecker: 'The truth is that Jill Harth is obsessed with ME – and would do everything she could do to get into my pants! Her claims are extortion, pure and simple.'

After the 1993 American Dream Calendar Girl Model Search contest at Trump Castle in Atlantic City, the couple sued for breach of contract. Harth also made a sworn deposition concerning sexual harassment. In 1997, Trump settled the breach-of-contract suit for an undisclosed sum and the sexual-harassment case was dropped. By then Trump had bought controlling shares in Miss Universe, Miss U.S.A and Miss Teen U.S.A.

Trump was swift to pay attention to the finer details. 'When I bought [Miss Universe], the bathing suits got smaller,' Trump told *Vanity Fair*, 'the heels got higher and the ratings went up.'

What was also lacking in the organisation was the control that the military academy had instilled in him.

'Donald Trump walked out with his entourage and inspected us closer than any general ever inspected a platoon,' said one contest, 'it was as though we had been stripped bare.'

Miss Arizona Tasha Dixon told Los Angeles' CBS affiliate in 2016 that Trump entered the Miss U.S.A dressing room in 2001 when she was a contestant.

'He just came strolling right in,' Dixon said. 'There was no second to put a robe on or any sort of clothing or anything. Some girls were topless. Other girls were naked. Our first introduction to him was when we were at the dress rehearsal and half-naked changing into our bikinis.'

The contestants were soon in no doubt on which side their

bread was buttered. Dixon said that employees of the Miss Universe Organization encouraged the contestants to lavish attention on Trump when he came in.

'To have the owner come waltzing in, when we're naked, or half-naked, in a very physically vulnerable position and then to have the pressure of the people that worked for him telling us to go fawn all over him, go walk up to him, talk to him, get his attention,' she said.

Trump proudly admitted his intentions – indeed boasted about them – live on the Howard Stern Show.

'I'll go backstage before a show, and everyone's getting dressed and ready and everything else,' he said. 'I'm allowed to go in because I'm the owner of the pageant. And therefore I'm inspecting it… Is everyone OK? You know, they're standing there with no clothes. And you see these incredible-looking women. And so I sort of get away with things like that.'

He is aware that women think it is wrong. In 2001, he told a Women's Chamber of Commerce at this Mar-a-Lago estate in Palm Beach, Florida: 'I love looking at the models…. Isn't that disgusting? The women here are going to walk out saying, "Isn't that guy a terrible, terrible barbarian?"'

Even the Miss Teen U.S.A changing rooms, where there were girls as young as fifteen getting undressed, were not sacrosanct, Miss Teen Vermont 1997 told BuzzFeed.

The women in Trump's daily life, however, did not question this behaviour rather seemed to endorse it. Trump's daughter Ivanka hosted Miss Teen U.S.A one year. Second wife Marla Maples co-hosted Miss U.S.A and Miss Universe and third wife Melania was a judge at Miss U.S.A. As a spin-off from his beauty pageants, Trump opened a modelling agency, which gave him more access to arm candy – and women to step out with.

The Donald was a regular guest on the Howard Stern Show. As part of their locker-room banter, they would discuss which celebrity woman – from Cindy Crawford to Princess Diana – they would consider sleeping with.

Diana's rating was 'without hesitation', though Donald added the caveat: 'She was crazy, but these are minor details. She had the height, she had the beauty, she had the skin.'

After Diana split from Prince Charles in 1992, Trump didn't let a moment go to waste and bombarded her with flowers. In November 1997, three months after Princess Diana had died, NBC's Stone Phillips asked him: 'Do you think you would have seriously had a shot?'

'I think so, yeah,' Trump replied. 'I always have a shot.'

Age was no object. In 2003, he told Stern 'I've known Paris Hilton from the time she's twelve. Her parents are friends of mine, and, you know, the first time I saw her, she walked into the room and I said, "Who the hell is that?" ... Well, at twelve, I wasn't interested. I've never been into that. They're sort of always stuck around that twenty-five category.'

Trump and Stern were also appallingly rude about those women they did not fancy. Passing judgement on Kim Kardashian, The Donald said: 'Does she have a fat ass? Absolutely. Her boob job is terrible. They look like two light posts coming out of a body.'

Trump claimed to have known Kardashian for years and has met her husband Kanye West.

After meeting Melania Knauss, who would become the third Mrs. Trump, he called into the show to talk warmly about Melania to everyone listening to the show and say: 'We have incredible sex once a day, sometimes even more.' He went on to praise how hot Melania was in a 'very small thong'. Some years later, Stern asked the seventy-year-old Trump if he would stay with Melania if she was maimed and disfigured in an accident.

'How do the breasts look?' asked Trump.

Stern said they were okay.

'That's important,' said Trump, who appeared to have evolved from hair.

The distance between Trump and the world of soft porn and paid-for encounters remained paper thin. *Playgirl* named him one of the ten sexiest men in America in 1987. Readers also got a chance to sleep with him with the magazine running competition for a Donald Trump pillowcase (presumably one that Ivana, still married to him at that time, had not touched). It was apparently '[t]he contest that puts you in bed with the man of your dreams.'

He also appeared on the cover of *Playboy* magazine in March 1990, the year at the end of which he would divorce Ivana, with a cover girl dressed only in the jacket of his tuxedo, rubbing her naked backside on the front of his trousers while he plugged his hands deep into his pockets. And he made a celebrity appearance in the magazine's soft-porn video *Playboy Video Centerfold 2000*, which featured busty beauties bursting out of their bikinis, nude nubiles smearing themselves with honey and showering under a garden hose, and The Donald surrounded by a bevy of would-be Playmates – he is popping his champagne cork and pouring the spume over the *Playboy* logo in a way that it would be hard to misinterpret.

In the interview inside the magazine, he was asked: 'What is marriage to you? Is it monogamous?' His answer, 'I don't have to answer that.'

While declining to talk about his relationship with his wife, he admitted to enjoying 'flirtations'. The Trump marriage was already in trouble and Donald was again pushing for an open relationship. In front of Ivana at a concert at the Trump Plaza in Atlantic City, Trump asked Robert Libutti, a high-rolling horse dealer with links to John Gotti: 'Hey, Bob, do you play around on your wife?'

'I'm not married any more,' said the bald and portly Libutti. 'If I was, I probably wouldn't play around. Look at me. Any young girls that would go after me would just be after my money.'

Trump blanked the answer.

'But how about when you were married?' Donald persisted. 'Did you play around?'

'Sure, I guess I did some,' said Libutti.

'You see,' said Trump to Ivana with a huge grin. 'Every married man plays around on his wife.'

Ivana did not return his smile.

Perhaps by way of appreciation for Libutti's candour, Donald then tried to get the New Jersey mobster's thirty-something daughter into bed, plying her with expensive gifts. When Libutti found out, he said: 'Donald, I'll fucking pull your balls from your legs.' It was this threat that made Donald move his sights on to someone else according to David Cay Johnston's books *The Making of Donald Trump,*.

At the time, Donald and Ivana had not had sex for some sixteen months. The last time had been on a trip to London, which had been a thank-you present to having agreed to leave her post as president of the Trump Castle Hotel and Casino in Atlantic City to oversee the renovation of the Plaza Hotel in Manhattan.

Donald told the press about his gratitude: 'I pay her a salary of one dollar a year and all the dresses she can buy.'

That Christmas he gave her a $1-million ring, saying: 'This is for all the shit you've had to put up with.'

To friends Ivana, while grateful, confided that, while Donald could erect a tall building, he had trouble elsewhere. According Harry Hurt III's 1993 biography *Lost Tycoon: The Many Lives of Donald J Trump*: 'Donald had difficulty achieving and maintaining an erection.'

Ivana complained: 'He's only interested in the oral sex.' There was little in this for her. One day Ivana turned up to a ladies-who-lunch lunch at swanky East Side restaurant Le Cirque carrying a copy of *The G Spot And Other Recent Discoveries About Human Sexuality* by Alice Kahn Ladas, a sex manual about the Gräfenberg Spot and how its manipulation can result in orgasm. 'I have to give this to The Donald,' she told her companions. 'He can never find the spot.'

In frustration, Ivana asked for a revision in the prenuptial agreement, upping the amount of money she got in the event of a separator or divorce. This provoked another spat with Roy Cohn.

While Trump's name was being linked to those of movie stars, he vehemently protested his innocence and Ivana even discounted the evidence of her own eyes. One night when he was supposed to be watching an ice-hockey match at Madison Square Gardens with male friends, she switched on the sports channel to see her husband in the audience with a Hollywood starlet. Indeed, he even got a walk-on part opposite legendary beauty Bo Derek in the movie *Ghosts Can't Do It*. Ten years later Trump played himself in an episode of *Sex in the City* entitled 'The Man, the Myth, the Viagra.' He played himself again in a film for the annual Inner-Circle Press Roast put on by reporters at New York City Hall. A clip features then-mayor Rudy Giuliani in drag and their sketch culminates with Donald nuzzling Giuliani's (false) breasts.

'Oh, you dirty boy – Donald. I thought you were a gentleman,' said Giuliani, slapping him.

'You can't say I didn't try,' Donald replied.

The lunge for the mayor's breasts was apparently unscripted.

Despite the rumours that Trump was cheating on her, Ivana refused to believe it, putting his sexual dysfunction down to the 'male menopause'. He insisted that there was nothing wrong. A few years later, he told *Playboy*: 'I've always said, 'If you need Viagra, you're probably with the wrong girl.''

Some of the rumours were planted by Trump himself, using, in pre-Twitter days, his favourite method of unattributed briefings to the press. During a wrangle with business rival Leonard Stern, Donald leaked to the *Daily News* that Stern's wife Alison, a former model and TV producer, kept calling his office, asking for a date. When Stern threatened to sue, Trump persisted.

'She called,' he said. 'I wasn't interested.'

As for his marriage, according to Trump, his lack of sexual interest in Ivana was not his fault but hers.

'Your tits are too small… You're too skinny,' he told her repeatedly.

But when she went to a plastic surgeon and had boob-job done, he complained: 'I can't stand to touch those plastic breasts.'

According to Ivana, Donald had a bit of tidying up too. Dr Steven Hoefflin, the plastic surgeon who had transformed her into a Brigitte Bardot lookalike, performed liposuction on Trump's belly and chin. He then had to sleep in a corset to slim down his waist.

King of the comb-over, Trump was also terrified of going bald.

'The worst thing a man can do is go bald,' he told one of his top executives. 'Never let yourself go bald.'

But Donald himself was developing a bald spot. Dr Hoefflin performed scalp reducing on him. This involved simply cutting out the bald area, then sewing together the hair-bearing skin around it and pulling it tightly back together. The resulting pain set off one of Trump's famous temper tantrums.

'Your fucking doctor has ruined me,' he yelled at Ivana.

According to Harry Hurt's *Lost Tycoon* (1993), Trump then threw her down on the bed and began ripping her hair out. He tore off her clothes and raped her. Afterwards, she fled to another bedroom, crying. In the morning he asked her 'with menacing casualness: "Does it hurt"?'

Trump has denied both the suggestion that he had scalp reduction, and also the rape allegation. But Hurt said that the incident was confirmed by two of Ivana's friends and appeared in her divorce deposition. 'It was,' he pointed out, 'sworn testimony.'

On the eve of publication, Trump's lawyers pressured Hurt's publishers into pasting a statement by Ivana into the flyleaf of every copy of the book. In it, she confirmed that in her deposition she had stated that her husband had 'raped' her, but added that she did not want those words to be interpreted in 'a literal or criminal sense'. She also said: 'As a woman, I felt violated.'

Again Trump denied that the rape or the scalp reduction had ever happened. A spokesman called the allegation 'a standard lawyer technique, which was used to exploit more money from Mr Trump, especially since he had an ironclad prenuptial agreement'. Indeed, in her divorce settlement, Ivana reportedly received $14 million dollars in cash.

One secret of the Trump bedroom that Ivana did not walk back from was that Trump kept Adolf Hitler's speeches in a cabinet by the bed. Donald claimed that his friend Martin Davis, head of Paramount, gave him a copy, not of *My New Order* – the collected speeches of Hitler from 1918 to 1939 – but of *Mein Kampf* – 'and he's a Jew.' Davis insisted that it was *My New Order* and he was not Jewish.

'If I had these speeches, and I am not saying that I do, I would never read them,' Trump told *Vanity Fair* in 1990.

During the divorce, Trump was deposed too. The New Jersey Division of Gaming Enforcement examined the divorce records while investigating whether he was a fit person to hold a gaming licence. According to their report, Trump invoked his Fifth Amendment right against self-incrimination around a hundred times when Ivana's lawyers questioned him about adultery.

The marriage was finally blown apart when a photograph of blonde beauty queen and aspiring actress Marla Maples was sent to the *New York Post* with a note saying she was dating a prominent businessman who was married. *The Post*'s Page Six gossip column reported that this 'shapely blonde supposedly goes around the stores in Trump Tower saying, "Charge it to Donald".'

A lunch companion at Le Cirque mentioned the story to Ivana. She stormed out, vowing never to speak to the woman again. Then at a fancy party, *Post* gossip columnist Cindy Adams asked: 'I understand that you and Donald are having problems.'

Ivana was indignant.

'Absolutely not!' she screeched. 'Donald and I are happily married. Where did you hear such a thing?'

Again she fled, vowing never to speak to Adams again. However, *The Post* kept the lid on the story as editor Peter Kalikow's wife was a close friend of Ivana's. At the time, Donald himself was giving matrimonial advice to Mike Tyson who was about to divorce actress Robin Givens. When Tyson was convicted of raping eighteen-year-old beautify queen Desiree Washington, Trump was the first person he called.

Marla Maples had met Trump through her ex-lover Tom Fitzsimmons, a former New York City cop and struggling screenwriter who known Donald from the singles-bars scene back in the 1970s. Donald kept telling Tom that, with Marla, he was having the best sex he had ever had. Meanwhile Marla returned the compliment and said that Donald was a real animal in bed. But, curiously, she had never – or almost never – seen Trump naked, according to *Lost Tycoon*. When the time came to undress, he would send her into bathroom while he quickly stripped off and dived under the covers. He was, apparently, ashamed of his old and unsightly body, but his reticence made him seem all the more cute and cuddly to her.

Marla was safely ensconced in the Trump Castle in Atlantic City, now that Ivana was back in Manhattan. Even so Marla was sometimes seen at Trump events – even when Ivana was present – accompanied by Fitzsimmons or another walker. After doing the rounds of Trump properties, Marla was eventually secreted in the Hotel St Moritz just three blocks from the family triplex in Trump Tower.

Just after Christmas in 1989, Trump flew out to Aspen, Colorado with Marla and her friend Kim Knapp. Ivana was already there, but Donald knew that she enjoyed the après ski so much that she could not be coming to meet him at the airport. Marla and Kim were taken to a two-bedroom condominium Donald had rented, while The Donald himself went to Little Nell's, the luxury hotel he was staying at with Ivana.

The following day, the real estate agent phoned Trump at his suite and says: 'That Marla sure is a piece of ass.' Unfortunately, Ivana had picked up the extension in the bedroom. She misheard 'Marla' and insisted on knowing who this 'Moolah' was. Donald said that she was a woman who had been chasing him for the two years, but there was nothing between them.

Ivana's suspicions were not allayed and she began asking around. At lunchtime in a restaurant on the slopes, Ivana spotted Kim, who she had been told was a friend of Moolah's.

'I hear you have a best friend named Moolah who has been chasing my husband for two years,' Ivana said.

'I don't know anyone named Moolah,' Kim replied.

Donald then spotted Marla. Ivana followed the direction of his eyes and moved in for the kill.

'Are you Moolah?' she asked. 'Why don't you leave my husband alone?'

'I love your husband. Do you?' asked Marla.

'Stay away from my husband,' was Ivana's only answer.

Marla and Kim then made their escape. Donald tried to flee, too, but on the ski slopes he was no match for Ivana who quickly caught him up.

Trump accused Ivana of overreacting, but the row dragged on into the evening with Donald insisting that he was not in love with 'Moolah' and agreed to call her and break it off – not that there was anything to break off, he protested.

That night the Trumps were having dinner with publicist Eleanor Lambert who was shocked when, again in front of Ivana, Donald asked about a young woman who had joined them at their table with her date, saying: 'Is her figure as good as it looks?'

That night, though, Trump made love to his wife for the first time since the alleged rape nearly two months before. When it was over, he said curtly: 'Now you can't say that we didn't have sex.'

Back in New York, Ivana consulted attorney Michael Kennedy, but Donald kept hedging when asked whether he was in love with Marla Maples. Once more he raised the question of having an open marriage.

'You're trying to have it both ways,' said Ivana, who decided that they ought to see a therapist.

Donald insisted that there was nothing wrong with him, but agreed to go 'if you think it will fix what's wrong with you'. After one session, Donald quit, refusing to continue the therapy.

Liz Smith, a gossip columnist for the *New York Daily News*, had also heard the rumours about the Trumps' troubled marriage. But she, too, was a friend of the Trumps. At parties, Donald would always hug her and say: 'She's the greatest.' Trump would change these words, however, and say: 'Liz Smith… used to kiss my ass so much it was downright embarrassing.'

This happened after she called him in early 1990 and told him that the story of him cheating on Ivana was doing the rounds and, if he gave her an exclusive, she promised to go easy on him. Trump declined. However, Ivana was keen. When Donald was in Japan, she invited Smith over and told her about the affair.

The story broke on the front page of the *Daily News* on Sunday 11 February 1990 under the headline 'LOVE ON THE ROCKS.' It continued: 'Ivana Trump is devastated "that Donald was betraying her." Page 3 Exclusive.' News that Nelson Mandela had been released after twenty-seven years in jail was relegated to page 5 by the *Daily News*.

Ivana's friend Peter Kalikow, editor at the *Post*, now had no reason to hold back. The following days, 'SPLIT – Trouble in paradise as Donald Trump walks out on Ivana' was splashed across the front page. The *Post* then gave Donald's side of the story and an all-out tabloid war broke out.

The *Daily News* reported Ivana demanding a better deal and branding Trump's prenuptial agreement 'a fraud', while the *Post* dubbed him 'Don Juan' who trysted with model Marla at a hotel hideaway. The *News* then put Ivana and Donald in a journalistic head to head, with her saying: 'I am afraid. I know the children and I will be Donald's next project', while Donald was saying: 'Ivana doesn't want the money. She wants Donald. She totally loves me.' The *Post* responded with: 'THEY MET IN CHURCH.'

The *News* reported that a truce was possible, while the *Post* blew it out of the water with a picture of a grinning Trump and Marla, with Marla boasting: 'BEST SEX I'VE EVER HAD.' There was some doubt about whether she ever said that, but the headline was considered libel-proof. Even if it was untrue, Donald was hardly going to sue. In fact, he later offered to fly editor Lou Colasuonno out for a weekend in Atlantic City and 'get a couple of chicks'. The 'best-sex' story had continued: 'We always knew that Donald Trump was a tiger in the corporate boardroom, but now we know he's a wildcat in the bedroom, too.'

Then the *News* had Donald flying into Florida for Ivana's birthday party, only to be trumped again by the *Post's* headline:

'SEPARATE BEDS'. The *News* drew up lists of each side's celebrity supporters, while the *Post* compared vital statistics under the strapline 'Tale of the Tape in the Battle of the Belles'...

A lot of the information for these stories was leaked by 'John Barron' and Trump's other alter ego 'John Miller'. This John Miller told Sue Carswell, a reporter at *People* magazine: 'Actresses, people that you write about just call to see if they can go out with him and things. Important, beautiful women call him all the time.'

Carswell said: 'He mentioned basically every hot woman in Hollywood.' One of the names that came up in the conversation was Madonna. 'She called and wanted to go out with him,' said Miller. 'He's got zero interest in Madonna,' Miller said. 'I mean, he's living with Marla and he's got three other girlfriends.'

Carla Bruni was another quarry. She had just dumped Eric Clapton for Mick Jagger. 'Then she dropped Mick Jagger for Donald, and that's where it is right now,' gossiped Miller.

Bruni went on to marry French president Nicolas Sarkozy and has been described as a female Don Juan. Trump's former attorney Jay Goldberg, who worked closely with Donald at the time, said that he was a workaholic rather than an overheated Casanova.

'I never heard him speak romantically about a woman,' he said. 'I heard him speak romantically about his work. I only remember him finishing the day going home, not necessarily with a woman but with a bag of candy... not Godiva, just something from the newsstand. Give him a Hershey's bar and let him watch television.'

Trump always denied that he was Miller, but Carswell had taped her interview. When she played the tape to Marla, she recognised his voice and burst into tears. Later forensic audio specialist Thomas Owen told CNN: 'I can conclude with a fair degree of scientific certainty that it is Donald Trump's voice.'

It was tough on Donald Jr, then a boarding school in Pennsylvania, to have his father's mistress in increasingly scanty outfits being plastered all over the newspapers. He did not speak to his father for a year. Meanwhile Marla stayed out of the way in Guatemala, working to calm tempers there for the UN Peace

Corps.

With Donald's Atlantic City behemoth Trump Taj Mahal – America's first casino to feature an in-house strip club – about to open, a helicopter crash killed three top executives. Both Marla and Ivana turned out at a funeral in Mount Vernon, New York. There were fears of a fistfight before Donald pulled Ivana away.

As the divorce proceeded, Donald became more philosophical about his own short-comings.

'My marriage was the only area of my life in which I was willing to accept something less than perfection,' he said.

His mistake, he realised, had been after all to employ Ivana in his business. When he got home at night, they would talk about work rather than 'the softer subjects of life'. He vowed never to give a wife any responsibility in his businesses again. Marla had no such ambitions. Besides Trump's attorney Jay Goldberg said: 'It had obviously been a tawdry affair, but I did not see it lasting.'

Meanwhile Marla had to be given a makeover to adopt the role of Donald's new playmate. The hair and make-up had to be perfect, and there were designer dresses and jewellery to be worn. A former winner of the Miss Resaca Beach Poster Girl contest from Dalton, Georgia, she became known as the 'Georgia Peach'.

In July 1991, Trump presented her with a 7.5-carat emerald-cut diamond ring. With three of his casinos in bankruptcy, the bankers who were bailing him out were outraged. They wanted to know where the money had come from, but Trump insisted he had borrowed the ring from Fifth-Avenue jeweller Harry Winston in return for free publicity. The banks also had to sit by while he handed over a certified cheque for $10 million to Ivana. Meanwhile, the Taj Mahal slipped into bankruptcy and his airline Trump Shuttle foundered when women travellers shunned it due to his womanising.

'Yeah, but the guys love it,' he smirked.

Trump was sanguine about the newspaper reports of his failing businesses.

'You know, it really doesn't matter what they write as long as you've got a young and beautiful piece of ass,' he told *Esquire* in 1991.

He blustered his way through the various bankruptcies in faux presidential style with a faux-Marilyn Monroe singing 'Happy Celebration to You' at a 'comeback' party at the Taj Mahal in Atlantic City.

After signing a prenuptial agreement, Marla wore an (also) borrowed $2-million tiara to marry Donald in December 1993 in the Grand Ballroom of the Plaza, which Ivana had only recently redecorated. Howard Stern said: 'I give it four months.'

Another guest, O.J. Simpson, commented: 'I think everybody in the country believes if their relationship can work, then anyone's relationship can work.'

Of the wedding, *The New York Times* remarked cynically: 'There wasn't a wet eye in the place.'

Uncharacteristically, Trump himself had his doubts about his own behaviour.

'I was bored when she was walking down the aisle,' he said. 'I kept thinking, "What the hell am I doing here"?'

Once married, Marla performed the wifely duties – such as cooking his dinner, which he appreciated – to his satisfaction. But soon he said in his 1997 book *Trump: The Art of the Comeback*: 'I realised that this is a marriage coming to an end. It just doesn't seem to be working out. Maybe it's my schedule, and probably it's my fault. But you've just got to really look forward to going home, and if you don't something is critically wrong.'

The couple formally separated that year. According to biographer Robert Slater, in a precursor to Trump's White House years, Marla learnt that Trump was divorcing her from a headline on the *New York Post*. However, Trump forced Slater to remove reference to this from his book *No Such Thing as Over-Exposure: Inside the Life and Celebrity of Donald Trump* before it was published. Not that it mattered. Even before they split Marla had begun an affair with the bodyguard Trump had hired for her.

It wasn't just single women who were ostensibly irresistibly drawn to the billionaire Trump. In *Trump: The Art of the Comeback*, he was candid about his ongoing appeal to married women since his bachelor days. He had to fight off the aggressive moves by these women to have sex. As a married man, it was clear to him that morals stood in the way.

'If I told the real stories of my experiences with women, often seemingly very happily married and important women, this book would be a guaranteed bestseller (which it will be anyway),' he wrote.

In the book, he related how women would not stop throwing themselves at him even when he was married. He recalled attending a magnificent dinner being given by 'one of the most admired people in the world'. He was seated next to a 'lady of great social pedigree and wealth... one of the biggest of the big...'. Her husband was sitting on the other side of the table.

'All of a sudden I felt her hand on my knee, then on my leg. She started petting me in all different ways,' he said, shooting her a quizzical look. 'I didn't want to make a scene in a ballroom full of five hundred VIPs.'

She then asked him to dance.

'While we were dancing she became very aggressive, and I said, "Look, we have a problem. Your husband is sitting at the table, and so is my wife".'

But her passion was too intense.

'Donald,' she said. 'I don't care. I just don't care. I have to have you, and I have to have you now.'

He promised to call her, provided stop her amorous behaviour immediately.

Trump told another tale of his irresistibility. He had given a lift in his limo to another 'truly great-looking and sexy' wealthy woman who was about to get married. 'Within five seconds after the door closed,' he said, 'she would be jumping on top of me wanting to get screwed.'

Even though he now had a ring on his finger, women were still falling at his feet.

'The level of aggression was unbelievable,' he said. 'This is not infrequent, it happens all the time.'

Trump wanted to show that he really admired women for their strength and wiles. 'The smart ones act very feminine and needy, but inside they are real killers....' It was a tired myth that they are the weaker sex, he observed.

'... I have seen women manipulate men with just a twitch of their eye – or perhaps another body part.'

Nonetheless, he didn't fear their killer power. In *Playboy* magazine in 2004, he said about Viagra: 'I just never needed it. Frankly, I wouldn't mind if there were an anti-Viagra, something with the opposite effect. I'm not bragging. I'm just lucky. I don't need it.'

Apart from the trappings of wealth that surrounded him like neon lights, this was his secret power he reckoned: 'Women find his power almost as much of a come-on as his money.' Though how they might be able to show how much they were turned on by the latter before having done the math on the former he did not explain.

Donald was a great fan of fellow-womaniser Bill Clinton – in the beginning at any rate. When Paula Jones sued Clinton for sexual harassment, Trump empathetically called her 'a loser'. Then there was Clinton's impeachment over Monica Lewinsky. The *Washington Post* asked Donald whether he would face the same onslaught if he ran for president.

'Can you imagine how controversial that'd be?' Trump replied prophetically. 'You think about him with women? How about me with women?'

But Donald also phantasised about the upside – what if Lewinsky had instead been one of the 'arm candy' that agencies would supply Donald with for publicity shots: 'There are those who say that if [Clinton] had a fling with a supermodel, he would be everyone's hero.'

A new promising chapter started for Donald with *The Apprentice* in 2004. 'All of the women on *The Apprentice* flirted with me – consciously or unconsciously,' he announced. 'That's to be expected.'

Later he added chivalrously: 'It's certainly not ground-breaking news that the early victories by the women on *The Apprentice* were, to a very large extent, dependent on their sex appeal.'

When on more familiar turf, he felt he could be more direct and told *Playboy* model Brande Roderick on *Celebrity Apprentice*: 'Must be a pretty picture, you dropping to your knees.'

TV reality suited Trump's outlook well. In 2007, Fox announced that he would be executive producer of another reality show called *Lady or a Tramp*, a version of the British series *Ladette to Lady*, where 'rude and crude party girls' would be sent to charm school. Having himself climbed the greasy pole from Queens via Le Club to Trump Tower, he knew what he was talking about. Donald pledge personally to troll nightclubs to pick up suitable candidates, but despite another opportunity to have more girls at this beck and call, the show was never made in the end.

Donald then got involved with professional wrestling in a proxy bout called the 'Battle of the Billionaires' against WrestleMania's impresario Vince McMahon, who had put WrestleMania IV and V at Trump Plaza in Atlantic City. In a warm-up encounter, McMahon boasted he would win because of the size of his 'grapefruits'. Trump countered with the simple put-down: 'Your grapefruits are no match for my Trump Towers.' Both picked representatives to fight for them and no grapefruits or towers were harmed in the process, which was perhaps the moral of the programme.

By now Trump knew through trial and error who he needed by his side. He had, he said, long been looking for what he called a 'no-maintenance woman'. He found it one night in 1998 in the Kit Kat Klub where a modelling agency was hosting a party. When he saw five-foot-eleven Yugoslav Melania Knauss – née Melanija Knavs – he dumped his date, Celina Midelfart. A beautiful Norwegian heiress, Midelfart also had a degree from the London School of

Economics and ran a billon SKR company. Cruel to be kind was better for all. Donald asked Melanie for her number.

Reluctant at first, Melania soon discovered an interesting side-effect of Trump's interest. Donald and his celebrity pals attracted the paparazzi like flies – which did wonders for her fledgling modelling career. Donald soon boasted that she was 'a very, very successful model'. And then she was when *Sports Illustrated* featured her in it swimsuit issue. Soon after that the swimsuit came off and Melanie was featured nude except for a diamond choker, bracelets and handcuffs, lying on a fur throw on the bed in Trump's customised Boeing 727, in the British *GQ* magazine. The cover line was subtle and read: 'Sex at 30,000 feet: Melania Knauss earns her air miles.'

'She was obviously so keen to be featured in *GQ*, we came up with a rather kitsch and camp story for her to feature in,' said its editor Dylan Jones.

Trump requested that photographs be delivered to his office. 'We framed the cover and a selection of prints and sent them as soon as we could,' said Jones.

Melania had done nude photo-shoots before, on one occasion with Scandinavian model Emma Eriksson both naked on a bed. They were shown embracing. In another shot, the twenty-five-year-old was covering her private parts with her hands and her breasts completely exposed. Yet another shows Eriksson in a black negligée brandishing a whip and grabbing Melania by the arm as if she were about to flog her.

'I always loved women together, because I have been with a lot of women who desired the *ménage à trois*,' said photographer Alé de Basseville defending the pictures with an appeal to providing a service to female needs. 'This is beauty and not porn. I am always shocked by the porn industry because they are destroying the emotion and the essence of purity and simplicity.'

He noted that Melania did not seem uncomfortable posing nude with perhaps a hint of surprise. In any case, they both drew inspiration from Renaissance paintings, though tantalisingly de

Basseville didn't disclose which ones could have given him the idea for a *ménage à trois* with whips. The photographs appeared in the now-defunct French men's monthly *Max Magazine*. That was three years before she and Donald first met.

The *New York Post*, nonetheless, saw what de Basseville meant to achieve and republished them in August 2016 under the headline: 'The Ogle Office.'

Donald and Melania married in January 2005 at Mar-a-Lago. The celebrity-packed guest list including Bill and Hillary Clinton. For this photo-shoot – for *Vogue* – Melania wore a $100,000 Dior dress and was so low maintenance that the older children called her 'The Portrait'. They had a son the following year. He was named Barron, after his father – Donald Jr was already taken.

By then, The Donald's sex life was public property. At a Comedy Central Roast, Lisa Lampanelli told him: 'You've ruined more models' lives than bulimia.'

Jeff Ross topped this with: 'Donald Trump's ego is so big, he videotapes himself masturbating and then masturbates to that video.'

After complimenting Melania, who was also there that night, Ross said: 'These two are so compatible, because they both yell out Donald's name when they climax.'

It seemed that Donald finally had the low-maintenance marriage that he craved with his new wife, who was twenty-three years his junior.

On the presidential campaign trail she would say in 2016, 'We give ourselves and each other space'. That didn't mean, however, Melania wasn't a business woman like Ivana or Donald. One of her opening shots as first lady was to sue the world's largest news website for libel. Melania as a 'brand', her lawsuit complained, had suffered the loss of 'significant value', in particular 'to launch a broad-based commercial brand in multiple product categories' now that she had become 'one of the most photographed women in the world'.

On 4 November 2016, just four days before the election, the

Wall Street Journal reported that in early August that year Karen McDougal, 1998 Playmate of the Year, had received $150,000 from the *National Enquirer* for the story of her consensual relationship with The Donald in 2006, a year after he married Melania. As it was, the *Enquirer* did not run it.

American Media Inc, which own the *Enquirer*, issued a statement saying the $150,000 was payment for exclusive life rights to any story related to a relationship McDougal may have had with a married man – and for fitness columns written by her. None appeared.

The contract kept McDougal from disclosing her story on other outlets and established damages of at least $150,000 if it appeared elsewhere. Naturally, Donald had nothing to do with this, even though David Pecker, CEO of American Media Inc, was a long-time friend and fixer. Yet two years later, billionaire David Packer was granted federal immunity in exchange for all information about the hush money paid to squelch stories implicating The Donald. The Donald's private lawyer, Michael Cohen, received no such immunity and had to admit, after pleading guilty of federal crimes, that he and Packer suppressed stories 'at the request of the candidate'.

McDougal, who continued modelling after appearing in *Playboy*, told several of her friends she had a relationship for about ten months with Trump, beginning in 2006 and lasting into 2007, according to people familiar with her account. Another friend told the *Journal* that Karen's relationship with Trump lasted about a year. The two of them had attended the Miss Universe Pageant at Trump's invitation. Karen had previously tweeted a picture of herself with Trump at the Miss Universe pageant in Los Angeles and at another event in Las Vegas. If the alleged affair with Karen is true, Trump would have been with her a year after marrying third wife Melania.

It was baffling. Once Trump was in the presidential race, there were twelve women who had accused Donald of sexual assault. Could anyone care less about a consensual extra-marital, sexual relationship between Trump and woman a year younger than his new wife? Nonetheless, David Pecker must have thought he was getting something for the $150,000 the *Enquirer* paid for McDougal's unpublished kiss-and-tell story.

As the disclosure of Donald's sexual career would intensify during the Trump presidency, Melania would remain portrait-like. In 2018, her White-House spokesperson would categorise them as 'just noise' and another advisor spoke about the 'unspoken affinity' between the couple. Melania would just disappear from view as the news cycle would plough through more sexual antics. Although Donald was too busy to buy Melania a present for her birthday that year, he called in to TV-show Fox&Friends to say that she got a 'beautiful card'. Around that time, he also dashed off a tweet to his 50-plus million followers that he 'wouldn't be the man today without her by my side.'

During his presidential campaign Donald clarified to his sympathetic home base at Fox News how he dealt with high-maintenance, successful women. At the first Republican debate, presenter Megyn Kelly had remarked, 'You've called women you don't like fat pigs, dogs, slobs and disgusting animals.'

Afterwards, he was quick to deal with question: 'You could see there was blood coming out of her eyes. Blood coming out of her wherever.' He later denied that this was a reference to her menstrual cycle, conceding to NBC's Chuck Todd on *Meet the Press* that 'only a deviant would think that'.

Donald's campaign manager weighed in and complained that the problem lay with Kelly who was 'totally obsessed with Mr Trump'. She was apparently another tragic case of an attractive, successful, married blonde woman falling for the Donald.

To protect himself from any further advances, Trump boycotted the next GOP debate that Kelly was moderating, warning Megyn off to cool her infatuation by calling her 'a bimbo'. While it was clear that Trump had no interests in 'bimbos', he, confusingly, also posted seductive photographs of Kelly from a 2010 *GQ* magazine shoot on his official twitter page. In the end though, he had to give in and agree to a one-on-one interview. He was the 'loser' in this instance, though Kelly's career subsequently declined.

It would be wrong to think that Trump treated all smart, rich, accomplished women the same way, nonetheless. When he was asked on ABC's *The View* how he would react if his twenty-four-year-old daughter and former teen model Ivanka posed for *Playboy*, he said: 'It would be really disappointing – not really – but it would depend on what's inside the magazine.' What's inside the magazine? Donald didn't explain. But he did add: 'I don't think Ivanka would do that, although she does have a very nice figure. I've said if Ivanka weren't my daughter, perhaps I'd be dating her.'

'Who are you, Woody Allen?' quipped *The View*'s co-host Joy Behar.

It was a pregnant question. Later, he spoke about Ivanka to *Rolling Stone* magazine: 'She's really something, and what a beauty, that one. If I weren't happily married and, ya know, her father…'

When Ivanka was just twenty-one Donald was already boasting about how hot she was on The Howard Stern Show, saying: 'You know who's one of the great beauties of the world, according to everybody? And I helped create her. Ivanka. My daughter, Ivanka. She's six feet tall, she's got the best body. She made a lot money as a model – a tremendous amount.' Proudly he told *New York* magazine: 'Every guy in the country wants to go out with my daughter.'

While Trump embraced a sleazy lifestyle rife with sexual innuendo, he knew that this was the Achilles heel of his political competitors, all of whom towed monogamy in one form or another. With the campaign for the nomination well underway, Trump accused rival contender Ted Cruz of cheating on his wife with numerous women. He also repeatedly tainted Hillary Clinton with accusations that Bill had been accused of sexually abusing women, even appearing at a press conference with Paula Jones, and Kathleen Willey, who accused Clinton of inappropriate sexual behaviour, and Juanita Broaddrick, who claimed that Bill Clinton had raped her.

It worked. At the Republican debate in Detroit, Senator Mario Rubio followed Trump's lead to make an off-colour joke about the size of Donald's hands.

'He's like 6'2', which is why I don't understand why his hands are the size of someone who is 5'2'',' said Rubio. 'And you know what they say about men with small hands.'

This was the type of attack Trump relished.

'Look at those hands, are they small hands?', he asked as if Rubio had made an important point about the national debt. A long-standing master of self-inflation, he dunked his bar-room shot 'And he referred to my hands – "If they're small, something else must be small." I guarantee you there's no problem. I guarantee.'

The issue continues to create column inches by predominantly male writers. The *Hollywood Reporter* then rushed to prove that Trump's hands were disproportionately small. In 1997, a team from Madame Tussauds had taken measurements of Trump's body parts to make a life-size wax sculpture. The waxwork was no longer on display, but there is a bronze mould of his hand on the wall of the company's museum in New York. The hand there is just 7.22 inches long, which is smaller than average, especially for someone of his height. The average man's hand is 7.44 inches long, larger than Trump's, but the average American man was 5 foot 10. So given that Trump was 6 foot 2, his hands must be considered rather small. The *Reporter* thoughtfully put a printable graphic on line so that others could see how they measured up. It spoke to the imagination of half of Washington. As late as 2018, former F.B.I. chief James Comey raked over the issue.

Sleaze was now a mere campaign topic, up for debate as if it was a policy matter. Trump's past had become the stuff of showmanship instead of a big ball around his ankle. It came to pass when a tape was leaked of Donald talking about blonde-haired actress Arianne Zucker and sexual assault with Billy Bush from *Access Hollywood* aboard a bus on the set of *Days of Our Lives* in 2005.

Donald said: 'I moved on her, actually. You know, she was down on Palm Beach. I moved on her, and I failed. I'll admit it.... I did try and fuck her. She was married.' Apparently he took her furniture shopping to press his advantage.

'I moved on her like a bitch,' he continued, 'but I couldn't get there, and she was married. Then all of a sudden I see her, she's now got the big phony tits and everything. She's totally changed her look.'

Then they spotted Arianne waiting for them.

'I better use some Tic Tacs just in case I start kissing her,' Donald continued. 'You know, I'm automatically attracted to beautiful – I just start kissing them. It's like a magnet. Just kiss. I don't even wait. And when you're a star, they let you do it. You can do anything... Grab them by the pussy. You can do anything... Ooh, nice legs, huh?'

Donald's defence was: 'This was locker room banter, a private conversation that took place many years ago. Bill Clinton has said far worse to me on the golf course – not even close. I apologise if anyone was offended.'

He went on to deny the things he had been bragging about. During the second presidential debate, moderator Anderson Cooper asked: 'Have you ever done those things?'

'No, I have not,' Trump insisted.

All it did was become known as 'pussy-gate'. In the campaign it opened the floodgates on further accusations of sexual misconduct against Trump. At least twenty-four women accused the Republican presidential nominee of inappropriate sexual behaviour over the previous thirty years. Of those, twelve accused Trump of actual sexual assault, including groping and kissing them without permission.

No criminal investigation was or had been brought and Donald dismissed their accusations as 'lies' and 'fabrications', and his accusers 'horrible, horrible liars'. For good measure Trump went on to claim that the allegations were either orchestrated by the Clinton campaign or the product of women seeking 'ten minutes of fame'.

In 2016, seventy-four-year-old Jessica Leeds told *The New York Times* that, in 1980, when the thirty-four-year-old Trump was at the end of his married-women phase, he groped her on a plane when she sat next to him in a first-class cabin during a business trip to New York. She said Trump lifted the armrest between them and then grabbed her breasts and tried to put his hands up her skirt.

'It was an assault,' she told the *Times*. 'He was like an octopus… His hands were everywhere.' Three years later they met again at a fundraiser, and he called her a 'cunt'.

Trump responded during a rally, 'Believe me, she would not be my first choice.'

Next in the news came Ivana Trump's rape in 1989. She wrote in a 1993 statement, '[O]n one occasion during 1989, Mr Trump and I had marital relations in which he behaved very differently toward me than he had during our marriage. As a woman, I felt violated, as the love and tenderness, which he normally exhibited towards me, was absent.' Michael Cohen, in 2015 Trump's personal lawyer and gopher, responded 'you cannot rape your spouse.'

In a video from 1992, the forty-six-year-old Trump was heard talking to a young girl. In an aside, he said: 'I'm going to be dating her in ten years. Can you believe it?'

The Harth allegations came from 1997 when he was fifty one. She repeated them to the *Guardian* in July 2016, saying: 'He pushed me up against the wall, and had his hands all over me and tried to get up my dress again, and I had to physically say: 'What are you doing? Stop it.' It was a shocking thing to have him do this because he knew I was with George, he knew they were in the next room. And how could he be doing this when I'm there for business?'

Harth said that Trump's inappropriate attentions damaged her marriage. 'Trump did everything in his power to get me to leave him,' she said. 'He constantly called me and said: "I love you, baby, I'm going to be the best lover you ever had. What are you doing with that loser, you need to be with me, you need to step it up to the big leagues".' Trump was seeing Marla Maples at the time.

Then came the testimony of Kristin Anderson, a photographer

and former model that Trump had actually grabbed her vagina. She told the *Washington Post* in 2016 she was at China Club, a Manhattan nightclub in the 1990s, when Trump reached down her skirt while she sat on a couch speaking with friends.

'This is the vivid part for me,' she said. 'The person on my right, who unbeknownst to me at that time was Donald Trump, put their hand up my skirt. He did touch my vagina through my underwear. As I pushed the hand away, I got up and I turned around and I see these eyebrows. Very distinct eyebrows of Donald Trump.' Others confirmed that it was Trump, though he denied it.

Anderson said she and her companions were 'very grossed out and weirded out' and thought, 'Okay, Donald is gross. We all know he's gross. Let's just move on.'

Hope Hicks, then Trump's spokesperson, responded that Anderson was 'looking to get some free publicity.'

Other allegations of Trump's behaviour towards attractive women feeling up strangers in different ways then surfaced.

Lisa Boyne, a think-tank employee who went on to become a health-food entrepreneur, told the *Huffington Post* in 2016 that in 1996 she had been at a dinner with Trump and modelling agent John Casablancas, who brought five or six models with him. According to Boyne, they were seated at a semi-circular table with Trump on one end and Casablancas on the other. The women couldn't get out of their seats without one of the men getting up – which they refused to do. Instead, Boyne said, Trump insisted that the women walk across the table, allowing him to peer up their skirts while they did so. Trump 'stuck his head right underneath their skirts' and made comments on whether they were wearing underwear and what their genitalia looked like. He didn't do it to her though, because she was not a model, she said.

In *Model: The Ugly Business of Beautiful Women*, author Michael Gross detailed Casablancas's numerous affairs with the ingénues he represented. Under his name in the index was a separate reference purely for 'extramarital affairs'. While in *Shut Up and Smile: Supermodels and the Dark Side*, Ian Halperin wrote of Casablancas:

'Countless stories were floating around about how some of the girls he recruited as models were being steered into the party life of drugs, alcohol and sex.'

Samantha Holvey, a contestant in the 2006 Miss USA pageant, which Trump owned, told CNN that Trump personally inspected each of the pageant contestants individually.

'He would step in front of each girl and look you over from head to toe like we were just meat,' adding that it made her feel 'the dirtiest I felt in my entire life.'

Then a twenty-year-old student at a private Southern Baptist college, Holvey said that after that inspection she 'had no desire to win when I understood what it was all about.'

Disproving that this might have been naïve girls speaking, Mariah Billado, Miss Teen Vermont 1997, claimed that, as Trump barged into the dressing rooms where underage girls were changing, he said: "Don't worry, ladies, I've seen it all before".'

Billado also told *Buzzfeed*: 'I remember putting on my dress really quick because I was like, "Oh my God, there's a man in here".' Victoria Hughes, a former Miss New Mexico confirmed that Trump would barge into the contestants' dressing room unannounced.

In his April 2005 Howard Stern interview, Trump had, in fact, confirmed he would habitually do just that and 'sort of get away with' it.

However, Trump himself, Billado and Hughes were apparently wrong as the Trump campaign stated in 2016 that these facts 'have already been disproven by many other individuals who were present.'

Nonetheless, more beauty-pageant contestants came forward.

Bridget Sullivan was competing as Miss New Hampshire at the 2000 Miss U.S.A contest when Trump came backstage while contestants were changing.

'The time that he walked through the dressing rooms was really shocking. We were all naked,' she told *Buzzfeed*.

Another 2001 Miss U.S.A contestant told the *Guardian* that

Trump walked into a dressing room shared by two of the contestants while they were changing, even though security had warned him that the women were naked.

'Trump just barged right in, didn't say anything, stood there and stared at us,' she recalled. 'He didn't walk in and say, "Oh, I'm so sorry, I was looking for someone." He walked in, he stood and he stared. He was doing it because he knew that he could.'

Kissing strangers on the mouth was another theme in the accusations that came forward.

In 1997, Cathy Heller told the *Guardian* she was attending a Mother's Day brunch at Mar-a-Lago when she met Trump and he immediately kissed her on the lips, fighting with her when she pulled away.

'He took my hand, and grabbed me, and went for the lips,' she said. She leaned backwards to avoid the kiss. 'And he said, "Oh, come on." He was strong. And he grabbed me and went for my mouth and went for my lips.'

Trump then kissed her on the side of her mouth, she claimed.

'He was pissed. He couldn't believe a woman would pass up the opportunity,' she said.

Temple Taggart, former Miss Utah told *The New York Times* in 2016 that in 1997 when she was a twenty-one-year-old pageant contestant, the fifty-one-year-old Trump kissed her on the mouth when she was introduced to him.

'He kissed me directly on the lips. I thought, "Oh my God, gross",' she said. 'He was married to Marla Maples at the time. I think there were a few other girls that he kissed on the mouth.'

Trump also kissed her on the mouth during a meeting at Trump Tower to aid her career, she told the newspaper, where he recommended the twenty-one-year-old lie about her age to advance her career.

'We're going to have to tell them you're seventeen,' she recalled him saying.

Claiming to be a 'germophobe', Trump parried these accusations himself and told *The New York Times* that it could not be true as 'he is reluctant to kiss strangers on the lips'.

In 2005, Rachel Crooks was a twenty-two-year-old receptionist at real estate firm Bayrock Group, whose offices are in Trump Tower. She told *The New York Times* that she introduced herself to Trump outside the building's elevator one morning. When they shook hands, he would not let go. He began kissing her cheeks, and then 'kissed me directly on the mouth,' she said.

'I was so upset that he thought I was so insignificant that he could do that.' Trump threatened to sue the *New York Times* if they reported on the allegations.

Yet there was also testimony from Trump-friendly women. Juliet Huddy, a former anchor of Trump-friendly Fox News, said on the 'Mornin!!! With Bill Schulz' podcast in December 2017 that Trump kissed her on the lips after a meeting in Trump Tower in Manhattan in 2005 or 2006.

'He went to say goodbye and he, rather than kiss me on the cheek, he leaned in on the lips,' she said.

'Now that I've matured, I would've said, "Nope." At that time, I was making excuses,' Huddy said.

And Jennifer Murphy, a former contestant both in Miss USA and Trump's reality TV show *The Apprentice*, as well as Trump supporter, told *Grazia* magazine in December 2016 that Trump kissed her unexpectedly following a job interview in Trump Tower in 2005.

Murphy was 'very taken aback at the time,' but she later created a Katy Perry parody video in which she sang, 'I was kissed by Trump and I liked it.'

Trump with a group of men brought out the worst of him.

Yoga instructor and life coach Karena Virginia said she was waiting for a car after the U.S. Open in New York in 1998, when Trump approached her. She was then twenty eight and had never met Trump before.

'He was with a few other men,' she said. 'I was quite surprised when I overheard him talking to the other men about me. "Hey, look at this one," he said. "We haven't seen her before. Look at those legs." As though I was an object rather than a person.'

In a press conference with her lawyer, Gloria Allred, Karena Virginia said Trump then walked up to her, 'reached his right arm and grabbed my right arm. Then his hand touched the right side of my breast. I was in shock. I flinched. "Don't you know who I am? Don't you know who I am?" That's what he said to me. I felt intimidated and I felt powerless.'

Trump dismissed Virginia's lawyer Allred as a 'discredited political operative'.

Mindy McGillivray told the *Palm Beach Post* that in 2003 Trump groped her while she was assisting a photographer friend working backstage at a Ray Charles event at Trump's Mar-a-Lago estate. Ken Davidoff, who was Mar-a-Lago's official photographer, said he remembered McGillivray telling him on the night: 'Donald just grabbed my ass!'

'All of a sudden I felt a grab, a little nudge,' she told the *Post* in 2016. 'I think it's Ken's camera bag, that was my first instinct. I turn around and there's Donald. He sort of looked away quickly. I quickly turned back, facing Ray Charles, and I'm stunned.'

Asked whether she thought the contact could have been accidental, she said: 'This was a pretty good nudge. More of a grab. It was pretty close to the centre of my butt. I was startled. I jumped.'

She recalled another occasion when he had come on to her, but she had been saved by the arrival of Melania.

Ninni Laaksonen, a model and former Miss Finland, told Finnish newspaper *Ilta-Sanomat* that Trump groped her backstage at the *Late Show with David Letterman* in 2006.

'Trump stood right next to me and suddenly he squeezed my butt,' Laaksonen said. 'He really grabbed my butt. I don't think anybody saw it, but I flinched and thought, "What is happening"?'

'Somebody told me there that Trump liked me because I looked like Melania when she was younger. It left me disgusted.'

Cassandra Searles, a contestant in Miss U.S.A 2013, posted a picture of herself and fellow contestants posing with Trump on

Facebook, asking: 'Do y'all remember that one time we had to do our onstage introductions, but this one guy treated us like cattle and made us do it again because we didn't look him in the eyes? Do you also remember when he then proceeded to have us lined up so he could get a closer look at his property?'

Paromita Mitra, Miss Mississippi 2013, added, 'I literally have nightmares about that process,' while Shannon McAnally called Searles's account 'so extremely true and scary'. Anna Horne also noted, 'Scares me so much.'

Searles also said: 'He probably doesn't want me telling the story about that time he continually grabbed my ass and invited me to his hotel room.'

Trump on his own with an attractive woman was even bolder.

People magazine reporter Natasha Stoynoff said she was sent to Mar-a-Lago in December 2005 to interview Trump for a story about his first wedding anniversary with Melania, when he forced himself on to her. He wanted to show her a 'tremendous' place at the resort.

'We walked into that room alone, and Trump shut the door behind us,' she said. 'I turned around, and within seconds he was pushing me against the wall and forcing his tongue down my throat.'

At the time, Melania, who was pregnant, was changing upstairs. Regardless, Donald was expecting big things.

'You know we're going to have an affair, don't you?' she said Trump told her. He then turned up at the salon where she was due to get a massage the following day.

Donald knew however that money at times speaks louder than actions. Actress in pornographic films Jessica Drake said Trump kissed her and two female friends on the lips uninvited and then offered her $10,000 to have dinner with him and attend a party, after they met at a golf event in 2006.

'He asked me for my phone number, which I gave to him,' she told a press conference. 'Later that evening, he invited me to his room. I said I didn't feel right going alone, so two other women came with me. In the penthouse suite, I met Donald again. When we entered the room he grabbed each of us tightly in a hug and kissed each of us on the lips without asking for permission. He was wearing pyjamas.' A bodyguard was with him.

'He asked me about my job as an adult film star and about our personal relationships,' said Jessica. 'It felt like an interview. About thirty or forty five minutes later we left.'

A man later called on Trump's behalf asking her to return to his room, she said, and she refused. Trump then called her.

'Donald then asked me "What do you want?" "How much?"' said Jessica. After she left a man called and offered her $10,000.

'I declined again and once more gave as an excuse that I had to return to Los Angeles for work,' she said. 'I was then told that Mr Trump would allow me the use of his private jet to take me home if I accepted his invitation.'

As well as issuing his standard denial, Trump said on WGIR radio, 'She's a porn star. You know, this one that came out recently, "He grabbed me and he grabbed me on the arm." Oh, I'm sure she's never been grabbed before.'

Summer Zervos, a contestant on *The Apprentice* in 2007, accused the sixty-one-year-old Trump of groping and kissing her on two occasions. During a meeting at Trump Tower, she said, Trump greeted he and said goodbye to her by kissing her on the mouth. Later that year, she said, she was to have dinner with Trump in Los Angeles, and met him at his hotel beforehand.

'He came to me and started kissing me open-mouthed and he pulled me towards him,' she said. 'He then grabbed my shoulder and began kissing me again very aggressively and placed his hand on my breast... he walked up, grabbed my hand, and walked me into the bedroom.'

After she made it clear that his attentions were unwelcome, she said he thrust his genitals at her. Trump denied having met her at a hotel.

By this time, the debate no longer was about these women coming forward against a man in a powerful position. Instead, it had fizzled out to their word against his.

Even a report by a well-known veteran journalist no longer made a dent in Trump's career of sleaze.

CNN anchor Erin Burnett said she had been told by a female friend about a meeting in a boardroom at Trump Tower in 2010 where Trump tried to kiss her on the mouth.

According to Burnett, the woman said: 'Trump took Tic Tacs, suggested I take them also. He then leaned in, catching me off guard, and kissed me almost on lips. I was really freaked out. After, Trump asked me to come into his office alone. Was really unsure what to do. … Figured I could handle myself. Anyway, once in his office he kept telling me how special I am and gave me his cell, asked me to call him. I ran the hell out of there.'

There was no need to comment on or dismiss these allegations. After all what was to be expected under circumstances?

Apart from experiences disclosed to the media there was only one actual civil challenge against Trump. It dated from early summer 2016. The woman alleged that Trump and billionaire Jeffrey Epstein had raped her when she was just thirteen. In 2008, Epstein had pleaded guilty to soliciting sex from underage girls and went to prison for eighteen months.

A tentative court date for the civil lawsuit had been set for 16 December 2016 when the case was halted on 4 November, the eve of the election. The anonymous accuser cancelled plans to speak publicly about the allegations because of 'numerous threats', according to lawyer Lisa Bloom.

The lawsuit against Trump included affidavits from two anonymous women who said they were witnesses, the *Huffington Post* reported. Earlier her attorney Cheney Mason told *Buzzfeed*: 'This case, based on the sworn declarations of the victim and two corroborating witnesses, will be tried in court, where the defendants will be required to answer questions under oath and pursuant to the rules of evidence.'

The aspiring model claimed that she was raped at a party at Epstein's New York apartment in 1994. One of the witnesses said she acted as a recruiter to find young women to attend Epstein's parties and claimed she saw Trump rape the accuser several times. The other witness claimed the accuser had told her about the assault a few months after it was alleged to have occurred

In a *New York* magazine profile of Epstein before he went to prison, Trump acknowledged that he knew Epstein.

'I've known Jeff for fifteen years. Terrific guy,' Trump said. 'He's a lot of fun to be with. It is even said that he likes beautiful women as much as I do, and many of them are on the younger side. No doubt about it – Jeffrey enjoys his social life.'

Trump's attorney Alan Garten dismissed the 2016 allegations, telling *LawNewz.com* that the claims were 'an obvious publicity stunt aimed at smearing my client'.

So far, it seems, Donald had stayed on the right side of the law – and that was what the American voter seemed to care about most.

Even the religious right, which usually takes a more pre-lapsarian view, could live with Trump's morals.

Nor, it seems, had the F.B.I. or any state prosecutors ever opened a criminal investigation that included the presidential hopeful in one capacity or other.

Throughout his life The Donald was raunchy and a sexual predator but he had never fallen on the wrong side of the law.

Nonetheless, now that Trump had been elected the highest official in the U.S. government legal scrutiny of him intensified.

It started with a secret memo prepared by a former British spy (with a solid reputation writes James Comey in his 2018 book), initially for anti-Trump Republicans during the primaries, later adopted by pro-Clinton Democrats during the election, which had then found its way into the hands of Senator John McCain, who handed it over to the F.B.I. to investigate.

The report stated that Trump engaged in 'perverted sexual acts'. These included the golden-shower incident where prostitutes were said to have been hired to urinate on the bed in the Presidential Suite of the Ritz Carlton hotel in Moscow where Obama and his wife Michele had slept during an official visit. Trump allegedly engaged in other 'unorthodox' behaviour in Moscow.

Published on *Buzzfeed*, the relevant section of the memo read, his 'conduct in Moscow included hiring the presidential suite of the Ritz Carlton Hotel, where he knew President and Mrs Obama (whom he hated) had stayed on one of their official trips to Russia, and defiling the bed where they had slept by employing a number of prostitutes to perform a "golden showers" (urination) show in front of him.'

Donald pooh-poohed the story. When staying in hotels, the proprietor of the chain of Trump hotels notably said, 'I tell people, be careful. There's cameras all over the place and you don't want to see yourself on television.'

Donald Trump missed the point of the dossier when during the first meeting in 2017 with F.B.I. chief James Comey. Comey had come to inform the president-elect of the existence of the dossier before it hit the media. Trump himself brought up the scene of 'hookers peeing on each other' and was keen to point out it wasn't true. Donald also offered a perspective on the odds that he paid for sex.

The real issue, however, was not that scene but that, in the words of the dossier, 'the hotel was known to be under F.S.B. [The Russian Secret Service] control with microphones and concealed cameras in all the main rooms to record anything they wanted to.' In Comey's view, the F.B.I. 'really didn't care if he had cavorted with hookers'. The point, however, was 'to protect the presidency from any kind of coercion.'

Comey's visit happened in the context of an F.B.I. investigation whether Russian hackers had tried to tilt U.S. election results with the same methods they used in Russia.

This investigation had started in 2016 and there were admissions from people involved in the Trump campaign of financial links to the Russian government. It was precisely the scenario that would have spooked the founding fathers and that they had provided for in the Constitution.

The fact that Vladimir Putin leapt to Trump's defence did not help matters. 'Trump organised beauty contests,' he said. 'I find it hard to believe that he rushed to some hotel to meet girls of loose morals, although ours are undoubtedly the best in the world.'

Trump was piqued by his sex dossier. Obama had had no meetings after he had appointed Comey as F.B.I. director – a presidential custom since the time of Watergate – but Trump was to have no fewer than three private conversations in the space of a few months to talk about the prostitutes and make the Russia investigation go away.

When Donald fired Comey, special Counsel Robert Mueller was appointed to lead the Russia investigation. Government officials knew that if they made the inquiry go away they would potentially open themselves up to criminal liability. A president unhappy about a sex dossier was preferable over a life behind bars. A criminal investigation, once underway, had to run its course; at least that was how the founding fathers had hoped to tunnel it into the U.S. system of government.

Now that Donald had entered the White House, his attitude to women became a fixture in the American news cycle.

The American public was not to be disappointed. In *Fire and Fury*, author Michael Wolff revealed in August 2017 that Trump liked to say that one of things that made life worth living was getting your friends' wives into bed. He would use a simple tactic. He would get his secretary to invite the friend to his office, then initiate sexual banter with him.

'Do you still like having sex with your wife? How often? You must have had a better fuck than your wife? Tell me about it. I have girls coming in from Los Angeles at three o'clock. We can go upstairs and have a great time. I promise... And all the while, Trump would have his friend's wife on the speakerphone, listening in,' said Wolff.

As well at Jeffrey Epstein, Trump had a number of raunchy friends. One was Tom Barrack, who he wanted as his White House chief of staff. He was a friend from Donald's swinging days in the

1980s and 1990s.

'Barrack, on his fourth marriage, had no appetite for having his colourful personal life – often, over the years, conducted with Trump – become a public focus,' said Wolff.

He had a point. While Donald seemed Teflon-coated those near him were less fortunate. There was key adviser Roger Ailes, the former head of Fox News who was forced to resign after sexual harassment accusations were levelled at him. Then there was Bill O'Reilly, the Fox News anchor, who was sacked after six sexual harassment suits against him were settled for some $45 million. Meanwhile Donald tweeted that he wanted a 'consensual presidency'. David Petraeus slipped from the list of potential Secretaries of State, due to his extramarital affair, while Antony Scaramucci lasted just ten days as White House Director of Communications, quitting after saying: 'I'm not Steve Bannon, I'm not trying to suck my own cock.'

There was even Tony Blair, who was accused of having an affair with Ivanka's best buddy Wendi Murdoch, causing the break-up of her marriage to media mogul Rupert – something Blair strenuously denied.

Hope Hicks, Donald's twenty-six-year-old personal PR woman, fled from the room when Trump told her not to fret about her on-and-off boyfriend, campaign manager Corey Lewandowski whom he had just fired, saying: 'You've already done enough for him. You're the best piece of tail he'll ever have.' Then, in 2018, there were Michael Cohen, Trump's private lawyer, who pleaded guilty to eight criminal charges, and Paul Manafort, Trump's former campaign chair, who was guilty of 10 criminal charges.

Not that Trump minced his presidential words when it came to women. Sally Yates, the Acting U.S. Attorney General, who he fired in January 2017, was 'such a cunt'.

Meanwhile lawyer Marc Kasowitz, a lawyer who also acted for several Russians with close ties to Vladimir Putin, was dealing with the ever-growing list of women accusing Trump of molesting and harassing them. Steve Bannon, then White-House Chief Strategist, had every confidence. 'Look, Kasowitz has known him for twenty-five years. Kasowitz has gotten him out of all kinds of jams. Kasowitz on the campaign – what did we have, a hundred women? Kasowitz took care of all of them.'

There was also the hush-money that was paid to sex workers. Michael Cohen, paid former stripper and sex Stormy Daniels $130,000, a week before election day when she was considering appearing on ABC's *Good Morning America*, at a time when other sex allegations were stacking up against Trump.

This was a tricky one for president Trump. Not because she was an attractive blonde woman and a sex worker – that seemed to burnish the Trump brand with U.S. voters – but because complaints had been filed with the Department of Justice and the Federal Election Committee that this payment constituted 'an unreported in-kind contribution to President Trump's 2016 presidential campaign committee in violation of the Federal Election Campaign Act'. After denying all and sundry at first, Michael Cohen confirmed he had paid it from personal funds and, after first denying knowledge of the payment, Trump conceded Cohen had acted for him personally in the week before the election.

In the Autumn of 2016 Daniels talked to the editor of *Slate* magazine, Jacob Weisberg, several times about her relationship with Trump, but she cut off all contact with him days before the election.

'Daniels said she was talking to me and sharing these details because Trump was stalling on finalising the confidentiality agreement and paying her,' Weisberg wrote in *Slate*. 'Given her experience with Trump, she suspected he would stall her until after the election, and then refuse to sign or pay up.'

Daniels had given examples of Trump's broken promises in the past.

'She claimed he'd offered to buy her a condo in Tampa, Florida, and that he'd said he wanted to feature her as a contestant in an upcoming season of *Celebrity Apprentice*,' Weisberg said, adding, 'She intimated that her view of his sexual skill was at odds with the remark attributed to Marla Maples.' Weisberg then provided a link to a Reddit post featuring Maples infamous' quote about her relationship with Trump: 'Best sex I've ever had!'

The encounter between Daniels and Trump was said to have taken place at a hotel during a celebrity golf championship in July 2006.

'He kept looking at me and then we ended up riding to another hole on the same golf cart together,' said Stormy, adding that he later asked for her phone number. 'Then he asked me if I wanted to have dinner that night. And I was like, "Yeah, of course"!'

Ms Daniels, aka Stephanie Clifford, previously told the celebrity magazine *In Touch* about the affair in 2011. She said she agreed to go back to his hotel room where he was watching TV in his pyjamas – 'black silk pyjamas and slippers' she wrote later in her 2018 book *Full Disclosure.*

'I was like, "Does Mr Hefner know that you stole his outfit"?' she said. 'I was actually really mean to him. He got all huffy and tried to play it off and was like, "Oh I just thought we would relax here".'

Stormy then asked Trump about Melania who was at home in Trump Tower nursing their newborn son Barron.

'He goes, "Oh, don't worry about her",' she said.

They had dinner in his room and she teased him about his hair.

'He thought that if he cut his hair or changed it, that he would lose his power and his wealth,' she said. 'I laughed hysterically at him.'

Then he began pressuring her to get closer.

'He was sitting on the bed, and he was like, 'Come here.' And I was like, 'Ugh, here we go,' and we started kissing,' she said. 'I actually don't even remember why I did it, but I do remember while we were having sex, I was like, 'Please don't try to pay me.' And then I remember thinking, "But I bet if he did, it would be a lot".'

According to the magazine, The Donald was ordinary in bed. She described the sex as 'textbook generic'.

'It was nothing crazy,' she said. 'He wasn't like, 'chain me to the bed' or anything. It was one position, what you would expect someone his age to do? I can definitely describe his junk perfectly, if I have to.'

Afterwards, she said, 'He definitely seemed smitten after that. He was like, "I wanna see you again, when can I see you again"?'

He started phoning her every ten days, calling her 'Honeybunch' and promising to get her on *The Apprentice*. He told her: 'People would think you're just this idiot with blonde hair and big boobs. You would be perfect for it because you're such a smart businesswoman.' She also suggested in *Full Disclosure* that Trump offered to arrange a cheat to allow her to survive through more episodes.

He also said that she reminded him of his daughter Ivanka, who Trump now thinks of as the real first lady.

'He told me once that I was someone to be reckoned with – beautiful, smart, just like his daughter,' Daniels said.

In *Full Disclosure*, Daniels added that Trump's penis was 'smaller than average' but 'not freakishly small'.

'His penis is distinctive in a certain way, and I sometimes think that's one of the reasons he initially didn't tweet at me like he does so many women', Daniels wrote. 'He knew I could pick his dick out of a line-up. He knows he has an unusual penis. It has a huge mushroom head. Like a toadstool.'

Trump was hardly Don Juan.

Daniels said she went to the bathroom in his suite. When she came out, Trump had stripped down to his underwear. Then came the action.

'I lay there, annoyed that I was getting fucked by a guy with Yeti pubes and a dick like the mushroom character in Mario Kart,' she wrote. 'It may have been the least impressive sex I'd ever had, but clearly, he didn't share that opinion.'

However, it appears that 'textbook generic' sex was not all The Donald was up for. After the news broke the website the *Daily Beast* reported that Trump was after a threesome.

A second porn star named Alana Evans (*Britney Rears III*) said that Stormy called her from Trump's room.

'Stormy calls me four of five times,' said Alana, former stripper and star of some 287 porn films including *Britney Rears 3: Britney Gets Shafted* and *Lesbian Adventures: Older Women, Younger Girls 5*. 'By the last two phone calls she's with Donald and I can hear him and he's talking through the phone to me saying, "Oh come on, Alana, let's have some fun. Come to the party, we're waiting for you".'

'And I was like, "OMG it's Donald Trump!" Men like him scare me because they have so much power and this was way before his presidential nomination. So I bailed on them and turned my phone off.'

Later she told Megyn Kelly: 'This was 2006, he wasn't president, there was nothing in the foreseeable future at that time that looked like that was going to be the future.'

'If you're inviting me to a hotel room to hang out with another man and a girlfriend of mine,' Evans said, 'it's very easy for you to, you know, believe that there's going to be more going on than just, you know, playing cards or Scrabble.'

Next morning Alana called Stormy to apologize for her no-show and asked how the evening went.

'She tells me: "All I'm going to say is: I ended up in with Donald in his hotel room. Picture him chasing me around his hotel room in his tighty-whites",' said Alana. 'I was like, "Oh I really didn't need to hear that." Then she said he offered her keys to his condos in Florida, and I was like, "Wow, guess you had a good night", and that was the last we ever spoke of it.'

Afterward the sex, Trump asked Daniels to sign a copy of her X-rated film *Three Wishes* and kept saying: 'I'm gonna call you, I'm gonna call you. I have to see you again. You're amazing. We have to get you on *The Apprentice*.'

Stormy said she continued seeing Trump in his private bungalow in Los Angeles, in his office in Trump Tower and at a vodka brand launch in Hollywood. She claimed he then invited her to a 'meeting' at the Beverly Hills Hotel in July 2007 when he tried to get her into bed once again. But the relationship soured when he admitted there would be no place for her on *The Apprentice.*

Stormy said: 'He kept kissing my neck and was like, "Can you stay?" I was like, "No, I gotta go." He kept calling me less and less.'

The last call was in 2009 and 2010. Her story was supported by her ex-husband Mike Moz and a lie-detector test.

Refusing any further kiss-and-tell details, Stormy remained loyal, saying: 'Whether you're a fan of his or not, which I never really was, you gotta admit he's pretty fascinating. We had really good banter.'

Clearly she was in two minds about the encounter.

'At the time, I didn't think that much about it,' she told the magazine, 'but now I have a baby the same age that his was at the time, I'm like, "Wow, what a dick".'

The sex was unprotected. 'It was kind of in the moment,' she said. 'And I was really kind of upset about it because I am so, like, careful.'

Then there was the 2009 Forbes email. Back then, Daniels was planning to run against Senator David Vitter, a Louisiana Republican whose phone number had been found in the records of a Washington madam. The budding Democrat's proposed campaign slogan was: 'Stormy Daniels: Screwing people honestly.' Supported by leaders in the adult entertainment industry, she hired political consultants who were surprised that she knew Donald Trump.

'Yep,' said an email dated 8 May. 'She says one time he made her sit with him for three hours watching *Shark Week.* Another time he had her spank him with a *Forbes* magazine.'

It was the Autumn 2006 edition listing the Forbes 400 Richest People in America with a picture of Trump, flanked by Ivanka and Donald Jr, on the cover.

'He kept talking about this magazine that he was on the cover of, like "Look at this magazine, don't I look great on the cover?"' she said.

Daniels has appeared in about 150 porn films including *Saturday Night Beaver, Breast Side Story, The Da Vagina Code, Butt I Like It, Missionary Impossible* and *Good Will Humping,* an X-rated spoof of

Good Will Hunting. She cashed in on the scandal by making a 'Make American Horny Again' tour of U.S. nightclubs.

Michael Cohen initially denied the *Wall Street Journal* report that Daniels had been paid hush money and released a statement, signed under Clifford's professional name, which said: 'Rumours that I have received hush money from Donald Trump are completely false. If indeed I did have a relationship with Donald Trump, trust me, you wouldn't be reading about it in the news, you would be reading about it in my book.'

But Stormy Daniels is not the only porn star who has warranted The Trumpster's attentions. Ukrainian-born Victoria Zdrok, star of *Lesbians in Lust, For Your Ass Only* and *Three's Cumpany*, claimed she had several dates with Donald in the early 2000s when she was a *Playboy* Playmate and a model for *Penthouse*, but said she never slept with him because she was put off by his bragging about giving 'the best orgasms'.

In a 2004 interview with celebrity interviewer Chaunce Hayden, reprinted in the *Daily Beast* in 2016, she said Trump had called *Playboy* to get a date with her. Playboy Promotions said Trump was 'looking for a new girl for his ad campaign for one of his casinos in Atlantic City… It turns out he was never actually looking for a model. He was just trying to pick me up.'

They went out four times. The job interview was not a success. 'First of all, he's really arrogant,' Zdrok told Hayden. 'He's really into himself. On a date all he does is talk about himself. He loves himself. The first thing he says to me on our date is that he's taller and better looking than what he looks like in pictures, and that people don't realize it. He said, "People don't realize how handsome I am." He actually loves himself! I never met a more narcissistic person than Donald. You feel just like a piece of jewellery when you're with him. For him it's all about looks, appearances, and signing autographs. He just loves it.'

All Donald's tried-and-tested techniques fell on barren soil. 'He would try to kiss me and say what a great lover he is,' she said. 'He never once asked about me. That's the worst turn-off for a girl. He just doesn't get it. I found him empty, shallow, phony and ostentatious.' Victoria said Trump spent the entire time telling tales of women who were all falling over themselves to date him.

'He would always talk about this one girl, a supermodel, and how he would give her the best orgasms of her life. And how she misses him so much,' Victoria said. 'He told me he really likes this girl but he would never go out with her because he found out she was half-black and that would be bad for his reputation. I thought that was very racist. He didn't like that she was some weird ethnic mix so he wouldn't go out with her publicly, but that he really missed her and she was wonderful in bed. He needed somebody more mainstream.'

As well as rattling on about ex-girlfriends, ex-wives also featured in their intimate conversation. 'He couldn't stop talking about Ivana and Marla and how skinny and horrible Marla looks now and that she looks like shit since she cut her hair off.'

Victoria said she did not sleep with Trump 'because I wouldn't be another notch on his belt. We made out a little bit and that's it. I just couldn't relax with him because he never lets his hair down.'

'His orange hair was very odd,' she said. 'He uses so much hair spray. I would never dream of touching it. But he doesn't care. He really thinks he's one of the most handsome people on earth. He really does.'

In 2004, Trump denied any liaison with Zdrok, telling Hayden she was 'full of shit'. 'Chaunce, this person, I don't even know who the hell she is,' he said. 'I never took her out. I don't know who she is.'

She was not even his type. 'Give me a break. I have good taste in women,' Trump protested. 'Take a look at her picture. It's all bullshit. I never took her out. She looks like a fucking third-rate hooker.'

Donald was fifty-eight at the time. Hayden explained that Victoria had appeared in both *Penthouse* and *Playboy*, the only girl to do both. In fact, Zdrok was *Penthouse*'s Pet of the Year that year,

Trump scoffed.

'*Penthouse*? Who the hell wants a *Penthouse* Pet? *Penthouse* is garbage, it's bankrupt, it's over,' Trump replied. 'She's a thirty-five-year-old *Penthouse* Pet? That's pretty pathetic.'

He had standards. He would never use a *Playboy* centrefold to advertise his New Jersey casino business.

'I use models for that, I don't use *Playboy* people for that,' he said, adding, 'It's total bullshit.'

As usual, it was Zdrok, actually, who was after him. 'I know one thing. She called up the office like ten different times, years ago, this like five years ago, that's the only reason I recognized her name because it was an unusual spelling, I never took her out, she wanted to go out,' Trump said. He then asked the magazine publisher if he had discussed the matter with one of Trump's employees who fielded his business calls.

Trump told Hayden that this was the fourth time in two weeks that a woman had given an interview about dating Donald Trump – just as *The Apprentice* was topping the ratings. Two of the women, Trump explained, he had actually dated – 'they said great things about me' – while one, who had said bad things, he had never heard of. Zdrok, he said, he had heard of, but never dated.

Donald said that he could just have ignored the story, but the reason he was calling Hayden was: 'It's just so fucking false. I don't like her to get away with this crap.'

Stormy Daniels' attorney declared that the $130,000 non-disclosure agreement she signed with Michael Cohen was invalid as the president did not sign the document personally and that Cohen had broken the agreement by speaking about it publicly. She then went on CBS' *60 Minutes* to talk about her erotic encounters with the president while also claiming that a man had tried to scare her into silence. He had come up to her in a parking lot and said: 'Leave Trump alone. Forget the story.' Then he l looked at her daughter and said: 'That's a beautiful little girl. It'd be a shame if something happened to her mom.'

Marc Kasowitz's magic didn't help with defending Trump in the

Russia investigation and he resigned in July 2017. Since then there has been a revolving-door policy on lawyers representing Trump which culminated with the appointment of former side-kick Rudy Giuliani, whose fake breasts Donald once so fondly fondled.

Giuliani promptly admitted that Trump had repaid the $130,000 that Cohen had paid Stormy Daniels a week before his election.

So, having gained a lot of experience over his life, here is The Donald's advice to a friend who, like him, found himself being accused of sexual assault?

'You've got to deny, deny, deny and push back on these women. If you admit to anything and any culpability, then you're dead.'

II
Barack Obama, #44
I switched careers. That's it.

When Barack Obama came to power in 2009, he was hailed as a breath of fresh air. With a beautiful wife and two young daughters, he was a (relatively) young man of African-American descent papped in a bathing suit emerging from the sea and, unusually for a politician, showing a well-trained James-Bond-like physique.

Within fifteen months of his arrival the White House, the *National Enquirer* published rumours about the new president and attractive young campaign worker Vera Barker, who worked tirelessly to raise millions for Obama's U.S. Senate race in 2004.

According to the U.S. supermarket tabloid, that would later helpfully bury The Donald's peccadilloes, a limo driver who preferred to remain anonymous – discretion being the better part of valour – claimed he drove Ms Baker to a secret hotel rendezvous with the thrusting young then-senatorial hopeful. He said he chauffeured Vera 'from a friend's home in the D.C. area to the Hotel George where I learned later that Obama would be spending the night'.

The driver recalled that he 'waited in the lobby while she went to change her outfit. But to the best of my knowledge she did not have a room at the hotel and she was not staying there so I thought that it was a bit odd.' He said he also picked up Barack Obama at the airport and drove both him and Ms Baker to various locations where they were raising money.

'About 10.30 pm, I drove them to the hotel and they went in together,' he said. 'My services for the evening were done.' So the driver left, but he added: 'There was absolutely no indication she was going to leave the hotel that night.'

The *Enquirer* said the driver's account had been independently corroborated by investigators who believed the couple spent the night together there.

The story of the alleged affair had surfaced before. On 11 October 2008 – just three weeks before the presidential election – Britain's *Daily Mail* ran the rumour that Obama had a 'close friendship with an attractive African-American female employee… who in 2004 was hired to work on his team for his bid to become a senator'.

This caused problems in the Obama household, apparently. 'The woman was purportedly sidelined from her duties after Senator Obama's wife, Michelle, became convinced that he had developed a personal friendship with her.'

The *Mail* also reported that the rumours had first circulated in August, just two weeks before the Democratic Party convention where he finally wrested the nomination from Hillary Clinton. The newspaper went on to say that the woman concerned had been 'exiled' to the Caribbean island of Martinique because Michelle Obama objected to her continuing to work with her husband on the 2004 campaign. According to the *Mail*'s sources 'she was removed from her position and the political scene because Michelle got wind of the fact that she had a close friendship with her husband. She disappeared, then she reappeared in the Caribbean.'

The paper did not reveal the name of the mystery woman, but had contacted her in the Caribbean.

'Nothing happened,' the woman insisted. 'I just left at the end of the campaign… I have no comment on anything. I switched careers. That's it. I'm a Democrat and I support Senator Obama…. I don't have anything to say.'

A lawyer representing her said: 'Although her duties on the [2004] campaign changed over time, there was never any hint that Mrs Obama had any concerns about her relationship with the Senator or played any role in recommending a change in her duties.'

The next day, on 12 October 2008, the *Enquirer* exclusively reported Barack Obama's long-time mentor and 'father figure' was a 'sex pervert'.

For seven years, Obama had had a 'father-son' relationship with Frank Marshall Davis, who, the *Enquirer* said, had confessed to having sex with children, sadomasochism, bondage and indulged in a wide array of other sexual proclivities.

In his 1995 memoir *Dreams from My Father*, Obama identifies his childhood mentor only as 'Frank', but it has since been revealed that he was referring to Davis. Mr Davis, a journalist and poet, was a pal of Obama's maternal grandfather, Stanley Dunham. Frank Marshall Davis admitted in his private papers that he had secretly authored a hard-core pornographic autobiography called *Sex Rebel: Black*, published in 1968. The author of the book is billed as 'Bob Greene', but Davis later confessed to its authorship after a reader noticed similarities in style and phraseology between that book and Davis' poetry.

Neither allegation did anything to dent Obama at the polls the following month. But the *National Enquirer* was far from satisfied. In 2010, it claimed that 'on-site hotel surveillance video camera footage could provide indisputable evidence… investigators are working to obtain the tape'. And 'top anti-Obama operatives are offering more than $1 million to witnesses to reveal what they know about the alleged hush-hush affair'. The tape never surfaced and the $1 million is, as yet, unspent.

There seemed to be more to write about his male relatives. Obama's grandfather, Hussein Onyano Obama, was married five times. Two of his wives he divorced and he had at least ten additional brief live-in lovers. His tribe, the Luo, have an expression for this type of revolving relationships door. They say he had 'ants in his bum'. Onyano's relationships were short-lived because he would beat wives and lovers he found unsatisfactory.

Obama's father, Barack Hussein Obama, Sr, was said to have an irresistible sexual magnetism. His stepmother said: 'He could always talk very sweetly to girls and promise them all that they dreamed of.'

It certainly worked on Obama's mother, Ann Dunham, a free-thinking white woman from Kansas. The seventeen-year-old found herself pregnant just after Thanksgiving, 1960, within a few weeks of meeting him. They married, although Sr had a wife back in Kenya who had two children with. He did not tell Ann about his first wife until later and then claimed he had divorced her. Later, the story was that his Kenyan spouse had given her permission for him to take a second wife in accordance with Luo custom.

After Ann divorced him, he took a third wife, Ruth Baker, who had met him in Cambridge, Massachusetts. She followed him back to Kenya, where they married. They would hang out with the prostitutes at the Starlight Club in Nairobi. Pretty soon he was running about with other women and passed on to Ruth a sexually transmitted disease, whereupon she fled back to the U.S. with their son.

Following her divorce from Obama Sr, Ann married an Indonesian and she took the young Barack to live in Jakarta. At the age of ten, Obama returned to the United States to live with his grandparents in Hawaii. There he played basketball and smoked pot.

'I inhaled…', he said, '… frequently. That was the point.'

He later snorted cocaine, though Obama seemed to be doing it more for the social bonding experience than for any lasting affinity for the drug, according to David J. Garrow, author of *Rising Star: The Making of Barack Obama*.

Moving to Los Angeles, he attended Occidental College. Until then Barack had been called Barry, but he used his real name for the first time in the college poetry magazine *Feast*, possible in an effort to impress one of the editors, a white girl named Alexandra McNear. She was lithe and popular. Her father was the president of the Mystery Writers of America and her mother was a former editor at *Playboy* magazine. However, Barack found himself at the back of a long line of would-be suitors.

According to one classmate at Oxy: 'Barry dated girls, but there was no one who came close to being his girlfriend or anything like that. Barry wasn't at all shy, and women liked him, but he seemed too focused on himself to really get involved with someone romantically.'

He transferred to Columbia, sharing an apartment in New York with Sohale 'Hal' Siddiqi, a Pakistani he had met through mutual friends in Los Angeles. Together they would cruise some of the more notorious singles bars on the East Side, Donald Trump's old stomping ground.

'We were always competing,' Siddiqi recalled. 'We would go to bars and try hitting on the girls. He had a lot more success. I wouldn't out-compete him in picking up girls, that's for sure.'

Several of Siddiqi's girlfriends considered Barack something of a 'hunk'.

Then one summer Alex McNear came to Manhattan to take a theatre course at New York University and contacted Barack. She admitted that she had always 'thought he was interesting in a very particular way' and that she was physically attracted to him.

She was staying in her mother's apartment on East 90th Street and Madison Avenue, just a short walk from the apartment Obama shared with Siddiqi on East 94th Street between First and Second Avenues. Alex called and they met in an Italian restaurant on Lexington Avenue.

'We sat and talked and ate and drank wine, or at least I drank wine,' Alex recalled. 'I think he drank something stronger. It was one of those dark old Italian restaurants that don't exist in New York anymore. It was the kind of place where they leave you alone. I remember thinking how happy I felt just talking to him, that I could talk to him for hours. We walked slowly back to my apartment on 90th and said goodbye. After that we started spending much more time together.' Usually after dark.

Initially she would spend the night at his apartment, then when her mother left for swanky Nantucket for the summer, they would sleep at hers. For the next two months, they were lovers until Alex had to return to Occidental. They remained in contact through a series of passionate letters, while he burned off his physical energy on an indoor running track.

In December 1982, they reunited in Los Angeles, barely stirring from her apartment for two weeks.

'I really loved him,' she said, 'but didn't know if we could sustain a relationship.'

By April she was writing that she feared he was cooling towards her. He explained that he was 'burning the midnight oil' with his studies and fantasised about running off with her to Bali or Hawaii. He was soon complaining that his salary as a community organiser was too little to survive on – let alone get married on.

Soon after the relationship ended, Obama met another girl, this time one slightly older with an income of her own. She was an Australian named Genevieve Cook. They met at a Christmas party in the East Village. She had brought a bottle of Baileys Irish Cream, which she swigged straight from the bottle.

She had exchanged a few words with him early on. He had been standing in the kitchen, wearing jeans, a T-shirt and a leather jacket. Only after midnight, when she had finished the Baileys and was about to leave, did he approach her again. He was taken with her accent, he said. His mother had mixed with a number of Aussies in Indonesia. Genevieve's stepfather had been a diplomat and she had lived in Jakarta briefly, while Barack had been there, though they had not met at that time.

Although she was three years older than him, they found they had a lot in common. Both had parents who were divorced and both had lived in a number of places where they had never really felt at home. Soon they were deep in conversation. When their hosts finally got round to evicting them, they exchanged phone numbers. Things moved fast and, the following Wednesday, she came around to his apartment.

'I think maybe he cooked me dinner,' she recalled. 'Then we went and talked in his bedroom. And then I spent the night. It all felt very inevitable.'

Obama was still partying with his Pakistani friends, but within a few weeks he and Genevieve would be spending the night together on Thursdays and weekends. At the time he had a room in an apartment on 114th Street leased by Dawn Reilly, a dancer, who later recalled Obama lounging around her flat, drinking coffee and filling out *The New York Times* crossword puzzle, bare-chested and wearing a blue and white sarong.

Cook kept a diary of their time together, including candid intimate details.

'Intercourse was pleasant, and in bed he neither came off as experienced or inexperienced,' she later recalled. 'Sexually he really wasn't very imaginative, but he was comfortable. He was no kind of shrinking "Can't handle it. This is invasive" or "I'm timid" in any way; he was quite earthy.'

Cook wrote two poems for him. One, 'in alphabetical form, progressed from "B. That's for you" to "F's for all the fucking that we do" to "L I love you… O is too".'

His bedroom was conveniently near to the front door. Genevieve recorded in her diary: 'I open the door, that Barack keeps closed, to his room, and enter into a warm, private space pervaded by a mixture of smells that so strongly speak of his presence, his liveliness, his habits – running sweat, Brut spray deodorant, smoking, eating raisins, sleeping, breathing.'

However, she had only been dipped her toe in the water, so to speak. On 10 January 1984, she wrote in her journal: 'Wonder where it will go with Barack. He's not "my man" – but I wonder if I will always know him.'

Two days later, things were heating up.

'This really strong feeling that Barack has offered me something,' she wrote, 'but what's interesting is that I'm not couching it in terms of need or emotional dependence or love (maybe a little bit).'

Ten days after that, she was sad that the 'original bliss is dissipated' and wondered if they can 'continue being friends despite sexual convolutions'.

On 19 February, she described him sitting 'on the edge of the bed – dressed – blue jeans and luscious ladies on his chest'. It appears that he had a T-shirt with a picture of bosomy women on the front which, presumably, Michelle got rid of long before he entered the White House.

The following day Genevieve said she felt that he was 'kindling something in me'. That Sunday, she had woken and written for a bit, waiting for him to wake. But over breakfast, she felt 'severed from him... lack of physical connection – it means so much more than lust, after all'. Then she read poetry with her eyes close and 'words lapping, lapping through my tongue and soul'. Her head was in Barack's lap.

Later, she was 'sensing his need stronger than I'm ready to believe [and] being drawn by it'. She also found him 'very beautiful – more than he thinks himself to be'.

He also understood her British humour, which was lucky.

Nevertheless, she wanted to get out for a walk around New York, or to meet him in a bar. Instead, 'it's all too interior, always in his bedroom without clothes or reading papers in the living room.' Despite his sweet words and general coolness, 'the sexual warmth is definitely there'.

Complimenting her, he said she 'was growing to be a fine strong young woman' and that she was sweet and kind. On the other hand, she found him 'young and defenceless', as well as guarded, 'as if behind a veil' – just one, not seven. On 5 March, she recorded crying while he bought her butter.

In his memoir *Dreams from My Father*, Obama included a reference to Genevieve but without naming her.

'There was a woman in New York that I loved,' he wrote. 'She was white. She had dark hair, and specks of green in her eyes. Her voice sounded like a wind chime. We saw each other for almost a year. On the weekends, mostly. Sometimes in her apartment, sometimes in mine. You know how you can fall into your own private world? Just two people, hidden and warm. Your own language. Your own customs. That's how it was.'

Although the description fits, during an interview in the White House, Obama said that this recollection comprised a 'compression' of girlfriends, including another white woman he had later had in Chicago.

By May, Barack found he was pushing his own mother away, finding her too needy and dependent. His need for mothering seemed to have shifted to Genevieve. On 4 June she said she found him 'round and soft and young' and provided 'continual comfort' to him, recording on 10 June: 'I tried to give a lot of it to B. today.'

By then, Genevieve had moved out of her mother's apartment on the Upper East Side and moved into a brownstone in Brooklyn which she shared with a fitness trainer. She and Barack then alternated between their two apartments. Genevieve was now telling Obama that she loved him. His response was a lukewarm 'thank you', she complained, not a passionate 'I love you too'. They cooked and read together and hung out with his Pakistani friends.

Early in their relationship, Obama had told her that, during his adolescence, he had an image of his ideal woman and had searched for her. It was becoming plain to Genevieve that she was not his ideal woman. Rather, that paragon was black. She saw a likely candidate while running in Prospect Park – a 'light skinned black woman, close cut hair, strong small body, very pretty, and she would be challenging and vivacious in company'.

Obama was struggling with his racial identity at the time. In *Dreams from My Father*, he described his break-up from his New York girlfriend: 'One night I took her to see a new play by a black playwright. It was a very angry play, but very funny. Typical black American humour. The audience was mostly black, and everybody was laughing and clapping and hollering like they were in church.

After the play was over, my friend started talking about why black people were so angry all the time. I said it was a matter of remembering – nobody asks why Jews remember the Holocaust, I think I said – and she said that's different, and I said it wasn't, and she said that anger was just a dead end. We had a big fight, right in front of the theater. When we got back to the car she started crying. She couldn't be black, she said. She would if she could, but she couldn't. She could only be herself, and wasn't that enough.'

This episode did not happen with Genevieve. The only time

they went to the theatre together was to see Billie Whitelaw perform the monologues *Rockaby* and *Footfalls*, written for her by Samuel Beckett. And the only time they found themselves surrounded by a black audience, the mood was anything but angry. They were watching Eddie Murphy in *Beverly Hills Cop* in the Fulton Street Cinema in downtown Brooklyn.

Again Obama acknowledge that the bust-up he described had not happened with Genevieve, though he insisted that it was an incident that had happened, perhaps with a girl he dated in Chicago – he preferred to be discreet.

In another scene designed to show the inevitability of their split, Obama described a visit to her parent's estate in Connecticut.

'The house was very old, her grandfather's house. He had inherited it from his grandfather. The library was filled with old books and pictures of the grandfather with famous people he had known – presidents, diplomats, industrialists. There was this tremendous gravity to the room. Standing in that room, I realized that our two worlds, my friend's and mine, were as distant from each other as Kenya is from Germany. And I knew that if we stayed together I'd eventually live in hers. After all, I'd been doing it most of my life. Between the two of us, I was the one who knew how to live as an outsider.'

But who tells the unvarnished truth about their sex life? By the time he was writing this he had Michelle's feelings to consider. Though Genevieve's stepfather was rich, their summer cottage dated from the 1920s and was on an altogether smaller scale. Life there was informal and, while Obama went on to live in a world where he was surround by presidents, industrialists and diplomats, that was a world where Genevieve would have been far from comfortable. She was arguably the outsider.

Briefly, Barack moved in with her. They did not get on. By 4 February, she was asking: 'Who is this boy/man/person, Barack Obama? We communicate, we make love, we laugh. I insulted him the other night – a retaliatory fuck you for having passed comment on my always wimping out at dinners with the gang….'

Soon after they both moved out. She found another apartment in Brooklyn, while he moved back to Manhattan, to a sublease on Eighth Avenue in Hell's Kitchen, then a grim part of the island. She was relieved. Nevertheless, they continued seeing each other regularly.

By May, though they were still lazing around in bed together, he did not feel like making love to her. On 23 May 1985, Genevieve realized that Barack was leaving her. She reviewed her journals and figured out that he had always been guarded about his feelings. She had hoped that he would let go and fall in love with her. But that had not happened and she thought a 'lithe, bubbly, strong black lady is waiting somewhere'.

Meanwhile, she confided to a colleague: 'I just wanted to chop his dick off. I called him a prick.'

He was already thinking about moving to Chicago, where another girl friend waited. Genevieve phoned him a couple of times after he moved there, but he soon made it clear that her calls were unwelcome.

In *Dreams from My Father*, Barack related telling his half-sister Auma about his split with Genevieve.

'I pushed her away,' he said. 'Maybe even if she'd been black it still wouldn't have worked out. I mean, there are several black ladies out there who've broken my heart just as good.'

In May 1986 – after telling a friend he had gone almost a year without 'female companionship' – he met twenty-two-year-old Sheila Jager, who was half-Dutch, half-Japanese. Obama was smitten, writing that she had 'specks of green in her eyes.'

During a weekend away, friends discovered how passionate they were. The couple 'went back and forth, having sex, screaming yelling, having sex, screaming yelling,' to the point where those nearby had to move 'to the other side of the porch just to be able to talk,' Garrow recorded.

They moved in together and seriously considered marriage. They went out to spend Christmas with her parents in California. But her father was a Republican who made is clear that he did not approve of Obama marrying his daughter. It was also clear that Barack had already set his sights on becoming President and he had to identify fully as an African-American, which meant a white or oriental wife would not do.

'Barack's political destiny meant that he and Sheila could not have a long-term future together, no matter how deeply they loved each other,' Garrow said. 'He felt trapped between the woman he loved and the destiny he knew was his.'

They broke up in 1988 when she read something about another woman in his journal and she moved out.

Another failed relationship did not seem to put Obama off women though. Obama's mentor in Chicago, Jerry Kellman said: 'Barack definitely dated, but he was just too driven to get deeply involved with a woman.'

However, for several months he lived with a dark-haired white woman, though her identity remained a mystery to the older women at his church who liked to mother him.

'They were obviously both very private people when it came to that,' said Loretta Augustine-Herron. 'They obviously wanted to keep the details of whatever it was they had to themselves.'

He broke it off on Loretta's advice when he decided to move to Boston to study law at Harvard.

Returning to Chicago after completing his first year at law school, Obama took a summer job in a law firm where Michelle Robinson was assigned to be his mentor. She resented having to babysit the new guy, figuring she would have nothing in common with him. She had never met anyone from Hawaii. He was biracial and, after studying his personnel file, concluded that he was a nerd – 'a little strange, a little weird, a little off-putting'. She figured her employers were impressed with any black man who had his own suit. But when she met him, she was taken aback.

'He was a lot cuter than I thought he'd be,' she said. Besides he was not even wearing a suit, but a loud, ill-fitting sports jacket and slacks.

He liked the fact that she was tall and it was easy to make her laugh. Maybe it was the sports jacket.

She took him to lunch to get better acquainted, but held him at bay.

'Here's this good-looking, smooth-talking guy,' she said warily. 'I've been down this road before.'

Michele was a difficult woman to impress. All men were judged against the impossibly high standards of her father Fraser Robinson III who suffered from multiple sclerosis but nevertheless struggled, uncomplaining, to do the best for his wife and children. It was no coincidence that her first serious boyfriend, David Upchurch, bore more than a passing resemblance to her father. He took her to the senior prom but admitted after the relationship faltered: 'I was a screw-up.'

As a test, Michele's suitors were sent to play basketball with older brother Craig, a two-time Ivy League Player of the Year at Princeton, who then played professionally for the Philadelphia 76ers and the Manchester Giants in the UK, before becoming a college coach and an analyst at ESPN. Few passed muster.

Craig told his parents: 'My sister's never going to get married because each new guy she meets, she's going to chew him up and spit him out.'

He said she would simply fire guys, one after another.

'It was brutal. Some of them were nice guys, but they did not stand a chance.'

Obama had yet to face these strictures. But when he began talking about his background, she found him intriguing.

'We clicked right away,' she said.

Barack was equally captivated. Bought up in Chicago's South Shore, Michelle had the authentic African-American roots that he lacked. She was from the 'hood' and her parents had worked overtime to send her to Princeton. What's more she had been a friend of Jesse Jackson's daughter Santita since childhood.

'Man, she's hot,' Barack told a friend. 'I'm going to work my magic on her.'

But Michelle quickly made it clear that she had no time for

magic or distractions – particularly of the male variety. She held out for a month, while he bombarded her with flowers, notes and phone calls, asking her out on a date.

Finally, she agreed to go along to one of his community-organising meetings in a church basement. When he took off his jacket and addressed a crowd of single mothers, she was impressed by his fervour. Otherwise, she found his clothes cruddy and his car was a rust-bucket.

She still refused to go out with him, as employees' dating was against company policy. But when he threatened to quit his job so that he could take her out, she finally agreed to spend a day with him.

A skilled seducer, he took her to Chicago's Institute of Art, where there would be plenty of nudes, including Edgar Degas' 'Woman at Her Toilette'. After lunch he took her to see Spike Lee's *Do the Right Thing*. At least it wasn't *She's Gotta Have It*. Nevertheless, they reached another milestone – she let him touch her knee.

A few days later, they stopped off for an icecream on the way back from a company picnic and Barack asked permission to kiss her. Barack remarked that she tasted of 'chocolate'. Despite her concern that he was mixed-race, she let the comment slide.

Soon after, she took him home to meet her parents and gave him the Craig basketball test. The verdict: the boy could shoot hoops. She kept his mixed-race heritage and the fact that he smoked from her family. From then on Barack and Michelle were inseparable, but they managed to keep their hands off of one another at work – just about. Others noted hushed conversations and found them flustered when caught alone in an office together.

He shared with her his one big secret – not that he planned, one day, to run for President of the United States. He told everyone about that and everyone thought he was nuts. His big secret was that he planned to become the first black president of the *Harvard Law Review*. Secrecy was required because he wanted to be seen as a last-minute compromise candidate between the conservative and liberal factions in the membership. The strategy worked like a charm. Another big secret was that he had continued seeing Sheila Jager on and off through 1990, while he was dating Michele. 'I always felt bad about it,' Jager said later.

Now his dating days were drawing to a close and it was Obama's turn to introduce her to his family. They flew to Honolulu where his grandfather's immediate reaction was: 'She's quite a looker.'

Despite her general concern about race mixing, Michelle had no problem with Barack's white family as they were fellow midwesterners. However, she was determined to stop Obama smoking. He valiantly resisted.

'You have to keep at least one vice,' he said. (This begged the question; which one did he keep after Michelle finally got him to give up cigarettes?)

It was no secret that he had fallen for her hook, line and sinker. He told anyone who would listen: 'I'm hooked, I'm in love.'

When Michelle's father died, Barack rushed back from Harvard to be by her side. After graduating, he was determined to return to Chicago to be near her, so he sat the Illinois bar exam. When he passed, they celebrated in the then-famous Gordon restaurant in Chicago.

By then, he was determined to marry her and copied the same tactics he had successfully used at the *Harvard Law Review*. Over dinner, he pretended not to be interested in marriage. Over dinner at the Gordon, he maintained that marriage did not mean anything. It was just a piece of paper. Then when she grew annoyed and protested that she was 'not that sort of girl', the waiter came to the table with a small velvet box. In it was a diamond engagement ring.

'That sort of shuts you up, doesn't it?' concluded Obama.

Before they married, Barak took Michelle to Kenya to meet his father's family there. Their engagement dragged on for eight months but then they had to put their wedding plans on fastforward so it would not clash with the 1992 elections.

They married in Trinity United Church and held their reception in the South Shore Cultural Center, which had once been a whites-only country club. After honeymooning in California, they moved in with her mum, until they found a two-bedroom apartment in a condo costing $277,500. And as his political career blossomed, their two daughters were born.

While Obama was out on the campaign trail, Michelle stayed home watching *Sex and the City*. They kept in touch via webcams and, in moments of stress, he secretly smoked a cigarette after all.

In the 2008 presidential election, Obama found himself running against Republican Senator John McCain. He had had a formidable sex life of his own. Shot down over Hanoi in 1967, during the Vietnam war, the badly injured McCain had refused early repatriation on account of his father's seniority and spent five-and-a-half years in captivity, during which he was repeatedly tortured. This was impressive, though Vietnam draft-dodger Donald Trump didn't think this made him a hero of any kind.

Presumably he had been deprived of the comforts of love during this period. But when he returned home to find his wife Carol had been crippled in a car accident, McCain embarked on a string of extramarital affairs, effectively terminating his marriage. He and Carol divorced and McCain married former cheerleader Cindy Lou Hensley.

Elected president in 2008, Obama finally gave up his one vice – smoking – as the White House is a smoke-free zone. He was celebrated as the United States' first African-American president – though, as we shall see, he was not. But he was, perhaps, the first openly African-American President.

Running for a second term, Obama found himself up against Mitt Romney, a Mormon....

III
George W. Bush Jr, #43
'So, what's sex like after fifty anyway.'

'When I was young and irresponsible, I behaved young and irresponsible,' said George W. Bush. It was for once a pthy statement that he didn't need Dick Cheney to draft for him. Unlike teetotaller Donald, Dubya, until he was married, was a notorious drinker. Moreover, his turnover of attractive playmates has more than a passing resemblance to The Donald – with the minor difference that he was patrician privilege to Trump's *nouveau riche*.

Perhaps George Jr was trying to make up for lost time. Born in New Haven, Connecticut, the ersatz Texan went to an all-male prep school in Houston called Kinkaid (was it know to its pupils as 'kink aid'?) in 1959. Two years later, like Bush Sr, he was sent east to Phillips Academy in Andover, Massachusetts, which modelled itself on British public schools and prided itself on turning out 'homogeneous boys' – known in America as 'cookie cutters'. A popular boy who liked to party, Dubya was elected 'chief cheerleader'.

'Texans have a hard time relating to a male cheerleader,' he would say. George W.'s nickname was 'The Lip'.

He played baseball too. Each dorm fielded a team with names such as the Crotch Rots and Stimson Steams, after the former Secretary of War, Henry Stimson, and the way a fresh dog's turd steams in the snow.

At Yale – still an all-male institution while George Jr was there – he was known as a hard drinker. The life of the party, he was elected president of the Delta Kappa Epsilon fraternity by acclamation, and embarked on his 'Big Man on Campus' career.

'The DKE frat house was the site of soul bands and dancing and dates. There was a lot of alcohol,' recalled a friend of junior's.

Another denizen said: 'If he didn't use marijuana at that point, he wasn't alive.' This frat-house was Yale's precursor to gross-out 1978 comedy *Animal House.*

As frat pack leader, George Jr got into trouble when he stole a Christmas wreath to hang on the door of the frat house. More publicised trouble came when *The New York Times* accused DKE of a 'sadistic and obscene' initiation process, and junior only escaped being arrested for stealing Princeton's goal post before a varsity match because his father had just been elected to Congress. He was run out of town and has not returned to Princeton, New Jersey since. George Jr was merely 'making up for lost time,' it was said. But it could not have helped having a father who had been nicknamed 'Rubbers' in Congress because of his stance on family planning.

While George Jr was at Yale, he got engaged to Cathryn Lee Wolfman. She had been at the all-women Smith College in nearby Northampton, then transferred to Rice University in Houston – maybe because Rice was a mixed-sex college. The *Houston Chronicle* announced: 'Congressman's Son to Marry Rice Co-Ed.' And, as the engagement had been announced at Christmas, the gossip columnist claimed: 'Cupid Hitched a Ride on Santa's Sleigh.' They planned to marry in the summer of 1967. It was for hippies the first Summer of Love in San Francisco, and the start of their endeavour to live a life of drugs and sex beyond their college days – Bush Jr sympathised, a lot.

Bush must have felt the hippy vibe all the way in New England, for the marriage knot with Wolfman was never tied.

'I was crazy about her for a year', Bush said later, 'but we decided not to get married in between my junior and senior year in college.'

Wolfman joined the CIA and married a Harvard M.B.A. two years later, but did not forget her entanglement with the 'Big Man on Campus'.

'I loved him,' she said. 'But I have no thoughts of "what if" – no regrets. I was engaged to him. I was glad I was engaged to him. The relationship died and that was that.'

However, friends say that among the old-money social circle that the Bushes moved in there were some 'nasty, snobbish whispers' about Wolfman's 'merchant' family background, as both her grandfathers ran clothing stores.

The Bushes are Episcopalians, as was Wolfman. However, 'given her last name and her stepfather's prominence in the garment industry, the Bush family pressured their son to call off the wedding because the prospective bride had a Jewish background,' said a friend. 'They both took it hard, especially George. He was always a wild and crazy guy, but losing the woman he loved, combined with the fear of going to Vietnam, kind of pushed him over the edge.'

George Jr got over his heartache by hooking up with Tina Cassini, the teenage daughter of veteran movie actress Gene Tierney and the reputedly Russian-aristocratic fashion designer Oleg Cassini who had styled Jacky Onassis.

'She was a real sweet, pretty girl and when she was in town we were all rushing to take her out,' recalled a friend who dated her.

It is thought that George Sr was the matchmaker. 'Mr Bush knew exactly what he was doing,' said a friend. 'He would set up guys and girls that he thought belonged together.'

For George Dubya himself it was 'a real salvation to have a woman that everyone wanted to be with', a comment that all his previous girlfriends could ruminate over if they cared for it.

'There was that kind of thrill there,' brayed a fellow Yale alumnus enthusiastically. 'She was a real show pony, and George latched on to her. They paraded for a summer. Tina was spectacular.... It was a good fling.'

However, Tina was a good deal younger than Dubya and had to go back to school at the end of the summer.

After graduation from Yale, he was liable for the draft. Instead he joined the Texas National Guard and somehow found himself fast-tracked to become a fighter pilot like Sr who won his wings during World War II. Although he would theoretically be on active service, he stood little chance of being sent to Vietnam. In his defence, not one square inch of Texas was conceded to the Viet Cong while George Jr was defending it.

In the National Guard, Dubya was also going to be the 'Big Man'. Dubya made it his business to 'flyhard, play-hard, drink-hard' and generally continued 'being the wild Bush son', compared to his father 'Rubbers'.

'He basically continued the partying tradition postcollege,' recalled one Yale classmate. 'He graduated one day, enlisted in the National Guard the next, went to basic training in San Antonio for a few weeks, and then never let his foot off the accelerator of life.' But there was a new sexual element to his reckless behaviour: 'He flew jets, drove fast cars and screwed more women than Hugh Hefner.'

In 1968, he packed up his sporty, blue Triumph TR-6 and drove to flight training school at Moody Air Force Base near Valdosta, Georgia. The comparison with The Donald continues as he also favoured a British sports car in his youth, in his case a red Austin-Healey. At Moody, Bush was known as a good pilot and, probably equally importantly, also as 'a guy who could hold his own at the bar'. In fact, there was only one bar in town, and one whorehouse, both reputed to be owned by the local sheriff.

'Friday night at the officers club was a big deal,' said Valdosta graduate Colonel Ralph Anderson. 'There was draft beer, and all the girls from town came in.'

And it was not just local girls. Young females were bussed in from all over the state to meet the pilots.

'There were the aviation groupies that would come to the club a lot,' said fellow trainee Roger Dahlberg. 'Some were very nice girls, and some you just knew what they were there for. It wasn't a bad place to spend a Friday night.'

Dubya beat Trump fair and square when clubbing – Dubya oozed confidence. 'Everybody got crazy,' said Anderson. Especially George Dubya. On more than one occasion, he stripped off and danced on the bar naked, lip synching to the tune on the jukebox. He was one tight little Bush.'

George Jr himself has conceded that he 'worked hard and played hard' during flight training in Georgia. But, he still had time to have a government jet pick him up from the air base to ferry him to Washington for a date with President Nixon's oldest daughter Tricia. Apparently the President's matchmaking was part of a sweetener to persuade George Bush Sr to give up his seat in the House of Representatives and run for the Senate.

And, in order to date a 'Georgia peach', who some of his friends 'thought would become Mrs Dubya', junior ostensibly ended his career as a Full-Monty extra in the Officers' Club on a Friday night.

Years later, Bush thought, too, that there had been such a woman from Georgia; but he could only remember her first name, which was 'Judy'.

Others agree that whoever she was she had left no impression on 'The Big Man at the National Guard', in fact, that he never had any intention of marrying her, and was just stringing her along, although he repeatedly promised to take her back to Texas as his wife when drunk.

'He was very much in love back then,' said a flightschool drinking buddy, 'but junior wasn't about to settle down and raise a family, which was exactly what she wanted. He'd get drunk and promise her a big church-wedding with all the trimmings, but when he sobered up he'd say, "I must've been out my goddamn mind when I told her that".'

Certainly family life held no appeal. Like The Donald he was more at home in seedy nightclubs. There was talk of marijuana and cocaine use too. But that did not stop him making speeches on his father's behalf in the 1970 Senate race when he returned to Texas. Bush Sr lost, but junior gained a reputation of being a 'Winston-bumming preppy with a disarming smile and an eye for young women and a taste for beer, Jack Daniels and martinis' in his ersatz home state. Later he said with civic-minded restraint: 'I choose not to inventory my sins because I don't want anybody to be able to say, "Well, the governor of Texas did it, why shouldn't I"?'

'We all experimented back then,' recalled one of his many

girlfriends from the early seventies. 'But you have to remember that George was just living for the moment. He never dreamed or schemed of running for governor, let alone president.' That makes all the difference.

By this time, he had moved into a one-bedroom bachelor flat in a singles-orientated apartment complex called Chateau Dijon on Beverly Hills Street in Houston. It was inhabited by girls from Rice University and smalltown Texan women who had come in to the city to work as secretaries for the downtown oil companies.

In his own waspish way, he followed the ad-man path Don Draper might have before getting married. Co-ed volleyball games, impromptu water-polo matches and poolside beer-blast parties were the order of the day. And he liked the company of young women. Spying an older woman, a friend of the family, one night in the nearby Milieu Club, he asked drunkenly: 'So, what's sex like after fifty anyway.'

Friends said he spent 'enormous amounts of time courting women' – it was becoming a Trump-size obsession of Dubya. Bush came and conquered and was never without a date with a nice privileged background. One of them was the sister of his tennis partner Peter Knudtzon, who was negotiating the purchase of horticultural interests in the U.S. and Central America.

Already known universally as 'Dubya', he worked on another failed senate race, this time for a friend of his father's in Alabama. He criss-crossed the state as an unmarried man and was remembered as a 'party boy who couldn't keep is hands off the girls'. It was said that he was 'addicted to strong drink and women'.

Then he went to Harvard Business School, where he boasted: 'I've got my daddy's eyes and my mother's mouth.'

'We all had steady girlfriends,' said a classmate, 'one week at a time. Drinking and womanising – what else is there to do in your spare time? George was no different than anyone else.'

Having to make a career beckoned and he went into the oil business in Texas at a time when OPEC had hiked up the oil price and there were lines at gas stations. A speed limit of 55 mph was applied to the freeways to cut oil consumption and a jovial Texan bumper sticker read: 'DRIVE 95, FREEZE A YANKEE.'

Though a yankee Dubya had no time to freeze. A friend in the oil industry recalled his 'constant bed-hopping with West Texas bimbos'. It seemed that he had to hop around other people's beds because his own bed was broken, possibly by too much hopping. With a nice touch that tells its own story, his bedframe was lashed together with neckties.

In another departure from Trump, George Jr was not successful in the oil business – despite the favourable conditions – and often let his date pick up the bar bill.

It didn't matter. 'All the ladies were going crazy over him,' recalled Julia Reed, who met him at a wedding and later became a writer for *Vogue*.

George Jr was eye-candy in the 1970s. 'When coupled with the young George's bad-boy good looks, the total package was enough to send the many eligible twenty-somethings into a collective swoon,' she said.

Moving the centre of his operations to the Midland Country Club, he spent nights in the sweaty honky-tonks of Odessa, twenty minutes to the west.

'Wherever he went, he would have a date,' recalled an admiring friend, 'and she would be a pretty good-looking one too.' And when he did not – or even when he did – friends would furnish him with fresh phone numbers of eligible girls.

Dubya turned thirty in 1976. By that time both his father and grandfather had been war heroes, academic overachievers and self-made millionaires. When asked what he had done with his life up to that point, Dubya responded candidly: 'Drinking and carousing and fumbling around.'

Then at a backyard barbecue he met public-school librarian Laura Welch. She was also a resident of Chateau Dijon. Miraculously, they were engaged within days. Then, without telling anyone, he introduced her to his family. Not knowing the situation, brother Jeb went down on one knee, as if making a mock proposal.

Dubya flushed.

'Did you pop the question to her, George, old boy?' asked Jeb, equally embarrassed.

'Yes, as a matter of fact he has,' said Laura, 'and I accepted.'

'We didn't even know he wanted to get married until he showed up at the door with this beautiful creature, Laura, and announced that she was going to be his wife,' said his mother Barbara.

The Welches feared he would blow it by being too eager.

'I was afraid George was going to ruin the whole thing because he was rushing it,' said Laura's mother. 'In the past, when Laura brought home these nice young men from SMU [Southern Methodist University], that had turned her off.'

But this time she was not turned off. Three months later they were married. There was no time even for a honeymoon.

The reason? Dubya had politics on his mind – his own. He was running for Congress, embarking on a career to become the second son in the history of the United States to succeed his father after John Quincy Adams.

At Laura's behest, the story goes, he sobered up, became a born-again Christian into the bargain, and acquired respectability. However, his new-found faith did not stop him smearing televangelist Pat Robertson who was contesting the 1988 primaries against Bush Sr Dubya dished the dirt on another televangelist and Robertson supporter, Jimmy Swaggart, who had been caught, several times, watching pornography in sleazy motels with prostitutes. He also stuck up for his father when Bush Sr was accused of having an affair with his secretary, Jennifer Fitzgerald. Then he bought the baseball club, the Texas Rangers. And what red-blooded Texan does not fantasise about cheerleaders – even if he had been one himself?

When George Dubya ran for President in 2000 against incumbent Vice President Al Gore, sex never reared its head in the election coverage.

All sorts of other corruption surfaced, though, with brother Jeb's state delivering its decisive electoral-college votes for Jr despite, it seemed, the wishes of the majority of its voters.

In office, though, Dubya failed to deliver a sex scandal of Trumpian proportions. But with a background as colourful as George Dubya's he was never going to have an easy ride and there was already movement under the covers.

During the 2000 election, Tammy Phillips, a thirty-five-year old stripper and model for *Playboy*, came forward, claiming she just ended an eighteen-month affair with one George W. Bush. According to the *National Enquirer*, the *New York Post*, and Tony Snow on FOX TV, the affair has lasted from late 1996 until June 1999 when he decided to run for president. She told the *Enquirer* that she met Dubya at a hotel in Texas. She was wearing micro-mini skirt.

'It was instant combustion,' she said and told how Dubya had been born-again as a womaniser once more. They made love that day, she said, and a few days later they met again at a Houston motel. Phillips claims there were six more trysts over the next eighteen months, the final one in San Diego in June 1999 when he decided to run for president.

Rather than turning into a sex scandal, the Bush campaign skilfully buried the allegations as a campaign smear.

According to the Russian news agency *Pravda*, people who knew George W Bush very well in his pre-presidential life were not really surprised when Margie Schoedinger, a thirty-eight-year-old African-American woman of Missouri City, Texas, filed a lawsuit against Bush, alleging sexual abuse and harassment. She said that she had been strongly recommended to keep her mouth shut and, when she did not, three unknown men attempted to kidnap her. The kidnap was thwarted, but she claimed neither the police nor the F.B.I. took any action against the perpetrators.

Schoedinger maintained that she and her husband were drugged and she was raped by the then governor of Texas George Dubya in October 2000 at the height of the presidential campaign. Her husband may have been raped too. She does not know. Nevertheless, she alleged 'race-based harassment and individual sex crimes committed against her and her husband'.

A seven-page document was filed at Ford Bend County Court Texas, which claimed that Bush also drugged and beat her. She furthermore suggested that she 'dated George W. Bush as a minor', and that the president may have been the father of the child she miscarried as a result of the alleged rape. Her husband was fired from his job. He has been unable to find work since and was denied federal unemployment benefit. Pravda said that a background investigation revealed Margie Schoedinger had no criminal record, though police said they had no record of any investigation into her allegations.

Working as her own counsel, Margie Schoedinger was looking for $1 million dollars in damages plus $49 million in punitive damages for 'emotional distress, loss of freedom and ability to pursue her own dreams, alienation of affection from her spouse, loss of privacy, being disparaged on the internet, and loss of her ability to be a Christian writer'.

To Russian ears, and with Donald Trump in the White House still a decade away, this accusation against a U.S. president had the sonorous ring of truth.

'It is hard to say if this woman's story is true or not,' argued *Pravda*, giving her the benefit of the doubt by a wide margin. 'Who knows, probably, she is one of thousands of American women who perform sexual favours to high ranking politicians of America.'

Most commentators dismissed her as a nut case nonetheless, despite the thoughtful Russian analysis. But then it was reported that Schoedinger had died on 22 September 2003, of a gunshot wound to the head, nine months after filing the suit. The Houston Harris County, Texas, Medical Examiner's office ruled the death a suicide rather than that the then president had any involvement in the tragic event.

Can a leopard change his spots? For Donald Trump the idea of change never arose. But if you want to be 'The Big Man in the White House'…?

IV

Bill Clinton, #42

'If I had, I wouldn't tell you.'

The young Bush Jr was more Trump-like than the young Donald – Queen's wide-boy haunting Manhattans's East-side clubs. Big Man Dubya lacked Trump's status anxiety. But what about America's 42nd president Bill Clinton, the third notorious ladies' man in recent times to become President?

Bill Clinton is doubtless the acknowledge master of the sex scandal (up to now, at any rate) in American politics as the only president to be impeached as a result of woman. The only other impeached president, Andrew Johnson, was impeached for defying an act of Congress about a minister of war. Even though Clinton had served five terms as governor of Arkansas, he was unknown nationally. That changed during the New Hampshire primary in February 1992, when the supermarket check-out scandal sheet *The Star* ran the banner headline, 'Dems front-runner Bill Clinton had an affair with Miss America.'

As with The Donald, Bill's intimate association with America's obsession with beauty pageantry splashed across the front-pages led to no lasting harm to the candidate.

Quite the opposite, as with Donald Trump, it rocketed him to fame. *The Star* went on to name another five women whom Clinton was alleged to have had affairs with – apart from Miss America it included former *Playboy* centrefold, Elizabeth Ward Gracen.

Where did this private information hail from? *The Star*'s column inches came courtesy of a lawsuit filed by a Larry Nichols, a disgruntled former state employee who linked Clinton to the five named women and made the as yet unsubstantiated charge that he had been fired as part of an attempted cover-up involving a secret fund used to facilitate Clinton's trysts.

Clinton fought the suit, and when asked by a local TV station in New Hampshire whether he had ever had sex outside his marriage, he turned on the charm and purred with a twinkle in his eye: 'If I had, I wouldn't tell you.'

Hillary Rodham Clinton, his long-standing wife of seventeen years whom he had met at law school, held the line for him. She told the crowd that their marriage was strong, even though an Arkansas-state trooper Roger Perry later would testify that he had overheard her complain loudly: 'Bill, I need to be fucked more than twice a year.'

The Star hit back at Bill with a new headline, 'My 12-year Affair with Bill Clinton.' The subtitle was 'Mistress Tells all, the Secret Love Tapes That Prove It.'

This was an entirely new allegation. *The Star* wheeled out Gennifer Flowers, a former nightclub singer from Little Rock, Arkansas. Clinton's campaign manager David Wilhelm immediately dubbed her the 'smoking bimbo'. Though it was widely reported that Clinton denied having had an affair with Flowers, Bill, a master of precision, himself merely stated: 'That allegation is false.' So it was only an eleven-and-a-half-year affair then?

Unlike Trump's lovers, who all seemed measured if not calculating in their praise of The Donald, Clinton however was showered with narrative praise by Flowers.

'We made love everywhere,' Gennifer gushed to *Penthouse* magazine, 'on the floor, in bed, in the kitchen, on the cabinet, the sink. I called his testicles "the boys" and he called my breasts "the girls".'

She also said that he once tried to have sex with her in the men's room in the governor's mansion while Hillary was entertaining on the lawn outside. He even used his jogging as cover – he jogged over to her apartment, made love to her and jogged home. That way, him being a bit sweaty did not arouse Hillary's suspicions.

'I admired his stamina,' Flowers said warmly, 'being able to make love with such enthusiasm after running. I used to tease him about running back much slower.'

A good time was had by both parties, it seemed, unsullied by even a whiff of money as they do with the amorous relations of Donald, the 45th President. But Bill did get Jennifer a job on the Arkansas-state payroll.

'If they ever ask you if you've talked to me about it, you can say no,' he said in a telephone conversation that was taped.

Gennifer's mother Mary corroborated the story of her daughter's affair, as did her one-time roommate, Lauren Kirk, who told the *New York Post*'s Cindy Adams with lawyerly precision, 'There can be no doubt that she and Bill Clinton had sex with one another.' Surprisingly, her lawyerly take against a Democrat received a cold-shoulder in Texas, and Kirk was fired from her job as a realtor in Dallas after speaking to the press.

The media couldn't believe its luck. All of a sudden the 1992 presidential election was about a theme that engaged every American, a rare thing before social media flooded the world with fluffy animal clips and angry conspiracy theories. In a press conference, one reporter brought the house down by abandoning serious political questioning and asking Flowers as if the nation's health was on the line: 'Did the governor use a condom?'

As the story had gone global for similar reasons, big money was on the table. British tabloids were offering up to $500,000 for the next kiss-and-tell on Clinton.

Instead of trying to make it go away, Clinton exploited it as Trump would do it his way during the 2016 campaign. Bill managed to secure an interview on CBS's *60 Minutes* directly after the Super Bowl. This was airtime you could not pay for. The slot guaranteed a huge audience that was feeling good after watching the game and, more than likely, tanked so full of beer that any harsh judgments would struggle to clear the surface.

With Hillary by his side, Clinton was asked wide-eyed: 'Who is Gennifer Flowers and why is she saying these things?'

Using well-rehearsed lines, Clinton admitted that there had been problems in his marriage. Flowers was only 'a friendly acquaintance', but he acknowledged unspecified 'wrongdoing' and 'causing pain in my marriage'. When asked whether that meant that he had committed adultery, Hillary answered coolly: 'People who have been married a long time know what it means.'

The producer of *60 Minutes* Don Hewitt, kneeling off camera near Clinton, twice prompted him to admit he had had sex with Gennifer Flowers. Clinton did not take the bait.

It was a riveting performance. In one fell swoop, the two of them blew every other candidate for the Democratic nomination out of the water. Hillary made only one slight slip when she said that she was not there just to 'stand by my man like Tammy Wynette'. She later apologised smoothly to Tammy – the word 'misspoke' had not yet been coined to suck the last bit of personal responsibility for political pile-ups –when Clinton spindoctors feared Bill risked losing the country-and-western vote.

Hewitt quickly realized what *60 Minutes* had done, apart from getting good ratings for their elated advertisers. 'The last time I had something as important was the Nixon-Kennedy debate, and I like to think we helped create a president,' he said. 'I'd like to think we'll do it again.'

You'd think Bill was pleased too. His past behaviour could have spelled the end of his political life as it had done for other presidential hopefuls. Instead he had dodged a bullet and ended up in the lead.

Not a bit of it.

On the flight back to Arkansas, Clinton was ebullient if a bit edgy as was to be expected of someone whose private life had been turned into a reality show.

But when they got home and watched the broadcast with their daughter Chelsea, he was furious. The segment was much shorter than he had been led to believe, and he thought the best bits had been cut out. He was so incensed that he did not sleep that night. He was even madder when he woke up.

'It was a screw job,' Bill fumed. 'They lied about how long it was going to be. They lied about what was going to be discussed. They lied about what the ending would be. It couldn't have been worse if they had drawn black Xs through our faces.'

America, however, liked what it could remember the next sober day. The polls soon showed that eighty two percent of people thought enough had been said about Clinton's private life – and, also, now everyone knew who 'Bill Clinton' was.

As with Trump's campaign, other scandals soon surfaced. Like Bush and Trump he was accused of not pulling his weight on Vietnam, in fact, dodging the draft altogether by studying abroad at Oxford University, and smoking marijuana. Though American university students on home turf had long sustained economies around the world with their impressive drug consumption, marijuana was considered a big red flag. Cued by Ronald Reagan's long-sustained campaign it was seen as a gateway addiction to hell.

Bill's response was to prevaricate, even though it made him seem highly implausible: 'I did not inhale.'

In any case, as Clinton had puffed on the joint while he was a student at Oxford, he hadn't strictly spoken broken any U.S. law. At Oxford, he did fell for arch-feminist Germaine Greer but was instantly blown off when he propositioned her.

It was an aide of Democratic rival Bob Kerrey, who had won the Medal of Honor and lost part of his leg in Vietnam, who spiked the press corps' guns over the draft dodging charge. On Valentine's Day, Bill Shore dashed off an ornery ditty for the baby-boomers in the press pack: 'Roses are red, violets are blue/Clinton dodged the draft and most of you did too.' It neatly pegged Vietnam's electoral relevance.

Paul Tsongas won the New Hampshire primary. Clinton came second and he promptly dubbed himself the 'Comeback Kid'. After that, there was no stopping him. Like Trump, he was fire-proof against any further sexual allegations. Admittedly, he was in a better state than Trump whose campaign had looming allegations of sexual impropriety that were potentially criminal in nature. Asked by TV talk-show host Phil Donahue whether his sexual peccadilloes were a thing of the past, he said: 'I've told you the only facts I think you're entitled to know. Have I had any problems with my marriage?

Yes. Are we in good shape now? Yes.' His pants didn't self-combust, so it must have been true.

Nevertheless, four months before the election, Clinton campaign aide Betsey Wright told the *Washington Post* that she was on full-time alert of quell potential 'bimbo eruptions'.

And she had her work cut out. In July 1992, former Miss Arkansas Sally Perdue claimed to have had an affair with Clinton in 1983 when she was a radio-show host in Little Rock. She said that the governor of Arkansas would cavort around her apartment in her nightie. After the affair was over, she claimed a Democratic Party official had promised her a $40,000 job if she 'behaved like a good girl'. And if she did not? In a precursor to what Stormy Daniels was to allege against Trump associates, Betsey claimed that a Democratic Party staffer told her that 'they knew that I went jogging by myself and he couldn't guarantee what would happen to my pretty little legs'.

Other stories were circulating in the news trough. Rock 'n roll groupie Connie Hamzy claimed that she had had a brush with Clinton back in Little Rock. She told *Penthouse* magazine that an Arkansas state trooper had approached her on behalf of the governor as she lay sunbathing by a hotel swimming pool in a bikini. She claimed that she and Clinton had looked for 'a place where they could have some privacy for an assignation, but couldn't find one'. She also boasted that she had fondled the future president.

Clinton's had a different story. He said Hamzy had approached him in a hotel lobby, flipped down her bikini top, and asked him, 'What do you think of these?' Clinton's senior political advisor George Stephanopoulos secured affidavits from three staffers who had been with Clinton, telling the same story. That corked the Hamzy eruption for the time being.

Bill Clinton won despite the sex headlines. But almost as soon as he entered the White House journalist David Brock unearthed 'Troopergate' by chance. After the inauguration, Brock received a tip that a number of Arkansas state troopers assigned to the now former Arkansas governor were considering coming forward to tell everything they knew about the Clintons, including extensive first-hand knowledge of Clinton's relations with women other than Hillary.

Two of them, Larry Patterson and Roger Perry, were eventually persuaded to go on the record. As a result, in January 1994, *American Spectator* published 'His Cheatin' Heart'. In the article, the two state troopers revealed that their motive for going public was signature rage.

'We lied for him and helped him cheat on his wife, and he treated us like dogs,' Patterson said. When one of the troopers asked Clinton to sign some photographs for his family after the election, he said the President-Elect snapped: 'I don't have time for that shit.'

More saliently perhaps, Clinton had also assured Patterson that he would get him a lateral transfer within the state police before leaving office but had never found the time to make the call said the aggrieved trooper.

Both troopers confirmed that Clinton had had an affair with Gennifer Flowers. It lasted several years in their recollection. She called the governor's mansion regularly, asking for 'Bill'. If Hillary was not at home, he would take the call. But if Hillary was there, the troopers were told to tell Flowers that he would call back. A little later, he would come down to the troopers' guard house and disappear into a back room where he could use a line that Hillary could not be intercepted from inside the residence. This became his regular method of handling calls from women.

Patterson often drove Clinton to the Quapaw Towers in Little Rock, where Flowers lived. He would wait in the parking lot for up two hours for Clinton's return. According to Patterson, everywhere they went, even a private party, the troopers would go in with him, except if they went to her house. Patterson speculated that this was because he had begun his relationship with Flowers long before he acknowledged the relationship to the troopers. Clinton wasn't as close then to the troopers as he would become overtime, and he had a cover story for them. He would tell them that he was visiting Maurice Smith, director of the Arkansas highway department, who lived in the same building, though most of the visits were late at night, a damned unsociable hour to make a social call.

In an interview with Brock, Gennifer Flowers said that, initially, Clinton would come enter the building through the lobby, then take the elevator to her apartment on the second floor. But gossip spread, so when she saw the governor's Lincoln arrive outside, she would go down to the first floor and prop the fire exit open with a newspaper so that he could enter from the rear without being seen.

Gradually, Clinton loosened up in front of his bodyguards, they said, for some male bonding. Once, after a particular memorable visit at Flower's, Clinton warmly praised her oral accomplishments with the phase that she 'could suck a tennis ball though a garden hose'.

Troopers Patterson and Perry also heard Clinton organising a job for Flowers when he was planning to run for president. (She lost the job again when she did not turn up to work three days running after her story first broke in *The Star*.) In the weeks, running up to *The Star* interview, the men knew something was up though. Flowers began calling several times a day. It made them suspicious that she was trying to tape the calls. So when she called and said 'Gennifer Flowers', Perry would say 'Gennifer Fowler?' According to Patterson, Hillary had the phone logs destroyed. But it was too late. Flowers had already taped their calls.

Meanwhile Bill was alternately worried and angry. He had believed that Flowers would stick by him through thick and thin and was upset about being betrayed. In the back of his Lincoln, he was overheard to muse unkindly: 'What does that whore think she's doing to me?' And he dismissed Flowers even less charitably as a 'fucking slut'.

'If they ever hit you with it just say "no" and go on,' he was heard to say on Flowers' tapes. He would be free and clear on the sex issue so long as 'they don't have pictures'.

It turned out that Bill was indeed addicted, but not to a marijuana hell. Far from adultery being confined to the early part of his marriage, the troopers revealed that, for at least a decade, Clinton had been continually seeing other women, often more than one at a time, along with numerous one-night stands. One trooper estimated that Bill had had clocked up bedroom relations with hundreds of women.

Clinton's long-term girlfriends since 1987 included a staffer in Clinton's office; an Arkansas lawyer Clinton appointed to a judgeship; the wife of a prominent judge; a local reporter; an employee at Arkansas Power and Light, a state-regulated public utility; and a cosmetics sales clerk at a Little Rock department store. Their ages ranged from the early thirties to the early forties. Patterson and Perry said Clinton's extramarital encounters took place at least two or three times a week.

By then each girlfriend had been assigned a designated trooper whose job it was to call her and find out when Clinton could see her at her home. He would also have to drive her to various events where Clinton was appearing and deliver gifts to her. Or they would come to the residence to see him and be given a 'personal tour of the mansion' if Hillary was out. If all else failed, he would visit them or in the early morning, perhaps while he was out jogging.

It was the jogging that first broke down the barriers between him and the troopers. 'He would jog out of the mansion grounds very early most mornings and then we would go pick him up at a McDonald's at 7th Street and Broadway,' Patterson said. 'When we picked him up, half the time he would be covered in sweat and the other half of the time there wouldn't be a drop of sweat on him, even in the middle of July in Little Rock. Sometimes I'd ask him, 'How far did you run today governor?' And he would say, 'Five miles.' I'd tell him there must be something wrong with his sweat glands because he didn't have a drop of sweat on him. He'd say, "I can't fool you guys, can I?"'

'There would hardly be an opportunity he would let slip to have sex,' Patterson said. And Bill's sex appeal to the women he met was magnetic.

The troopers ran quite a procurement service during their office hours, they said. While they were out-and-about, Bill regularly instructed them to approach women and get their telephone numbers. They would also organise hotel rooms and scout out other places where he could have sex with them.

One day, for example, Clinton eyed a woman at a reception at the Excelsior Hotel in downtown Little Rock. Clinton asked one of the troopers to approach the woman, who he remembered only as Paula, and tell her that the governor found her attractive. He was then to take her to a room in the hotel where Clinton would be waiting. The standard procedure was for one of the troopers to tell the hotel that the governor needed a room for a short time because he was expecting an important call from the White House. The encounter with Paula lasted no more than an hour. As she left, she told the trooper that she would be available to be Clinton's regular girlfriend if he was interested.

Parking lots were fine for such quick assignations. On more than one occasion Patterson saw the department-store clerk fellating Clinton in a car – in the grounds of the governor's mansion or in a parking lot, including the one at Chelsea's elementary school. On that occasion, there was only one other car parked on the school's lot. The sales clerk was in it. Patterson parked blocking the entrance about 120 feet away. The parking lot was well-lit and Patterson told Brock, 'I could see Clinton get into the front seat and then the lady's head go into his lap,' said Patterson. 'They stayed in the car for thirty or forty minutes.'

On another occasion she drove up to the governor's mansion. He came out and got into her vehicle. The troopers then zoomed in the security cameras and the image of Bill Clinton being given a blowjob was projected on the twenty-seven-inch screen in the troopers' guardhouse. While they were enjoying this, Chelsea's babysitter turned up. Patterson stopped her and, explaining that there was a security alert, directed her another way. When Clinton was finished he came running over to the guardhouse.

'Did she see us? Did she see us?' he asked.

Patterson told him what he had done and Clinton said: 'Atta boy.'

According to the state troopers, Clinton would also go out on the prowl late at night several times a month. After the lights clicked off in the first couple's bedroom, he would get out of bed.

Hillary was a heavy sleeper and rested in the eye of the storm of all this frenzied activity. The troopers would sneak women into the governor's mansion while she and Chelsea were sleeping, then mount a 'Hillary watch'. It was also their job to keep tabs on Hillary as she went about her business, lie to her about her husband's whereabouts, and generally aid the cover-up.

Hillary, they said, nonetheless knew what they were up to and cold-shouldered them, keeping the details of her schedule to herself which made their job of covering Bill's tracks harder than they wanted it to be.

Their general impression was that Hillary was more protective of his political fortunes than he was himself.

'I remember one time when Bill had been quoted in the morning paper saying something she didn't like', Patterson said. While enjoying Bill's hose-pipe-and-tennis-ball jokes, Patterson didn't enjoy Hilary's expressions: 'I came into the mansion and he was standing at the top of the stairs and she was standing at the bottom screaming. She has a garbage mouth on her, and she was calling him motherfucker, cocksucker, and everything else. I went into the kitchen, and the cook, Miss Emma, turned to me and said, "The devil's in that woman".'

It was not the only time that she came up short in the troopers' estimation. In the morning of Labor Day in 1991, Hillary was just leaving the governor's mansion. It was early and the flag was not flying, so she did a U-turn and sped back, squealing to a halt in a cloud of dust.

'"Where is the goddamn fucking flag?' she screamed. "I want the goddamn fucking flag up every fucking morning at fucking sunrise".'

It came furthermore as an unpleasant surprise to the troopers that, despite their procurement for Bill, Hillary would seek to wind them up at times. She would refer to their guns as 'phallic symbols' and send them to fetch her sanitary towels, which they didn't like. It was Patterson, listening to the audio monitor at the rear porch of the main house, who eaves-dropped on Hillary tell Bill in argument about the frequency of their marital relations.

On one of Bill's prowling nights Hilary woke up to find him gone, flicked on the bedroom light and called down to the guardhouse looking in salty language for 'the sorry-damn-son-of-a-bitch'. When Clinton arrived home there was a screaming match in the kitchen. Examining the battlefield later, Perry found that the kitchen was a wreck – one of the cabinet doors had been torn off its hinges. No governor was hurt, though, in this anecdote.

Hillary would also complain bitterly, he said, when Bill lingered with an attractive woman at a public event, a common occurrence by all accounts.

'Come on Bill, put your dick up,' she was heard to quip. 'You can't fuck her here.'

According to the state troopers, Bill's secret sexual encounters continued during the President Elect's final days in Little Rock, Arkansas. By then, the Secret Service had already moved into the governor's mansion. Still on Bill-duty the troopers faithfully smuggled women through an outer security cordon by saying they were staff or relatives. 'Three times after the [presidential] election I called [the judge's wife] to see if she was at home for the governor,' Patterson said. (Patterson eventually did get his autographs by insisting on a signature each time Clinton sent for him to pick up a gift for a woman.)

On the day the Clintons headed off to Washington, Bill asked Patterson to bring one of his women friends to the send-off at Little Rock airport.

'When I got there with [the judge's wife],' said Patterson. 'Hillary turned to me and said, "What the fuck do you think you're doing? I know who that whore is. I know what she's doing here. Get her out of here".'

Clinton was standing right there and just shrugged, so Patterson dropped her off at a nearby Holiday Inn.

The troopers agreed that Clinton treated the women he met

courteously. There were dozens of them – some married with children – but all willing and there was no impropriety, they said. There were no indications that he used drink or drugs to seduce them. Clinton even once said that he was in love with one of them, but they could not make out which one it was.

At the end of Bill's two presidential terms, an entirely new allegation would surface – that Hillary was an accessory to Bill's sex addiction. Juanita Broaddrick, claimed in 1999 that Bill Clinton had raped her during the 1978 gubernatorial race. She also said that at a fundraiser after the incident, Hillary had offered her hand and said: 'I just want you to know how much Bill and I appreciate what you do for him.' When Juanita moved her hand away, she said, Hillary Clinton held on to her and said: 'Do you understand? Everything that you do.' To Juanita's mind, Hillary had just thanked her for keeping quiet about being raped by her spouse.

Juanita claimed that in 1991 she met up with Bill again and that he pleaded with her more forthrightly: '"Juanita, I'm so sorry for what I did. I'm not the man that I used to be, can you ever forgive me? What can I do to make this up to you?" And I'm standing there in absolute shock. And I told him to go to hell, and I walked off.' Soon after his plea to her, Juanita said, Bill released his statement that he was running for president.

Over the years, the Clintons had apparently almost turned the governor's mansion into Carry-On Arkansas. It was generally assumed among its staff that Hillary herself was having an affair with Vince Foster, a partner of her Arkansas law firm. When Clinton was out of town, the married Foster would turn up to see Hillary, staying until the early hours. They would also spend time alone together in a mountain cabin in Heber Springs maintained by their law firm. On several occasions furthermore, it was rumoured the two had been caught alone, embracing and French kissing.

Trooper Patterson also saw Foster squeeze Hilary's bum on the way to the men's room in a French restaurant one day. Foster winked at Patterson and made an 'OK' sign at him. On his way back, when their female companion, also a partner of their law firm, was not looking, Foster squeezed Hillary breast for good measure and made the same 'OK' sign for Patterson's benefit. Meanwhile, Hillary cooed in response: 'Oh Vince'. Not having seen the breast-squeeze, their female colleague must have filed these words away as Hillary's Lucille Ball impression.

When Clinton became president, a job was found for Foster as Deputy White-House counsel. Yet he was later found dead with a gunshot in his mouth in Fort Marcy Park in what looked like mysterious circumstances. Subsequent investigations concluded that he committed suicide, but still. A person who thuggishly ripped a kitchen-cabinet door off its hinges, was probably capable of a whole lot more if they wanted to silence someone else.

In spite of his own CV, Clinton was not above getting his hands dirty and stir the pot of sexual relations of his opponents. During the 1990 Arkansas gubernatorial race, he asked Patterson to locate a woman whose child, it was rumoured, had been fathered outside of marriage by one of his opponents in the primaries. Although it was illegal for state troopers to take part in political campaigns, Patterson said: 'Clinton told me to go to the Holiday Inn at the airport, find the woman, and offer her money or a job to sign a statement [about the illegitimate child].' Patterson followed Clinton's instructions and offered the illegal bribe, but the woman declined the offer and never came forward.

Soon after Brock's first interview with the troopers, Perry (and two others who wished to remain off the record) received telephone calls from their former supervisor on the governor's security detail, Captain Raymond L. 'Buddy' Young, who had then just been appointed by Clinton to head the regional Federal Emergency Management Agency office in Texas. Perry said Young told him that he was aware that they were thinking of going public with their stories about the Clintons private lives. According to Perry, Young told him: 'I represent the President of the United States. Why do you want to destroy him over this? You don't know anything anyway…. This is not a threat, but I wanted you to know that your own actions could bring about dire consequences.'

Patterson said Young sent him a handwritten note expressing concern for his health. That, apparently, was not a threat either.

Young confirmed that he had been in contact with Perry and Patterson, but denied making threats. Nonetheless, another two state troopers had been given jobs at a company in Little Rock that Young part-owned.

According to Patterson, Young told him that he had been assigned to deal with the women.

'If one more came out, they knew Gennifer would be credible,' said Patterson. 'He said they could weather the storm on one, but not two. He told me he went to Texas to talk to Elizabeth Ward.' Young denied this.

But if Young was there to keep the lid on the other women, he had his hands full.

The publication of Brock's 'Troopergate' article prompted Arkansas-state employee Paula Jones to file suit against Clinton for sexual harassment. She came forward as the 'Paula' that the state trooper had picked up in the Excelsior Hotel. The alleged event took on 8 May 1991 and she filed suit on 6 May 1994, three days before the three-year statute of limitations ran out. She sought $700,000 in damages for 'wilful, outrageous and malicious conduct' at the Excelsior Hotel. Her court papers accuse Clinton of 'sexually harassing and assaulting' her, then defaming her with denials. She named state trooper Danny Ferguson, the man she said led her up to Clinton's room, as co-defendant. Jones also claimed that when she got to the room Clinton whipped out his cock and, after one look, she politely declined, saying: 'I'm not that kind of girl.'

She claimed 'severe emotional distress' and said that she could substantiate her allegations by describing distinguishing characteristics of Clinton's genitals.

The White House responded to Paula Jones's oral allegations by trying to trash her. The Republicans gave her a makeover to make her look at her best and she pressed on. She did not want money, she said, she wanted an apology. But an apology would mean an admission by Bill.

Clinton tried to keep the lid on things by claiming that, as president, he could not be taken to court in a civil matter while in office. That squeezed him by the 1996 election as his Republican opponent, Bob Dole, could hardly play mister clean. He was a twice-married divorcee and had also been known to have relations outside his marriage. Besides, he was 73-years old and dared not risk playing the sex card against a younger politician who seemed to be attractive to women from Miss America onwards. He kept his powder dry until 1998 when he became the front man for Viagra.

The pundits had spoken. It was up to the voters. In the polling booths in November 1996, the American people gave a second overwhelming endorsement to Bill. Well, the economy was booming, stupid. While appreciating the colourful view of Clinton's bedroom antics, ostensibly the majority of voters didn't think it mattered. Besides, Clinton had that little-boy smile. And when he turned on the charm, the country – like Hillary – would forgive him anything.

The question of presidential immunity in the Paula Jones case reached the Supreme Court in 1997 and they didn't think the president could use the U.S. Constitution as a shield. The august institution was itself no prude with regards to thorny revelations of a bedroom nature. Supreme Court Judge Clarence Thomas had had to answer the accusation in 1991 that he enjoyed and vividly discussed bestiality and rape porn as well as the work of the prodigiously-shaped pornstar Long Dong Silver with his colleague Anita Hill at the Equal Employment Opportunity Commission. In fact, the #MeToo hashtag would in 2016 yield a new allegation against Supreme-Court Justice Clarence Thomas by attorney Moira Smith. She met Thomas in 1999 at her boss's home and said that as she, a star-struck twenty four year old, was introduced to him at the beginning, he groped her twice and tried to make her sit next to him.

A hearing in the Paula Jones case was set for May 1998. Paula Jones's lawyer, conservative-activist Susan Carpenter-McMillan, then went on the offensive, calling Clinton on national television a 'liar', a 'philanderer' and even 'un-American'. 'I do not respect a man who cheats on his wife, and exposes his penis to a stranger,' she said. I don't think the Puritans who landed on Plymouth Rock spoke like that.

The president's lawyer came close to stopping the lawsuit with an eleventh-hour compromise with Slick Willy and, as with Trump, it was all water off of a duck's back.

But hubris intervened. A White House aide told CNN that Paula Jones was pulling back because she knew her case was hopeless.

That characterisation by the aide riled Paula and her advisors. She put her foot back on the pedal and, for the first time, she painted in graphic detail a picture of America's First Genitals. When Bill dropped his trousers and exposed his penis back in Little Rock, she said it was erect – and bent. At the same time, she served up a bill for $2 million for emotional distress at the sight. Was it a veiled compliment or a crushing comment? It was left for the world to ponder, although by all accounts there were a lot of women who could compare notes with Paula Jones.

Either way, Bill and Hillary didn't dwell on the question for too long. As a damage-limitation exercise they took another honeymoon in, of all places, the Virgin Islands. They brought along half the world's press to witness these intimate moments of bliss. The happy, if slightly overweight, couple were pictured dancing on the beach in their cozzies. This touching, seemingly spontaneous act of affection was memorialised by a thousand lenses that drowned out talk of a sexual insult valued at $2 million.

There had long been talk inside the DC Beltway that Bill and Hillary had made a pre-presidential pact. She would stand by him and cover up for his bedroom relations, if she got a big job in government. Unlike previous First Ladies, Hillary was indeed given the enormous task of reforming U.S. healthcare within days of Bill taking office. For a policy wonk such as Hillary that was as hot as it got, her equivalent of Trump getting to erect a beautiful wall against Mexicans.

Some commentators were enamoured by the Caribbean

romance of the Clintons. They argued that Hillary had actually fallen in love with Bent Willy again. There were also rumours that Bill would settle the civil suit with Paula Jones, on humiliating terms if necessary because he did not want to risk disrupting his new-found marital bliss with Hilary. Well...

First off, Clinton had to testify under oath in a six-hour, closed-door hearing as part of the discovery phase of the Paula Jones case, while Paula sat only feet away. Under tough cross-questioning by Jones's lawyer, Clinton was asked whether he had been in, er, 'close proximity' to Paula.

The Comeback Kid came out shooting from the hip. He said he could not recall meeting her. There had been so many, one supposes.

He denied dropping his trousers and asking her to 'kiss it'. His attorney added: 'In terms of size, shape, and direction the President is a normal man.' Though the attorney did not say how this had been determined.

The President was cross-examined generally about his sex life. Wild Willie admitted, humbly, that he was as pure as the driven snow.

Trial judge Susan Webber Wright threw the net wider, ruling that Jones was 'entitled to information regarding any individuals with whom President Clinton had sexual relations or proposed to or sought to have sexual relations and who were, during the relevant time frame, state or federal employees'.

Enter a young woman named Monica Lewinsky. She had started as a twenty-one-year-old intern in the White House. She was asked whether she had had sexual relations with the President. This was relevant because, if Clinton had asked her for sex, it would show that he made a practice of importuning employees. Monica stoutly denied any such sexual relations had taken place.

Jones' private investigators also interviewed Juanita Broaddrick in her home, but she refused to discuss the rape allegation, saying she did not want to relive it and that, if subpoenaed, she would deny everything.

But then in a summary judgement Judge Webber Wright found the case without merit. Jones' appeal was dismissed when Clinton settled out of court for $850,000, though Paula's share of it had shrivelled to only $201,000.

'Bimbo eruptions' continued to pop up – though the next one was not by a state or federal employee, or even a bimbo. Unlike Trump, Bill didn't have just one type.

Blonde power-company executive Marilyn Jo Jenkins denied having an affair with Clinton, but his phone records showed that he telephoned her eleven times in one day. One of the calls, at night, lasted ninety four minutes. Bill evidently liked what he heard. According to Gennifer Flowers, Clinton liked to indulge in mutual masturbation sessions on the phone, though she claimed she faked it because his voice on the phone did not turn her on. In any case, Watergate journalist Carl Bernstein claims that Clinton thought about divorcing Hillary and marrying Jenkins.

The Jenkins eruption was followed by the 1999 story of an African-American prostitute called Bobbie Ann Williams who claimed that she bore a child by Bill after one of thirteen sex sessions starting in February 1984. This had legs as there were rumours Clinton had had several liaisons with African-American women, including allegedly Lencola Sullivan, who had been Miss Arkansas in 1980. At the time of the affair, she was a reporter on a TV station in Little Rock. When the relationship became too hot, she was shipped off to New York, where the governor, ostensibly on state business, would fly in to see her. Later she dated Stevie Wonder.

According to Bobbie, she was patrolling her regular patch with two other prostitutes in Little Rock when Clinton, who was jogging, stopped for a chat. She said he returned three days later and told her to walk a hundred yards down the street and wait behind a row of hedges, just yards from the governor's mansion. There she performed a sex act and he paid her $250 instead of her usual $80.

After that, she said they either had sex behind hedges, or his aides would drive her out to a forest cabin around Hot Springs (not the one that Vince and Hillary were using for their trysts). She even said that he took part in an orgy there with her and two other prostitutes.

Then there was Deborah Mathis a reporter on the *Arkansas Gazette* who, conveniently went on to become a White-House correspondent. Both women denied any sexual involvement with Clinton. But then, a gentleman never asks and a lady never tells.

When Bobbie Ann was four months pregnant, she said she told Clinton. He rubbed her swollen belly and said: 'Girl, that can't be my baby.'

That November she gave birth to a ten-pound boy. Although she had an impressive list of customers, she claims Clinton was the only white man she had sex with the month she conceived. Her son grew up tall and fair skinned. In 1991, she went to a lawyer. She underwent two lie-detector tests and gave graphic accounts of the sex sessions she had with Clinton. She also described the aides that drove her out to the cabin and the cabin itself. Reporters tracked down the cabin and it was exactly as she described.

On 3 January 1999, the *New York Post* ran with the front-page headline: 'Clinton Paternity Bombshell.' It claimed that DNA test conducted by *The Star* had shown that a sample from Bobbie Ann Williams' thirteen-year-old son Danny matched Clinton's – though the *Post* admitted: 'It was unclear how the magazine obtained Clinton's DNA and whether it was a fresh specimen.'

However, the following week *Time* magazine said that there was no match and *The Star* did not publish the story. Clinton had ducked under another one.

Then, finally, details of the Monica Lewinsky affair hit the media fan.

The daughter of a wealthy Californian physician, she said that the affair had begun soon after she had arrived in the White House. She was just twenty-one, still relatively fresh from school in Beverly Hills. The video of her high school prom shows her in clinches with a string of boys. At college in Portland, Oregon, she was considered 'a bit flash' at the raucous barbecues the students held. There were also rumours of an affair with one of her professors. After graduating in 1995, her mother arranged for her to be an intern, or trainee, in the White House – a prestigious if unpaid position.

'There goes trouble,' said the White House staffer who had interviewed her. That July, the twenty-two-year-old graduate got a position as an unpaid intern in the office of the White House chief of staff Leon Panetta. She was given a desk that lay between the Oval Office and the President's private apartment. Every time he walked by, it was plain that the President noticed her. She wore dresses or blouses with at least the top three buttons undone. But what particularly attracted Bill's attention was the Essex-style thong that, on occasion, was known to rise suggestively above her waistband.

According to Lewinsky, she caught the President's eye on 15 November when she flashed her thong at him. It was, she said, 'a small, subtle, flirtatious gesture'. At first, White House wags put his attentions down to innocent heavy chatting. Later, the romantic moment of mutual seduction was recorded in forensic detail for the benefit of the U.S. nation by Special Counsel Ken Starr, with questions about the exact pornographic detail formulated by Supreme Court Judge and rape-accusee Brett Kavanaugh: 'At one point, Ms Lewinsky and the President talked alone in the Chief of Staff's office. In the course of flirting with him, she raised her jacket in the back and showed him the straps of her thong underwear, which extended above her pants.'

Things moved fast. On her way to the restroom at about 8pm, she passed George Stephanopoulos's office. The president was alone inside, and he beckoned her to enter. She told him that she had a crush on him. He laughed, then asked if she would like to see his private office – a euphemism, perhaps, for 'the boys'?

Through a connecting door in Stephanopoulos's office, they went through the President's private dining room towards a small study off the Oval Office.

'We talked briefly and sort of acknowledged that there had been a chemistry that was there before,' she said. 'We were both attracted to each other and then he asked me if he could kiss me.'

Lewinsky said yes. In the windowless hallway adjacent to the study, they kissed. Before returning to her desk, Lewinsky wrote down her name and telephone number for the President.

Two hours later, she was alone in the chief of staff's office and the President approached. He invited her to rendezvous in Stephanopoulos's office in a few minutes, and she agreed. When Monica was asked if she knew why the President wanted to meet her, she said: 'I had an idea.'

They met in Stephanopoulos's office and again went to the President's private study. This time the lights in the study were off. According to Lewinsky, she and the President kissed. She unbuttoned her jacket and either she unhooked her bra or he lifted her bra up to expose her breasts. She said he touched her breasts with his hands and mouth.

Then official duty called and the president had to take a phone call, so they moved from the hallway into the back office. Then, 'he put his hand down my pants and stimulated me manually in the genital area,' Monica said. But for the president it was business as usual and he continued talking on the phone. As he was talking to a senator or some other member of congress, she performed oral sex on him.

When he finished his call, after a moment's thought, he told her to stop. She said that she wanted to finish what she was doing, but he said he wanted to wait until he trusted her more. Then he said he had not had 'that' for a long time. She took this as a joke. According to the phone records, he talked to two Southern-Democratic congressmen while she was going down on him.

Two days later Monica was working late when some of the staff sent out for a pizza. A piece of it landed on her jacket and she went to the restroom to wash it off. On the way back, the President waylaid her and they kissed. When she said she had to go back to her desk, he told her to come back with a slice of pizza. His secretary Betty Curie ushered her in. Again he got her breasts out.

It was now full-on Carry On Up the White House. The door had remained ajar and Ms Curie came to tell him that the President had a phone call that was more urgent than his meeting with the intern. While the president was on the phone, he deftly unzipped his pants and exposed himself and she went down on him. Again he stopped her before he came. Kenneth Starr did not record whether the phone call was from a Republican or a Democrat.

Their brief encounters were touching a nerve. Bill said he like her smile – and told her: 'I'm usually around on weekends, no one else is around, and you can come and see me.'

Bill was genuine about it. In December she moved to a paid position in the White House Office of Legislative Affairs in December 1995.

On 31 December 1995, Clinton had decided how he wanted to see the old year out – or the New Year in. Monica told him that he had promised her one of his cigars, so he gave her one. She had thought that he had forgotten what had gone on between them six weeks earlier as he called her 'Kiddo' rather than using her name. He apologised, saying that he had lost her phone number, though he had tried to find her in the phonebook…. So he demonstrated beyond doubt that he did remember. He took her into his study.

'And then… we were kissing and he lifted my sweater and exposed my breasts and was fondling them with his hands and with his mouth,' she revealed.

She went down on him again and, once more, he stopped her before he came. Something must still have been on his mind.

On 7 January 1996, he must have found that illusive phone number because he called her at home.

'I asked him what he was doing and he said he was going to be going into the office soon,' said Lewinsky. 'I said, oh, do you want some company? And he said, oh, that would be great.'

So she went to her office, then they made plans over the phone for a clandestine rendezvous. He would have the door to his office open, and she would pass by the office with some papers.

'Then… he would sort of stop me and invite me in,' she continued her testimony to Kenneth Starr.

Unfortunately, this little drama went awry. There was a uniformed Secret Service officer named Lew Fox outside the Oval Office. But plainly the president was in the mood. He popped out of and said: 'Have you seen any young congressional staff members here today?'

Officer Fox said, 'No, sir.'

So Clinton said, 'Well, I'm expecting one. Would you please let me know when they show up?'

It worked like a dream. A few minutes later Monica stopped by and told Fox: 'I have some papers for the president.'

Fox informed the President she was there and he said: 'Oh, hey, Monica, come on in.'

Then he said to Fox: 'You can close the door. She'll be here for a while.' He must have thought he was talking to an Arkansas-state trooper.

Monica and Bill talked for about ten minutes in the Oval Office.

'Then we went into the back study and we were intimate in the bathroom,' she said.

He gave her the breast treatment again, she said, and he talked about going down on her. But as she was having her period they decided that this might not be a good idea. So Monica went down on him again.

Back in the Oval Office, they had another little chat.

'He was chewing on a cigar,' she said. 'And then he had the cigar in his hand and he was kind of looking at the cigar in… sort of a naughty way. And so… I looked at the cigar and I looked at him and I said, we can do that, too, some time.'

The following week they had 'phone sex'. This made her feel a little bit insecure. She did not know whether he had liked it or not. Nor did she know whether their affair was developing into some kind of a longer-term relationship, or did he have some regular girlfriend who was furloughed? At the time, following a dispute with the Republican-dominated Congress, Clinton had vetoed a spending bill and all non-essential government workers had been furloughed. Not Monica, however.

On 21 January, the President saw Monica by the elevator and he invited her into the Oval Office. She was quite shirty.

'I asked him why he doesn't ask me any questions about myself,' she said. 'Is this just about sex? Or do you have some interest in trying to get to know me as a person?'

No, the President laughed and said that 'he cherishes the time that he had with me'. But even Monica at the time thought this was curious statement.

Then, as he took her into the hallway by the study, 'he just started kissing me' as Monica was mid-sentence. He got her breasts out, then 'unzipped his pants and sort of exposed himself', and she went down on him once more. Conversation about getting to know Monica the person had ceased by this point.

Just then someone came into the Oval Office. Bill quickly zippered up. 'I just remember laughing because he had walked out there… visibly aroused,' she said. 'I just thought it was funny.'

After dealing with the intrusion, he remembered that an old friend from Arkansas was going to drop by. He gave her a kiss and bundled her out.

Nevertheless on 4 February, he was up for more play-acting. He called her at her desk and she suggested that they bump into each other in the hall. That would be convincing. Then they scurried though into his private study.

'He unbuttoned my dress and unhooked my bra,' she said. 'He was looking at me and touching me and telling me how beautiful I was.'

After working his magic on her breasts, he went where Trump would have gone without asking, first stroking her vagina through her panties, then directly, she said. And, just when they are getting somewhere, she performed oral sex on him. According to her sworn testimony, the Leader of the Free World was still holding back.

Afterwards they talked for about forty five minutes – Bill was 'trying to get to know me'. Then he kissed her arm and said he would call.

'Yeah, well, what's my phone number?' she said touch of residual petulance. Then a miracle happened – 'He recited both my home number and my office number off the top of his head.'

However, the course of true lust never runs smooth. On 19 February, President's Day, he called her at her apartment in the Watergate building – a good choice for a political scandal. She knew from the tone of his voice that something was wrong. She said she wanted to come and see him, but he said he did not know how long he was going to be there. Nevertheless, Monica headed for the White House and stormed into the Oval Office, despite the 'tall, slender, Hispanic plain-clothes agent on duty near the door'. In his defence, agent Nelson U. Garabito said Monica was carrying a folder and said: 'I have these papers for the President.' A trick that apparently never gets old.

Bill said that he no longer felt right about their intimate relationship and was going to put an end to it. They could go on seeing each other, but just as friends.

After the break-up Monica said that they kept on flirting, as he did with the American people. After passing in a hallway one night in late February or March, the Clinton telephoned her at home and said he was disappointed that, as she had already left the White House for the evening, they could not get together. Monica thought that the call 'sort of implied to me that he was interested in starting up again'.

Some added inducement was needed, she reckoned. When a friend named Natalie Ungvari came to town, Monica took her to the White House. They bumped into Bill who seemed to know all about Natalie.

There were more subtle Bill signs that whatever it was they had might rekindle itself. On 29 March, she spotted that he was wearing a necktie that she had given him.

'Where did you get that tie?' she asked seductively.

'Some girl with style gave it to me,' he replied. He even wore one of her ties giving the State of the Union address she said.

Hillary was away, so Bill phoned Monica at her desk and asked her to come to watch a movie with him. What she had to do was hang about outside the White House movie theatre, he would then bump into her accidentally and invite her in. Monica thought this was none too subtle. Instead, she asked to meet him over the weekend. He said he would try.

Again she used the old 'I've got some papers for the President' ploy to get into the Oval Office. This time she had a new Hugo Boss necktie in the folder for the chief executive. Then in the hallway by the study 'he focused on me pretty exclusively', kissing her bare breasts and fondling her genitals, as Kenneth Star faithfully recorded in his blow by blow account.

At one point, she said, the President stuck a cigar in her vagina, then put the cigar in his mouth and said: 'It tastes good.' After the encounter she needed a walk through the White House rose garden to cool off.

The Secret Service, whose job it was, and White House staffers, whose it wasn't, had noticed that Ms Lewinsky was spending a lot of time loitering with intent around the West Wing. On one occasion, she had brushed passed one member of presidential protection detail, saying breathlessly: 'The President needs me.' No doubt they were well aware of his needs.

White House tongues started wagging like beagles when Monica turned up one night with a private visitor's pass, something that is extremely difficult to get hold of. She said she was visiting a close personal friend in the Chief of Staff's office, but the person whose name she wrote in the security log had already gone home. After receiving the private visitor's pass, she would regularly turn up late at night in figure-hugging dresses.

The White House walls at times leak like a sieve; and Secret-Service men were overheard complaining that she should not be visiting the President's apartment so often – especially not when Hillary and Chelsea were away. Speculation thickened when Monica also appeared on the guest list at Camp David. Now the story spread throughout the whole of the White House like wild fire. White House deputy chief of staff Evelyn Lieberman said Monica was 'always someplace she shouldn't be' and had her transferred from the White House to another job in the Pentagon. On Easter Sunday, 7 April, she told the president tearfully that she had been removed.

'Why do they have to take you away from me?' he complained as his re-election battle loomed.

They had a 'sexual encounter' and he promised to bring her back into the White House after the election.

According to Ms Lewinsky: 'I think he unzipped... because it was sort of this running joke that I could never unbutton his pants, that I just had trouble with it.' She went down on him and, still, he did not come.

Again she did it to him while he was on the phone – this time to Dick Morris, Clinton's aide who resigned after being caught with a prostitute. Then they were interrupted by deputy chief of staff Harold Ickes who stormed into the Oval Office, hollering: 'Mr President.' They always left the door to the anteroom ajar during their sexual encounters.

Clinton 'jetted' back into the Oval Office, while Monica slunk off. The Secret Service officer noticed that Monica, still clutching her manila folder, was 'a little upset'.

Later Bill called her and asked why she had run off.

'I told him that I didn't know if he was going to be coming back,' she said. 'He was a little upset with me that I left.'

Though they did not meet again privately for the rest of the year, he did call to ask how her new job was going. She began getting disillusioned though, when she discovered that there may have been other women in Clinton's sex life. She began to record her own phone calls with the President. Some of the conversations were very explicit indeed. There were hot telephone-sex sessions. Memorably, the Chief Executive expressed a desire to 'coat you with my baby gravy'.

Lewinsky was left with a big legal problem though. In her deposition in the Paula Jones case, Monica had denied fooling around with the Commander in Chief under oath. She had, in effect, perjured herself.

They did see each other at public functions. On one occasion when he reached past to shake the hand of another guest, she reached forward and grabbed the commander-in-chief's crotch in a 'playful' fashion. Another time, she yelled out as one does to the President: 'Hey, handsome – I like your tie.'

That night he called. The following day she was going to be in the White House on Pentagon business. He told her to drop by the Oval Office while she was there. But Ms Lieberman was nearby so she did not dare. Then came the famous photograph of Monica shaking hands with the president. Though he was re-elected, she did not hear from him. Nor was she recalled to work in the White House.

Her other problem was that Monica felt she was in love with Bill. 'I kept a calendar with a countdown until election day,' she wrote in an unsent letter. 'I was so sure that the weekend after the election you would call me to come visit and you would kiss me passionately and tell me you couldn't wait to have me back. You'd ask me where I wanted to work and say something akin to 'Consider it done' and it would be. Instead I didn't hear from you for weeks and subsequently your phone calls became less frequent.'

However, Bill Clinton put their renewed encounters on a more formal basis, having his secretary Betty Currie arrange them. Betty would even come to the White House at weekends to make sure that everything went smoothly. She said they were usually alone together in the Oval Office for fifteen to twenty minutes, though once she had to wait thirty or forty minutes because he had another visitor.

This in itself was not unusual. But Monica also sent letters and packages via Ms Currie, who suspected that something was going on.

'He was spending a lot of time with a twenty-four-year-old young lady,' she said. 'I know he has said that young people keep him involved in what's happening in the world, so I knew that was one reason, but there was a concern of mine that she was spending more time than most.' Ms Currie knew that 'the majority' of the President's meetings with Ms. Lewinsky were 'more personal in nature as opposed to business.'

Monica even discussed the matter with Ms Currie. Monica said: 'As long as no one saw us – and no one did – then nothing happened.'

'Don't want to hear it,' said Ms Currie, flustered. 'Don't say any more. I don't want to hear any more.'

It was a reality check. Bill eventually got Ms Currie to invite Monica to the White House where he told her that he must end the relationship. He admitted that, early in his marriage, he had had hundreds of affairs, but since turning forty, he had made an effort at any rate to not have new sexual relations. He was now fifty. They kissed and hugged, but there was to be no more sex, she said. This was three days before the Supreme Court ruled that the Constitution did not give the president immunity against civil law suits.

Things got ugly.

Clinton was still trying to get Monica a job back at the White House, but he was obstructed by Ms Currie and other women staffers. The claws came out. Monica said she felt 'used' and reminded him in a letter that she had 'left the White House like a good girl in April of '96,' when other people might have threatened disclosure to hold onto their job. Ouch. His response was swift. At a very emotional meeting the next day, he said lugubriously: 'It's illegal to threaten the President of the United States.'

'He remarked… that he wished he had more time for me.' 'And so I said, well, maybe you will have more time in three years.' 'And he… jokingly said, well, what are we going to do when I'm seventy-five and I have to pee twenty-five times a day? 'I left that day sort of emotionally stunned,' the twenty-six-year-old Monica confided to Special Counsel Kenneth Starr. 'I just knew he was in love with me.'

In fact, another woman had entered their love frame. Monica told Bill that *Newsweek* were working on an article about Kathleen Willey, a volunteer at the White House. Monica had been told about this by Linda Tripp, a colleague in the Pentagon's public affairs office who was speaking to *Newsweek*. Tripp, who had formerly worked at the White House, said that she saw Willey emerge from the Oval Office 'dishevelled – her face red and her lipstick was off'. *Newsweek* was to claim that Clinton had sexually harassed Willey in the Oval Office. In words that could have been spoken by Trump, Bill told Monica that the harassment allegation was ludicrous, because he would never approach a small-breasted woman like Ms Willey.

Nevertheless, the President urged Monica talk to Linda Tripp to try and shut her up. This was a tricky move. Tripp was not only a former Bush aide, but, oddly, she had also served Hillary's partner Vince Foster his last hamburger before he committed suicide – or was ruthlessly gunned down through the throat by the Clintons' hired assassins if one sides with the conspiracy rumours. Unbeknownst to Clinton, Tripp, as Monica's confidante, also knew about the many blow jobs on-and-off phone calls, including one with the Mexican President.

Willey refused to comment publicly, however, and Tripp was denounced as a liar by the President's lawyers. Reluctantly, Willey was forced to make a deposition in the Paula Jones case. She later let TV in on her secrets as well. The President, she said, had taken her hand and placed it on his member. Were the First Genitals aroused? she was asked. Yes, she conceded.

In a tantalising sideways move, Tripp thoughtfully extended Monica's circle of trust to literary agent Lucianne Goldberg. A long-time Clinton-baiter Goldberg had previously been a $1,000-a-week Republican spy in the McGovern camp in the 1972 Nixon dirty-tricks campaign. She had gone on to represent Mark Fuhrman, the racist cop caught lying in the O.J. Simpson trial. She was an all-round person, full of sound advice.

Goldberg lapped up Tripp's salacious White House gossip. But for it to stick, she said, she needed hard evidence. Lewinsky had turned to Tripp as a shoulder to cry on and so, in return, Tripp began taping Lewinsky's phone calls, and pumping her for as much pornographic detail as she could on these calls. Tripp also advised Monica not to clean the now infamous navy-blue dress that had caught America's First Semen.

The fun was fizzing out of Carry On Up the White House at this time, though Monica was still eager to revive their affair.

On 16 August 1997, three days before Bill's birthday, she visited the White House again, where she managed to get into the President's back office (another day of tight presidential security that day too). There she stuck a candle in an apple square. When he came in, she sang 'Happy Birthday' and gave him his presents. Then she asked for a birthday kiss. He said 'we could kind of bend the rules that day. And so... we kissed.'

But it was not going to end there as far as the twenty-five-year-old Monica was concerned. She grabbed his penis through his pants and went to go down on him, but this time he stopped her. 'He said, "I'm trying not to do this and I'm trying to be good".'

Linda Tripp had by now heard from a friend at the National Security Council that rumours were spreading about Monica and that she would never get another job in the White House. Her advice was to 'get out of town'. Clinton independently arranged for Monica to be offered a job at the United Nations in New York, but she stubbornly turned it down preferring to stay near her love interest.

On 15 December Paula Jones' attorneys asked Clinton to 'produce documents that related to communications between the President and Monica Lewisky [sic]'.

Clinton's friend and legal adviser Vernon Jordan said he would find her an attorney. But first he asked Clinton one question: 'Mr President, have you had sexual relations with Monica Lewinsky?' Bill, having a dry-run at the question, said to his friend: 'No, never.'

Before Christmas Monica turned up at the White House with some presents and, while she had to wait for some forty minutes, the Secret Service officer let slip that Clinton was in a meeting with blonde sizeably-breasted thirty-seven-year-old actress and TV personality Eleanor Mondale. The *Washington Post* was later to imply in the same article that Mondale was having an affair with the president and to report Lewinsky had 'stormed away, called and berated Ms Currie from a pay phone.'

Monica's final visit to the Oval Office came after Christmas when she gave Bill his presents. He was overwhelmed, she thought. She said that the president rewarded her with a 'passionate' and 'physically intimate' kiss – a mysterious term that the otherwise pornographic Starr accepted without prodding further.

That same day Betty Currie drove to Monica's apartment and collected all the gifts that Clinton had given her (though a subpoena required Monica to produce all the gifts he had given her). Vernon Jordan advised her in addition to throw away any correspondence she had had with the president.

Monica later went around to Betty Currie's home to deliver yet another present for Bill – a book called *The Presidents of the United States*. It made an eclectic collection with her earlier gifts: a marble bear's head, a Rockettes blanket, a black dog stuffed animal, a box of chocolates (small), a pair of joke sunglasses, and a pin with a New York skyline on it... The book itself included a love note inspired by the movie *Titanic* and said that she wanted to have sexual intercourse with him at least once. But the president conceded later that he cautioned her not to write such notes.

Meanwhile, Clinton was questioned about his relationship with Monica Lewinsky. Judge Wright specified, for the purposes of his deposition, that a person engages in 'sexual relations' when the person knowingly engages in or causes... contact with the genitalia, anus, groin, breast, inner thigh, or buttocks of any person with an intent to arouse or gratify the sexual desire of any person... 'Contact' meant intentional touching, either directly or through clothing.

To Clinton's mind however, 'any person, reasonable person' would recognise that oral sex performed on the deponent falls outside the definition. So if Monica performed oral sex on the President she was engaged in sexual relations, but he was not. He did admit that direct contact with Monica's breasts or genitalia would fall within the definition, but he denied touching them. His definition would even explain the semen on Monica's dress without inviting a charge of the president perjuring himself in court. He could come all over her as many times as he wanted and still not have sexual relations. In order to run the world's only superpower you need that level of logic, or at any rate that assumption held water until the Trump Presidency.

The President then had a word with Betty Currie. He said: 'You were always there when she was there, right?... We were never really alone.... Monica came on to me, and I never touched her, right?... You can see and hear everything, right?' Ms Currie said that she got the distinct impression that the president wanted her to agree with him.

Sensing they had another –gate on their hands, on 21 January 1998, the *Washington Post* unleashed Zippergate with a story headlined: 'Clinton Accused of Urging Aide to Lie; Starr Probes whether President Told Woman to Deny Alleged Affair to Jones's Lawyers.'

Meanwhile Bill consoled his staff with the repeated assertion: 'I want you to know I did not have sexual relationships with this woman, Monica Lewinsky. I did not ask anybody to lie. And when the facts come out, you'll understand.'

He meant, elliptically, that when his definition of 'sexual relations' came out they would understand.

It was vitally important for his job, and theirs. Adultery is a misdemeanour in the District of Columbia with a maximum penalty of $500 or 180 days in jail. But it is a felony in Idaho, Massachusetts, Oklahoma, Wisconsin and Michigan, where the maximum sentence is life. As recently as 1980, a Massachusetts couple were spotted having sex in a van and, when they admitted they were married but not to each other, they were arrested for adultery and fined $50. If it were proved that Clinton had an affair with Lewinsky or anyone else while he was President, it would constitute one of the 'misdemeanours' identified in the Constitution as criteria for impeachment.

Hence Bill's preference for oral sex. There is no mention of oral sex in the Bible. So it is not, in a very technical sense, adultery.

It is true that some states specifically define adultery as sexual intercourse outside marriage. But the District of Columbia leaves adultery undefined, so the biblical definition would apply in that state. That meant that Bill Clinton could enjoy oral sex in the White House with as many women as he fancied, though he would have to avoid Kansas and a few other states where oral sex is expressly part of the criminal code. And he would have been well advised to steer clear of Maryland, where Montgomery County Circuit Court Administrative Judge Paul Weinstein had ruled that adultery should be understood to include any other sexual acts as it was essentially a breach in the trust between a married couple, regardless of the precise nature of the sexual act involved.

The polls showed that the American public wasn't too bothered about extra-marital relations but that they would not forgive perjury or obstruction of justice. So Clinton urged his aides to go easy on Monica Lewinsky in the hope that she would not co-operated with the Starr investigation.

'We don't want to alienate her by anything we put out,' he said.

But alienate her the master of verbal pyrotechnics inadvertently did himself. On 26 January 1998, he tried to draw a line under the affair, once and for all. At a televised news conference, he said defiantly: 'I did not have sexual relations with that woman, Miss Lewinsky.' Subconsciously he had swapped the well-rehearsed 'this' with an exasperated 'that'. Ouch.

Determined that the moment had come, Linda Tripp went to Kenneth Starr and handed over the tapes of intimate conversations between Monica and Bill. Starr began to request testimony from the Secret Service agents who had guarded the President and also testimony from Bill Clinton, who was characteristically interesting.

Clinton insisted to Starr he had been telling the truth when he told his top aides that 'there is nothing going on' between him and Monica Lewinsky. Looking back, his aides realised that Clinton had always used the present tense. So he was right. He was not having a relationship with Monica Lewinsky at the time he was talking to them as he had put an end to it.

Things moved to the next scene. Starr had spent $25 million and three years on investigating the Clintons without success and could afford a wiretap hidden in Tripp's capacious frontage. Tripp then invited Lewinsky for cocktails at the Ritz Carlton in Crystal City for some more secretly-taped girl talk.

Monica began complaining to Tripp that the President was cheating on her with four other women – three of whom worked in the White House. The Carry On show was still continuing, just not with her. She was not content and called him 'The Creep' and 'El Sicko'.

Monica also said she had asked Bill Clinton why he did not settle the Paula Jones case out of court. He apparently replied: 'I can't – because then they would all come out of the woodwork.'

'Were there that many?' Lewinsky had asked.

'Hundreds', replied Bill to Monica.

The latest 'bimbo eruption' had reached unprecedented proportions. Who were these four other women the President was currently seeing? Who were the hundreds he had had intimate relations with during his political career? There were plenty of candidates.

The press quickly tracked down former Miss America and *Playboy* centrefold Elizabeth Ward Gracen. Then there was forty-eight-year-old Dolly Kyle Browning, who said her high school affair with Clinton lasted into his White House days. She claimed to have made love to him three times in a senator's hotel room. And, while he was governor, they had sex in the basement of the gubernatorial mansion, frolicked in houses borrowed from friends and made love in a neighbour's backyard.

Another friend, Susan McDougal, went to gaol for eighteen months for refusing to testify against Clinton. Her husband, Jim, said that he had intercepted an 'intimate' phone call between his wife and the President, and that she later admitted the affair. But she contradicted him and told the press, 'I'm a small-town girl, a

Southern Baptist, I wouldn't do that.'

Sheila Lawrence was then accused of having sex with President Clinton. In return for ignoring what was going on, her millionaire husband Larry was made U.S. Ambassador to Switzerland. When he died, Clinton rewarded Sheila's discretion by having her husband's remains interred in Arlington National Cemetery, where John F. Kennedy is buried (Lawrence was later moved when it was discovered that he had lied about his military service).

Other girlfriends past returned to the lime light. Gennifer Flowers now told CNN chat-show host Larry King that Clinton had made her pregnant and she had had to have an abortion. Meanwhile, the tennis ball and garden hose tape aired. And thirty-three-year-old Bobbie Ann Williams took a lie detector test in an attempt to get child support for her seven-year-old son and Clinton-lookalike, Danny.

But Clinton's affair with Monica Lewinsky remained completely different as one false move could trigger a perjury charge. The young intern seemed to be able to bring the most world's powerful man to his knees. Bill fessed up to having been 'emotionally close' to Monica.

Politically, things were rosier. To impeach a president, the House of Representatives has to pass a Bill of Impeachment. But House-Majority Leader, right-wing Republican Newt Gingrich, was a chip of the same sex block. In a bitterly contended divorce case, he had denied 'sleeping with a lover' on the grounds that he had only had oral sex with her.

In the Senate things were no different. It was packed with old roués. Where would Ted Kennedy stand on this one? After all, he had gone down with, if not on, an intern at Chappaquiddick in 1969.

Then there was the legendary Dixiecrat Strom Thurmond, a nonagenarian and still in the Senate. He was famed for his sexual antics. When he was judge he picked up a woman, who he had recently been condemned to death, from the county jail and drove her to death's door, making love to her on the way. He was twenty three years older than his first wife and forty four years older than his second. He was sixty eight when he married a twenty-four-year-old former South Carolina beauty queen and they had four children. Well known for groping women in the elevator in the Senate building, he kept a baseball bat in his office so that, when he died, the undertaker could use it to beat down his penis so they could close the lid of the coffin.

The Republicans did not even want Clinton out. They would prefer to keep him on as a lame duck.

Hillary was again wheeled out to hold the line. She went on the chat shows and said she still loved and trusted her husband! It did her no favours to step in the firing line and say there was a right-wing conspiracy to bring her husband down. She was promptly dubbed 'the world's most powerful doormat'.

Legally, things were a little more hairy.

If Clinton had lied under oath in his deposition, he was still guilty of perjury. And if he had put pressure on Monica Lewinsky to lie too, he was guilty of suborning a witness. And if he had had some gifts he had given Monica Lewinsky removed from her apartment – as was now being alleged – he was guilty of obstructing justice. As President, Clinton was the chief law officer of the United States and he had to obey the law.

Starr struck his deal with Monica Lewinsky. If she testified in graphic detail to the Grand Jury, holding nothing back, he would guarantee her immunity from prosecution. But if she did not testify, he would charge her with perjury over her testimony in the Paula Jones case. Monica had no choice. She took the deal.

Courtesy of *The Star*, Bobbie Ann Williams had her son's DNA compared with that provided to the Starr Committee by Bill Clinton, but it was found that the President was not his father.

After the Senate acquitted Clinton from impeachment, N.B.C. aired Juanita Broaddrick's story. She had finally agreed to go on the record, saying that he had inveigled his way into her hotel room and suddenly kissed her. She pushed him away and said she was a married woman and not interested.

'Then he tries to kiss me again. And the second time he tries to kiss me he starts biting my lip,' she told *Dateline* interviewer Lisa Myers. 'He starts to, um, bite on my top lip and I tried to pull away from him. And then he forces me down on the bed. And I just was very frightened, and I tried to get away from him and I told him "No," that I didn't want this to happen but he wouldn't listen to me.... It was a real panicky, panicky situation. I was even to the point where I was getting very noisy, you know, yelling to "Please stop." And that's when he pressed down on my right shoulder and he would bite my lip.... When everything was over with, he got up and straightened himself, and I was crying at the moment and he walks to the door, and calmly puts on his sunglasses. And before he goes out the door he says "You better get some ice on that." And he turned and went out the door.'

Norma Rogers, who was sharing an apartment with Juanita, said she returned to find her on the bed 'in a state of shock,' her pantyhose torn in the crotch and her lip swollen as though she had been hit. Norma also said that Juanita had told her Clinton had 'forced himself on her'. She confided the same to three other friends.

Clinton's attorney denied Broaddrick's allegations. Ken Starr's investigation had been wound up. There was nothing to add. Except that, it all came back again during Hilary's presidential campaign against Trump in 2016 and as a result of the #WeToo movement.

Ironically, Hillary married and ran against the same type of man as her husband. As always in politics, the winner takes all. Had she become president we might have discovered whether she is a lesbian – or at any rate what her definition of the term is – and how that rumour might relate to the other rumours of her and the salty affair with Vince Foster.

When Hillary first entered the White House as First Lady, she admitted going up to the roof to commune with Eleanor Roosevelt. Gennifer Flowers quoted Bill about Hilary: she has 'probably eaten more pussy than I have'.

V

George H.W. Bush Sr, #41

'I'm not going to take any sleaze questions'

As unlikely as if may seem George Herbert Walker Bush was in the centre of a sex scandal. In truth, back in the 1960s, when 'Rubbers' Bush Sr was banging on about contraceptives in Congress, it was said that he set up an Italian woman in an apartment in New York. Then during the 1988 election, it was alleged that George Bush had had a long-term affair with Jennifer Fitzgerald, an aide on his vice-presidential staff. She was no bimbo. She was in her mid-fifties and bore a striking resemblance to the matronly Barbara Bush who at times was mistaken to be George's mother. Nevertheless, *LA Weekly* ran a story naming Fitzgerald as Bush's long-time mistress and quoting an unnamed source that Fitzgerald had spoken openly of the affair.

Jennifer Fitzgerald denied the story. However, in the hot house that is Washington, rumours of Bush's extra-marital dalliances and his association with a mysterious 'Ms X' continued.

It might be considered the first seed that was to lead to the #WeToo era. At the time, this sort of press enquiry into the sex lives of the presidential candidates was unprecedented. Newsmen had deliberately hushed up sex scandals of John F. Kennedy and Franklin D. Roosevelt. In fact, anything to do with a President's body was off-limits. Even mentioning that FDR was confined to a wheelchair was a no no.

The reason reporters had broken with tradition and began reporting on the sex lives of the candidates was the Democratic hopeful Gary Hart. A handsome young Senator from Colorado, Hart liked to think of himself as another Kennedy. He had the same effect on women voters, leading one Republican to quip 'my heart is for Bush, but my bush is for Hart'.

Hart had a reputation as a womaniser which the press kept quiet about until he made an astonishing challenge. In 1987, he told *The New York Times* that he had nothing to hide and invited journalists to follow him.

Reporters from the *Miami Herald* took him at his word. They staked out his Washington townhouse and discovered that, while his wife was away, Hart was entertaining twenty-nine-year-old model Donna Rice overnight. When the story hit the front pages, Hart's wife Lee rallied to his defence.

'I made a mistake in my personal life,' Hart admitted on the TV. 'I've also insisted, as I think I have a right to, that my mistake in my personal life be put against the mistakes of this administration – selling arms to terrorists, lying to Congress, shredding documents.'

It would not wash. The *Washington Post* came up with another unnamed young woman who claimed to have had an affair with Hart. The *National Enquirer* followed up with pictures of Hart, Rice, Hart fundraiser William Broadhurst and Rice's friend Lynn Armadt at a cosy drinks party on board a yacht called, aptly, *Monkey Business* in Bimini. In *People* magazine, Lynn Armadt claimed that Hart and Rice shared the master bedroom. The Hart campaign quickly disappeared under a landslide of fresh allegations. From then on, nothing in a politician's bedroom was safe from the American press.

Thus, on the eve of the 1992 Republican convention in Huston, Susan B. Trento published the book *The Power House* which named British-born diplomat Jennifer Fitzgerald as 'First Mistress'.

In 1955, Jennifer Patteson-Knight, the daughter of a British officer, had married a U.S. Army private, Gerald FitzGerald, but divorced him in 1959. She kept his surname, though she made the G lower case. Fitzgerald first met Bush during the Watergate scandal in 1974 and quit her job in the White House to become his secretary when he was appointed ambassador to China and went on to work with him at the CIA and on his vice-presidential staff.

According to the book, U.S. Ambassador Louis Fields claimed 'first-hand knowledge of the affair'. He had arranged for then Vice

President George Bush and his former appointments secretary Jennifer Fitzgerald to share a private cottage during an official visit to Geneva in 1984.

'It became clear that the Vice President and Mrs Fitzgerald were romantically involved and this was not a business visit,' said Fields. The couple had adjoining bedrooms but the rendezvous was 'so heavy handed' that it made him feel 'very uncomfortable'. At the time, the First Lady Barbara Bush was in the U.S. faithfully promoting her book about the family dog, *C. Fred's Story: A Dog's Life*.

During the 1992 campaign, Hillary Clinton brought up the name of Jennifer Fitzgerald when allegations of infidelity were being made against her own husband. The scandal broke when the story made the front page of the *New York Post*, who cited two other sources – a lawyer and a former reporter – who had also heard versions of the story.

When CNN reporter Mary Tillotson broached the topic at a joint news conference Bush was holding with Israeli Prime Minister Yitzhak Rabin at the family estate at Kennebunkport, Maine, Bush grew heated and declared himself to be outraged.

'I'm not going to take any sleazy questions like that from CNN,' said Bush. 'I am very disappointed that you would ask such a question of me, and I will not respond to it. I haven't responded in the past. Nevertheless, in this kind of screwy climate we're in, why, I expect it. But I don't like it, and I'm not going to respond other than to say it's a lie.'

Barbara Bush looked on with disgust.

Later in the day when Bush returned to Washington, he was interviewed in the Oval Office by Stone Phillips, who asked him straight out: 'Have you ever had an affair?'

'I'm not going to take any sleaze questions,' Bush replied. 'You're perpetuating the sleaze by even asking the question, to say nothing of asking it in the Oval Office. And I don't think you ought to do that, and I'm not going to answer the question.' Ironically the interview went out on NBC's *Dateline*.

Not being able to take advantage of the situation without harming himself, and obviously without a hint of self-interest, the Democratic presidential nominee Bill Clinton condemned the lowering of the tone of presidential campaign with allegations of marital infidelity. Referring to rumours of his own adultery earlier that year, Clinton said: 'I didn't like it when it was done to me, and I don't like it when it's done to him.'

He had said nothing when Hillary was fuming over stories about her husband's alleged affair with Gennifer Flowers and complained to *Vanity Fair* in May that everyone knew there was also a 'Jennifer', in Bush's life, but that no one was reporting it.

Ms Fitzgerald was then deputy chief of protocol in the State Department, an appointment arranged by Bush when he entered the White House. When the scandal broke, she was said to be out of the country on business, but her mother, eighty-six-year-old Frances Patteson-Knight, said Jennifer was 'devastated'.

'She had a very unhappy marriage, and she can't stand men,' she said, and she recalled helpfully that her daughter once told her, 'I've been through so much. I couldn't have sex with anybody.'

VI

Ronald Reagan, #40

'Let's just get to know each other.'

Like Donald Trump, Ronald Reagan did not dye his hair, but went prematurely orange, according to former President Gerald Ford. But while The Donald was a TV reality show star before he became president, Ronnie had been a movie star, of sorts.

A well-known ladies' man back in his home state of Illinois, his first publicity shots in Hollywood show him bare-chested and surrounded by a bevy of bathing beauties. Indeed, one of Reagan's first jobs was as a lifeguard.

'He was the perfect specimen of an athlete, tall, willowy, muscular, brown, good-looking,' a friend remembered. 'Of course, the girls were always flocking around him.'

In church, he could not take his eyes off Bee Drew. She had a boyfriend, so Reagan would go out with them as a foursome with Bee's friend Margaret Cleaver. He later claimed to be in love with Margaret but 'she was grown-up enough to know we weren't grown-up enough to call this anything but friendship'. Members of their church thought they would wed nonetheless. They went on to college together. With other couples they dated at the graveyard nearby, where they could huddle together against the old gravestones.

After college, 'Dutch' Reagan became a radio announcer in Des Moines, while Margaret went to spend a year with her sister in France. This left him one of the most eligible bachelors in the city. He soon found himself a new girlfriend, the sleek and glamorous Mary Frances from Monmouth, Illinois. However, one was not enough.

Reagan began to be a man about town, hanging out at Cy's Moonlight Inn 'with many girls'. He broke up with Mary Frances and began dating the shapely Miss Schnelle and the beautiful Jeane Tesdell. Then came Joy Hodges, who accepted his invitation to go horseback riding, but found she had nothing to wear.

When he moved out to Hollywood, he maintained his friendship with Joy, but fell under the spell of the green-eyed beautiful June Travis, who played alongside him in his first movie *Love Is On The Air*. When the shooting was over, so was their romance.

He escorted Lana Turner – then renowned as the 'sweater girl' for her figure-hugging sweater in *They Won't Forget* – to the premiere of *Jezebel* in 1948. He also dated Ila Rhodes, a striking blonde contract player who appeared with him in *Secret Service of the Air* and *Hell's Kitchen*.

It was in *Brother Rat* the he met 'pretty, pert' Jane Wyman. She fell in love with him. He thought of her as 'a good scout' and 'loads of fun to be with'. She sourly complained that he was 'about as good in bed as he was on screen'. Nevertheless, they married in 1940.

Reagan's movie career peaked in 1942 when he played a small-town playboy who awakes to find his legs have been amputated by a sadistic surgeon in *Kings Row*. His character's immortal waking line: 'Where's the rest of me?' became the title of Reagan's 1965 autobiography.

After World War II, Reagan found it harder to get starring roles and, in 1947, became president of the Screen Actor's Guild, though he continued making B-movies.

In 1948, Jane Wyman filed for divorce, citing 'continual arguments on his political views', and began a torrid affair with Lew Ayres, her co-star in *Johnny Belinda*. Given her comment on his bedroom performance, there had obviously been other failings in their marriage.

After the divorce, Reagan reverted to the bachelor life he had led in Des Moines, only better. A free man again, he was out on the pull – in a town that was full of starlets and other hopefuls. He also had access to some of the most beautiful women in the world. Though

John Loves Mary contains passionate kissing scenes with Patricia Neal he was thought of as something of a gentleman.

Arlene Dahl remembered his 'paternal' kindness which she compared to that of Gary Cooper. Virginia Mayo complimented him on his gallantry.

'He did have, occasionally, young ladies on the set,' Mayo recalled. 'His charm was overwhelming and I think that was the basis of his career as an actor.'

He chatted openly about sex to Viveca Lindfors, his Swedish co-star in *Night unto Night*, maintaining it was 'best in the afternoon after coming out of the shower'. However, fellow actor Eddie Bracken remembers him around that time as a lonely guy.

'He was never for the sexpots,' Bracken said. 'He was never a guy looking for the bed. He was a guy looking for companionship more than anything else.'

Four years after his divorce, Reagan married another movie actress, Nancy Davis, a woman with a history of her own. Her mother Edith Luckett was an actress and her godmother was famous silent-era lesbian movie star Alla Nazimova. According to Kitty Kelley's *Nancy Reagan: The Unauthorized Biography*, Nancy had a lesbian affair with a classmate when she was majoring in theatre at Smith College in Massachusetts. As a debutante, she fell in love with a young man who committed suicide and this had left her scarred.

During World War II, she got engaged to a naval officer, a distinctly feminine character, but she broke the engagement off after a couple of months. After that, she started a period of sexual experimentation and became what men at that time called 'accessible' to the point including to the married men who were friends of her parents.

Escaping to New York, she began hanging out with gay men, taking one, with some mild bisexual tendencies, as her lover. In 1946, she won a role in the Broadway musical *Lute Song* and began an affair with one of the dancers who, until then, had slept with only two other women in his life. During her time on Broadway, she also had three dates with Clark Gable.

Nancy's phone number was being passed around, guaranteeing a regular supply of dates. Spencer Tracy, a notorious womaniser, drunk and friend of her mother's, organised a screen test for her, which led to an offer from Hollywood.

At MGM, she had an affair with Bernard Thau the casting director and her career took off. In an interview shortly before he died in 1983, Thau said that Nancy was renowned for giving oral sex in the movie company's offices to powerful men who expected it in return for career advancement. It was one of the reasons she got a contract, according to Thau. It bolstered her popularity among those men on the MGM lot.

Thau was not the only one. In *The Peter Lawford Story: Life With the Kennedys, Monroe and the Rat Pack*, written by Lawford's widow Patricia, Lawford is quoted as saying Nancy's 'avocation was to have a good time'. Patricia Lawford went on: 'Peter was watching the news right after Reagan was elected. He went over to the set, laughing and calling Mrs Reagan a vulgar name. I was shocked and wanted to know what was bothering him. He laughed again and said that when she was single, Nancy Davis was known for giving the best head in Hollywood.'

Lawford told his wife of a drive to Phoenix with Nancy and Bob Walker, who he said was Nancy's lover at the time.

'Nancy would visit her parents, Dr and Mrs Loyal Davis, while Peter and Walker picked up girls at Arizona State University in Tempe, a Phoenix suburb,' Patricia wrote about her husband's first-hand knowledge. 'He claimed that she entertained them orally on those trips, apparently playing with whichever man was not driving at the moment. I have no idea if Peter was telling the truth, though I have to assume he was because Peter was not one to gossip.'

Nancy appeared in eleven movies. In her last film, *Hellcats of the Navy*, she played opposite her future husband. At the time, Reagan was running around with a number of women – starlets, singers, models, beauticians and some big stars – most of them around ten years younger than him.

Betty Powers, one of the bevy of models and starlets Reagan was seen with at the time, said that Reagan was so obsessed with his ex Jane Wyman that he was impotent.

Reagan's type was big, blonde, outdoor women like actress Doris Lilly, author of *How to Marry a Millionaire* and *How to Make Love in Five Languages*, and thought to be the inspiration for Holly Golightly in Truman Capote's Breakfast at Tiffany's. They had a brief affair, but she complained that he was 'passive… very gentle, very square' and, seemingly, more interest in drinking than sex. Reagan would send her flowers and love letters. Two of these letters later came up at auction. They were bought by millionaire publisher and Trump adversary Malcolm Forbes. He gave them to Nancy Reagan, but she asked him to wait until Reagan had left office before he handed them over, so she would not have to declare them as gifts. Lilly believes that Nancy probably destroyed the letters out of jealousy, so that no one would know that he had anyone else in his life.

Starlet Jacqueline Park, later the mistress of Warner Bros studio boss Jack Warner, told a similar story. When the two began dating, Reagan 'couldn't perform sexually,' she said. 'I think he was still suffering withdrawal pains from Jane Wyman.'

Throughout their liaison, Park said, 'He never took me out in public, never gave me a present and never ever paid for a cab for me.' Nonetheless, Park, became pregnant.

'When I told him I was pregnant, he said he didn't want to have anything to do with me anymore,' she said. 'He just ran out on me. He was a swinger in those days. He went out with this girl and that girl. But the moment he married Nancy and became a Republican, he was reformed, and there's nothing more boring than a reformed swinger.'

According to Reagan's own account, he was tiring of the never-ending round of beauties he was having sex with. 'I woke up morning and I couldn't remember the name of the gal I was in bed with,' he told a friend. 'And I said get a grip here.'

Reagan first proposed to glamour girl Christine Larson, who

turned him down. Soon after, Nancy told him she was pregnant which settled the question who to get a grip with.

The old swinger in Reagan had one final wobble. Before the nuptials, he encountered nineteen-year-old blonde Selene Walters. They met a Hollywood nightclub.

'Although I was on a date,' Walters said, 'Ronnie kept whispering in my ear, "I'd like to call you. How can I get in touch with you"?'

Reagan was then president of the Screen Actors Guild and she hope that he could give her a leg up in her career, so she gave him her address and was surprised when he came calling at 3 am.

According to Kitty Kelley, Walters told her: 'He pushed his way inside and said he just had to see me. He forced me on the couch… and said, "Let's just get to know each other." It was the most pitched battle I've ever had, and suddenly in a matter of seconds I lost… They call it date rape today.'

Selene Walters later confirmed Kelley's account of what happen, except she said that Reagan did not force his way in.

'I opened the door,' she told *People Magazine*. 'Then it was the battle of the couch. I was fighting him. I didn't want him to make love to me. He's a very big man, and he just had his way. Date rape? No, God, no, that's her [Kelley's] phrase. I didn't have a chance to have a date with him.'

Walters said she bore Reagan no ill will, and even voted for him.

'I don't think he meant to harm me,' she said.

A week later, Reagan announced that he was going to marry Nancy. They married in March 1952. Two months later, they announced that Nancy was expecting a baby in December. In fact, the child, Patti, was born in October. (When she grew up, her name was to be linked romantically to that of presidential hopeful John Kerry). Reagan was not present at the birth as he was with Christine Larson. Their affair ended shortly after, when Reagan arrived at her apartment one afternoon to be greeted by a French actor wearing no more than a bath towel.

Once married Nancy quit Hollywood and stopped working to dedicate herself to being a housewife.

'A woman's real happiness and real fulfilment come from within the home with her husband and children,' she said.

However, according to Kitty Kelly's biography, Nancy did not attain this real happiness with Reagan. While he was governor of California, Nancy began an affair with Frank Sinatra that 'continued for years.'

As First Lady, Kelley wrote, Nancy entertained Frank Sinatra privately to 'lunch' in the White House while Reagan was away. The entered the back way and these private 'lunches' never appear in the First Lady's schedule. He would stay from 12.30 to 3.30 or 4pm. While he was there the family quarters were off limits to everyone. Kelley quotes a staffer, saying: 'She was not to be disturbed. For anything. And that included a call from the President himself.'

Sinatra would also accompany the First Lady to fundraisers. At White House parties she would dance dreamily with her 'Francis Albert', annoyed if her husband cut in. She would take up so much of his evening that even his wife Barbara complained.

According to Peter Lawford, Sinatra hated Reagan almost as much as he hated Nixon. A life-long Democrat, Sinatra despised Reagan as a turncoat after his defection from the Democratic party in 1962. During Reagan's governorship of California, he would change the words of 'The Lady Is a Tramp' to: 'She hates California, it's Reagan and damp… that's why the lady is a tramp.'

Reagan had already left office when Kitty Kelley's damning book came out and his Alzheimer's may already have been too advanced for him to take it all in. It was well before the #WeToo movement and the Selene Walters Hollywood-rape accusation came and went.

VII
Jimmy Carter, #37

In the 1976 presidential campaign, Carter took the bold step of giving an interview to *Playboy* magazine.

'Committing adultery according to the Bible – which I believe in – is a sin,' Carter told the magazine, 'For us to hate one another, for us to have sexual intercourse outside marriage, for us to engage in homosexual activities, for us to steal, for us to lie – all these are sins.'

However, he admitted: 'I've looked on a lot of women with lust. I've committed adultery in my heart many times.'

He married Rosalynn Carter on July 17, 1946 after he planted a surprise kiss on her cheek in the backseat of a car.

VIII
Gerald Ford, #38

Vice President Gerald Ford stepped in after Richard Nixon resigned as President. At college, he had fallen instantly in love with stunningly beautiful Phyllis Brown. She went on to become a model in New York and he and Phyllis joined forces to model ski clothes together for *Look* magazine. After what Ford himself describes in his autobiography as a 'torrid four-year love affair', they split when Ford turned down offers to practise law in New York or nearby Philadelphia and returned to his home town, Grand Rapids, Michigan.

He met his wife Betty there during the local 1948 congress election campaign for the House of Representatives. She had been born in Chicago but was brought up in Grand Rapids. She studied modern dance at Bennington College in Vermont and joined the Martha Graham company, supporting herself by working as a fashion model. She married for the first time at twenty-four, but divorced five years later. She married Gerald Ford three weeks before the election, beginning a sojourn in Washington that lasted nearly thirty years.

Although she was already ill when they entered the White House, Betty Ford rose to the challenge of becoming, unexpectedly, First Lady in 1974. Later that year she underwent radical surgery for breast cancer. Explaining her decision to discuss this openly she said: 'If I as First Lady could talk about it candidly and without embarrassment, many other people would be able to as well.'

Her autobiography, *Betty: A Glad Awakening* published in 1987, discusses publicly her drug and alcohol dependency. Asked why his wife's life story, rather than his own, had been made into a TV movie, Gerald Ford replied: 'My wife is much more interesting.'

IX
Richard Nixon, #37

'That old cocksucker.'

On the Trump scale, Richard Milhous Nixon was sexually, as well as politically, enigmatic. Olga, his steady girlfriend at college, said: 'Most of the time I just couldn't figure him out.' They had met at Whittier College when Nixon was standing in the student-union's presidential election. Startlingly, she wrote in her diary: 'Oh, how I long to hate Richard Nixon' and voted for his rival.

A few weeks later, they were both in a college production of *The Aeneid*. As they were as Dido and Aeneas, Nixon was supposed to declare his love for her and embrace her before they threw themselves on the funeral pyre. Sadly he was not up to exhibiting that much passion on stage. He tiptoed around her, gave her a simpering kiss, then tugged at her toga. It was more than the teenage audience could stand. His performance as a classical lover was greeted with boos and catcalls. It was, he conceded, 'sheer torture'.

'I was never so embarrassed in my whole life,' Olga recalled on her part. Still, they started going out together.

At Duke University, Nixon was stiff and stilted with women. 'Let's face it,' said one co-ed, 'he was stuffy.' But he could come up with a date if he was forced to.

'I don't believe that girls were as important to Dick as they were to the rest of us,' a fellow student said.

Later, when he was a partner in the law firm Wingert and Bewley in Whittier, California, he admitted that he was embarrassed when it came to handling a divorce case.

'This good-looking woman, beautiful really, began talking to me about her problem of sexual incompatibility with her husband,' Nixon confided. 'I turned fifteen colours of the rainbow.'

On 16 January 1988, he met twenty-six-year-old school teacher Patricia Ryan. It was love at first sight. He asked her for a date. She said she was too busy and he blurted out: 'You may not believe this but I am going to marry you some day.'

Gradually, she got to like him and agreed to date him provided he 'made no declarations of love or proposals of marriage'.

One night, they went to Topsy's in East Los Angeles with another couple. It was a striptease joint, one of Nixon's enduring passions. Nixon made them dress for the occasion. He wore his mother's raccoon coat. It was surely the oddest date for a future First Lady to meet her President. The entrance fee was $3 that night because the famous 'Burlesque's ball of fire' Betty Roland was performing. Her act ended in shambles when some guy in the front row touched her butt with a cigarette lighter. Despite this, Pat fell in love with Nixon and married him in 1940. They had two daughters

Even after they were married, Nixon could not stay away from strip shows. One night they went to Earl Carroll's nightclub in Los Angeles where, for $2.50, men competed to see who could throw the most garters on to the legs of the cancan dancers.

Nevertheless, Nixon always appeared rather asexual. Nixon's closet friend was Cuban-exile Bebe Rebozo. They were friends for forty four years. After losing the 1962 gubernatorial race in California, he told the press: 'You won't have Nixon to kick around anymore because, gentlemen, this is my last press conference.' Then he said he was going to go home spend some time getting to know his family again. Instead, he spent three weeks alone with Rebozo on Paradise Island in the Bahamas.

White House chief of staff General Alexander Haig joked about the two men having a homosexual affair, even aping Nixon's limp-wristed manner. But there is no evidence that they were gay. They were both fiercely anti-homosexual in an old fashioned way. Indeed, being gay was a smear Nixon liked to use against political opponents.

'The World's Greatest Girl Reporter' Adela Rogers St Johns said she once saw Nixon at a Republican rally where he was surround by some of Hollywood's most beautiful movie stars.' It was straight out of a Trump scenario, but without the lecherousness.

'You never saw such beautiful flesh,' she said. 'And he acted like a man utterly unsexed. It was as if he did not know they were there.

After only four months in office, Trump fired F.B.I. director James Comey, F.B.I. deputy director Andrew McCabe followed ten months later.

For over three years, Nixon tried to fire legendary F.B.I. Director J. Edgar Hoover, though he was well over retirement age. Each time Nixon emerged from the meeting ashen-faced with Hoover still in place. Clearly, Hoover had something on him – as he had on previous presidents and, indeed, most people in Washington.

Then Nixon got lucky, or at least he thought he did. On 2 May 1972, Hoover died. Nixon greeted the news with characteristic expletives the public learnt about from the Watergate tapes.

'Jesus Christ!' he said of Hoover, who was rumoured to have a relationship with his assistant Clyde Tolson, 'That old cocksucker.'

Later, at the height of Watergate, Nixon cursed his luck. If Hoover had still been alive, he could have contained the scandal and Nixon would have stayed on at the White House.

But, riding high in May 1972, Nixon sent his aides scurrying over to F.B.I. headquarters to retrieve his own file and other incriminating documents. The file was bulging. It turned out Hoover had even bugged the Oval Office.

But even before Nixon entered the White House, Hoover had a fat file on him. President Lyndon Johnson had read it and especially enjoyed one item. It was the story of Nixon's illicit affair with a modern-day Mata Hari.

In 1958, Nixon, then Vice President, met a twenty-three-year-old tour guide in Hong Kong named Marianna Liu. Nixon was forty five, eighteen years into his marriage and travelling alone. They met again in 1964, 1965 and 1966 when Nixon returned to Hong Kong as a private citizen. Liu was working as a hostess in the Den, the cocktail bar of the Hong Kong Hilton. Naturally, Hoover had managed to obtain photographs of the two of them together.

Their meetings were not limited to the cocktail lounge. Liu and a waitress friend visited Nixon in the suite of his friend Bebe Rebozo at the Mandarin Hotel. He also sent her flowers and a bottle of her favourite perfume when she was ill in hospital, along with a note giving her his address in New York.

The F.B.I. took a particular interest because there were suspicions that Liu was a spy of the Communist Chinese government in Beijing. She had already been seen fraternising with U.S. Navy officers. As Vice President, Nixon had had a top-secret briefing on the People's Republic of China, and any contact with Liu could be classified as a security risk.

Liu was also being watched by British intelligence. At the request of the CIA, the Hong Kong Special Branch had photographed Nixon through his bedroom window, using an infra-red camera.

Despite the F.B.I.'s attempt to monitor any visa application from Liu, she turned up at the White House at Nixon's inaugural ball in 1969. Her visa application had been given top priority. She became a U.S. permanent resident and went to live in Nixon's home town of Whittier, California. After they had been seen together, a newspaperman asked Liu about her relationship with Nixon. She said: 'Are you trying to get me killed?'

When Nixon had tried to sack Hoover, Hoover had taken great delight in personally showing Nixon Liu's file. This, presumably, was how he kept his F.B.I. job, but Liu's file, good as it was, was too blunt an instrument to use to pressure the White House on day-to-day business.

Instead, Hoover leaked rumours about White House aides. He produced a report saying that Watergate conspirators H.R. 'Bob' Haldeman, John Ehrlichman and a third aide, Dwight Chapin, were lovers and that they had attended gay parties in the Watergate building. The source was a barman and regular F.B.I. informant. The three men denied the allegations, but it was enough to keep Nixon's White House in line.

It was only after Nixon fell from power over Watergate that the

National Enquirer ran a story about his 'hot and heavy' romance with Liu. She threatened to sue, but admitted to *People* magazine that she had met Nixon when she was a 'hostess' in the cocktail lounge of the Hong Kong Hilton, that she went to see him in Rebozo's suite in the Mandarin Hotel, that he had sent her flowers and a note when she was ill, and that he had given her legal advice on emigrating to the U.S..

Liu's lawyer says Nixon is so angry about the accusations that he has volunteered to take the stand on Marianna Liu's behalf. The editor of the *Enquirer* said: 'We hope he does.'

X

Lyndon Baines Johnson, #36

'I can't stand a woman who looks like a cow
that's gonna sit on her own udder.'

John F. Kennedy's successor Lyndon Baines Johnson had been a
rival of Kennedy's in every way and considered it unjust that
Kennedy's reputation as a womaniser outstripped his own.

'I have had more women by accident than he has had on
purpose,' he said. It would not be hard to imagine that statement as
a late-night tweet emanating from the Trump White House.

Johnson openly boasted of his conquests, which were
numerous, but what was more remarkable about him was his ability
to keep two long-term relationships going, without his wife suing
for divorce.

Johnson's womanising career began early when he was fortunate
enough to go to a college at San Marcos, where the women on
campus outnumbered the men by three to one. It was easy to get a
date. His brother, Sam Houston Johnson, recalled visiting him
there. Lyndon came back to his room naked after taking a shower.
He took his penis in his hand and said: 'Well, I've gotta take Ol'
Jumbo here and give him some exercise. I wonder who I'll fuck
tonight.'

He was inordinately fond of exposing himself, whipping out
'Jumbo' at the slightest excuse. Once when flying out of Thailand
during the Vietnam war, an unwary journalist asked him how he
had enjoyed Bangkok. Cue the presidential penis. No friend of the
highfaluting British politicians, who would not back him in the
Vietnam war, he would interview the British ambassador while
sitting on the john.

He also loved to boast about his sexual conquests and was
graphic in his descriptions of his partner's anatomy and blow-by-

blow accounts of the action in the crudest terms.

But Lyndon had his eye on the main chance. A poor country boy, if he wanted to get on he had to marry for money. He first dated Carol Davis, daughter of a rich businessman. Johnson would brag that when they went out, she picked up the tab. The relationship ended when she got engaged to someone else. Later Johnson courted Kitty Clyde Ross, daughter of the richest man in Johnson City.

From a young age, Johnson had been passionate about politics. When he began his political career, he worked so hard at it that he had little time for enduring relationships. For relaxation, he would pick up waitresses and spend the night with them. His sexual encounters were episodic, one-night stands.

Too busy for conventional wooing, Johnson resourcefully asked a woman friend who had refused him a date to fix him up with someone else. She introduced him to Claudia 'Lady Bird' Taylor, the daughter of a prominent businessman who owned 15,000 acres of cotton fields and two general stores. When she turned him down, he issued an ultimatum. Either she marry him or he would never see her again. It seemed to work, miraculously. Reluctantly she accepted and they married in 1934.

In 1938, four years later, when he was a freshman U.S. congressman, Johnson met Alice Glass, the live-in lover of newspaper magnate Charles E. Marsh. Marsh had left his wife and children for her. Alice did not believe in marriage, but she and Marsh had two children together.

Their Virginia home, an eighteenth-century-style manor known as Longlea, was a meeting place for politicians and journalists. At the time, Alice was involved in organising efforts to get Jews out of Germany. Johnson lent a hand. Sometime in 1938 or 1939 they became lovers, meeting often in the Mayflower Hotel in Washington or at the Allies Inn.

It was an extraordinarily dangerous gamble as Marsh had also become Johnson's political patron. His paper ran pro-Johnson articles and, when Marsh found out Johnson was having trouble getting by on his $10,000-a-year congressman's salary, Marsh helped out. At Alice's behest Marsh even facilitated land deal that made Johnson independently wealthy. He sold Johnson a tract of land at a knock-down price. It was actually Lady Bird's money that paid for the acreage, but that one deal secured the Johnsons' financial future. It was almost as good as having a rich daddy.

It was clear that Lady Bird knew what was going on between Alice and LBJ. When he went to spend the weekend at Longlea, she would discreetly fly back to Texas or stay in Washington and busy herself with domestic chores.

Alice's sister Mary Louise said: 'Lyndon would leave her on weekends, weekend after weekend, just leave her home. I wouldn't have stood for it for a minute. We were all together a lot – Lyndon, Lady Bird and Charles and Alice. And Lady Bird never said a word. She showed nothing, nothing at all.'

But while others were sniggering behind her back, Lady Bird went on to become First Lady. She gave birth to his two daughters and she seems to have loved Johnson deeply. Jackie Kennedy said dismissively: 'Lady Bird would crawl on broken glass down Pennsylvania Avenue for Lyndon.'

It was a high-stakes game. When Johnson spent the weekend away with Alice in New York, he left his number with one of his staff. Marsh needed to contact Johnson and insisted that the man give him the number. Johnson was furious and gave the staffer a dressing down on Monday. Marsh eventually found out nonetheless.

One night, when very drunk, Marsh confronted Johnson and ordered him out of the house. But by then Johnson was too powerful to tear down and when Johnson returned later, Marsh said no more about it. The affair lasted until 1967 and only ended, when Johnson and Alice fell out over the Vietnam war. She burned his love letters and then married Marsh. And then divorced him.

Not that Johnson was faithful to his mistress. In Washington, his aide Bobby Baker ran the Quorum Club, a private member's club, and there was a continuous stream of new women to entertain him.

There was also Johnson's other enduring love – Madeleine Brown. He met her at a reception in Dallas in 1948 when he was a congressman. She was twenty three and an assistant in an advertising firm.

'He looked at me like I was an ice cream cone on a hot day,' she told *People* magazine.

They began a twenty-one-year affair. Three years after they met, Madeleine also bore Johnson a son, who they called Steven.

Madeleine said her love for Johnson was 'purely physical'. Their affair was kept well hidden from his wife Lady Bird and their two children. In return, Madeleine was furnished with a two-bedroomed house, a live-in maid, an unlimited charge card and a new car every two years.

When Johnson was in Texas they would get together. At one of their assignations at Austin's Driskill Hotel, when Johnson was Kennedy's Vice President, he explained that they were in trouble. At that time Kennedy was still trying to remove Hoover as head of the F.B.I. and Hoover wanted Johnson to exert his influence with Kennedy. He knew about Madeleine and her son Steven.

Johnson's proposed solution was for Madeleine to marry someone else – on paper at least. 'I want you to go through with the marriage,' he told Madeleine, 'to help me get my balls out of Hoover's vice grip.' But the affair continued for another five years nonetheless.

Johnson had been friends with Hoover since he first came to Washington in the 1930s. They were neighbours. Hoover would invite the Johnsons over for dinner or Sunday brunch and sometimes babysit their daughters. Privately, Johnson disparaged Hoover as 'that queer bastard'. But with his own closet bulging with skeletons – women, bent business deals and allegations of ballot-rigging in the 1948 election – he had to keep on the right side of his neighbour.

This also had other advantages. Hoover was wildly indiscreet and would lend Johnson F.B.I. files for light, bedtime reading. Johnson revelled in the sexual peccadilloes of his colleagues and the information he gleaned helped him in his spectacular rise to power. He would regularly simply walk up to a senator and say: 'How about this little deal you have with this woman?'

At the 1960 Democratic Convention in Los Angeles, Johnson used some of what Hoover had told him in the dirty fight for the nomination.

LBJ, it was said, at the times, stood for 'Let's Block Jack'. When John F. Kennedy's money and superb organisation nonetheless won him the nomination, Johnson was furious. Early editions of the newspapers gave the names of three men Kennedy was considering as his running mate. Johnson's was not one of them. Johnson changed all that.

He went to Kennedy and he said he would use the F.B.I. material to blow Kennedy's 'family man' image out of the water if he was not included on the ticket. Most explosive was Kennedy's wartime affair with Danish beauty-queen Ingrid Arvad, whom Hitler had praised as the perfect example of Nordic beauty. According to an F.B.I. report, she had actually been to bed with the Führer. She had also been the mistress of a Swedish journalist who had been pro-Nazi. The war had only been over fifteen years and revealing that Kennedy had slept with a woman so closely involved with Hitler and the Nazis could, at the very least, have lost the Democrats the vital Jewish vote.

Kennedy and his brother Bobby agonised over the decision, but could see no way out. Johnson had boxed them into a corner.

In the end, Kennedy conceded defeat. 'I'm forty three years old,' he told Johnson. 'I'm not going to die in office. So the Vice Presidency doesn't mean a thing.'

Johnson saw it differently. 'I looked it up,' he said. 'One of every four presidents has died in office. I'm a gamblin' man, and this is the only chance I got.' The next day Johnson was named as vice-presidential nominee.

As Vice President, Johnson developed a close relationship with Kennedy's younger sister Jean. They travelled together to India in 1962. Jackie Kennedy was also very fond of Johnson, finding him 'very gallant, courtly'. At White House parties, she made a point of dancing with him. After Kennedy's funeral, she wrote to Johnson, thanking him 'for the way you have always treated me... before, when Jack was alive, and now as President'.

Johnson's partnership with Hoover continued when he became Vice President, with Hoover providing him with any sleaze he could, especially if it concerned the Kennedys. Kennedy had been having sex with one of the hostesses on the family plane and brought her into the White House as assistant press secretary. Hoover supplied a full field investigation report on her, including some nude pictures she had posed for when she was still in high school. When she came into the Oval Office to clear the Teletypes, Johnson would take the pictures out of their folder and examine them. Nowadays, it would be a lawsuit for harassment, but at the time it became quite a joke in the White House.

When a young aide urged the President to fire Hoover, Johnson refused, replying famously: 'If you've got a skunk around, it's better to have him inside the tent pissing out, than outside the tent pissing in.'

Once in the Oval Office, he followed in the Kennedy tradition and used the White House secretaries as his personal harem. White House press secretary George Reedy said: 'He may have been 'just a country boy from the central hills of Texas', but he had 'many of the instincts of a Turkish sultan in Istanbul.'

It was constantly on his mind while seeking to extend his White House pool of secretaries. One highly qualified woman was denied a position on his staff when Johnson said: 'She's got everything but good looks.'

In a primer for the Trump song-book Johnson said, 'I put high marks on good looks, I can't stand a woman who looks like a cow that's gonna sit on her own udder.' When he spotted an attractive journalist at a press conference, he told her: 'You're the prettiest thing I ever saw.' The next day she had a job on his staff and the press corps called him the 'Lochinvar of the Pedernales' – Johnson's valley homestead.

Of the six pretty secretaries he hired he had an affair with five of them. In a precursor of Bill Clinton's presidency, one 'very pretty young' White House secretary had sex with Johnson on the desk in the Oval Office. Another was caught sitting on his lap claiming that she had tripped over a rug. And it wasn't just in the Oval Office that things got raucous. LBJ also had sex with his the secretaries on Air Force One and *Sequoia*, the presidential yacht.

Johnson was unashamed and reckless. If he spotted a pretty woman outside the White House gates, he would send an aide out to get her.

Johnson's approach was a straightforward line of assault. When one woman staffer on secondment to the Johnson ranch in Texas had to stay overnight at Johnson's ranch after working late, she awoke in the middle of the night to find a naked man climbing into bed with her.

'Move over,' he would say. 'This is your President.'

'One way, you could visualise Lady Bird as the queen in Anna and the King of Siam,' said one journalist who knew him well. 'It worked that way; you know the scene where she sits at table and all the babes – Lady Bird was the head wife.'

Lady Bird accepted her husband's sexual exploits. One Secret Service agent even claims that she caught Johnson having sex with one of his secretaries on a couch in the Oval Office.

'That's just one side of him,' she said. Years later she explained to a television producer: 'You have to understand, my husband loved people. All people. And half the people in the world are women. You don't think I could have kept my husband away from half the people?'

Even Esther Peterson, head of the Women's Bureau in the Johnson administration, found that she 'had to bend a lot'. Johnson's humour, she noted, was largely based on women's sexual features. This was said before the word 'sexism' had entered the American language.

In many ways Trump's views are exchangeable with Johnson's in the 1960s. When one aide reported that Congresswoman Green was giving a member of the administration trouble over an education bill, Johnson said: 'Tell him to spend the afternoon in bed with her and she'll support any goddamn bill he wants.' He told another aide to adopt similar tactics with a woman journalist who was criticizing his government.

Johnson happily took his own advice. He had regular sex in the Oval Office with a female reporter from the *Washington Star*. Towards the end of his administration, gossip also circulated that he was having an affair with a blonde graduate student from Harvard named Doris Kearns, who had famously written a 'Dump Johnson' article for *The New Republic*, because he spent so much time alone with her.

In a precursor to Donald Trump's pussy remark, Johnson told one young aide that he saw nothing wrong with having sex outside marriage. He bragged about his extra-marital affairs and sought constantly to impress his cronies with tales of his sexual prowess. Nothing, not even the most intimate details of his partners' anatomy, was held back.

Given Johnson's promiscuous behaviour, it is curious that the only sex scandal to hit his administration was a homosexual one. On 14 October 1964, just weeks before the election, Johnson's White House chief of staff Walter Jenkins was arrested for 'disorderly conduct' with a sixty-year-old man in the toilets of the YMCA. It was soon discovered that he had been arrested five years before doing the same thing in the same toilet. During the ensuing scandal, one kindly journalist enquired whether he was suffering from overwork or was it 'combat fatigue'.

At the time, security guidelines stipulated that 'homosexuals and other sex perverts' were not to be employed in government on the grounds that they were a security risk. When the story broke, Johnson's legal adviser had Jenkins check into a hospital. Johnson then called Hoover, who issued a report saying that Jenkins had not compromised national security. The scandal died down, but Republican wits suggested Johnson change his campaign slogan from 'All the way with LBJ' to 'Either way with LBJ'.

The extent of Johnson's sexploits only became clear in 1987, fifteen years after his death, when his illegitimate son Steven Brown stepped into the lime light with a $10.5-million suit against Lady Bird for his inheritance and demanding to change his name to Johnson. Standing six feet four tall, he certainly looked like his putative father. Earlier in February 1987, his mother Madeleine Brown had had a heart attack. Fearing she was going to die, she confessed all and told him about his parentage.

Madeleine had married a soda jerk when she was very young. He was later confined to a mental hospital, but, being a Catholic, she had not divorced him. Johnson's pick-up line at a party in the Driskill Hotel in 1948, the second time they had met, had been nothing if not to the point.

'He said after a while, "Well, I'll see you up in my apartment",' she recalled the Congressman saying. "He had a certain amount of roughness about him, and maybe that's what I liked, you know. He commanded. I've been told that every woman needs to act like a whore in bed and I guess that's what I did".'

There was another parallel with Trump. LBJ 'was a little kinky and I loved every second of it,' Madeleine said. Johnson was an aggressive lover, highly sexed and liked to play games in bed. 'We spent our time doing, not talking. Once, after he was through, he went to the window and opened it and bellowed like a bull, yelling, "My God, I love Texas in the morning".' She used the memorable phrase as the title of her memoir *Texas in the Morning: The Love Story of Madeleine Brown and President Lyndon Johnson*.

The two never discussed politics as the affair was only about sex. 'He told me from the beginning,' she said. '"You see nothing, you hear nothing, you say nothing".' She was never to be publicly acknowledged.

They communicated via Jesse Kellam, the manager of the radio station in Austin where they had first met, and a close friend of Johnson's. When Johnson was home from Washington, D.C., Kellam would call Madeleine. She would fly in from Dallas. Met at the airport by the radio station's mobile news unit, she would be taken to the Driskill Hotel and smuggled up to his suite.

Johnson was a busy man. It would all be over in half-an-hour. Only once did he dawdle and stay three hours.

Madeleine, nonetheless, had her own ambitions to be First Lady. 'Sometimes, when I'd hint around, he'd just say, "Today's today, tomorrow's tomorrow." That was his favourite answer. I guess it could have meant anything. I like to think it meant someday I'd be in the White House. I would have been like Nancy Reagan. I wouldn't have stood it if he had other women.'

As it was, she did.

Though she was upset and unhappy about it, the hit-and-run nature of their relationship meant Johnson had plenty of time to dally elsewhere.

When in spring 1950 she fell pregnant with Stephen, Johnson, by then a senator, went incandescent with rage. He called her 'dumb Dora' and blamed everything on her. But, after he had calmed down, he said he would look after her and the child, leaving his attorney, Jerome Ragsdale, to tie up the details.

Steven was born in December 1950. As Madeleine was still married, she put her husband's name on the birth certificate. Ragsdale picked up all the expenses, though Madeleine continued to work as a media buyer for any advertising agency in Dallas. Work colleagues were amazed when she turned up in an expensive mink coat. She coquettishly explained: 'I got my mink the same way minks get minks.'

There were other gifts and flowers between the snatched interludes in hotels in Austin, Houston and San Antonio, all arranged for by Kellam. After the death of her husband, and the marriage of convenience followed to protect Johnson, she never lived with her new husband.

On 21 November 1963 – the day before Kennedy's assassination – she claimed Johnson told her: 'After tomorrow those SOBs will never embarrass me again.' Brown believed that a plot to kill JFK had been hatched at the 1960 Democratic Convention, when Johnson lost the nomination to Kennedy.

'When they met in California, Joe Kennedy, John Kennedy's father, and [oil tycoon] H.L. Hunt met three days prior to the election – they finally cut a deal according to John Currington [an aide to H.L. Hunt] and H.L. finally agreed that Lyndon would go as the Vice President,' she said. 'This came from the horse's mouth way back in 1960 – when H.L. came back to Dallas I was walking… with him… and he made the remark, "we may have lost a battle but we're going to win a war", and then the day of the assassination he said "well, we won the war".'

As President, Johnson still found time to fly down to Austin for half hours in the Driskill Hotel. Then in 1967, she had a car accident, badly scaring her face, and she feared that she would never see her lover again. By that time, he was deeply unpopular across the country because of the Vietnam and was terrified that his illicit affair would be found out. Kellam, Johnson's lawyer, constantly reminded her to be a 'good girl' and keep quiet.

After Johnson left office in 1969, he arranged to meet her as was attending a parade in honour of the Apollo 11 astronauts in Houston. They met in a room in the Shamrock Hotel. She was shocked how tired and old he looked. While the Secret Service agent waited outside, for once, they talked.

'We talked for almost two hours,' she said. 'I cried. We kissed. But we didn't even try to make love.'

She thought that he did not have much longer to live and urged him to recognised Steven as his son.

'I can't do that,' said Johnson. 'I've got the girls to think about.'

XI

John F. Kennedy, #35

'Slam, bam, thank you, ma'am'

Womanising while married was a family tradition for male Kennedys. JFK's father Joe Kennedy, pre-war U.S. Ambassador to London, was known as an ardent skirt-chaser. In a case of early #WeToo, he facilitated his sexual needs by investing heavily in Hollywood. There he could indulge himself in an endless stream of beauties willing to take a chance on stardom.

With the money he had made from bootlegging, the married Joe Kennedy bought the biggest movie star of the day, Gloria Swanson, by setting up Gloria Productions, Inc. in 1927, and financing her films. To his mind, he had not only bought her career but also her body.

'In two months, Joe Kennedy had taken over my entire life', Swanson said. One evening he turned up at the door of her room in a Palm Beach hotel. 'He just stood there, in his white flannels and his argyle sweater and his two-toned shoes, staring at me for a full minute or more, before he entered the room and closed the door behind him. He moved so quickly that his mouth was on mine before either of us could speak. With one hand he held the back of my head, with the other he stroked my body and pulled at my kimono. He kept insisting in a drawn-out moan, "No longer, no longer. Now." He was like a roped horse, rough, arduous, racing to be free. After a hasty climax he lay beside me, stroking my hair. Apart from his guilty, passionate mutterings, he had still said nothing cogent.'

In 1928, he did mouth a few words. At a party in New York, Joe Kennedy confessed to stunned guests that he wanted to have a baby with Swanson: there had been no Kennedy baby that year. He begged Swanson to visit Rose and the children with him, but she refused. Later he managed to get the three of them together on a ship returning from Europe. Rose Kennedy seemed oblivious to what was going on.

'Was she a fool, or a saint?' Swanson wondered. 'Or just a better actress than me?'

In 1929, Cardinal O'Connell paid Swanson a visit and warned her not to go on seeing Joe Kennedy. Joe had sought the religious permission to separate from Rose and set up a second household with Swanson, as divorce from Rose was out of the question for the catholic Kennedy.

The affair ended after two box-office bombs and the cheap fact that Swanson discovered that the gifts joe was plying her with were actually charged to her own company.

Jack Kennedy was well aware of the actresses and showgirls in his father's life. Joe often brought his mistresses home with him. One even stayed for a month and joined in family activities.

Nor did Joe Kennedy limit his sexual radius to Hollywood starlets and showgirls. No good-looking woman was off-limits – not the wives of business associates or the girlfriends of his own sons. Later, when Joe was ambassador to London, Jack warned women guests: 'Be sure to lock your bedroom door at night. The Ambassador has a tendency to go wandering.' His old age made no difference either. In the 1950s, he made a pass at Grace Kelly while in his early seventies, he was seen fondling a young prostitute brought to a Kennedy party by playboy Porfirio Rubirosa.

Jack was given a detailed sex education of sorts by his father. Once when he got home from school, he found his bed covered with sex magazines the old man had bought. They were all opened to display naked women in the most explicit of poses. This was 'Dad's idea of a joke,' the young Kennedy explained to a friend.

Jack Kennedy had lost his virginity at the age of seventeen with a prostitute in a brothel in Harlem which he had visited with his schoolfriend Lem Billings. The girl, who was white, charged them $3 each.

Back at school, the boys panicked. Convinced that they had

contracted a venereal disease, they covered themselves with creams and salves. Even this was not good enough for Kennedy, who woke a doctor in the middle of the night, demanding an examination.

Kennedy quickly overcame his fear of STDs and went to visit a number of other brothels. He especially favoured those south of the Rio Grande. In May 1936, Jack wrote to Billings about his adventures with schoolfriend Smokey Wilde.

'Got a fuck and suck in a Mexican hoar-housse [sic] for 65c, so am feeling very fit and clean,' he boasted. 'Smoke and I set out yesterday, went over the border and arrived at a fucking Mexican town. Met a girl there who is really the best thing I have ever seen but does not speak English. Am writing to her tonight to get a date with her because she wouldn't go out with me last time and it is really love at first sight. They have the best-looking girls in those towns. Anyways Smoke and I ended up in this two-bit hoar-house and they say that one guy in five years has gotten away without just the biggest juiciest load of clap – so Smoke is looking plenty pallid and even I occasionally think of it, so boys your roomie is carrying on in true 9 South style and is upholding the motto of "always get your piece of arse in the most unhealthy place that can be found".'

This escapade did indeed result in a dose of clap. His next letter to Billings was signed 'your gonnereick roomie'. Back at college, the action continued and his interests were not confined to prostitutes.

'Went down to the Cape with five guys from school,' he wrote. 'EM [Eddie Moore] got us some girls thru another guy – four of us had dates and one guy got fucked three times, another guy three times (the girl a virgin!) and myself twice – there were all on the football team and I think the coaches heard because they gave us one hell of a balling out. The guy who got the virgin just got a very sickening letter, letting [him know] how much she loved him etc and as he didn't use a safer he is very worried. One guy is up at the doctor's seeing if he has a dose and I feel none too secure myself. We are going down next week for a return performance, I think. Regards to Ripper and the boys – the name of the drug store where I buy my rubbers is Billings & Stower – Regards, Kennedorus.'

Sadly, a new coach 'found out about our little party and I am now known as "Playboy".' Kennedy complained about the crack down and lamented: 'I will have to wank plenty to "tame" it down.'

Billings was in awe: 'He was very successful with girls. Very.'

At Harvard, Kennedy devoted much of his time to chasing women, successfully it seems.

'I can now get tail as often and as free as I want which is a step in the right direction,' Kennedy boasted to his friend. When he was intending to visit Billings at Princeton he asked: 'Get me a room way away from all the others and especially from your girl as I don't want you coming in for a chat in the middle as usual and discussing how sore my cock is.'

Moving on to Stanford, in California, one of the first co-eds to be 'branded' by Kennedy's 'red-hot poker' was Susan Imhoff.

'Because of his bad back he preferred making love with the girl on top,' she recalled. 'He found it more stimulating to have the girl do all the work. I remember he didn't enjoy cuddling after making love, but he did like to talk and had a wonderful sense of humour.'

Like his father before him, Jack Kennedy got no further than a quick grope and eschewed any emotional attachment.

'He was like a kid,' recalled Boston Democrat Tip O'Neill who went on to become speaker of the House of Representatives. 'He really liked girls. But Kennedy never got emotionally involved. He'd sleep with a girl and he'd have Billy take her to the airport the next day.'

A friend of his sisters explained choice of partner: 'The young girls, the secretaries and the air hostesses – they were safe grounds. They were not going to make any intellectual or strong demands on him which he wasn't ready to fulfil.'

He used to call his penis 'Lay More', but after he was circumcised in 1938 he began calling his newly renovated member 'JJ' Soon, he told Billings it 'has never been in better shape or doing better service'.

He also began courting high society girls with a half-hearted view to marriage. He pursued Frances Ann Cannon, a rich beauty from

North Carolina studying at Sarah Lawrence. Next came Charlotte McDonnell, daughter of a New York stockbroker. There was rumour of an engagement, but Charlotte's father disapproved. He called Kennedy a 'moral roustabout and forbade him seeing his daughter again.

Olive Crawley dropped him when he disappeared during a date to seduce the hatcheck girl at the Stork Club. He dumped Harriet 'Flip' Price when she would not put out. There had been talk of marriage, but Kennedy confessed he was not that serious. His favourite expression, was, 'slam, bam, thank you, ma'am'.

In 1938, Kennedy and his older brother Joe Jr accompanied their father to the U.S. embassy in London, where he continued to his sexual activities. Even Joe Sr was exhausted and imposed a curfew on his two sons to curb their pursuit of women.

In the autumn of 1941, Kennedy joined the U.S. Navy and was posted to the Office of Naval Intelligence in Washington, where he quickly spread his reputation as a playboy. It was there that he met Ingrid Arvad. As a journalist, she had interviewed Hitler, accompanying him to the Olympic Games in Berlin in 1936, and he was much taken by her.

Suspected of being a German spy, Ingrid's phone was tapped and her apartment bugged by the F.B.I. F.B.I. boss J. Edgar Hoover got tapes of Kennedy making love to his 'Inga Binga'. She called him 'Honeysuckle' or 'Honey Child Wilder'. Early in his political career, Kennedy boasted that when he got to Washington he would get the tapes back. He never managed it.

'He'd always be walking around with a towel around his waist,' Ingrid's son Ronald said his mother told him. 'That's all he ever wore in the apartment – a towel. The minute he arrived, he'd take off all his clothes and take a shower… If he wanted to make love, you'd make love – now. They'd have fifteen minutes to get to a party and she'd say she didn't want to. He'd look at his watch and say we've got ten minutes, let's go.'

Ingrid also told her son that she was pregnant when she married and she did not know whether his father was her husband or

Kennedy.

After just ninety days with Naval Intelligence in Washington, Kennedy was on the verge of being cashiered as a security risk. Political influence kept him in uniform. He was quickly posted to Charleston, South Carolina. That did not stop the young Kennedy from seeing Ingrid though. On numerous occasions, they made love in Room 132 of the Fort Sumter Hotel, South Carolina. Once he even went AWOL to visit her in Washington. The F.B.I. soon had the hotel rooms where they met for their trysts bugged. J. Edgar Hoover got still more tapes of the future president's activities. On one memorable recording, Ingrid told Kennedy that she was pregnant and accused him of enjoying the pleasures of youth without the responsibility.

Kennedy wanted to marry Ingrid and took her to Hyannis Port, but his father opposed the match as Ingrid was not a Catholic — though that did not stop the old man from trying to seduce her himself while she was there. The marriage off, Ingrid went on to have an affair with British member of parliament Robert Boothby (the long-term lover of the wife of the prime minister Harold Macmillan), who also enjoyed homosexual orgies laid on by East End gangster Ronald Kray.

When he was finally posted to active duty, commanding a PT boat, fellow officers nicknamed him 'Shafty' and complained that he spent more time chasing models than chasing enemy submarines.

'Girls were an obsession with him,' one recalled. 'We liked them too, but we didn't make a career out of it.'

At a Hollywood party after the war with Ingrid, he tried to woo actress Olivia de Havilland. She resisted his charms and said she was leaving. Unlike his father, he did not go for rape but leapt to the door to open it for her, only to find that it led to a closet. Rackets and tennis balls rained down on him.

After Ingrid, Kennedy filled the void with a series of chorus girls and models, notably Angela Greene who went on to become an actress.

Kennedy had met the twenty-four-year-old model Florence 'Flo'

Prichett in the Stork Club in 1944. She was a divorcee so there was no question of them ever marrying. Their affair went on for years. In his appointment book for 28 June 1947, she wrote: 'Flo Prichett's birthday: SEND DIAMONDS.' Family friend Betty Spalding said that, perversely, for Kennedy 'Over a long period of time, it was probably the closest relationship with a woman I know of.'

That same year Florence married four-forty-year-old stockbroker Earl E.T. Smith, whom President Dwight Eisenhower appointed as ambassador to Cuba.

In 1957 and 1958, in the run up to the Cuba revolution, Kennedy made over a dozen visits to Havana to see Florence and also to meet up with prostitutes in the Hotel Commodoro. Later, they had adjoining properties in Palm Beach and their affair continued into his presidency. According to one account: 'JFK would elude the Secret Service on occasion in order to have trysts with women. He did this in Palm Beach when he hopped a fence to swim with Flo Smith. The Secret Service agents couldn't find him and called in the F.B.I. They finally turned to Palm Beach Police Chief Homer Large, a trusted Kennedy family associate. The Police Chief knew exactly where to find Jack – next door in Earl E.T. Smith's swimming pool. Jack and Flo were alone, and as Homer put it, "They weren't doing the Australian crawl".'

After the war, Kennedy was briefly a journalist, though he appeared in the gossip columns more often than that he contributed writing as he spent most of his time at parties, trying to seduce rich, often married women. There were ice skaters, Hollywood starlets and strippers such as Tempest Storm. Divorcees were his particular favourite as, being a Catholic, there was no danger of marriage. The names were legion – one that stood out was English actress Peggy Cummins. With her, he made gossip columns though he never got her into bed.

Anita Marcus outlined the Kennedy technique: 'I think that the main thing was that when he talked to you, he looked you straight in the eye and his attention never wandered. He was interested in finding out what I was doing there – why I was there. It was a drawing-me-out thing. It was undivided attention. I was the most envied girl in the room. He had a way with women. There is no question about it.'

When he began his political career, he ran on his good looks and charm. Women responded viscerally.

'The older ladies seemed to mother him,' a volunteer said, 'all of the young ones fell in love with him.'

During his 1946 congressional campaign, he was caught in the act of congress on his desk with a young campaign worker on the desk in his office. The girl later missed her period. Kennedy said: 'Oh shit.' And moved briskly on.

Kennedy used his sexual charisma to good effect in the congressional election and he did not turn off the charm once in office. When he arrived in Washington, three hundred correspondents voted him 'the handsomest member of the House'. Fellow congressman Frank 'Toppy' Thomson of New Jersey said: 'I could walk with Jack into a room of a hundred women and at least eighty-five of them would be willing to sacrifice their honour and everything else if they could get into a pad with him.'

State Department official Lucius Battle recalled having to drag his wife away from him.

Campaigning for Kennedy's second congressional term, Massachusetts Governor Paul Denver told a crowd: 'I hear it being said that my young friend Jack Kennedy isn't working down there in Washington, that he's too fond of girls. Well, let me tell you ladies and gentlemen, I've never heard it said of Jack Kennedy that he's too fond of boys.'

In his book *The Dark Side of Camelot*, Pulitzer Prize-winning investigative journalist Seymour Hersh said that, around this time, Kennedy married Palm Beach socialite Durie Malcolm. At the time, the marriage was hinted at by the *New York World-Telegram* society writer Charles Ventura. Hersh quotes Charles Spalding, a retired New York stockbroker who had known Kennedy since World War II. It was 'a high-school prank,' said Spalding, that lasted 'twenty-four hours. They went down and went through the motions. I remember saying to Jack, "You must be nuts. You're running for president and you're running around getting married".'

As early as 1947, Kennedy was being groomed for the White House by his father who 'had a haemorrhage' when he heard about the prank marriage. Not only was Malcolm twice divorced, she was an Episcopalian. According to Spalding, Joe 'demanded that it be taken care of. They were afraid the whole thing was going to come out.'

Spalding said that Jack asked him to go had get the marriage papers from Florida.

'I went out there and removed the papers,' said Spalding. He told Hersh that he got the documents with the help of a lawyer in Palm Beach. The marriage was officially never terminated. In other words, Kennedy later became a bigamist. But even if it had been terminated, Kennedy would have been something equally scandalous for a Catholic – a remarried divorcee. After Kennedy became president, *Newsweek* got wind of the story which had been circulating in small Republic journals across the country. Kennedy's friend Ben Bradlee, Washington bureau chief for *Newsweek*, personally vetoed the *Newsweek* article.

In 1951, Kennedy had another brush with marriage, this time with Alicia Darr, the estranged wife of English actor Edmund Purdom. The anti-British Joe put a stop to that. When Jack became president, she told the Italian magazine *Le Ore* about the affair. She was divorcing her husband at the time. Kennedy paid $500,000 to have the whole thing hushed up. It further alleged that she was pregnant. Danger did not end there. In the summer of 1960, during the presidential race, Alicia's divorce finally came to court. Her husband countersued, naming Kennedy as co-respondent. A friend of the Kennedy's contacted Alicia. A discreet divorce was arranged in Mexico and the whole thing was hushed up.

Kennedy continued taking crazy risks. In 1952, at a benefit dinner after defeating the long-term incumbent Henry Cabot Lodge in the Massachusetts senatorial race, Kennedy disappeared with his date to a closet and the guests had to wait to retrieve their coats until the junior senator had finished his grope in the dark.

He liked to make love on the floor of his office and, on his desk, he kept a photograph of himself with several nude girls, taken on a yacht. The press took a shine to it and were soon calling him the playboy senator.

Clearly, if he was going to run for president, Kennedy was going to have to take a wife. The pose, charm and sophistication of Jacqueline Bouvier fitted the vacancy. She was also the daughter of John Vernon 'Blackjack' Bouvier III, an alcoholic and another notorious womaniser. Jackie would, at least, know what family life with Jack would be like.

Jacqueline Bouvier herself was the classic virgin princess. In every way, her education surpassed Kennedy's own. She was beautiful and classy. Whenever he used words like 'prick', 'fuck', 'nuts' and 'son of a bitch', she was shocked. Nonetheless, on their first date, Jack had Jackie where he wanted her. They were making out in Kennedy's convertible in Arlington, Virginia when they were spotted by the police. Fortunately, the patrolman recognised 'the playboy senator' and left the couple alone to complete their tête-à-tête.

Jackie quickly broke off her engagement to John Husted, but there were no flowers or candies from Kennedy. He proposed instead by telegram. The wedding in 1953 was the society event of the year. The beautiful Jackie perfectly complemented the handsome young senator, it was said, and they became Washington's most glamorous couple.

In fact, the marriage was strained to start with. Though Jackie was catholic by background, she was raised as a patrician and wasp by her stepfather. Kennedy on the other hand was a bog-trotting, street-fighting politician like his father. To expect her to fit into his world was, a friend said: 'Like asking Rocky Graziano to play the piano.'

Kennedy's sexual obsession was the biggest sticking point. She had not expected fidelity. She had witnessed her father's many affairs. But she had not prepared herself for the industrial scale of her husband's gropes. These were not just chance entanglements. Kennedy and his congressional friend George Smathers established an apartment at the Carroll Arms Hotel in Washington, where they could entertain young women.

'Jack liked to go over there and meet a couple of young secretaries,' Smathers recalled. 'He liked groups.'

JFK would often bring his sex partners along to receptions where Jackie would be present. Sometimes he would employ a beard such as his brother-in-law, actor Peter Lawford or he would employ other tactics to maintain secrecy. While Jackie was away in Europe, he arranged to go to various house parties in Maine. Uneven numbers of men and women at these parties were supposed to throw the press off the scent, or a respectable elderly lady would be employed to take a jejeune Kennedy to Mass on a Sunday morning to allay suspicion.

In 1954, when Kennedy was required to declare against the communist witch-hunt of Senator Joe McCarthy – a friend of his father's – he got, diplomatically, ill. For years, Kennedy had suffered problems with his back and Addison's disease, a disorder of the adrenal glands. This meant he spent a lot of time bedridden in hospital, though he found comfort in being surrounded by female nurses.

In his New York hospital room this time, there were also visits from a series of young 'cousins' to be enjoyed. Playing along, Jackie hired Grace Kelly to pretend to be his night nurse to see his reaction. When Jack opened his eyes, he thought he was dreaming, especially as his father shared his infatuation.

In 1956, Kennedy met divorcee Joan Lundberg, a mother of two, in a bar in Santa Monica. They began by discussing the record she was about to put on the jukebox, then moved on to a party at Peter Lawford's home.

Lundberg said that Kennedy loved sex with two girls. She also said that he was a voyeur. The affair lasted three years. He paid her bills and for an abortion when she got pregnant. They even made love in Jackie's marital bed at their house in Georgetown. The affair ended amicably when he won the Democratic nomination in 1960.

One night in 1958, a couple called Leonard and Florence Kater were disturbed by a man throwing pebbles at the window of their twenty-year-old lodger, Pamela Turnure, a secretary at Kennedy's Senate office. It was the senator himself, who, thereafter, became a regular nocturnal visitor.

Devout catholics and peeping Toms, the Katers took pictures of Kennedy sneaking out in the middle of the night and rigged up a tape recorder to pick up sounds of the couple's lovemaking. In 1959, when Kennedy was running against Lyndon Johnson for the Democratic nomination, they mailed details of the affair to the newspapers. The press shied away from the story but J. Edgar Hoover heard about it, got the pictures and tapes from the Katers and gave them to Lyndon Johnson to use in his campaign. In fact, Hoover had a bulging file on Kennedy which included 'affidavits from two mixed-race prostitutes in New York'. At that time, Kennedy also maintained a private suite in Washington's Mayflower Hotel, which an F.B.I. informant referred to as 'Kennedy's personal play-pen'.

When Kennedy won the nomination and then the election, the Katers, in frustration, demonstrated outside the White House, with placards complaining that there was an adulterer in charge of the country. Nobody took any notice.

Pamela Turnure's nocturnal visitor continued to step by for over three years. When Kennedy entered the White House, she was promoted to press secretary to Jackie. Jackie knew what was going on, but did not object, figuring that if she made it that easy for her husband, he would get bored. When Kennedy was asked what it was like having his mistress work for his wife, he replied: 'Like living life on a high wire.'

Turnure moved away from the Katers' house and moved in with Jackie's friend, the artist Mary Meyer, who knew of the affair. As Jackie had guessed, after a while Kennedy grew tired of Pam and so he turned to Mary instead. During their lovemaking session in her studio, in the homes of friends and, later, in the White House, they experimented with marijuana and LSD. Peter Lawford also supplied them helpfully with cocaine and amyl nitrate or 'poppers', which they first tried out on two White House secretaries to gauge the effect.

The President and the First Lady both developed a strong dependence on speed by the summer of 1961 and Kennedy was high on it during the Cuban missile crisis. (Kennedy was also on novocaine and cortisone to dull the pain in his back. Dr Max Jacobson – known as 'Dr Feelgood' to his high-class clientele – travelled with Kennedy to give his shots of amphetamine and steroids. He was struck off after one of his patients died.)

Thus, the Kennedy marriage was damaged beyond hope of repair long before they entered the White House. It was effectively over when Jackie gave birth to a still-born child in 1956. At the time, Kennedy was cruising in the Mediterranean with George Smathers and several infatuated young women. One of them, a stunning but not particularly bright girl named 'Pooh', fascinated Kennedy. Rather than fly back to be with his grief-stricken wife, he chose to stay on in the Mediterranean. He only returned home three days later, after Smathers convinced him that any further delay would ruin his political career.

His callousness ruined their marriage, especially after Jackie learnt what Kennedy had been doing. She would bring it up repeatedly.

In fact, Jackie was so upset that, when she left hospital, she did not go home. Instead she went to stay on her step-father's estate. Things got worse when she heard that their fifteen-year-old babysitter, supplied by a veteran newsman, was pregnant and named Kennedy as the father (she was quickly despatched to Puerto Rico for an abortion).

As always, Joe Kennedy stepped in to patch things up. He offered Jackie a financial settlement, provided that she did not leave Jack. Having little money of her own, she agreed but from then on it was guerrilla warfare. She would constantly be on his back about the pretty women in his life, go on shopping sprees and flaunt herself in public with male friends to incite his jealousy. Once, in the White House, she got drunk on champagne and danced with every man in sight. This was very effective as Kennedy was jealous of men who were mere acquaintances of Jackie's.

His jealousy did not stop JFK's own sex activities though. 'I don't think there are any men who are faithful to their wives,' Jackie told a friend. 'Men are such a combination of good and bad.'

She may have had affairs of her own. Kennedy's secretary Evelyn Lincoln talked of a 'dashing Italian count'. There were rumours that she had succumbed to the owner of Fiat Gianni Agnelli, after Kennedy had flirted openly with his wife, and even fallen for one of her security guards.

Indeed, Jackie was always one step ahead of her husband. At White House dinners, she would not hesitate to seat one of his lovers on either side of him. That way, at least, he would have no access to new women.

Jackie was so popular with the American public that she felt that nothing could hurt her – 'unless I run off with Eddie Fisher,' she said. Fisher was a singer who dumped Debbie Reynolds for her best friend Elizabeth Taylor.

The marriage worked for Kennedy, anyway. When a friend of his was contemplating divorce, Kennedy advised: 'Try it the way I am doing it.'

The friend replied: 'I go home five nights a week. You're in this Arabian Nights never-never land of the White House. Some nights you don't go home at all.'

Kennedy thought about this. A few nights later, he called and said: 'You're right. If I had to go home three nights a week, I'd go up the wall.'

Kennedy's secretary Evelyn Lincoln also believes that Jackie had begun her affair with Aristotle Onassis in October 1963, one month before her husband was assassinated in Dallas, Texas.

Kennedy was doubtless a sexual exhibitionist. One F.B.I. informant said that he saw Kennedy and Senator Estes Kefauver have sex with two women in their apartment in front of other guests, then switch partners and do it again.

Stories of his reckless womanising circulated in the Senate. He would hold orgies in his apartment at the Carroll Arms Hotel across the road from the Senate Office building while his colleagues were voting on various pieces of legislation. 'I am not through with a girl till I have had her three ways,' Kennedy told a colleague in the Senate.

'Jack felt he could walk on water so far as women were concerned,' Senator Smathers said. 'There is no question about the fact that Jack had the most active libido of any man I've ever known. He was really unbelievable – absolutely incredible in that regard, and he got more so the longer he was married.'

Smathers even remembered a time when he, Kennedy and two girls had gone back to their private apartment, when a call came that he was wanted back at the Senate. He was halfway there when he realised that the Senate was no longer in session. When he got back to the apartment, he found Kennedy having sex with both women.

As with Joe, 'No one was off limits to Jack,' Smathers said. 'Not your wife, your mother, your sister.'

During the 1960 election, Hoover suppled some material on Kennedy's sex life to Republican candidate Richard Nixon. This included a picture of Kennedy naked with an attractive brunette on a beach. But Kennedy wasn't bothered. He hung out in Las Vegas with Frank Sinatra during the filming of the Rat-Pack movie *Ocean's 11*. One F.B.I. report stated that 'showgirls from all over the town were running in and out of the Senator's suite'. One of these showgirls, a tall brunette, was later observed visiting the White House.

Then he began the most scandalous affair of his career. In February 1960, Sinatra introduced him to twenty-five-year-old Judith Campbell, a wealthy divorcee Sinatra had picked up the previous year. Edward Kennedy also fancied her, but Jack met her first. The following month Kennedy and Campbell spent four days together in the Plaza Hotel in New York while Sinatra also introduced her to the Mafia boss Sam Giancana – and she became his lover too.

Campbell said that the President's persistent back pain eventually made their lovemaking rather perfunctory and one-dimensional. Writing in her memoir *My Story*, Campbell said Kennedy always lay on his back with her on top, and 'the feeling that I was there to service him began to really trouble me'.

At the beginning of April, Jackie was pregnant again and had gone to Florida, so Judith was free to visit Kennedy in his house in Georgetown. Despite Joe Kennedy's enormous wealth, the Kennedy campaign was short of funds. Kennedy asked Campbell whether she could arrange a meeting with Giancana, whose Chicago Crime Syndicate – former proprietor Al Capone – turned over $2 billion a year. She did and, according to F.B.I. wiretaps, the Mafia made huge campaign contributions which were used to pay off key election officials. Giancana later boasted to Judith that her boyfriend would never have made it to the White House without his help.

As the 1960 primaries drew to a close, Judith Campbell met up with Kennedy at Peter Lawford's suite in the Beverly Hilton Hotel for a late-night party. He lured Judith into a bedroom, where another woman was waiting, and suggested that the three of them make love together – 'I know you'll enjoy it', Jack purred. 'He assured me that the girl was safe and would never talk about it to a single soul,' Judith recalled, but she tearfully rejected him.

Later Jack wooed her back with flowers, telephone calls and a ticket to the convention. If he failed to win the nomination, the two of them would take off to a remote island, he promised, where they would never have to wear clothes. Judith got the impression that Jackie intended to leave him if he was not elected. The most Kennedy ever said about their marriage was that it 'had not worked out as they had hoped'. It would have been a political bombshell had it come out. Jackie was one of Jack's greatest assents on the stump.

On the campaign trail, women other than his wife mobbed him. One student in Louisville shouted at him: 'We love you. You're better than Elvis Presley.' Young women swooned over his pearly teeth and a teenage girl said that if she had the vote, she would vote for him, then fled into the school locker room in embarrassment.

Journalists began writing of the female 'jumpers', 'leapers', 'clutchers', 'touchers', 'screamers' and 'runners'. One wrote of the 'groans and moans and a frowzy woman muttering hoarsely to herself, 'Oh, Jack I love yuh, Jack, I love yuh, Jack, Jack, I love yuh', or the harsh-faced woman peering over one's shoulder glowering, 'You a newspaperman? You better write nice things about him or you watch out' (and she meant it)'.

Although Jackie continued to play the part of the adoring political wife, her husband's relentless womanising sent her into depressions. She could not escape from her gilded cage. Her beauty and grace were seen as vital vote catchers and she had to be at the candidate's side constantly.

At the Democratic convention in Los Angeles that summer, Kennedy had won the nomination, much to Judith's chagrin, and Lyndon Johnson's knowledge of Kennedy's sexual history had got him on the ticket as Vice President. With that tied up, Kennedy found time to party, usually at Peter Lawford's beach house north of Santa Monica. Dean Martin said that Lawford acted as Kennedy's pimp and that 'the things that went on in that house were just mind-boggling'.

Lawford himself refused to talk about Kennedy and his 'broads… all I will say is that I was Frank's [Sinatra's] pimp and Frank was Jack's. It sounds terrible now, but then it was a lot of fun'.

Some in the know though spotted a problem. Lawford's mother put it succinctly: 'I find it difficult to place my complete trust in a president of the United States, who always has his mind on his cock.'

There were rumours about his involvement with the beautiful brunette Janet des Rosiers, who travelled on the Kennedys' plane with him. She was his 'girl Friday' – or 'our stewardess' as Evelyn Lincoln called her – and massaged the candidate and combed his hair in a private compartment on board. It was a family thing. Previously she had been employed to perform the same functions for Kennedy's father, having been his mistress for nine years and practically living at Hyannis Port. She said she had been seduced by Joe when she was a twenty-four-year-old virgin. He was not a religious man, she said. 'He did not go to confession. Oh God! If a priest heard his confession.'

The 1960 election is famous for having the first televised debates between the two principal candidates. Those who heard the debates on the radio thought the Nixon had won; those who saw them on TV thought Kennedy was the winner. Nixon was famous for his five-o'clock shadow. He looked tense and awkward, and perspired under the hot television lines. Kennedy appeared relax and totally in control.

The night before the first debate, Kennedy was so chilled he said to his aide Langdon Marvin: 'Any girls line up for tomorrow?'

A beautiful prostitute was laid on. Marvin took the girl to Kennedy's room and stood guard outside. Fifteen minutes later, Kennedy emerged grinning from ear to ear. The pre-show sex gave him a glow that the cameras picked up. He looked relaxed and in control. Before each subsequent debate, his aides made sure that a prostitute was provided.

The press knew all about these activities, but chose to keep quiet. In those days unless a politician's thirst for strong drink, womanising or homosexual activities affected his performance in office, the press corps simply refused to report them. Nevertheless, Kennedy ruefully noted: 'I suppose if I win, my poon days are over.' ('Poon' is the navy term for vagina he had picked up while in uniform.)

He was wrong, of course. Once elected, the press gave him even more latitude. Sometime before his inauguration, Kennedy slipped off for two or three days in Palm Springs with actress Angie Dickinson, famed as TV's 'Sergeant Pepper'. They disappeared into a holiday cottage and never emerged. A *Newsweek* reporter who travelled with the Kennedys barged in and caught Dickinson relaxing on the bed, but he promptly forgot what he had seen.

Angie Dickinson has been credited with saying of sex with Kennedy: 'It was the best twenty seconds of my life.' Indeed, it has been widely reported that Kennedy, like his father, was a quick and inconsiderate lover, more interested in the conquest than the consummation.

This was unexpectedly confirmed in 2014 by Marlene Dietrich. Fifteen years older than JFK, she related their assignation over White House drinks to the critic Kenneth Tynan, who recorded it in his journals on April 4, 1971. Dietrich said she was in a hurry as '2,000 Jews were waiting to give her a plaque at 7 p.m., and it was now 6:30.'

'That doesn't give us much time, does it?' said the President.

'No, Jack, I guess it doesn't…. And then [after] he went to sleep. I looked at my watch and it was 6:50.'

Dietrich woke Kennedy up, 'because I didn't know my way around the place, and I couldn't just call for a cab.' Dressed in a towel, JFK took her to an elevator and ordered the staff present to get her a car – but not before asking her 'just one thing… Did you ever make it with my father?'

'No Jack… I never did," Dietrich said.

'Well that's one place I'm in first.' was his parting response.

Dickinson has, in fact, maintained a respectful silence on the subject of her affair with Kennedy. Then there was actress Gene Tierney and stripper Blaze Starr, whom he made love to in a closet while her regular boyfriend, Democrat Governor Earl Long, was at an election party next door. Judith Campbell was invited to Kennedy's inaugural ball, but declined. She said she would not feel right as his wife and children would be there.

Angie Dickinson did attend and went to a private dinner party with Kennedy.

'From the moment I met him, I was hooked, like everyone else' she told *TV Guide* in 1987. 'He was the sexiest politician I ever met…. He was the killer type, a handsome, charming man – the kind your mother hoped you wouldn't marry.' But she refused to say whether they had had an affair. 'He was a married man and president of the United States,' she said. 'I'm not going to tell anyone what happens in my bed. That's ridiculous.'

Jackie herself avoided many of the inaugural functions, having no wish to stand by while her husband was squeezed, hugged and pawed by the numerous actresses who had been invited. Jackie did, however, attend one ball with her husband at the Statler-Hilton. Even then he could not resist slipping out of the presidential box to attend a private party with Frank Sinatra, Angie Dickinson, Janet Leigh and Kim Novak. He returned sheepishly with a copy of the *Washington Post* under his arm as if the newly inaugurated President of the United States had simply gone to buy a newspaper.

Later that night, JFK celebrated his inauguration in proper Kennedy style. He attended a party at columnist Joe Alsop's Georgetown house, where the first thing he asked was: 'Where are the broads?'

The place was packed with young girls and Hollywood starlets. The niece of one European ambassador was also available. Peter Lawford lined up six candidates. Kennedy picked two of them and went to celebrate his inauguration in his favourite style.

Once in the White House, Kennedy was bombarded with the F.B.I. files of people in his administration. At first, he enjoyed reading them as it told him which of the White House secretaries were 'available', but when he realised the extent of Hoover's snooping, he swore he would never read another dossier – though he admitting ruefully: 'I'd like to see what they have got on me.'

Judith Campbell was a regular visitor to the White House. She tells of a visit there one Saturday afternoon, kissing and cuddling in his bedroom to the sound track of the musical *Camelot*. She went into the bathroom to undress and when she returned, he was already in bed, lying in his favourite position on his back, awaiting servicing. This was one of over twenty visits Judith Campbell made to the White House, smuggled in by the Secret Service.

Despite Hoover's regular warnings about Judith Campbell's connections with the Mafia to the Attorney General Bobby Kennedy, the affair continued. They also met in Palm Springs, where he would go to search out new girls. Campbell also recalled sitting in a hotel bathroom while Kennedy and Giancana discussed the assassination of Fidel Castro – the Mafia's attempt on Castro's life is thought to have backfired and led to Kennedy's own assassination. Meanwhile the F.B.I. continued to keep track of Kennedy's every move. They bugged Judith Campbell's phone and did security checks on the prostitutes hired for Kennedy's parties.

The painter Mary Pinchot Meyer visited the White House too. Veteran journalist Ben Bradlee and his wife often accompanied her to soirees there, but there were clandestine visits too, when they smoked marijuana together. A woman known only as Susannah M. claimed on a TV documentary to have had a four-year relationship with Kennedy, which included visits to the White House.

In fact, the stream of attractive young women making their way to the Presidential Mansion was endless. Kennedy would often take them nude swimming in the White House pool. Male friends would send over nubile volunteers. One was a *Playboy* centrefold sent over by a columnist. Kennedy replied in a note saying: 'Got your message – both of them.'

At one nude swimming party, Kennedy and a tall beautiful blonde were joined by Bobby Kennedy, a male friend and several more naked girls. Suddenly they got a message that Jackie, who had left for Virginia, was on her way back to the White House. Everybody scrambled. But when Jackie had collected the things she had forgotten and was on her way again, the nude party resumed.

White-House kennel-keeper Traphes Bryant also recalled that, one day when he was making a routine trip to the basement, the doors of the elevator opened and a naked office girl came flying out so fast that she almost knocked him down. She stopped just long enough to ask where the president was. On another occasion, two presidential aides had urgent business with the president. They knocked on the door of the Lincoln bedroom. Kennedy let them in. There was a young woman in the bed. He slumped down in a chair, read the classified telegrams they had brought, issued his orders, ushered them out, then went back to what he had been doing.

There was a strict code of silence about these goings-on. Any mention of them, particularly to Jackie, was considered disloyal, if not downright unpatriotic.

'That's just the way Jack is; it doesn't matter,' said the wife of one of Kennedy's older male friends. 'Everyone at court knows it. No one minds, of course, unless they're jealous of the ones he chooses – or they feel bad for Jackie.'

But even the nude parties began to pall. At one, he slumped down in a chair to read the syndicated columnist Walter. Lippmann. Later, he phoned a friend saying that he was in the Oval Office with two naked young women and he was reading the *Wall Street Journal*.

'Am I getting too old?' he asked.

The sheer numbers of women going through the White House gave the Secret Service major headaches. They were supposed to give every visitor a full security check. It proved impossible to keep up and the Secret Service codenamed Kennedy 'Lancer' – ostensible for its associations with Camelot.

White-House staff were instructed to comb the presidential apartments for lipsticks, dropped hairpins or other incriminating evidence. They disliked Kennedy's penchant for blondes. Telltale hairs got everywhere: if he had slept with brunettes like Jackie it would be much easier to cover his tracks. And sometimes things went massively awry. Jackie once found a pair of panties stuffed in a pillow case. She held them between her forefinger and thumb and presented them to her husband.

'Would you please shop around and see who these belong to?' she said. 'They are not my size.'

There were two mistresses Jackie definitely knew about. When showing Italian journalists through the White House, she opened a door to an office. There were two attractive blonde secretaries inside.

'Those two are my husband's lovers,' she said.

They were twenty-one-year-old Priscilla Weiss and Jill Cowan, twenty three, former college roommates who had joined the Kennedy campaign, then got jobs are the White House, ostensibly working for Kennedy's press secretary Pierre Salinger and Evelyn

Lincoln. They were lively and often dressed alike. The Secret Service codenamed them 'Fiddle' and 'Faddle'. They were on call twenty four hours a day and took it in turns to accompany him everywhere he went, and were the ones who had first tried amyl nitrate 'poppers' for Kennedy. Washington insiders had long come to the same conclusion as Mrs Kennedy.

Kennedy's need for sex was a pathological condition. At a Summit meet on the Bahamas with British Prime Minister Harold Macmillan and Foreign Secretary R.A.B. Butler, Kennedy complained: 'If I don't have a woman for three days, I get terrible headaches.'

He told others that he could not sleep properly unless he had had a lay.

'We're a bunch of virgins, married virgins,' said Fred Dutton, secretary to the cabinet, 'and he's like a God, fucking anybody he wants to any time he feels like it.'

Sex quickly became the currency of American diplomacy. When he visited the President, the French ambassador Hervé Alphand was often accompanied by two young women said to be his nieces, though it was hard to see the family resemblance. This was to counter the British who had installed Kennedy's old friend David Ormsby-Gore as their ambassador to Washington, at the president's request. He supplied Kennedy with embargoed Cuban cigars and was so close to the family it is said that he had an affair with Jackie after the assassination of JFK.

Even during the Cuban missile crisis, Jack's mind was on women. During a tense meeting when the fate of the world hung in the balance, Kennedy spotted an attractive secretary. He told Secretary of Defense Robert McNamara: 'I want her name and number. We may avert war tonight.'

Kennedy had had his eye on Marilyn Monroe ever since she first appeared in movies in the early 1950s. In 1954, when he was incapacitated after back surgery, he stuck her picture on his wall. It showed her standing feet apart, wearing shorts. He stuck it on the wall upside down, so that her legs were in the air.

They began their affair in the late 1950s. They were certainly lovers during the 1960 election campaign and made love in Los Angeles when Kennedy was there for the Democratic National Convention that year. Around that time Peter Lawford remembered taking photographs of Kennedy and Monroe together, naked in the bathtub. Marilyn was performing oral sex on Kennedy at the time. Another time, Kennedy aide Peter Summers saw them emerge from the same shower.

They appeared together at a nude swimming party at Lawford's beach house the night of his acceptance speech. Still Kennedy was shocked when he found that Marilyn wore no underwear when he put his hand up her dress that night at a dinner party.

On other occasions, heavily disguised with a black wig and sunglasses, Monroe was smuggled into Kennedy's suite at the Carlyle Hotel in New York and on to Air Force One. They made love on the beach at Santa Monica, spent the night at the Beverley Hilton and spent time together at Bing Crosby's estate in Palm Springs. She even called her masseur when they had an argument about anatomy and she put Kennedy on the phone to settle the point.

As newspaper reporters covered the lobby of the Carlyle, the Secret Service found another way into the hotel via a series of tunnels that ran from a nearby apartment building. The President of the United States would have to clamber past huge steam pipes, accompanied by two Secret Service men with torches and a map, for half an hour with Marilyn or his latest playmate. But this was a better option than letting him get away with his usual trick – simply giving them the slip. Sometimes Kennedy left behind the army officer who had the nuclear security codes handcuffed to his wrist.

The F.B.I. had Peter Lawford's house bugged and in November 1961, agents taped Kennedy and Monroe talking, disrobing and having sex on the bed. Hoover was delighted. He had overheard Bobby Kennedy discussing the possibility of firing him. Now he knew he was safe. Hoover, himself kept a nude photograph of Marilyn in a basement, along with other cheesecake pictures, to counter the oft repeated rumour that he was gay.

There were other guests at the Carlyle Hotel. Lawford brought high-priced New York callgirl Leslie Devereux there for Kennedy. She was not told who the client was to be and was surprised to discover it was the President. She returned their on four other occasions.

'I'd been with a number of powerful politicians and the one thing they always liked was mild S&M,' she said. 'So we did a little of that. I tied his hands and feet to the bedposts, blindfolded him and teased him first with a feather and then with my fingernails. He seemed enjoy it.'

Devereux also visited Washington where she spent fifteen minutes a small room off the Oval Office. Kennedy knew that this was where his Republican predecessor Warren Harding had made love to his mistress Nan Britton. He had once told Blaze Starr about it. On her second visit, they repaired to the Lincoln bedroom. She questioned the propriety of making out in Lincoln's bed. He said that if you made a wish in Lincoln's bed, it always came true. As he had to be careful with his back, he lay back and she climbed on top. 'See,' he said. 'It never fails.'

When Marilyn Monroe, fatally addicted to alcohol and pills, became mentally unstable she became a dangerous liability to the president. At one point during the 1960 election campaign, Marilyn was on a binge with liquor and pills and Kennedy had to send Charles Spalding to Los Angeles to make sure she did not speak out of turn. On another occasion Smathers had to send a mutual friend to 'talk to Marilyn Monroe about putting a bridle on herself and on her mouth and not talking too much, because it was getting to be a story around the country'.

'She devised all sorts of madcap fantasies with herself in the starring role,' said Lawford. 'She would have his children. She would take Jackie's place as First Lady.'

When no divorce seemed to be on the horizon, she began calling Kennedy's private apartment in the White House. When Jackie answered, she would hand the phone to her husband and go on about her business.

In March 1962, Hoover learned that Kennedy had visited Monroe again in California and the two of them had spent the night together. They met again in May in New York when she sang her famous 'Happy Birthday, Mr President' at a Democratic Party fundraiser at Madison Square Garden.

On the night of this birthday party, Marilyn appeared, sewn into a dress that veteran diplomat Adlai Stevenson described as 'skin and beads – only I didn't see the beads'. The sexual electricity between Kennedy and Monroe was visible even to the TV cameras. Afterwards the press was full of speculation about Kennedy and Monroe. Jack called on the inspector general of the Peace Corps William Haddad, a former reporter on the *New York Post*, and asked him to 'see the editors. Tell them you are speaking for me and that it's not true.' Photographs showing the President ogling Marilyn mysteriously disappeared from the picture agencies.

After Marilyn had finished her seductive rendition, Kennedy took the stage and said: 'I can now retire from politics after having had, ah, 'Happy Birthday' sung to me in such a sweet wholesome way.'

Kennedy could no longer risk seeing Marilyn. It was time to put an end to the affair and he told Marilyn bluntly: 'You're not really First Lady material.' Marilyn could not accept that the affair was over and fell into a deep depression. A scandal had to be avoided at all costs, so Kennedy sent his brother Bobby to reason with her. According to Peter Lawford, she took it pretty hard. Bobby felt for her. They met the following day and spent the afternoon walking along the beach.

'It wasn't Bobby's intention, but that evening they became lovers and spent the night in our guest bedroom,' said Lawford. 'Almost immediately the affair got very heavy… Now Marilyn was calling the Justice Department instead of the White House.'

Pretty soon Marilyn announced that she was in love with Bobby and he had promised to marry her. Hoover was delighted to hear this. Bobby Kennedy, as Attorney General, was Hoover's boss and, consequently, his arch-enemy. He proceeded to make things hot for Bobby. He told the Attorney General that the Mafia were intending to use their knowledge of his sexual exploits to prevent Bobby's continuing investigations into organised crime.

Jack was forced to give up Judith Campbell and Bobby had to abandon Monroe. For Marilyn, this was one blow too many. She attended some orgies at Lake Tahoe arranged by Lawford and Sinatra, but it did not help. When she died of a drug overdose, numerous theories about how this happened ensued. The latest is that Kennedy, Lawford and others goaded her into attempting suicide then, instead of saving her at the last minute, left her to die.

Jack got Lawford to arrange an introduction to Jayne Mansfield. With her forty-two-inch bust and her eighteen-inch waist, she was even more than Monroe the ideal woman of her era. According to Lawford, they met at least three times. On one occasion she was eight-months pregnant. He was 'very considerate of my condition,' she said. But she also said she found him cold. A week after an assignation in Palm Springs, she was having drinks with her press agent when Kennedy called. An argument broken out and she hung up on him after shouting: 'Look, you'll only be president for eight years, but I'll be a movie star for life.'

In 1963, in another sly attack on the President, Hoover leaked to the press information linking Kennedy to the Profumo affair. Kennedy had had sex, both in London and New York, with actress and model Suzy Chang who moved in the wealthy London circles associated with Profumo and his friends. Kennedy had met Chang at the 21 Club in London. After that, she took regular flights to the U.S. to meet up with him. Bleach-blonde Czech prostitute Maria Novotny was also involved.

The president turned to Bobby to keep a lid on the scandal. J Edgar Hoover contacted the F.B.I.'s legal attaché in London and told him to 'stay on top of this case and… keep bureau fully and promptly informed of all developments with particular emphasis on any allegation that U.S. nationals are or have been involved in any way'. The CIA were given similar instructions. The deputy chief of station Cleveland Cram said he spent the next 'three or four' weeks at MI5 headquarters going through the Profumo files.

'It was lots of fun,' he said.

At the time, he had no doubt that they were trying to find out whether 'one of the Kennedys' was linked to the Profumo girls. He noted that a special request had come from the President himself. They needed to know whether anything was about to be made public on the grounds that 'forewarned is fore-armed.'

Meanwhile, back in the U.S., the *New York Journal-American*, a Hearst newspaper, reported that: 'One of the biggest names in American politics – a man who holds a very high elective office – has been injected into Britain's vice-security scandal.' The reporters, James D. Horan and Dom Frasca, quoted Maria Novotny saying that the connection involved 'a beautiful Chinese-American girl now in London,' adding that the "highest authorities" had 'identified her as Suzy Chang'.

The story – which ran on the front page under the three-deck headline 'High U.S. Aide Implicated in V-Girl Scandal' – was pulled after the first edition. Horan, who died in the 1980s, told his sons that the story had been spiked due to pressure from Bobby Kennedy.

Bobby then called Warren Rogers, Washington correspondent for *Look* magazine, and told him to get on the phone to his fellow reporter to find out if anyone knew who the man mentioned in the *New York Journal–American* story was.

While Bobby was trying to cope with the scandal, brother Jack had gone to see the pope. On his way home, he had arranged to visit a villa on Lake Como where Gianni Agnelli's wife Marella would he waiting.

Bobby Kennedy summoned Horan and Frasca to the Justice Department and demanded to know who the high official involved in the Profumo scandal was. F.B.I. liaison officer Courtney Evans who was taking notes at the meeting said that Horan and Frasca were reluctant to answer, but eventually admitted: 'It was the President of the United States.'

Their source of the story was Peter Earle, a reporter on the *News of the World* in London. The Sunday paper had signed up Maria Novotny for her story, which Earle had been assigned to write. The attorney general then berated them for writing a story about the President of the United States 'without any further check being made to get to the truth of the matter'. But Frasca said he had 'other sources of a confidential nature'.

In 1987, Anthony Summers was researching his book *Official and Confidential*, a biography of J. Edgar Hoover, and tracked down Suzy Chang, then living under another name on Long Island. She said: "'We'd meet in the 21 Club. Everyone saw me eating with him. I think he was a nice guy, very charming." He asked for sex. She said yes. "What else am I going to say?"'

Maria Novotny had been arrested for prostitution in New York in 1961. She died in 1970, leaving the manuscript of an unpublished autobiography. In it, she claimed that Peter Lawford had recruited her to have group sex with Jack Kennedy a few weeks before his inauguration, and she and another prostitute had pretended to be a doctor and nurse, while the president-elect was their willing patient.

Kennedy had another affair with security implications. At the Quorum Club, an exclusive watering hole in the Carroll Arms Hotel where Suzy Chang and Maria Novotny had both worked, he asked to be introduced to Ellen Rometsch. Born in Kleinitz in 1936, at the end of World War II, she found herself in East Germany. She joined the Communist Party Youth Group. In 1955, she fled to the West Germany. Her first marriage ended in divorce. Then she married Rolf Rometsch who, in 1961, was posted to Washington as air attaché and Ellen began hanging out at the Quorum Club.

Bobby Baker, an aide to Lyndon Johnson who ran the Quorum Club, made the introduction. According to Burton Hersh, after Jack's first date with Ellen, the President phoned Baker to rave: 'That was the best blow job I ever had in my life.' Baker said the couple had several other sexual encounters. Ellen, he noted, was equally gratified during these encounters, telling Baker: 'Jack was as good as it got with the oral sex. He really was a satisfier… made me happy.'

In July 1963, the F.B.I. picked up Ellen and questioned her about her background. They quickly concluded she was a Communist spy. According to historian Michael Bechloss, Hoover told Bobby: 'We have information that not only your brother, the President, but others in Washington have been involved with a woman whom we suspect as a Soviet intelligence agent, someone who is linked to East German intelligence.'

Hoover even told Courtney Evans that Rometsch had worked for Walter Ulbricht, the Communist leader of East Germany. Bobby Kennedy promptly had her deported.

President Kennedy told J. Edgar Hoover, once again, that he was 'personally interested in having this story killed'. However, the *Des Moines Register* carried a story claiming that the F.B.I. had 'established that the beautiful brunette had been attending parties with congressional leaders and some prominent New Frontiersmen from the executive branch of Government…. The possibility that her activity might be connected with espionage was of some concern, because of the high rank of her male companions.'

Information about Ellen Rometsch was also leaked to John Williams, a leading Republican senator who was investigating the activities of Bobby Baker. Sensing danger, Bobby Kennedy sent aide La Verne Duffy to West Germany, where, in exchange for a great deal of money, he got Rometsch to sign a statement formally denying that she had slept with important people in Washington.

It was then a matter of quashing any senate investigation. Bobby had the senate leaders in. It was easy to persuade the Democrats to keep shtum. But only J. Edgar Hoover had the necessary firepower in his files to shut up the Republican senators. President Kennedy cut a deal with him. He agreed to bailout the President only on two conditions – that Kennedy would never fire him and that the F.B.I. could escalate its bugging of Martin Luther King.

Kennedy acceded and Hoover showed senate leaders the F.B.I. files he had on dozens of senators. He explained that if the Senate exposed the President's sex life, no one would be safe.

On the same day, the Senate leaders announced there would be no investigation into Ellen Rometsch. Soon after, Kennedy opined to Ben Bradlee: 'Boy, the dirt he has on those senators, you wouldn't believe it.'

The matter was dropped and the Kennedy's were now in Hoover's debt. After that, when Kennedy was asked why he did not fire Hoover, he would reply simply: 'You don't fire God.'

Forty years after Kennedy was assassinated in Dallas, his sex life made the headlines, yet again, when documents were released showing that he had an affair with a teenager while he was in the White House.

Nineteen-year-old Marion 'Mimi' Beardsley came to 1600 Pennsylvania Avenue to interview Mrs Kennedy for Jackie's old school paper, but the First Lady was too busy to see her. It seems that the President had more time for the young lady and hired her to work in the press office.

'Mimi had no skills. She couldn't type,' said former press aide Barbara Gamarekian. 'She could answer the phone and she could handle messages and things but she was not really a great asset to us.'

However, she did have her role as one of a group of girls who were invited to pool parties and went on presidential trips.

'We all went on trips one time or another, but Mimi, who obviously couldn't perform any function at all, made all the trips,' Mrs Gamarekian said.

She was then invited to pool parties and flown around the country on Air Force One to provide 'sexual release' for the commander-inchief. In the Bahamas, Mimi was spotted by aides after the Macmillan summit hiding in one of the cars waiting to take the president to the airport. According Mrs Gamarekian, 'they walked over and looked in the car and here seated on the floor was Mimi'. The aides said nothing and neither did the press. At that time, Mrs Gamarekian said, 'this is the sort of thing that legitimate newspaper people don't write about or don't even make any implications about. It was kind of a big joke.'

Bearded by the New York *Daily News* outside her Fifth Avenue Presbyterian church in Manhattan in 2003, Mimi said: 'From June 1962 to November 1963, I was involved in a sexual relationship with President Kennedy. For the last forty one years, it is a subject that I have not discussed.' She had told no one, not even her immediate family.

In August 1963, Jackie was rushed to hospital and gave birth to a boy six weeks premature. The child died after a couple of hours. In October, she flew to Athens to take a cruise on the yacht of Greek shipping magnate Aristotle Onassis. The trip had been organised by Jackie's sister 'Princess' Lee Radziwill – her husband was the Polish Prince Stanislaw Radziwill, though he had become just plain 'Mr' when he had taken British citizenship in 1951. Onassis's long-term mistress, the opera singer Maria Callas, was not on board as she had just discovered that Onassis had taken Jackie's sister Lee as his lover.

Bobby Kennedy was outraged when he heard about Lee's affair. But Onassis, who had already had several run-ins with the attorney general, knew about the Kennedy brothers' involvement with Marilyn Monroe and said: 'Bobby, you and Jack fuck your movie queen and I'll fuck my princess.'

Everyone was amazed when Jackie accepted Onassis's invitation. Her motivation seems to have been revenge on her husband. Onassis had already expressed an interest in the president's wife.

'There's something provocative about that lady. She's got a carnal soul,' he told a friend.

According to Evelyn Lincoln, Onassis and Jackie became lovers on that cruise. However, the trip brought her bad press and, when she returned, she agreed to travel with her husband to Texas the following month where he was killed.

Onassis's biographer Peter Evans told the *Daily Mail* that Onassis paid for Robert Kennedy's assassination. Jackie married Onassis four months after Bobby's death.

XII
Dwight D. Eisenhower, #34

'There's nothing I can do.'

While Roosevelt was womanising his way through the war and Truman was keeping himself to himself, General Dwight D. Eisenhower, commander of the largest amphibious assault force ever marshalled and soon to be the thirty-fourth President of the United States, was stationed in London.

Eisenhower's family life was strict and religious, but he was interested in girls from an early age. He was in luck — in his high school in Abilene, girls outnumbered boys by two to one. The boys tended to drop out before graduation, too, so in Eisenhower's graduation class there were twenty-five girls and just nine boys.

However, Ike was shy around girls and he wanted to impress his classmates that he was a regular guy. Paying the girls too much attention was not cool at all. So Ike deliberately dressed badly, mussed up his hair and, on the few occasions he was forced on to the dancefloor, proved to be a terrible dancer.

After graduating, Ike took a summer job in a creamery and began to lose his shyness. He had a half-serious romance with redhaired Ruby Norman.

Then, on his way to West Point, he stopped off to visit his brother Edgar at Ann Arbor. One evening, the two boys rented a canoe and paddled down the Huron River with a couple of college girls. It was 'the most romantic evening I had ever known,' Eisenhower later recalled.

That evening caused him to regret abandoning his plan to study law with Edgar at the University of Michigan in favour of a career in the army. 'It looked to me as if he were leading the right life,' he said.

Eisenhower was a keen sportsman who enjoyed fishing,

baseball, football and, later, golf, and a fanatic poker player. A knee injury sustained during a game at West Point put an end to his hopes of fame as a running back. Otherwise, Eisenhower was an average student, graduating 61st academically and 125th in discipline in a class of 164 in 1915.

He was posted to Fort Houston at San Antonio, Texas. There, one Sunday afternoon, as officer of the day, he was inspecting the guard. On the lawn outside the Officers' Club, there was a gaggle of women. One of them, Mrs Lulu Harris, wife of Major Hunter Harris, saw Eisenhower and called out: 'Ike, won't you come over here? I have some people 1'd like you to meet.'

He refused.

'Sorry,' he said. 'I am on guard and I have to make an inspection trip.'

'Humph!' said Mrs Harris, turning to her companions. 'The woman-hater of the post.'

Then she called out at Ike: 'We didn't ask you to come over to stay. Just come over here and meet these friends of mine.'

Ike walked over. Later he recalled: 'The one who attracted my eye instantly was a vivacious and attractive girl, smaller than average, saucy in the look about her face and in her whole attitude.'

She was nineteen-year-old Mamie Geneva Doud, the daughter of a Denver meat packer. He was twenty five. There followed a whirlwind romance and, on St Valentine's Day 1916, he proposed. In June, he organised a tenday leave. They married in the Douds' spacious home on 1 July. Eisenhower did not sit down until the ceremony was over, afraid of destroying the knife-edge creases in his pants. Afterwards, they had a two-day honeymoon in Eldorado Springs, Colorado.

Back at the post, Ike did not settle easily into married life. He often showed a marked reluctance to return to the married quarters, preferring to play poker in the evening with his friends instead.

Less than a month after her marriage, Mamie Eisenhower discovered that she would always be number two in her husband's life. As he was packing to move to a new posting, he told his nineteen-year-old bride matter-of-factly: 'My country comes first and always will. You come second.'

Despite frequent rows about this, they began a family.

Good to his word, he stuck with the army. Over the following thirty seven years' service to his country, Mamie estimated that they moved house twenty-seven times.

During World War II, Ike was appointed Supreme Commander in Europe and was posted to London. Because of the bombing, Mamie stayed behind in Washington, DC.

When Ike landed in Prestwick, Scotland, he was met by young driver Kay Summersby. She was a former model and movie actress, who had enlisted in the transport section of the Women's Royal Army Corps. She was assigned to Eisenhower because of her encyclopaedic knowledge of London. Though born in County Cork, Eire, Kay was a British subject.

'She is also very pretty,' Eisenhower wrote tactlessly in a letter home to Mamie. 'Irish and slender and I think in the process of getting a divorce, which is all that worries me.'

Fortunately, his aide Harry Butcher forgot to mail this letter. Butcher also recorded in his own diary that Eisenhower's feelings towards Kay were rather more carnal.

'Ike defines this member of the WAC as "a doublebreasted GI with a built-in foxhole",' he wrote.

Kay played an important part in Eisenhower's life. As well as driving him around, making his coffee and providing him with some well-earned relaxation, he turned to her for emotional support when the going got rough.

After the letter that was never sent, Eisenhower discreetly omitted any reference to Kay Summersby in correspondence with Mamie. As Supreme Commander, however, his every move was reported on and Kay appeared in almost every press shot of the General, close beside him.

Even though Kay was engaged to a young American officer, Colonel Richard A. Arnold at the time, gossip flourished. Some of it inevitably got back to Mamie. Ike constantly reassured her and told her that he wished she was there with him, if it was not for the bombing.

Eisenhower was ill at ease with women generally, but Kay Summersby made him feel comfortable. He enjoyed her charm, her good looks and her flirtatious manner, even if she was twenty years his junior. As well as being his driver, she was appointed his secretary at AFHQ and he drove her like a slave from dawn to dusk. They were seldom out of each other's sight. Her light touch with high-powered military men, royalty and senior politicians was invaluable. They went together on a trip to Algiers, Egypt and Palestine and would dine together. She would be his partner at bridge and they went horseback riding. Her youth and humour were a convenient escape from the pressures of war and death. She found it easy to fall in love with her middle-aged boss, while he found excuses to touch her, or brush her knee. Gradually their relationship grew into a full-blown affair.

Ike's deputy chief of staff, Brigadier General Everett Hughes recorded in his diary: 'Leave Kay alone, she's helping Ike win the war.' Nevertheless he foresaw a terrible scandal.

Mamie's letters continually harped on her worries about him being surrounded by attractive young women in London. He would tell her 'not to worry your pretty head about WAACs', but she was still concerned about 'tales I heard about the night clubs, gaiety and loose morals'.

The gossip, he said, was without foundation. How could anyone be 'banal and foolish enough to lift an eyebrow at an old duffer such as I am in connection with WAACs – Red Cross workers – nurses and drivers?' he wrote. Her suspicions and his prevarication continued.

'If you want me to get you a lot of vital statistics I'll have [his aide Tex] Lee form them up, march them in here, and I'll give each a questionnaire,' he wrote shirtily.

Then Mamie mentioned that she had read in *Life* magazine that his 'London driver' had joined him on a trip to Algiers.

'She is terribly in love with a young American colonel and is to be married to him come June, assuming both are alive,' Ike wrote back. 'I doubt that *Life* told that.'

Besides, he said ruefully: 'I'm old – my days of romance may be all behind me but I swear I think I miss you more and love you more than I ever did.'

Mamie's suspicions drove her slowly to drink.

Asked whether the affair was just a matter of rumour, war correspondent John Thompson of the *Chicago Tribune* replied: 'Well, I have never before seen a chauffeur get out of a car and kiss the General good morning when he comes from his office.'

The gossip had gone almost as far as it could when, on the eve of their wedding, Kay's fiancé was killed by a land mine. Eisenhower consoled her in her grief and told Mamie that she 'cannot long continue to drive – she is too sunk!' But she wasn't and they began a passionate affair.

'It was like an explosion,' Kay wrote in her memoirs. 'We were suddenly in each other's arms. His kisses absolutely unravelled me. Hungry, strong, demanding. And I responded every bit as passionately. He stopped, took my face between his hands. "Goddamn it", he said, "I love you".'

'We were breathing as if we had run up a dozen flights of stairs. God must have been watching over us, because no one came bursting into the office. It was lovers' luck, but we both came to our senses, remembering how Tex had walked in earlier that day. Ike had lipstick smudges on his face. I started scrubbing at them frantically with my handkerchief.'

One evening, he and Kay found themselves alone for a nightcap.

'Ike refilled our glasses several times,' she recalled, 'and then, I suppose inevitably, we found ourselves in each other's arms in an unrestrained embrace. Our ties came off. Our jackets came off. Buttons were unbuttoned. It was as if we were frantic. And we were.

'But it was not what I expected. Wearily, we slowly calmed down. He snuggled his face into the hollow between my neck and shoulder and said, "Oh, God, Kay. I'm sorry. I'm not going to be any good for you".'

Eisenhower could not get an erection. Kay put this down to the fact that he had a lot on his mind.

To help move things along his aides fixed up a rural retreat called Telegraph Cottage on Kingston Hill in Surrey and bought her a puppy they called Telek – the 'Tele' from Telegraph Cottage and the 'k' from Kay. They tried to make love several times at Telegraph Cottage, too, but again without success.

Kay was by Eisenhower's side as he saw off the D-Day assault force and witnessed the tears in his eyes. She toured the battlefields of Normandy with him and stayed with him at his new headquarters at Versailles. As late as March 1945, members of Eisenhower's staff discussed the General's affair, but slowly his relationship with Kay Summersby had begun to cool.

He travelled more, leaving her behind at his headquarters. Mamie was giving him hell, he told General Hughes. With the war drawing to a close there would be no further place for Kay in his life.

Nonetheless, in June 1945, he wrote to his superior, General Marshall, chief of the general staff, asking permission to divorce Mamie and marry Kay. Marshall was furious.

He threatened to break Eisenhower through the ranks and 'see to it that the rest of his life was a living hell' if he married Kay Summersby.

Mamie had known of Eisenhower's intentions and thought it for the best but Eisenhower accepted Marshall's decision, realising that 'from every stand-point of logic and public relations the thing is impossible'. He wrote to Mamie with the bad news and comforted her with the thought that 'you cannot be any more tired than I am of this long separation'.

Eisenhower was ordered home for a whirlwind tour of the United States. Mamie met him at the airport. After their years apart, she gave him only the briefest kiss and a hug before he was hustled off to the Pentagon. They had a week together at White Sulphur Springs before he went back to Germany alone, even though the

European war and the threat of bombing were over.

Their time together had done little to ease the situation. When Eisenhower had to pay a brief visit to Belfast, Mamie remarked in a letter that he seemed 'highly interested in Ireland'. Eisenhower explained wearily that he had travelled with two male aides and 'carried out a schedule that would kill a horse'.

Mamie was right to be suspicious. Eisenhower and Kay had one last attempt at lovemaking on his birthday, 14 October 1945. He had arranged for her to become a U.S. citizen so that she could continue working for him, telling her that she was going to be on his personal staff in the Pentagon. When he told her the news, she kissed him.

'We sat there on the sofa making daydreamy plans for the future, kissing, holding hands being quite indiscreet for the rest of the afternoon,' she wrote. 'Never in all the time I had known him had I had to hold Ike back. He had always been circumspect, but this afternoon he was an eager lover.'

The door was closed and she knew that nobody from the household would be walking in.

'The fire was warm. The sofa soft. We held each other close, closer. Excitedly, I remember thinking, the way one thinks odd thoughts at significant moments, wouldn't it be wonderful if this were the day we conceived a baby – our very first time,' she wrote. 'Ike was tender, careful, loving. But it didn't work.

'"Wait," I said, "you're too excited. It will be all right".'

'"No," he said flatly. "It won't. It's too late. I can't." He was bitter. We dressed slowly. Kissing occasionally. Smiling a bit sadly".'

'"Comb your hair," he said. "I'm going to ask then to serve supper in here".'

When Eisenhower returned to Washington, she found that she had been dropped from the roster of people going with him. Instead she was given a job in Berlin working for the Deputy Military Governor of Germany, General Lucius Clay, explaining to his friend Walter Bedell Smith that Kay 'feels very deserted and alone'.

After Kay was discharged from the Army, she began stalking Eisenhower who was then president of Columbia University in New York City. Bumping into him on campus one day, she said she was visiting a friend who was a student there. He did not believe her.

'Kay, it's impossible,' he said. 'There's nothing I can do.'

Mamie returned to Europe with her husband when he was appointed to head NATO and played hostess at their chateau there. Kay eventually reconciled herself to her loss and, in 1952, married.

That same year, just a few days before Eisenhower's presidential campaign began, a new woman took on the Kay Summersby role. Her name was Ann Whitman who had been at supreme allied headquarters with him during World War II. This time she stayed with him as his aide for eight years.

Mamie's last temporary quarters were the White House. Some say that the marriage never mended after his affair with Kay Summersby. Mamie began to have trouble with her balance, due to a problem in the inner ear. But rumour attributed it rather to alcohol abuse and 'visits to health spas' were seen as efforts to dry out.

However, in the White House, Ike and Mamie still slept together in the same bed room. Mamie said she liked to reach over in the middle of the night 'and pat Ike on his old bald head any time I want to'.

The couple retired to the farmhouse they had bought in Gettysburg, Pennsylvania, in 1948. It was the only home they ever owned together. Mamie died ten years after her husband in 1979 and was buried beside him in a small chapel beside the Eisenhower Library in Abilene, Kansas.

In 1948, Kay Summersby wrote *Eisenhower Was My Boss*. Then she threatened to tell the story of their affair in a series of articles in *Look* magazine. The affair caused a lot of sniggering when Eisenhower ran for president, but it was not until five years after his death in 1972 that she finally published *Past Forgetting: My Love Affair* with Dwight D. Eisenhower, revealing the full extent of their passionate but rarely consummated wartime romance.

XIII
Harry S. Truman, #33

Roosevelt's successor, Harry S. Truman married his childhood sweetheart and said that she was so beautiful he never looked at another woman. He was even embarrassed if they looked at him, which mostly they did not.

The courtship was one of the slowest ever. It began when he was six. They got engaged when he was thirty and married when he was thirty-three. In the eighty-two years they knew each other, they were only separated briefly by World War I. While in France as an artillery officer, he visited the Folies-Bergère, which he dismissed as a 'disgusting performance'. In Marseilles, though, the dancer Gaby threw him a bunch of violets, which he caught. He returned from the war fond of swearing and full of off-colour jokes.

His wife Elizabeth 'Bessie' Virginia Wallace Truman was a private person, though she stood by his side on election platforms and served as his secretary when he was elected Senator.

'She is worth every penny I pay her,' he quipped.

She said that she was not much interested in the 'formalities and pomp or artificiality which… surround the family of the President'. After nine months in the White House, *Newsweek* reported that she had done her Christmas shopping alone. No one had recognised the First Lady in Washington stores.

XIV
Franklin D. Roosevelt, #32

'Don't be a goose.'

While General Eisenhower's wartime affair was practically chaste, his wartime commander-in-chief's antics were almost as disorderly as Donald Trump's. The press knew what was going on, but appreciated that Franklin Delano Roosevelt had bigger fish to fry. First, he had to steer America through the Great Depression, then through World War II. They would no more print a story about his sexual relations than a picture of the callipers he needed if he was to stand or walk. Roosevelt was untouchable.

Like so many presidents, as a young man, Roosevelt had a reputation as a womaniser and drinker. At Harvard, FDR loved to dance and flirted outrageously with pretty women. Among his special favourites were Muriel Delano Robbins, his niece Helen Roosevelt, Mary Newbold and Frances Pell. His flirting once earned him a sharp slap from Alice Sohier, though he proposed to her nonetheless and she declined. He dated two girls from prominent Boston families, Dorothy Quincy and Frances Dana. He nearly married Frances, but she was a Catholic and his mother objected.

During his time at Harvard, Franklin fell under the influence of President Theodore Roosevelt, his distant relative, and met the President's niece Eleanor who had led a sheltered life. She was the ugly duckling of the family and she was shocked and delighted when such a tall, debonair young man as Franklin showered her with his amorous charm.

Many queried what first attracted Theodore to the President's niece, and considered him in no way good enough for her. From the start, he continued to womanise uninterrupted. On a trip to England, he wrote to his mother: 'As I knew the uncivilised English custom of never introducing people… I walked up to the best-looking dame in the bunch and said "howdy?" Things at once went like oil and I was soon having flirtations with three of the nobility at the same time.'

Eleanor burned all the letters of their courtship, but her letters to him survived. In one, she quoted from Elizabeth Barrett Browning: 'Unless you can swear, "For life, for death!" Oh, fear to call it loving!' He got the point and in 1903, they became engaged.

Roosevelt's mother, Sara, was against the match and took him off on a five-week cruise of the Caribbean in the hope that he would forget Eleanor. During the trip, he had a shipboard romance with an attractive older French woman, but this displeased his mother even more. As late as 1936, when he heard that she had moved to Trinidad, he tried to get in touch with her.

As planned, the marriage went ahead in 1905 with President Roosevelt giving away the bride. Their honeymoon was a European tour. They sailed on the *Oceanic*. In Brown's Hotel in London, they were ushered directly to the Royal Suite because of their kinship with the U.S. President. Roosevelt was delighted. Eleanor was not. It cost $1000 a day. He also began calling her 'Babs', short for 'Baby', the nickname he used for the rest of their life together.

On their honeymoon, she was further disturbed by two things – his sleepwalking, which was, she thought, a sign of an uneasy conscience, and his chatting up of other female guests on the ship.

Never a good sailor, she had a particularly miserable voyage on the way home. When they landed in New York, she went straight to the doctor who told her that she was pregnant. It was the first of six children (one of whom died in infancy).

During World War I, Roosevelt was in Washington where he spent a great deal of time partying with old friends from Harvard. Women flocked to him and there was the occasional entanglement. Meanwhile, Eleanor spent more time at their holiday home in Campobello, leaving him all the time he needed to have sex with other women. The married couple's sexual relations ended altogether in 1918 when Eleanor discovered that her husband was having an affair with her social secretary, Lucy Page Mercer.

Lucy was in her early twenties and extremely attractive. As she came from a prominent Maryland family that had fallen on hard times, it was not difficult for Roosevelt to woo her while Eleanor was away, and he courted her quite openly. When, later, Roosevelt was recovering from a bout of pneumonia, Eleanor decided to sort out his personal correspondence and came across a package of love letters from Lucy.

'The bottom dropped out of my own particular world,' she said.

She was devastated. His affair confirmed everything she thought about herself – that she was unattractive and unloved. After thirteen years of marriage, she offered Roosevelt a divorce.

'Don't be a goose,' Roosevelt replied.

At a family conclave, the couple agreed to stay together. A divorce would have finished his political career in those days. Sara, Roosevelt's mother, said that she would cut off her son without a penny if he left Eleanor. Foremost in Roosevelt's own mind was that Lucy was a Catholic. Even if he had divorced Eleanor, she would not have married him.

Although Eleanor agreed that she would remain married to Roosevelt, she would no longer share his bed. The truth was that she had never really enjoyed physical intimacy. Sex, she explained to her daughter, was a burden that a woman had to endure.

'Father and mother had an armed truce that endured until the day he died,' wrote their son James.

Eleanor had also insisted that Roosevelt give up his mistress. He agreed, but not really.

Behind Eleanor's back, and against his promise, he continued to see Lucy until his death, twenty seven years later.

In fact, the affair continued with hardly a pause for breath. Lucy had already left Eleanor's employment and joined the Navy as a yeomanette. She worked in the Navy Department in Washington and lived nearby. He, of course, was assistance secretary of the Navy. Although Eleanor delayed her departure to their holiday home at Campobello that summer to keep an eye on her wayward husband, as soon as she had gone, the affair resumed.

Roosevelt's letters talk of boat trips down the Potomac and long drives in the country with a circle of friends that usually included Lucy. To allay Eleanor's suspicions, he employed British diplomat Nigel Law as their beard. He was a good friend and would pretend to escort Lucy on any occasion the three of them might be seen in public.

However, Eleanor may not have been totally fooled. Her cousin Alice Longworth once spotted Roosevelt and Lucy out alone together for a drive. She told him: 'I saw you twenty miles out in the country. You didn't see me. Your hands were on the wheel but your eyes were on that perfectly lovely lady.'

Lucy and Roosevelt were physically well suited. She was beautiful. He was handsome. Young women in Washington would stop in the street to watch him ride by. Alice Longworth even had Roosevelt and Lucy to dinner at her home. Roosevelt 'deserved a good time,' Alice said, 'he was married to Eleanor.'

But that did not stop Alice trying to spill the beans to her cousin. She told Eleanor that Roosevelt had a 'secret'.

'She inquired if you had told me,' Eleanor told Roosevelt later, 'and I said that I did not believe in knowing things which your husband did not wish you to know so I think that I will be spared any further secrets.'

This may have been disingenuous. Roosevelt's son James said that his mother had evidence that Roosevelt and Lucy had checked in together in a hotel at Virginia Beach as man and wife and had spent the night together when Roosevelt was mobilising for war.

In 1919, Roosevelt risked scandal again when he took on her new secretary, Marguerite 'Missy' LeHand and promptly made her his mistress. Eleanor became aware of the liaison, but tolerated it, perhaps because she considered Missy of a different social class; or it may have been because, after 1920, Eleanor's interests had changed. Many of her own closest friends were lesbians, and she shared her husband's interest in having close female friends.

Eleanor even learned to tolerate his reputation as a bottom-pincher and knee-holder – a reputation that increased with age and was thought to reflect the innocent charm of the man. During the 1920 presidential campaign, Roosevelt joked about the 'lovely ladies who served luncheon for my husband and who worshipped at his shrine'. Missy LeHand was constantly on hand, being taken out on the campaign trail with him. Their affair went on for twenty years, with Missy playing hostess at the White House when Eleanor was away. Missy also had a room the family home at Hyde Park, upstate New York, and in Roosevelt's house in Manhattan. Later she lived in an apartment in the White House.

In 1921, while vacationing on Campobello Island in New Brunswick, Roosevelt went swimming in the Bay of Fundy and contracted polio. His mother wanted him to retire to Hyde Park but his advisers thought it best that he keep his interest in politics alive. While Roosevelt underwent a systematic programme of hydrotherapy at the hands of Missy LeHand, the two lived together more or less openly on a houseboat on winter holidays in Florida, where Roosevelt tried strengthening his legs by swimming. Florida was not Eleanor's scene at all and she seldom visited.

Although Missy ostensibly had her own room on the boat, she had to go through Roosevelt's bedroom to get to the bathroom. The houseboat's inhabitants were often to be seen lolling around in pyjamas, nighties and bathing suits. It was what one guest called a 'negligée existence'. When Eleanor visited, she usually came with one of her lesbian friends.

Roosevelt also established a foundation for the care of polio victims at Warm Springs, Georgia. Eleanor seldom went there either, and the Roosevelt cottage at Warm Springs was presided over by Missy LeHand. When Eleanor did stay, she was a guest and Missy the hostess.

Eleanor, instead, attended political meetings and acted as his eyes and ears. Throughout her life Eleanor remained a staunch supporter and political helpmate to her husband and gradually she used her position to begin a political career of her own.

Despite years of therapy in Georgia, Roosevelt never recovered the use of his legs and his suffering gave him a new determination. 'If you have spent two years in bed trying to wiggle your big toe,' he once remarked, 'everything else seems easy.'

After 1923, Roosevelt and Eleanor were rarely together. She had set up homes for herself in Greenwich Village in New York City and Val-Kill, near Springwood, his home upstate, but in her letters to him, Eleanor still addressed him as 'Dearest Honey', told him 'We all miss you dreadfully', and signed off 'Ever lovingly'. In his letters to her, Roosevelt expressed his growing admiration for her energy, determination and political activities.

Eleanor's interests there were not entirely Sapphic. In 1929, she took up with a young man named Earl Miller. She was forty five. He was thirty two, a body builder and a well-known womaniser. Roosevelt was Governor of New York state at the time and had assigned Miller, a former New York police sergeant, to Eleanor as a bodyguard.

They spent a great deal of time together, reading aloud, singing and playing the piano. An Olympic athlete and former Navy middleweight boxing champion, he coached her at tennis and taught her how to shoot and to dive. He was totally devoted to her, checking her bills and squiring her around her public duties. Some of her lesbian friends were distressed to see him 'manhandle' her, especially when they were in bathing suits. They would walk hand-in-hand and he would touch her knee. Again there was nothing secret about the affair. He squired her around her public duties, but the press made nothing of it. He claimed that she would have made a better president than Roosevelt and called her not 'Mrs Roosevelt', but 'Lady' or 'Dearest Lady'.

When it seemed likely that Eleanor would become First Lady, there was talk of her running away with Miller – she hated the thought of being imprisoned in the White House so much. It was then that Miller had an affair with Missy LeHand. Miller claimed that Missy had put him on night duty at Warm Springs so that he could come to her room. But after two years of clandestine romance, he says she found out that he was also 'playing around with one of the girls in the Executive Office', and took to her bed and cried for three days. There has been speculation that Roosevelt actually engineered the affair to prevent Eleanor running away with Miller, which would have destroyed his bid for the presidency.

Not only did Eleanor take Miller's affair in her stride, she actually encouraged his romances. She managed to keep a hold over him even during his three marriages, which all ended in divorce. After Roosevelt's death, the affair almost hit the headlines. On 13 January, 1947, the New York *Daily News* columnist Ed Sullivan wrote: 'Navy Commander's wife will rock the country if she names the co-respondent in her divorce action!!!'

While Earl Miller denied having a physical relationship with Eleanor Roosevelt, saying he preferred 'pretty young things', the aggrieved Mrs Miller threatened to name Mrs. Roosevelt as co-respondent, because she was in possession of some of Mrs Roosevelt's letters and knew that threatening to publish them would be the most likely way to win herself a lucrative settlement out of court – as she did eventually. Eleanor's son James wrote of his mother's relationship with Miller, 'I personally believed that they were more than friends.' However, Miller hardly rates a mention in Eleanor's autobiography.

Though Missy LeHand had her own suite in the White House, she was often seen visiting the President's room in her night attire. She shared meals with the family and, when alone together, she called him 'F.D.'

Meanwhile, on the north side of the White House, Eleanor lived with cigar-smoking Associated-Press reporter Lorena Hickok, a well-known lesbian who had openly lived with other women before. She had first met Eleanor in 1928. As a reporter, she had gone to interview the First Lady of the Empire State. In her report, she eulogised Eleanor's 'long, slender hands' and her 'lace-trimmed hostess gown'. Later she joined Eleanor on the 1932 campaign trail. The two of them became inseparable and her flattering columns – cooked up with Eleanor herself – were syndicated throughout the United States and helped build Eleanor's image. The other press syndicates soon realised that Associated Press were getting all the exclusives and assigned women reporters of their own to cover Eleanor's activities.

Lorena Hickok was not a traditional beauty. She was five foot eight but weighed almost two hundred pounds, smoked cigars, cigarettes and pipes, drank Bourbon on the rocks and was very much 'one of the boys'. In February 1934, *Time* magazine called her a 'rotund lady with a husky voice' who wore 'baggy clothes'.

By that time, in 1933, Lorena had quit her job, saying she could no longer be objective about the Roosevelts, now that they were about to enter the White House. Eleanor found her a job as chief investigator of the Federal Emergency Relief Administration. They had jealous lovers' tiffs. When Roosevelt was first elected they had walked across Lafayette Park to the White House together. On the day of FDR's inauguration, Eleanor was seen wearing a sapphire ring Lorena – or 'Hick darling', as she called her – had given her. Eleanor had also given Lorena one in what one might call an exchange of rings.

She and Eleanor went to great lengths to hide their affair otherwise. Hickok even edited and retyped Eleanor's letters, burning the originals. Still, explicit expressions of love slipped through. In letters Eleanor spoke of 'longing to kiss and hold' Lorena in her arms. 'I can't kiss you, so I kiss your picture good night and good morning!' she wrote. 'Goodnight, dear one. I want to put my arms around you and kiss you at the corner of your mouth. And in a little more than a week now – I shall.'

The White House staff soon cottoned on to what was going on. White House maid Lillian Parks recalled that Eleanor and Hickok would disappear together for long periods in Eleanor's bathroom, claiming that it was 'the only place they could find privacy for a press interview'. The staff considered this 'hardly the kind of thing one would do with an ordinary reporter, or even with an adult friend'.

In fact, coping with the Roosevelts' convoluted domestic arrangements was a nightmare for the White House staff, especially as FDR despised Hickok and was once heard yelling: 'I want that woman kept out of this house.'

Even as president, he was powerless against Eleanor, however, and in January 1941, Hickok moved into the White House, living there until 1945.

The only four-term president, Roosevelt certainly revelled in the role. Every year on his birthday, he would hold a drinks party at the Cufflinks Club. He would dress as a Roman emperor and his female guests would be expected to appear as Vestal virgins.

In 1940, when Roosevelt won an unprecedented third term in the White House, everyone was jubilant except Missy LeHand. She was concerned for his health and wanted him to retire, perhaps so that he could divorce Eleanor and marry her.

The pregnant atmosphere in the White House was not improved when 'Hick' took up with the Honourable Marion Janet Harron, U.S. tax-court judge who was nineteen years younger than Eleanor.

Eleanor got her own back by starting an affair with the young Joseph P. Lash, who later found fame as her biographer. This outraged the president. Lash was a socialist who had appeared before the House's Un-American Activities Committee. He had a security file and Eleanor was outraged when she discovered that the room where she had spent time with him in the Blackstone Hotel in Chicago had been bugged by Army Intelligence. The tapes 'indicated quite dearly that Mrs Roosevelt and Lash engaged in sexual intercourse', an F.B.I. report said. Later, Lash was refused an Army commission. A number of indiscreet letters from Eleanor to Lash surfaced, while Lash was engaged to be married at the time.

Eleanor and 'Hick darling' kissed and made up and Eleanor continued to find jobs for her within the Democratic Party. Hickok co-authored *Ladies of Courage* with Eleanor in 1954 and pumped out *The Story of Eleanor Roosevelt* in 1959. She lived in a cottage on the Roosevelt estate to be near to Eleanor. When she died there in 1968, she left half her papers to the FDR Library at Hyde Park. The rest went to the National Archives under the proviso that they be sealed for ten years after her death. When they were opened, they were found to contain 2,336 letters from Eleanor.

Meanwhile, a public sex scandal hit the White House from a most unexpected quarter. Roosevelt's special envoy, first to Hitler and Mussolini, then to Churchill, was Under Secretary of State Sumner Welles. In January 1941, F.B.I. Director J. Edgar Hoover outed Welles as a homosexual and produced a number of affidavits from two African-American porters on a Pullman train saying that Welles, while drunk, had propositioned them. Roosevelt stuck by Welles, but the matter leaked and Welles was forced to resign.

In 1941, Missy Lehand suffered a stroke. She was moved out of the White House and died three years later. Roosevelt had rewritten his will, leaving her half the income from his estate. In the end, since she died before Roosevelt did, the money went to Eleanor. The loss of Missy left Roosevelt short of female companionship. Laura Delano and Margaret Suckley, two unmarried cousins, stepped in and became such frequent visitors that Eleanor called them his 'hand-maidens'.

Margaret Suckley was told to burn his letters. In those that survive he writes, 'There is no reason why I should not tell you that I miss you very much – It was a week ago yesterday,' Roosevelt wrote her after spending time with her at Hyde Park. 'I have longed to have you with me,' he wrote another time during a cruise to Panama. 'He told me once,' she wrote in her diary soon after his death, 'that there was no one else with whom he could be so completely himself.' Meanwhile Roosevelt also had a wild flirtation with the exiled Crown Princess Martha of Norway.

Then Lucy Page Mercer, Eleanor's former social secretary, returned into the fray.

She had been at the Democratic National Convention in 1936 when Roosevelt made his acceptance speech and secretly attended all four of his inaugurations. Now, Roosevelt and Lucy began meeting again regularly. Secret service agents would drive him out to Canal Road, beyond Georgetown, where she would be waiting for him in her car. They would usually drive about for a few hours before he would return to the White House. On at least one occasion, they had an assignation at Hobcaw Barony, Bernard Baruch's estate in South Carolina, where Roosevelt had gone for a rest. There is a famous story of Roosevelt's railroad car being shunted off into a siding near the Rutherfurd estate at Allamuchy, New Jersey, for a secret rendezvous.

Lucy visited Roosevelt in the White House, while Eleanor was away with Lash. She was also at Roosevelt's side in the cottage in Warm Springs when Roosevelt died. Laura Delano and Margaret Suckley were there too, but while they stayed on, Lucy had to pack quickly and leave.

Roosevelt had just been re-elected yet again in 1944 by a popular majority of two-and-a-half million over Thomas E. Dewey of New York. He died of a massive cerebral haemorrhage, less than a month before the end of the war in Europe and four months before the fall of Japan.

When Eleanor left the White House, she told reporters: 'My story is over.'

She was wrong. Longtime friend Bernard Baruch proposed marriage. She refused, but continued her active sex life and went on to become a delegate to the United Nations and one of the authors of the Declaration of Human Rights. She died in November 1962 and was buried at Hyde Park alongside her husband.

XV
Herbert Hoover, #31

'We in America today are nearer to the final triumph over poverty than ever before in the history of any land,' said Herbert Hoover during the Presidential elections in 1928. Within months of his inauguration, the world was plunged into the Great Depression of 1929.

Herbert Hoover's sex life was nowhere near as dramatic or as bizarre as his namesake and contemporary F.B.I. Director J. Edgar Hoover. Only Edgar, allegedly, pored over pornography, liked dressing-up in women's clothing, gave oral sex to his deputy or liked being masturbated by a young boy wearing rubber gloves while another leather clad youth read passages from the Bible.

Herbert Hoover was born on 10 August 1874 in West Branch, Iowa, and was the first president to be born west of the Mississippi. His father, a Quaker, was a blacksmith, who died of typhoid fever when Hoover was six. His mother died of pneumonia three years later and at the age of ten Hoover travelled with his bedroll and a wire basket filled with chickens from West Branch to Newberg, Oregon, to live with his uncle. He earned his keep chopping wood, milking cows and caring for his uncle's horses.

Hoover attended a Quaker school and developed a crush on his teacher Miss Gray. With her help, he entered Stanford University in 1891 where he won a student election by marshalling the votes of the 'queeners' – that is, the co-eds.

Graduating with a degree in engineering in 1895, he went to work in a mine in Nevada. Two years later, he left for Australia where he headed goldmining operations for a British company and lived in rough mining communities.

There is evidence that Hoover had a torrid affair in Australia with a barmaid in Kalgoorlie. Years later, after his return to

America, he is said to have written her a love poem which was quoted in the book *Those Were the Days* by Arthur Reid, published in Perth in 1933. The poem speaks eloquently of their passion:

> While the starlight-spangled heavens rolled around us where
> we stood,
> And a tide of bliss kept surging through the currents of our
> blood,
> And I spent my soul in kisses, crushed upon your scarlet
> mouth,
> Oh! My red-lipped, sunbrowned sweetheart, dark-eyed
> daughter of the south.

Despite this great passion, Hoover returned to California where he married his Stanford sweetheart Lou Henry with whom he had two sons. After a successful career in mining, Hoover 'on the slippery slope of public life' organised relief during World War I.

Hoover called prohibition 'a great social and economic experiment, noble in motive, far-reaching in purpose'. At a baseball match, however, he was booed by his constituents and the crowd chanted: 'We want beer! We want beer!'

XVI
Calvin Coolidge, #30
'You lose.'

Calvin Coolidge was aptly named. Coolidge was as warm-hearted as granite. The title of William Allen White's biography of Coolidge describes him fittingly as *A Puritan in Babylon*.

Coolidge could not have been less Trump-like if he tried. He was the personification of traditional New England virtues of honesty, modesty, frugality and dry wit. His economy with words was legendary. Apocryphal stories circulated about it. One was that a young lady who sat next to him at dinner took a bet that she could get more than two words out of him. In an effort to strike up conversation with him, she told him about the wager. Coolidge simply replied: 'You lose.'

Born on 4 July 1872 in Plymouth Notch, Vermont, John Calvin Coolidge was a shy, industrious, redheaded boy. 'Calvin could get more sap out a maple tree than any of the other boys around here,' his father said approvingly.

As a young teenager, he attended parties where he played kissing games with girls, until his grandmother, who thought dancing was sinful, gave him a dollar if he promised not to.

He studied classics at Amhurst College where he led a rather solitary life. Most of his contemporaries were guilded youths, keen on parties and girls. As Coolidge did not dance, he became a wallflower at his college. He did not join in the social and sports events and, in his own words, 'did not seem to get acquainted very fast'.

Girls began to scare him and he was certainly not attractive to women. Theodore Roosevelt's daughter, Alice Roosevelt Longworth, said that Coolidge looked 'as if he had been weaned on a pickle'.

A college acquaintance wrote of Coolidge: 'In appearance he was splendidly null, apparently deficient in red corpuscles, with a peaked, wire-drawn expression... As he walked there was no motion of the body about the waist. The arms hung immobile.'

Shy with the college girls, sometimes he managed to overcome his reserve and go out with girls from the town. He even proposed marriage to one fellow-redhead. She turned him down.

Coolidge's wife Grace, however, was everything her husband was not – warm, friendly, outgoing and gregarious. She was brought up in Burlington, Vermont, and was teaching at a school for the deaf in Northampton, Massachusetts, when she met Coolidge. The first time she saw him was through the window of a friend's house, where he was staying. He was shaving, wearing just his long underwear and a hat.

In the relationship, she made the running, taking him out picnicking, buggy-riding and sailing. For her sake, he tried dancing and skating but was singularly unsuccessful at both of them. Nevertheless, she was the only woman who ever attracted his adult attention.

He was certainly not the wooing type, but Grace fell for him anyway. Later she explained: 'Mr Coolidge had deeper sentimental feeling than most people whom I have known, but he did not reveal it in outward manifestations.'

Coolidge's grandmother suggested that, as he had no other prospect, he marry Grace. He went straight to her father and asked for permission. He had not even informed Grace of his intentions; nor did he ask her for her hand. Once he had her father's consent, he told Grace simply: 'I am going to be married to you.'

He was so unromantic in his approach that Grace's mother tried to break up the match. But he fought for his bride and they were married in October 1905 in her parents' home. It was raining that day and someone remarked that it was a bad omen.

'I don't mind the weather if I get the girl,' he said gnomically.

They headed off to Montreal for a two-week honeymoon. It was plainly unsatisfactory. After a week, he told her he wanted to go home. He was running for a seat on the School Committee and he wanted to make a campaign speech.

Although restricted to the modest income of a small-town lawyer, Grace kept up appearances and worked tirelessly to promote her husband's political career. When he became Governor of Massachusetts, she stayed at home bringing up their two boys, while he lived in rented rooms in Boston.

Later in Washington, as Harding's Vice President, Coolidge was totally out of place. Not for him, the wild parties with chorus girls that Harding's cronies organised. He stayed at home with his wife, mooning over her like a lovesick schoolboy.

A contemporary noted: 'The man would not have been what he was without the woman, and most of all precisely because of her infinite, exquisite tact in effacing herself.'

Entering Washington society as the wife of Vice President during Harding's presidency, Grace quickly became the most popular woman in town. Once established in the White House after Harding's death in office, she introduced a more restrained and dignified air to entertaining after the excesses of the Harding years. Even the sudden death of her younger son did not distract her from her public duties. She was voted one of America's twelve greatest living women.

The White House under Coolidge was as different from Harding's administration as 'a New England front parlour is from a backroom speakeasy'. He kept the good men from Harding's cabinet and got rid of the corrupt remainder. The Republican Party rallied behind him and he mollified a fractious Congress, promising to continue the policy of returning to 'normalcy'. Above suspicion in the midst of a sea of corruption, he soon earned the confidence of the electorate. He went on to win the 1924 election with the slogan 'Keep cool with Coolidge'.

He certainly took little interest in other women. When an associate drew his attention to a pretty young woman whose stockings had been splashed up to the knee, Coolidge commented on the state of the pavement.

However, he was very jealous of his wife. In his autobiography he wrote, 'For almost a quarter of a century she has borne with my infirmities, and I have rejoiced in her graces.' He was deeply suspicious of the Secret Service agents detailed to protect her. One day in the Black Hills of South Dakota his wife went for a walk with her guard, James Haley. They got lost and turned up over two hours late. Coolidge was beside himself. Haley was sacked and Coolidge's tantrum made the headlines.

Soon after, there was a rumour that Coolidge and his wife planned to divorce after he left the White House. He decided not to contest the 1928 election, but stayed with his wife until, on 5 January 1933, he died of a coronary thrombosis. Hearing Coolidge was dead, humourist Dorothy Parker remarked: 'How can they tell?'

After Coolidge's death in 1933, Grace continued her work for the deaf and embarked on an adventurous life, travelling to Europe and flying in an aeroplane. She died in 1957.

XVII
Warren G. Harding, #29

'I can't say no.'

The election of Warren Gamaliel Harding promised a 'return to normalcy' after his predecessor Woodrow Wilson.

In a way, it was. Like Donald Trump and many early presidents, Harding was a tireless womaniser. He died in office before it came out that he had an illegitimate child by a young campaign worker. If any of that sounds familiar, wait for it – Warren Harding was America's first black president. Or, at least, that was the allegation made at the time by the Trumps of his time.

It had long been rumoured in Ohio that Harding's great-grandmother had been an African-American woman; that Harding's father's second wife had divorced him because he was 'must too Negro for her to endure'; and that Harding's father-in-law had denounced his daughter for 'polluting the family line'. This was at a time when the 'one-drop' rule applied in southern states – that is, when one-drop of slave blood meant that you were considered black and, thus, ineligible to vote or hold office.

When Harding became President in 1922, historian William Estabrook Chancellor had toured Ohio, compiling these rumours and accusations. The resulting book can be seen as the smear of a racial bigot. Nevertheless, there may have been some truth to it.

The dark-skinned Oliver Harding, said to be the President's great-uncle, appeared in *Abbott's Monthly*, a black-owned Chicago magazine, in 1932. As recently as 2005, a Michigan schoolteacher named Marsha Stewart made her own claim about Harding ancestry. 'While growing up,' she wrote, 'we were never allowed to talk about the relationship to a U.S. president outside family gatherings because we were "coloured" and Warren was "passing".' Harding himself appeared to believe it, but his political allies hit back against Chancellor, driving him out of his job and destroying all but a handful of copies of his book.

On the subject of womanising, his allies were more forthcoming. Harding's Attorney General Harry M. Daugherty said that no President had more 'woman scrapes' than Harding. Fearing that he might be found out, Harding himself stunned a private party of reporters at the National Press Club by confessing his carnal failings in graphic terms.

'It's a good thing I am not a woman,' the President said. 'I would always be pregnant. I can't say no.'

Like Trump, Harding never wanted to be President. He was a small-town politician who was forced into high office by an ambitious wife and a scheming party boss.

'I knew this job would be too much for me,' he admitted with candour when his administration was falling apart. 'I am not fit for this office and never should have been here.'

While a total failure as a president, overseeing the most corrupt government in the history of the Republic, he did manage to maintain two steady mistresses, see other women and attend drunken orgies – accomplishments unequalled by any U.S. President until John F. Kennedy.

Harding was the first journalist to become president. Born on 2 November 1865 in Blooming Grove, Ohio, Harding was educated at a local school and learned the printing trade in the offices of the *Caledonia Argus*, a newspaper which his father bought in 1875. In 1880, he went to Ohio Central College, where he was a horn player in the band and editor of the yearbook. He graduated with a BSc and after a short period as a teacher, he began work as a journalist on the *Marion Mirror*.

In 1884, Harding and two partners bought the *Marion Star* for $300. By 1886, he had bought them out. To improve the paper's profitability, he abandoned the *Star*'s non-partisan stance and began taking Republican advertising. In 1886, he was appointed a member of the Republican County Committee. After that, he left the running of the paper in the hands of his wife Florence.

'I went down there intending to help out for a few days and remained for fourteen years,' she said. Florence Harding used her immense acumen to make her hard-drinking, poker-playing husband President of the United States. But she herself had a shaky start. When she was just nineteen, Florence eloped with twenty-one-year-old Henry De Wolfe. He was a wastrel and spendthrift, and soon abandoned her. She returned to Marion, Ohio, with a baby son. Despite her plight, she refused to live at home, renting rooms and earning money by teaching the piano.

Despite the objections of her father, Warren and Florence married in 1891. Florence was thirty; Warren was twenty five. His motivation seems to have been sexual on the whole. Divorcees were considered racy in the 1890s, but he got less than he bargained for. As her early ardour had caused her so much grief, Florence had grown passionless.

Harding called her 'Duchess' and often followed her advice, which was sometimes based on her consultations with an astrologer. She was considered to be the power behind the throne and, when he became President, a cartoon depicted the couple as 'The Chief Executive and Mr Harding'.

There was little sex in their relationship and he began to look for release elsewhere. First he turned to Florence's childhood friend, Susan Hodder, who is thought to have given birth to his child Marion Louise Hodder in Nebraska in 1895.

Then he began an affair with another of her friends, Mrs Carrie Phillips, the wife of a neighbour. The affair began in 1905, when Florence was in hospital for the removal of a kidney, and continued for around fifteen years. Mrs Phillips was tall, high-breasted and had a reddish tinge to her golden hair. She was sophisticated, charming, mercurial and the love of Harding's life. At the time, she had an eight-year-old daughter, but she had just lost a son and needed consolation. Harding provided that and quickly fell deeply in love.

With Carrie Phillips, he experienced physical desire and emotional release together. He loved both her mind and her body.

They met and made love in her house on Main Street.

When they were separated, Harding bombarded her with letters, sometimes thirty or forty pages long, full of romantic verse, doggerel and rhymed jokes. He rhapsodised about the feel of her thighs, the sound of her voice, the warmth of her personality, her hair, her cheekbones, her earlobes, how he craved her kisses, how he yearned for her breasts, how he longed for her caresses. Indeed, with all his mistresses, Hardy was a passionate letter writer. In one of his missives to Mrs Phillips, he included a poem that read'

> I love your back, I love your breasts
> Darling to feel, where my face rests,
> I love your skin, so soft and white,
> So dear to feel and sweet to bite. . . .
> I love your poise of perfect thighs,
> When they hold me in paradise. . . .

At Florence's behest, Harding put his political career on a state-wide footing. Though no politician by desire, this suited him for other reasons. Florence would have to stay in Marion, Ohio, running the paper, while he could play away from home. Carrie could then find some excuse to get away from her doting husband and consummate her passion with Harding in hotel rooms in remote towns in the boondocks of Ohio.

No one suspected anything back in Marion, where the Phillipses and the Hardings would be seen socialising together. When Harding bought his first automobile, they would go out for an early evening drive together. They even went on holiday together to Europe in 1909. On the boat, Harding and Carrie would slip out of their staterooms and meet in the shadows on deck. Part of the excitement, it seems, was finding ways to have sex practically under the noses of their respective spouses.

Even at home in Marion, it was amazing what they got away with. The small town was sometimes abuzz with gossip about them but somehow the managing editor of the local newspaper,

Florence, did not seem to hear it. When she eventually found out in 1911, she considered filing for divorce, but then thought better of it when he agreed to end the affair.

Carrie begged him to leave his wife, but he was already too enamoured with his political career for that. She said she planned to take her daughter and go to live in Germany. At Christmas, Harding gave her a photograph of himself and begged her not to go. Carrie did go to Germany, briefly, but the outbreak of World War I forced her to return to his arms and they quickly became lovers again. Her husband John eventually found out about his wife's infidelity in 1920, but harboured no lasting resentment towards Harding. If Mrs Harding knew about that the affair was continuing despite her husband's promises, she did not make a fuss.

By this time, Harding was a Senator and was also having an affair with Grace Cross, member of his Senate staff. He had assorted other flings, including one with Augusta Cole, who said her pregnancy by Harding was terminated when he sent her to a Battle Creek Sanitarium, and one with Rosa Hoyle, who claimed to have given birth to his only illegitimate son and committed suicide when he would not leave Florence. He bedded an employee of the *Washington Post* known as Miss Allicott, and former chorus girls Maize Haywood and Blossom Jones – all procured by Harding's crony, Ned McLean, the owner and publisher of the *Washington Post*. Then there was the string of 'New York women' – including one who committed suicide after Harding wouldn't marry her, and another who had a stash of incriminating love letters that had to be purchased by Harding loyalists.

By far the most indefensible relationship was that with Nan Britton, a girl he had known since she was a child in Marion. At thirteen, Nan had become obsessed with Harding, who was running for the Senate at the time. Her father, a friend of Harding's, told him of her infatuation and, when she went round to his house with her mother to have a chat with the candidate. Nan admitted that she had decorated her room with Harding's campaign posters. Harding said that he was sure that she would like to have a real photograph of him to go with her collection. Florence neither smiled nor spoke and the atmosphere was as cold as ice.

In his book, *Warren Gamaliel Harding – An American Comedy*, Clement Wood claimed that Harding fell for her when she was a child and took her to his newspaper office where he bounced her on his lap, though it is generally accepted that the affair took a little longer to develop. However, according to her own account, while still in her early teens, though already well developed, she would hang around outside the newspaper office in the hope of bumping into him.

When Nan's father died, her mother turned to Harding for help. He found her a job as a substitute teacher and promised young Nan that, if he could ever do something for her, she only had to ask.

Three years later, she did just that. On graduating from secretarial school in New York, she wrote to him asking whether he remembered her and if he could help her get a job in Washington. He wrote back saying that he did indeed remember her – 'you may be sure of that, and I remember you most agreeably too,' he replied, and he would be delighted to help her. He would 'go personally to the War and Navy Department to urge your appointment'. He also mentioned that there was 'every probability' that he would be in New York the following week and that he would like to phone or to look her up and would 'take pleasure in doing it'.

Their letters progress by innuendo. She replied quickly saying that she thought that 'an hour's talk would be much more satisfactory', so that 'I could give you a better idea of my ability… and you could judge for yourself as to the sort of position I could competently fill'. This, she said, 'would please me immensely'.

The reply was a long, handwritten letter on Senate notepaper saying, 'I like your spirit and determination' and assuring her of 'my very genuine personal interest in your good fortune'.

Early the following morning, before she had time to reply, Harding phoned from Manhattan, saying that he had arrived in New York and she should meet him at his hotel. She hurried over.

They walked through the reception area arm-in-arm and sat down on a settee. She blurted out all her schoolgirl feelings for him. He suggested that they go up to his room so that they would not be interrupted. But there was a convention in town, he said. All the rooms were taken. Except for one – the bridal suite.

Harding's long game of grooming had paid off. 'We had scarcely closed the door behind us when we shared our first kiss,' she wrote later.

'Tell me it isn't hateful for you to have me kiss you,' said the fifty-year-old Senator, occasionally sighing 'God! God! Nan', as the two continued kissing.

Harding admitted that he had come from Washington solely to see her. He needed a woman. Nan pointed out that she was a virgin and was not ready to explore the 'lovely mystery' of sex despite the urgings of the antediluvian Harding. Nevertheless, the Senator tucked $30 into the top of her new silk stockings.

Somehow between kisses, they also managed to discuss her job prospects. He suddenly decided that it would not be a good idea for her to work in Washington. It was a goldfish bowl and her presence would attract gossip. Instead he would find her a job in New York.

After lunch he took her to the headquarters of U.S. Steel. In the taxi on the way he decided to test her shorthand.

'I'll dictate a letter to you and you tell me whether you get all of it,' he said.

It began: 'My darling Nan: I love you more than the world, and I want you to belong to me. Could you belong to me, dearie? I want you… and I need you so….' He could not finish it because Nan began smothering him with the kisses.

The head of U.S .Steel gave her a job on the spot. When they got back to the hotel, Harding tripped when he got out of the taxi.

'You see, dearie, I'm so crazy about you I don't know where I am stepping,' he said. Back in the bridal suite, she finally sat on his lap in a big armchair. 'I'd like to make you my bride. We were made for each other,' he argued.

Before she began her new job, Nan went to visit her sister in

Chicago. Harding sent her a picture of himself on the steps of the Capitol – another one for her collection – and a rambling forty-page love letter. In her reply, she made her first casual request for money. He sent $42. He always sent odd sums, as in the accounts, it would appear that she had run up some expenses on his behalf as a campaign volunteer.

Harding had a speaking tour of the Midwest lined and, within a week, Nan received a letter asking her to meet him in Indianapolis. He was at the station when she arrived. They checked into separate rooms at the Claypool Hotel. She pretended to be his niece. They spent most of the night together, but she still withheld what she referred to as 'love's sweetest intimacy'.

The next day they travelled to Connersville, where Harding had a speaking engagement. This time Nan checked in with Harding's secretary's name, Elizabeth N. Christian. Afterwards they travelled back to Chicago by Pullman. On the way to the station, he asked: 'Dearie, are you going to sleep with me?'

He booked a single berth, which they shared, but still she coyly resisted, according to her account.

'I had earlier reached his conclusion,' she wrote. 'People got married and undressed and slept together, therefore, one must be undressed in order for any harm to come to them. I remember that his belief was so strong in my mind that when, during our ride together from Connersville to Chicago, I experienced sweet thrills from just having Mr Harding's hands upon the outside of my nightdress, I became panic-stricken. I inquired tearfully whether he really thought I would have a child right away. Of course, this absurdity amused him greatly, but the fact that I was so ignorant seemed to add to his cherishment of me for some reason. And I loved him so dearly.'

Back in Chicago, they tried to book into a hotel as man and wife. A disbelieving desk clerk said that, if they could prove they were married, he would give them the room for free.

After their 'kissing tour' of the Midwest, Nan could resist no longer. Back in New York, she gave way to what she called 'climactic intimacy'. It was a hot July day in 1917 and Harding had taken her to the Imperial, a second-rate hotel on lower Broadway which friends had recommended for such 'unconventional' activities.

'I remember so well, I wore a pink linen dress which was rather short and enhanced the little-girl look which was often my despair,' she admitted. 'There were no words going up in the elevator. The day was exceedingly warm and we were glad to see that the room which had been assigned to us had two large windows. The boy threw them open for us and left. The room faced Broadway, but we were high enough not to be bothered by street noises.'

It was a torrid afternoon and they stripped off and got into bed. 'I became Mr Harding's bride – as he called me – on that day,' she said.

As they lay in bed together afterwards, the telephone rang. Harding answered it. 'You have the wrong party,' he said.

Then there was a knock on the door. A key turned in the lock and two detectives burst in. They demanded to know Nan's name and address. She turned to Harding. 'Tell them the truth,' he said her told her, disconsolately. 'They have got us.'

As the detectives wrote down her details, Harding begged them to let her go. The scandal would ruin his career.

'We've hurt no one,' he said.

'Tell that to the judge,' they replied, telling him that a paddy wagon was on its way.

Then one of the detectives picked up Harding's hat. He noticed the name W.G. Harding stamped on the sweatband and realized that they had just arrested a U.S. Senator. They became respectful, deferential – obsequious, even – and left the room while the lovers dressed. The detectives led them to a side exit. At the door, Harding slipped them $20. In the taxi afterwards, he said: 'Gee, Nan, I thought I wouldn't get out of that for under a thousand dollars.'

This brush with danger did nothing to dampen his ardour. He would travel up to New York once a week to sleep with her. And they were hardly discreet. She would meet him at Penn Station.

They would go and see Al Jolson at the Wintergarden or a musical comedy on Broadway, then have a romantic dinner for two in a nearby restaurant.

'We were so sweetly intimate and it was a joy just to sit and look at him,' she said. 'The way he used his hands, the adorable way he used to put choice bits of meat from his own plate on to mine, the way he would say with a sort of tense nervousness, "That's a very becoming hat, Nan," or "God, Nan, you're pretty!" used to go to my head like wine and made food seem for the moment the least needful thing in the world.'

In 1918, Florence started suffering from her kidney complaint again and left Washington for treatment at Camp Meade. With his wife out of the way, Harding grew bold, almost reckless. He brought Nan to Washington to show her off, parading her in public with extraordinary indiscretion. He even took her on a stroll down Pennsylvania Avenue, chewing gum and pointing out the sights.

Nan registered in various hotels under the name of Harding's secretary, though sometimes he took her over to the Senate Office building and made love to her in his office. He liked to see her naked there, so that he could fantasize about her when he was working.

Harding had long been convinced that he was sterile. As a boy he had had mumps and his testicles had swollen. The doctors told him that he was probably infertile. Neither his wife nor Mrs Phillips had been with child by him, though they had both had children with other men. He told Nan that he had wanted to adopt a child, but Mrs Harding would not hear of it.

In January 1919, Nan proved Harding wrong. She was thrilled and once she was sure she was pregnant, she wrote to him. He wrote back in a panic, but assured her that, however serious the trouble, he could handle it. Nan's sister in Chicago agreed and bought her some 'bitter apple' medicine. Nan refused to take it. Back in New York, Harding continued to visit as usual. They even made love in a secluded corner of Central Park and he bought her a sapphire ring. On the afternoon of 22 October 1919, Nan gave birth to a daughter, Elizabeth Ann.

Six weeks later, she went to New York to do some Christmas shopping and call Harding. She did not feel safe calling from Asbury Park. When she got him on the phone, he said hello, then nothing more. She began to cry. She said she wanted him to come to New York for a brief visit. He said that he was coming to New York, but he would not visit her there. He did not think it wise for them to be seen together. At the time, his political patrons had asked him to run for president.

In fact, Harding never once saw the child. Harry Daugherty, the skilful political manipulator who ran the Ohio Republican Party, had foreseen with astonishing accuracy that the Republican National Convention in Chicago in 1920 would be deadlocked. He told a reporter: 'After the other candidates have failed... the leaders, worn out and wishing to do the very best thing, will get together in some smoke-filled room about 2:11 in the morning. Some fifteen men, bleary-eyed from lack of sleep, and perspiring profusely with excessive heat, will sit down around a big table. I will be with them and present the name of Senator Harding. When that times comes, Harding will be selected.'

It happened almost exactly as predicted. Harding was asked whether there was any reason why he should not be given the nomination and he told the political grandees in the smoke-filled room: 'No gentlemen, there is no such reason.' It was a blatant lie of Trumpian proportions, of course, as the party bosses soon discovered.

Carrie Phillips and her husband – who now had to be told of his wife's adultery – were paid by the Republican Party to take a world cruise during the election. Harding's men also gave her an outright bribe of $25,000 and a monthly stipend of $2,000 a month through a secret bank account to be paid while he was in office, as long as she kept quiet about their affair. She accepted without a moment's hesitation.

Nan watched from the gallery as the cheering convention nominated Harding Republican candidate for the 1920 election. In a showdown in Marion, Ohio, Harding admitted to Nan's sister that he was the father of Nan's child. In return for their silence, he agreed to support Nan and offered her sister $500 a month if she and her husband would adopt the child.

Grace Cross proved more troublesome. They had already had one close scrap with scandal. While Harding was a senator they had had row and she cut his back. The police were called, but the matter was hushed up. So, after a late night assignation in the Willard Hotel on the eve of his inauguration, Grace Cross was told to pack her bags and leave town.

After a phoney affidavit claiming that she was a liar and a blackmailer failed to shut Cross up, Jess Smith, the bootlegger who provided booze for White House parties during prohibition, dragooned Cross's friend Bertha Martin to purloin the love letters Harding had sent to Cross in return for being made society editor of the *Washington Post.* When Ned McLean sanctioned the deal, Martin took Cross out to lunch, asked Cross to show her Harding's letters, then grabbed them and ran from the restaurant. Nevertheless, the two stayed friends and took a European vacation together, courtesy of Harding's secret blackmail fund. Martin was later found dressed in her fur coat, pearls and white gloves with her head in the oven, another alleged suicide.

Other mistresses were tracked down and were paid to sign affidavits denying their affairs. These all found their way to the First Lady

The enforced celibacy in the White House was too much for Harding. He sent for Nan. A White House aide was despatched to pick her up at the station. She was wearing a black crêpe dress with cerise braiding and a floppy picture hat. Driven direct to the White House, she was led in through the portico, down the main hall and into the Cabinet Room, where Harding was waiting.

'He introduced me to the one place where, he said, he thought we might share kisses in safety,' she recalled. 'This was a small closet in the anteroom, evidently a place for hats and coats, but entirely empty most of the times we used it, for we repaired there many

times in the course of my visits to the White House, and in the
darkness of a space not more than five feet square the President of
the United States and his adoring sweetheart made love.'

This small anteroom was later used by Bill Clinton and Monica
Lewinsky and... whichever else of the womanising presidents.

The assignations in the hat-closet were facilitated by Secret
Service agents James Sloan and Walter Ferguson. Unlike the
exhibitionist JFK, 'Harding hated to have them around, for he
despised being watched.' Proceedings came to an abrupt end when
another agent, Harry Barker, tipped Florence off, and she ran
downstairs for a confrontation. She almost caught them in
flagrante, but Sloan and Ferguson barred her way. When she
demanded that they stand aside, they told her it was a Secret-
Service rule that no one was allowed in when the President had
asked not to be disturbed.

Florence headed around to another door that gave access to the
Oval Office through his secretary's office. This gave the couple
enough time to curtail their lovemaking, put their clothes on and
for Harding to bundle Nan out of a side door.

Harding often complained of this sort of inconsiderate
behaviour by his wife. 'She makes my life hell for me,' he told Nan.

Things now took a turn that President Donald Trump can only
dream of. The First Lady hired a private detective Gaston Means to
investigate Nan Britton, which he duly did. She then summoned
the President to her rooms in the White House and confronted him
with the evidence. Harding turned on Means.

'By what authority have you put the President of the United
States under surveillance?' Harding fumed.

Means replied that he had not put the President under
surveillance, only the President's mistress and his illegitimate child.

That did not matter, said Harding. Means would be indicted
within twenty-four hours and Means eventually spent a term in
Atlanta Penitentiary.

Paradoxically, it put a spring in the Duchess's step and she took
on the duties of First Lady with renewed fervour. She opened the

White House and grounds to the public again – they had been closed since President Wilson's illness – and established garden parties for veterans as a regular event.

And so it did for Harding, if there was any need. The public were all too well aware of this when he was caught ogling Margaret Gormon, Miss District of Columbia and the first Miss America, after her crowning in Atlantic City in 1921.

Although prohibition was in force, liquor was served at private parties in the White House. Bootlegger Jess Smith and Harry M. Daugherty – now elevated to Attorney General and solicitous in a way that Donald Trump would have loved Jeff Sessions to be – laid on parties in a house they called the 'Love Nest' on Washington, D.C., H. Street, complete with a pink taffeta bedroom. One night some New York chorus girls were brought down to entertain a stag party. In attendance was the President. When glasses and bottles were being flung off the table so the dancing girls could perform, one Washington prostitute, identified only as a Miss Walsh, was knocked unconscious. Harding was hustled out. The woman died and was buried in a field.

Women who took Harding's fancy – and there were many of them – were given lucrative government jobs. Others, who turned up with incriminating letters, were paid off. One woman, a former campaign worker who was banned from the White House by Mrs Harding, tried to blackmail the President with some love letters he had written. This cost Daugherty $15,000.

Harry M. Daugherty's Justice Department, in fact, went the extra mile. The Department used to intimidate anyone who threatened to make a scandal. The civil servants even managed to seize and destroy a small, privately printed book, *The Illustrated Life of Warren Gamaliel Harding*, that revealed Harding's affair with Carrie Phillips, the blackmail payoff and Florence's out-of-wedlock child by a common-law first husband. It was the only book in the history of the United States to be suppressed by the government in peacetime.

The action was entirely illegal. The books were not even

impounded on government property. Rather they were taken to Ned McLean's estate where they were burnt. However, one escaped the conflagration. It can now be found among the papers of McLean's wife Evelyn in the Library of Congress, along with a letter from Harding to Grace Cross. It seems that Ned McLean had been made a special agent who sought to thwart any threats to Harding he heard about as publisher of the *Washington Post*. In the privacy of his editorial office, he even helpfully ripped the blouse off of Nan Britton trying to snatch letters she claimed to be carrying.

Like the Trump administration, Harding's was mired in other scandals and rumour of his impending impeachment was rife. His cabinet was, naturally, made up of poker and drinking buddies and people to whom he owed political debts.

Nonetheless, the Attorney General Harry M. Daugherty's relationship with bootlegger Jess Smith was investigated by the Senate. When Smith was brought to trial, the jury could not agree a verdict after sixty-six hours deliberation and he was acquitted. Jess Smith was found with a bullet in his head. Rumours were spread that he was homosexual.

The Secretary of the Interior Albert B. Fall was, however, found guilty of accepting a $100,000 bribe to lease U.S. Navy oil reserves at Teapot Dome to private interests. He was the first cabinet member to be sent to prison. And in an echo of today's headlines there were also scandals concerning corruption in the Veterans' Bureau, the Prohibition Bureau and the Bureau of Investigation – the forerunner of the F.B.I.

Like Trump, Harding liked to blame others for what went wrong. 'I have no trouble with my enemies,' Harding said. 'But my damned friends, they're the ones that keep me walking the floor nights.' It could have been a Trump tweet.

In 1922, the mid-term elections brought the Democrats back to power in Congress and in an attempt to shore up his sagging popularity, Harding set out on a nationwide whistle-stop tour. On the way back from Alaska, he stopped for a dinner in Vancouver, where he contracted food poisoning.

In San Francisco, he took to his bed in the Palace Hotel. On 2 August 1923, his wife was reading the newspaper to him when he suffered a fatal cerebral thrombosis after being given purgatives by Florence homeopath Charles 'Doc' Sawyer whose mistress was the First Lady's housekeeper.

In the face of the torrent of corruption scandals engulfing the Harding administration, his sudden death two years into his term seemed convenient and it was rumoured that it had been precipitated by his wife's intervention to save him from impeachment.

Florence Harding not only believed in homeopathy, she also consulted the capital's society psychic Madame Marcia. Marcia's diary, which surfaced in a barn auction in 1997, shows that Florence had gone to see her in February 1920. The seer accurately predicted that if Harding ran for president that year, he would be nominated – but that if he won the election, he would not live through his full term and instead die of 'sudden, peculiar, violent… death by poison'.

For weeks after Harding's death, while the President's corpse lay in state in the White House and then in the Capitol Rotunda, smoke could be seen curling from the White House chimney even though it was mid-summer. The First Lady was burning her husband's papers. She died fifteen months later, having done all she could to salvage his reputation.

Nan Britton was away in France, at Harding's expense, at the time of his death. When she returned to New York, she married a Norwegian sea captain who soon abandoned her with considerable debts. Three years later, Nan wrote a sensational 440-page book about her relationship with the President and the child she bore him. It was called *The President's Daughter*. Her co-author was Richard Wright, whose wife thereupon sued for divorce naming Nan as co-respondent.

The book was nearly suppressed when the Society for the Suppression of Vice entered the printing plant and seized the plates, but a magistrate's court ordered them to give them back. Bookshops refused to handle it, however, and reviewers ignored it. Nevertheless, Nan managed to sell 90,000 copies at $5 a piece under the counter. The great journalist and humourist H.L. Mencken took up the story in the *Baltimore Sun*, and used it to attack the Republican administration.

The Coolidge Administration quickly closed ranks. White House staff were paraded in front of the public saying that they had never heard of Nan Britton and that she was a liar. The former editor of the *Buffalo Times*, Joseph DeBathe, wrote a book called *The Answer*, claiming that Nan's book was a tissue of sexual fantasies, deliberate falsehoods and criminal libel. Nan sued and lost. Then Gaston Means, the private detective Mrs Harding had used to spy on her husband, came forward with a book called *The Strange Death of President Harding*, claiming that Mrs Harding had poisoned her husband and murdered other of his associates when she had discovered his affair. The book was also a runaway bestseller.

Carrie and John Phillips had lost all their money in the Great Depression and separated. John died in 1939, while Carrie supported herself by breeding Alsatian dogs. She moved to a house on Gospel Hill in Marion, nearer to Harding's old home. By 1956, she was so frail and decrepit that a court order was taken out to put her in Willetts Home for the Elderly in Marion, where she died in 1960. When her possessions were auctioned off, a box was found containing ninety-eight letters written by Harding. One letter, dated 1911, read: 'Carrie, take me panting to your heaving breast.'

XVIII

Woodrow Wilson, #28

The President spent much of the evening entering Mrs Galt.

Unlike Donald Trump, President Woodrow Wilson, a true WASP, publicly confessed he was 'ignorant of women' and, in fact, on the eve of his nuptials in 1884, he had a mental breakdown. The physical symptoms included an eye tic and a paralysed right hand, something Sigmund Freud, perhaps surprisingly, didn't make much of in his famous psychoanalytical study of Woodrow Wilson.

During their long engagement, Wilson wrote to his fiancée, Ellen Axson, confessing in barely concealed sexual terms: 'It isn't pleasant or convenient to have strong passions. I have the uncomfortable feeling that I am carrying a volcano about with me. My salvation is in being loved.' He was twenty eight and still a virgin.

Freud concluded that the cause of Wilson's breakdown was that he was tortured by the power and intensity of his own libido, as his periodic fits of depression continued during both his first and second marriages.

Wilson had been in love before he met Ellen Axson. When he was twenty three he had fallen for his cousin Hattie and he wrote ardent letters to her.

'His increased masculinity for the moment led him no closer to the body of a woman,' Freud wrote.

Headaches and indigestion plagued him that time too, so much so that he had to drop out of the University of Virginia without a degree. Acutely unhappy, he proposed to Hattie. She refused him.

There seems to have been some sexual activity even earlier. On vacation in Columbia in 1878, when he was twenty two, he wrote to friends that he was at 'the scene of some old love adventures' and joked about 'a walk and a kiss'. He also said that religious camp meetings he had attended made flirtation easy.

On that holiday, he certainly made a monumental effort to keep away from the many pretty girls who attended the amateur concerts and went for moonlight excursions on the river. In Wilson's young mind, sexual stirrings were the work of the devil. Nonetheless, shortly before he met his first wife to be, Wilson seems to have had a relatively happy date with Katie Mayrant, the attractive niece of Mrs J. Reid Boylston who owned the boarding house he stayed at in Atlanta, Georgia,.

The feelings of depression and loneliness that tormented Wilson throughout his life – attributed, by Freud and others, to his fear of his own powerful sex drive – didn't make his wooing of Ellen all gloom and doom. He wrote to her saying: 'I long to be made your master – only however, on the very fair and equal terms that, in exchange for the authority over yourself which you relinquish, you shall be constituted supreme mistress of me.'

He also joked that during a brief separation they formed 'an interstate love league (of two members only, in order that it may be of manageable size).'

In 1885, they married. He took various professorships at Bryn Mawr College, Pennsylvania, and the Wesleyan College, Connecticut. During separations they exchanged letters daily. Even ten years after his marriage, his correspondence indicates an intense passion. In 1895, he wrote: 'Then I come myself, to claim you, to take possession of you – of all the time and love you can give me: to take you in my arms and hold you till I have made sure, by feeling your heart beat against mine and by seeing once more the very depths of your eyes, that I am really at home once more, with the woman who has made me and kept me what I am. I tremble with a deep excitement when I think of it. I verily believe I never quivered so before with eager impatience and anticipation. I know that I was not half so much excited on the eve of our marriage.'

Elsewhere he called himself her 'intemperate lover' and, shortly before returning home one time, he asked: 'Are you prepared for the storm of lovemaking with which you will be assailed?'

In 1902, Woodrow Wilson became president of Princeton. During this time particularly, he made inordinate efforts not to be away from home at night. On the other hand, he spent time translating from the French a highly erotic bedroom scene from Théophile Gautier's *Mademoiselle de Maupin*, which was based on the life of a celebrated lesbian opera star.

At the same time, he seemed to have developed over-active sexual fears. When he heard that his wife's young sister, Margaret Axson, then eleven, was going to live with relatives in Athens, Georgia, he became alarmed that she would be in a college town where 'the restraints upon the intercourse of the two sexes are at a minimum' – though he conceded: 'It must be the riotous elements in my own blood that make me fear so keenly what even the most honourable young fellows might be tempted by mere beauty to do.'

He was concerned that, as an academic himself, his own daughters were also exposed to the attentions of students. At Princeton, he fenced them in. When a student lent one of them a volume of poems by Edward de Vere, Earl of Oxford, which celebrated love a little too lustily for a staunch Presbyterian like Wilson, he confiscated the volume and burnt it.

Like Coolidge, he was extremely jealous of his wife, envying men who sat next to her at dinner. He also told her that he was not worthy of her and that she should pray that he be less subject to temptation.

Even in 1908, after more than twenty years of marriage, Wilson was writing that his love continued to grow 'deeper and more passionate'. Around this time, his mother died and his father took up with a Mrs Gannis, which Wilson found disturbing. He was glad when they broke up.

A mass of sexual contradictions, Wilson was embarrassed

when he heard jokes about sex, but he was not above telling a risqué story himself. What's more, the uptight scholar Wilson had a mistress.

Wilson met Mrs Peck in 1907. She was a vivacious, witty, sophisticated woman of forty five, a gourmet cook, an accomplished pianist and an excellent dancer. Born in 1862, in Grand Rapids, Michigan, as Mary Allen, she married Thomas Harbach Hulbert in 1883. Their marriage was a happy one. She had one child, a son, before her husband died suddenly six years later.

The young widow went to live in Rome with her recently widowed father-in-law and his young woman companion, whom he later adopted. After two years, she quit this bizarre *ménage à trois* and returned to America to have an operation to correct injuries sustained during childbirth.

In 1890, she married Thomas Dowse Peck, a widower with two daughters, and moved to Pittsfield, Massachusetts. She found her husband to be cruel and mean, and fell into a deep depression. However, a sympathetic doctor recommended that she holiday alone on Bermuda, which she did each winter after 1892. It was there, in 1907, that she met Wilson. He was on his first vacation alone without Ellen. He found an 'instinctive sympathy' between them and one topic of conversation – and mutual interest – was marital unhappiness.

When Wilson returned to Princeton after his vacation, he continued to write to Mrs Peck. They met again the following year, when Wilson was holidaying in Bermuda once more. They walked along the beach together, reading verse. Soon they were deeply in love. One letter, which Wilson never sent, began: 'My precious one, my beloved Mary.'

At the same time, Wilson was writing home to Ellen, describing Mrs Peck and the platonic friendship they had struck up. Ellen was not convinced. When he returned to Princeton that autumn, there was a blazing row and Ellen refused to accompany her husband on his trip to Great Britain that year as she had in

1906.

However, when he returned from England, they made up as husband and wife and became lovers again. She even accompanied him on a visit to the Pecks in Pittsfield, and invited Mrs Peck to come and stay with them in Princeton. When Mrs Peck accepted the invitation and actually turned up in Princeton, it caused tensions to say the least.

In 1909, Wilson and Mrs Peck discussed separation and divorce from their respective partners so they could be together. Wilson urged caution and circumstances conspired to keep them apart. Wilson, though, wrote to Mrs Peck that he thought of her 'a thousand times' and he grew jealous when he heard that Mrs Peck was considering an invitation from the Governor of Bermuda, a bachelor whose name had also been romantically linked to hers.

That winter, there was no correspondence between Wilson and Mrs Peck. It is clear that he visited her in New York. He was in or near the city at least six times in November, December and January. His other correspondence indicates that sex was very much on his mind that winter. Mrs Peck's apartment was at 39 East 27th Street, only five blocks from the house where Wilson's father had received 'love ministries' from Mrs Gannis.

Mrs Peck began divorce proceedings in 1912. Wilson secured the Democratic nomination at the party's convention that same year and there were rumours that he might be named in the suit. It was even said that the judge had been given one of Wilson's love letters in evidence.

Wilson's presidential opponent Theodore Roosevelt, who was running for a third time, dismissed the gossip. 'You can't cast a man as a Romeo when he looks and acts so much like an apothecary's clerk,' Roosevelt said.

Mrs Peck's divorce was granted and she reverted to calling herself Mrs Hulbert. Wilson, however, was already well on his way to the White House and any whiff of scandal could have cost him the presidency. When he won the election though, he took his entire family to Bermuda for a holiday. Mrs Peck joined them there. She also visited Wilson in Washington, but the couple were always chaperoned by Ellen or Wilson's cousin, Helen Bones.

In the last year of her life, Ellen Wilson told Cary Grayson, the White House doctor, that the Peck affair was the only unhappiness that her husband had caused her during their long marriage. In 1915, he confessed to what he called the contemptible error and madness of a few months – November, December and January of 1909-10, perhaps? – that had left a stain on his whole life.

Mrs Peck and Wilson kept up a lively correspondence and she visited him at the White House in 1915, after Ellen had died from kidney disease. There was speculation that they might marry. Wilson certainly supported her financially, but by then he had already met Mrs Edith Bolling Galt.

Less than a year after his first wife died, Wilson turned his attention to the forty-three-year-old widow. They had met when Helen Bones, who had taken on the duties of First Lady after Ellen died, invited her to tea. Wilson was out playing golf, but came home early. He invited her to dinner; two months later, he proposed. Mrs Galt could give him no answer. Wits said she was so shocked that she fell out of bed.

Wilson was determined to marry her. He sent her flowers daily and had a private wire installed between her home and the White House so that they could communicate secretly. Their letters indicate that they became physically intimate during a secret vacation in New Hampshire.

Back in Washington, Wilson's colleagues found him hopelessly in love. He put aside all but the most pressing business of state to be with his sweetheart. With the European powers already embroiled in World War I, the last thing the country needed was a lovesick president.

His ministers were terrified of the political repercussions if Wilson married again so soon after the death of his first wife, but they dare not tell him that. Instead, to remind him of the political dangers he faced, they told him that Mrs Peck was circulating his letters around town. The plan backfired. Wilson rushed over to Mrs Galt's house, spilt the beans about Mrs Peck and begged her to stand by him. She did and agreed to marry him. Wilson wrote a sickeningly schmaltzy press release and sent it out to the papers.

Fortunately for the standing of the President, *The New York Times* chose to paraphrase his statement rather than print it in full. But his luck could not hold. On 9 October 1915, the *Washington Post* made one of the most embarrassing typos in history.

In a story about Wilson's first appearance in public with his fiancée, the *Post* intended to say: 'The President spent much of the evening entertaining Mrs Galt.' Instead, what it actually printed was: 'The President spent much of the evening entering Mrs Galt.'

The editors spotted the error once the first edition had hit the streets and recalled the paper from the newsstands, but some of the issue had already been sold. The story got around and it confirmed the public's worst suspicions.

Soon Wilson was facing a hostile press. Rumours circulated that he was neglecting Ellen's grave. It was even alleged that Mrs Galt had been behind a plot to murder the first Mrs Wilson. The outraged women of America began to protest.

To limit the political damage, Wilson decided to marry as soon as possible and he and Mrs Galt were wed in December 1915. The new Mrs Wilson was not as tolerant as the old one when it came to Mrs Peck. She was banned from the White House and there is evidence that Wilson paid Mrs Peck off. It was said that she was paid $15,000 never to reveal the details of their extra-marital affair in an echo of the Trump payments to stop talk about him.

However, within four years Mrs Peck was reduced to selling books door-to-door. Nevertheless, when she was offered $300,000 for his letters, she refused. Finally, in 1933, long after

Wilson was dead, she published her side of the story in her autobiography, *The Story of Mrs Peck*.

After World War I, Wilson proposed the setting up of the League of Nations, but Congress opposed him. Against the advice of this doctor, Admiral Grayson, Wilson started a nationwide tour to convince the population. He had gotten as far as Pueblo, Colorado, when he collapsed with a stroke affecting the left side of his body. The train turned around at Wichita, Kansas, and took him back to Washington. For months, the President was bedridden, unable to carry out his duties.

During the illness, his wife Edith was rumoured to be the 'secret president'. In her book *My Memoir*, published in 1939, she calls this period her 'stewardship'. Others talked of 'Mrs Wilson's regency', 'Petticoat government' and referred to Woodrow Wilson as the 'First Man'.

She effectively ran the White House but claimed: 'I, myself, never made a single decision regarding the disposition of public affairs. The only decision that was mine was what was important and what was not, and the very important decision of when to present matters to my husband.'

Wilson died three years after leaving office, but Edith lived long enough to ride in President Kennedy's inaugural motorcade.

XIX
William Howard Taft, #27
'Do say that you will try to love me.'

Weighing over three hundred pounds and standing six feet tall, William Howard Taft was the largest president ever. He makes the overweight Donald Trump at six-foot-three and 236 pounds, apparently (just shy of the medical definition of obese), look sylph-like. Despite his size, President Taft spent his life under the heel of two small, slim women. His first dominatrix was his wife Helen.

It began with Taft's domineering mother, Louisa. Louisa and her sister Delia travelled together as young women and had vowed not to marry. When Louisa nonetheless took up with Alphonso Taft (seventeen years her senior and a man who brought her the social status she craved), Delia wrote mournfully, 'Oh Louise, Louise, how can I live the rest of my life without you? I am but one half of a pair of scissors.'

Alphonso had been married before. His first wife described the marriage as an 'unbroken sea of unhappiness'. He was stiff and Victorian and his second marriage was equally cold. Louisa always referred to her husband as Mr Taft. When he died, the scissors were reunited and she resumed her travels with her sister.

Louisa constantly complained that Taft was large for his age, grew fatter every day and 'he has such a large waist that he cannot wear any of the dresses that are made with belts.' But it was her constant chiding that made him overeat.

When Taft left home, he found himself unhappy. He was used to Louisa chiding him and bossing him around. He found what he missed in Helen 'Nellie' Herron. He pursued her with ardour for two long years. She did not respond with passion initially, but slowly began to realise that Taft could help her to fulfil her lifelong ambition to become First Lady.

At the age of seventeen, Helen had stayed in the White House as a guest of President Hayes. She had not 'come out' yet, 'so I couldn't spend my time in the White House as I would have liked in going to brilliant parties and meeting all manner of charming people,' she lamented. However, she got a taste for Washington and in 1912 she told a *New York Times* reporter that she had vowed to marry only a man 'destined to be President of the United States'.

In fulfilling that ambition, Nellie has been compared to 'chilled steel', but otherwise, she was neurotic. As a girl, she shied away from any social whirl because she feared sexual relationships. Young men made her nervous and she hated them. She got on better with married men who were ten or more years her senior.

'This matter of fancying people is inexplicable,' she wrote in her diary. At twenty two, she still claimed to be 'utterly indifferent' to men. However, she and her girlfriend Sally visited a 'Bohemian' barroom opposite the Music Hall in Cincinnati, where they drank beer and smoked cigarettes. This, she boasted, was 'rather fast'.

The year after her visit to the White House, Nellie had invited her childhood friend William Taft to one of her 'salons', where they talked about Washington. From the beginning he adored her, but she tried to calm his passion. 'Friendship is infinitely higher than what is usually called love,' she wrote, 'that fatal idealisation which is so blind and, to me, so contemptible.'

'Oh Nellie, you must love me,' Taft pleaded ardently, despite the splashing of cold water. 'Any act, any expression, any look of yours, Nellie, that shows me you hold me dear… sets me wild with delight. Every such act, or expression or look I regard as evidence, with however little ground, that there is dawning in your heart the love I am so hungry for.'

Taft assured her that his love 'grew out of friendship' and was 'founded on a respect and admiration for your high character…

and your intellectual superiority'. If they married, he promised, she would be his 'senior partner' for life.

Even when they eventually got secretly engaged, she remained frigid towards him. He forgave her for this. Taft thought she was 'afraid I shall think you too cold and you want to be forgiven for it. Why, Nellie, dear, do you think I think you are any less tender in your feeling because you do not talk about it? Ah, my dear, I know you better than you think I do. You are reserved. That is your nature.'

Helen only conceded to marrying Taft in 1886 because, as she wrote to her mother, 'a lot of people think a great deal of Will. Some people even say that he may obtain some very important position in Washington.'

Taft's own ambition was to be Chief Justice of the Supreme Court, but Helen steered him relentlessly towards the presidency. When pleased, she called him 'the dearest sweetest boy that ever lived' or 'my dear darling, lovely, beautiful, sweet, precious boy'. He called her his 'guardian angel'.

But still she kept her distance. She frequently left him to go on trips and extended holidays alone. He felt lost if he was away from her for even a day or two and would bombard her with letters. She rarely bothered to reply, increasing his anxiety exquisitely.

'I shall understand silence, my darling, to mean that you are having a good time,' he bravely conceded.

When she did write, it did nothing to mend his feelings of inadequacy.

'I was very much puzzled by your letter,' he replied on one occasion. 'I read it over and over again. There was no word of endearment or affection from one end to the other and the tone of it sounded to me so hard and complaining.'

When he discovered the merest hint of affection, he exalted that it was 'all the sweeter that it is so unusual in you'.

She was more inclined to chide him on his excessive eating. She went straight for the jugular, saying that she found his obesity physically repulsive. But she did not try to reign it in as it gave her the excuse not to have sex with him. This in turn led him to seek his familiar comfort in food.

'Oh Nellie, do say that you will try to love me,' he begged. 'Oh, how I will work and strive to be better and do better. Oh Nellie, you must love me.'

Though this wish may never have come true, he did get one piece of satisfaction. After he left the White House – which he described as the 'lonesomest place in the world' – President Harding appointed him Chief Justice. So both Helen and Taft got what they were after all along.

XX

Theodore Roosevelt, #26

He stands in such abject terror of Edith.

As a 'Rough Rider' during the Spanish–American War of 1898, Theodore Roosevelt is the only U.S. President to have a condom named after him. Born on 27 October, 1858 at 28 East 20th Street, New York City, Roosevelt was an asthmatic child born in a family proud of its Dutch ancestry. Too ill to attend school; he was given private tuition at home, which he supplemented with voracious reading.

At thirteen, the young Roosevelt was unable to defend himself against two bullies and he persuaded his father to let him take boxing lessons. The incident, he said, 'did me real good' and he continued to use boxing to build up his strength.

At the age of sixteen, he became interested in girls. His sweetheart was Edith Carow. They had attended dancing classes together as children and Roosevelt mentioned in his diary that she was 'a very pretty girl'.

Meanwhile he picnicked with other girls: Annie Murray, went rowing with Nellie Smith and riding with Fanny Smith. Fanny later recalled being overwhelmed by the 'unquenchable gaiety' of his personality. 'As a young girl I remember dreading to sit next to him at any formal dinner lest I become so convulsed with laughter at his whispered sallies as to disgrace myself and be forced to leave the room,' she said.

While at Harvard, Roosevelt went to parties in all the best houses of Boston. 'I have been having a very gay time,' he wrote. 'Some of the girls are very sweet and bright.'

His name was linked with Miss Fiske, Miss Wheelright, Miss Andrews and Miss Richardson – 'the prettiest girl I have seen for a long time'. And there was still Edith Carow.

In fact, Roosevelt compared all other girls to Edith. During a sleigh ride he mentioned that 'one of the girls looked quite like Edith – only not so pretty as her Ladyship'. Later Edith came to visit him at Cambridge, Massachusetts. 'I don't think I ever saw Edith look prettier,' he wrote to his sister. 'Everyone admired her little Ladyship immensely and she behaved as sweetly as she looked.'

By this time, Roosevelt had become quite a dandy, with his English-cut suits, silk cravats, cameo pins, beaver hat, fob watch and cane. He agonised over the question whether he should wear a frock coat or a cut-away in the afternoon.

In the summer of 1878, Roosevelt asked Edith Carow to marry him. She refused and he discovered that she had a romance, they quarrelled and Roosevelt she recorded 'was not very nice'.

On the rebound he met Alice Hathaway Lee, the daughter of a Boston banker. 'See that girl? I am going to marry her,' he told a friend. 'She won't have me, but I am going to have her.'

It was true. Alice was not at all impressed by Roosevelt. She claimed that a faint smell of formaldehyde clung to him. She certainly had no intention of marrying him. But he said: 'I loved her as soon as I saw her sweet, fair, young face.' He called her 'enchanting', 'flowerlike', 'radiant' and even rhapsodised over her to Edith, once they had made it up after their romantic spat.

Roosevelt pursued Alice with the relentless energy he brought to bear on everything else in his life. Despite turning him down several times, she eventually consented to marry him after watching him box. Although he was totally outclassed in the ring, he showed such courage in the bout that everyone was impressed. Even when he had won her, he was so afraid of losing her that he bought a pair of French duelling pistols so he could take on any rival,

'How I love her,' he wrote. 'She seems like a star of heaven, she is so far above other girls; my pearl, my pure flower. When I hold her in my arms there is nothing on earth left to wish for.'

Roosevelt let his feelings run away with him and at least one teacher suggested that this was not entirely masculine. But

Roosevelt did not apologize for his sensitivity. Nothing, he said, disgusted him more than the 'male sexual viciousness', which made a wife the servant of her husband's lusts.

While Roosevelt's fellow students had been carousing in the seamier parts of Boston, he had held himself inviolate. In October 1880, when he married Alice, he was still a virgin. He wrote in his diary: 'Thank Heaven, I am at least perfectly pure.'

In other passages, he had asked God's help to stave off temptation 'and to do nothing I would have been ashamed to confess'. When his wayward cousin Cornelius 'distinguished himself by marrying a French actress!' Roosevelt was outraged. 'He has disgraced the family, the vulgar brute,' he wrote. 'P.S. She turns out to be a mere courtesan! A harlot!'

Alice, too, was a virgin. He called her his 'baby wife'. The picture of her he loved most showed her at fourteen. But of their wedding night, all Roosevelt would confide to his diary was: 'Our intense happiness is too sacred to be written about.'

Together, on their honeymoon in New York, they would devour the newspapers – 'our only intercourse with the outside world'. His attraction to her was passionate and physical. Their honeymoon was 'a perfect dream of delight'.

'When we are alone, I can hardly stay a moment without holding her in my arms or kissing her,' he wrote. 'She is such a laughing, teasing, pretty little witch... I cannot help petting and caressing her all the time.'

They travelled on to Europe by boat and Alice became so seasick that she thought she was going to die. In the National Gallery in London, Roosevelt admired the Rembrandts, but disapproved of the Rubens nudes. 'I do not believe that you can get a "grand Greek Aphrodite",' he wrote, 'by merely exhibiting a scantily attired Dutch housewife.'

Roosevelt had robust puritanical views. He condemned the realism of Emile Zola, saying: 'Of course, the net result of Zola's writing has been evil. Where one man has gained from them a shuddering horror at existing wrong which has impelled him to try to right that wrong, a hundred have simply had the lascivious, the beast side of their natures strengthened and intensified.'

Even Tolstoy was 'a sexual degenerate... for erotic perversion frequently goes hand in hand with a wild and fanatical mysticism'. This was largely because he saw Tolstoy as being against marriage, which Roosevelt thought was proper except for shiftless and worthless people. While divorce, he thought, should not be easy for anyone.

Roosevelt called Alice 'Sunshine'; she called him 'Teddykins'. However, their love life was not without problems. Alice had to undergo gynaecological surgery in 1882 before they could have children.

Then tragedy struck. On Valentine's day 1884, both Roosevelt's mother and his wife – who had given birth to a baby daughter just two days before – died of typhoid fever. He wrote in his diary: 'The light has just gone out of my life.'

His obituary of Alice was terse: 'Alice Hathaway Lee. Born at Chestnut Hill, July 29th, 1861. I saw her first in Oct. 1878; I wooed her for over a year before I won her; we were betrothed on Jan. 25th, 1880, and it was announced on Feb. 16th; on Oct. 27th of the same year we were married; we spent three years of happiness greater and more unalloyed than I have ever known to fall to the lot of others; on Feb. 12th 1884 her baby was born, and on Feb. 14th she died in my arms, and my mother had died in the same house, on the same day, but a few hours previously. On Feb. 16th they were buried together in Greenwood. On Feb. 17th I christened the baby Alice Lee Roosevelt. For joy or for sorrow my life has now been lived out.'

Later, Roosevelt published a book called *In Memory of My Darling Wife*. In it, he pays her a more glowing tribute: 'She was beautiful in face and form, and lovelier still in spirit; as a flower she grew, and as a fair young flower she died. Her life had been always in the sunshine; there had never come to her a single great sorrow; and none ever knew her who did not love and revere her for her bright, sunny temper and her saintly unselfishness. Fair, pure, and joyous as a maiden; loving, tender, and happy as a young wife; when she had just become a mother, when her life seemed to be just begun, and when the years seemed so bright before her – then, by a strange and terrible fate, death came to her. And when my heart's dearest died, the light went from my life for ever.'

Roosevelt lost three successive elections and left for Dakota, where he took up the life of a cowboy. He returned to New York two years later to marry again, this time to his childhood sweetheart Edith Carow. They had remained friends throughout Roosevelt's marriage to Alice. However, Edith secretly admitted that she was 'passionately in love with him' but had moved to England with her mother.

When Alice died in 1884, Roosevelt wanted to be true to her forever and avoided seeing Edith. But Edith was determined and returned to New York. The two of them met by accident and the old flame reignited.

'I have never loved anyone else,' Edith wrote to him. 'I love you with all the passion of a girl who has never loved before.'

Roosevelt went through torments of self-recrimination for not being constant in his heart to Alice.

'I utterly disbelieve in and disapprove of second marriages,' he wrote to his sister Bamie. 'I have always considered that they argued weakness in a man's character. You could not reproach me one half as bitterly for my inconstancy and unfaithfulness as I reproach myself.'

Secretly they got engaged and married in London in 1886. By the time, they returned to the U.S., Edith was pregnant. They settled at Sagamore Hill, in Oyster Bay, New York, in the house Roosevelt had originally built for Alice, and had five children over the next ten years.

In the 1890s, eager for high political office, the Roosevelts were drawn into the political circle of Henry Adams, the grandson of John Quincy Adams and great-grandson of John Adams. They met in Adams's book-lined living room in Lafayette Square near the White House in Washington, DC. Although they talked politics, the group was riven with sexual intrigue.

Adams was in love with the wife of another Senator J. Donald Cameron of Pennsylvania. She was said to be the most beautiful woman in Washington. John Hay, former secretary to Abraham Lincoln, who went on to become Secretary of State, though married, was having a clandestine affair with Nannie Lodge, the wife of Roosevelt's best friend Henry Cabot Lodge. Clarence King, the brilliant geologist, who secretly pretended to be an African-American Pullman porter in order to have a freedwoman as his common-law wife – she bore him five children without knowing the truth. Adams was also captivated by Edith, Roosevelt's 'sympathetic little wife'. She obviously had power over Roosevelt observed Adams: 'He stands in such abject terror of Edith'.

Then in 1892, Roosevelt was almost ruined by scandal.

Katy Mann, the former maid of Roosevelt's alcoholic brother Elliott, claimed that Elliott was the father of her illegitimate child and demanded $10,000 for the child's upkeep. She had a locket and letters to back her story, plus the testimony of the other servants. Elliott, who had been addicted to morphine and laudanum since an accident, vehemently denied the charges. The family hired an 'expert in likenesses' who examined the child and promptly concluded that Katy's story was true. The family paid her off.

Roosevelt thought that marital infidelity was a hideous crime which reduced its perpetrator to the level of a 'flagrant man-swine'. He believed that any sex between Elliott and his wife Anna should cease until Elliott's 'hideous depravity' had been expunged by 'two or three years of straight life'.

Elliott, however, collapsed under the pressure. He took another mistress, a Mrs Evans, and resumed his heavy drinking. Terrified of ruin, his wife wanted to seize control of Elliott's $170,000 estate before he blew it, and moved to have him declared legally insane. Roosevelt, himself, applied for the writ. The press found out and had a field day.

Later, Roosevelt got his own back. He made his famous assault on 'muckrakers'. In 1913, he sued the editor of the obscure

Michigan paper, *Iron Age*, who said that he frequently got drunk. Roosevelt won the case and just six cents in damages.

When the assassination of McKinley, six months into his second term, brought his Vice President Roosevelt to the presidency, Edith filled the White House with children and pets. She tried to keep the family in the background while reporters focused on her extravagant husband, though the debut of one daughter and the wedding of another took place in the White House. She was also an accomplished political hostess, aristocratic enough to play the game.

One of Roosevelt's closest friends in Washington was Jules Jusserand, the French ambassador to the U.S. from 1902 to 1924. The two men would go swimming together naked, in the Potomac, though Jusserand would keep his gloves on 'in case we meet a lady'. Roosevelt, though prudish, did not.

XXI
William McKinley, #25
'Receive my evening benediction of love.'

President William McKinley had a dizzying view of women. During his youth he repeatedly read *Noble Deeds of American Women*, one of the few books his father owned.

He was a staunch Unionist and vehemently anti-slavery. When the Civil War came, he joined up and fought fiercely. Returning as a war hero, McKinley was popular with women. He had a muscular body and dressed flamboyantly, with a black frock coat and purple ties. Eager to get married, he often escorted local eligible girls and his name was linked romantically with several of them. But then he fell for Ida Saxton.

McKinley first set eyes on her when she was working as a cashier in her father's bank. She was beautiful and attracted a number of young male depositors who often brought bouquets in with their money. Soon McKinley had vanquished his rivals and Ida's father said: 'You are the only man I have ever known to whom I would entrust my daughter.'

They married in 1871 and honeymooned in New York. Their first daughter was born later that year. At his wife's prompting, McKinley became a leader in the temperance movement, though as President he enjoyed whiskey, wine and a good cigar. Ida was very possessive and called her husband 'the Major', after the rank he attained during the Civil War.

Soon after their second daughter's birth in 1873, the child died, followed not long after by her older sister. They had no more children. Ida developed phlebitis and epileptic seizures. She believed that her illness was a punishment from God. If it was, he punished McKinley too. Ida's possessiveness turned into an obsession. She forbade him to leave her side and took bromides to sleep. Although she regularly seemed to hover on the brink of death, she always rallied and somehow managed to survive for another thirty-four years.

McKinley was nonetheless devoted to her. Opposite to the usual marital arrangement for (future) Presidents, he organised his burgeoning political career around her. She was never far from his side when he served as a Congressman and Governor of Ohio, spending most of her waking moments in a small rocking chair. If he could not be with her he would send a note saying: 'Receive my evening benediction of love.'

In the White House, she was lavishly dressed and received guests sitting in a blue velvet chair. She held a small bouquet so that she would not be expected to shake hands. Contrary to protocol, she would be seated next to her husband at formal dinners. If he saw a seizure coming he would throw a napkin over her face until it passed. Although it was known that Ida's health was 'delicate', the press did not report the facts of her illness and they only came to light long after she died.

During his presidency, McKinley would often leave important business to attend to his wife. His political patron Mark Hanna once remarked: 'President McKinley has made it pretty hard for the rest of us husbands here in Washington.'

However high he may have set the bar as a husband, he did have his vices. He was a vain man and, for example, never wore his spectacles in public. He had a huge wardrobe and changed his clothes three or four times a day when they became wrinkled. He also liked to dance and at this distant in time one can only speculate on how a man like him would feel dancing with a personable young female partner.

When President McKinley was shot by a Polish anarchist, his dying thoughts were of his wife. After his death, she was nursed by her younger sister in Canton. She died five years later, at the age of fifty nine, and was laid to rest beside her husband in a memorial tomb.

XXII
Grover Cleveland, #22 & 24

'Whatever you say, tell the truth'

Grover Cleveland survived a sex scandal to get into office and is the only president to get married in the White House. Yet this provoked its own scandal. He wed his twenty-one-year-old ward who was twenty eight years his junior, days after she had become of age legally.

Like Donald Trump, George W. Bush and Bill Clinton, Cleveland had dodged the draft. He was called up in 1863 to fight in the Civil War, but he exercised his legal right under the Conscription Act and paid a young Polish immigrant named George Benninsky $150 to fight in his place. While the war was on, Cleveland built up his law practice in Buffalo and spent a great deal of time eating, drinking and gambling. He was particularly fond of the beer, sausages and sauerkraut at Schenkelerger's restaurant and his weight soared to 250 pounds. The only exercise he got was on fishing and hunting trips, and his occasional visits to local brothels.

From 1871 to 1874, he was sheriff of Erie County and hanged murderers with his own hands, rather than inflict the onerous task on his deputies. He then returned to private practice. 'The law,' he said, 'is a jealous mistress.'

Not that jealous, it seemed. Around that time, he became involved with a widow, Mrs Maria Halpin. She was thirty six; he thirty seven. She gave birth to a son. There was no proof that the child was his. Indeed, she named him Oscar Folsom Cleveland after Cleveland's law partner Oscar Folsom, but the other men Mrs Halpin had been seeing were all married, so Cleveland gallantly admitted paternity. Mrs Halpin demanded marriage but Cleveland would go no further than offer child support.

In the 1884 presidential election, the Republican candidate was

James G. Blaine and the battle between Cleveland and Blaine was one of the dirtiest campaigns in U.S. history. While in Congress, Blaine had accepted $100,000 in bribes from the railroads. Even the corrupt New York Republican Boss Conkling, when asked why he had not backed Blaine's nomination, said: 'I do not engage in criminal practice.'

Democratic newspapers ran huge features showing how Blaine had gotten rich in political office. The Republicans countered weakly with stories about Cleveland's illegitimate child. Cleveland took the bold step of admitting all. He announced that he had once formed an 'illicit connection with a woman and a child had been born and given his name'. He denied that he had ever entertained a woman 'in any bad way' while he occupied the governor's mansion in Albany and refreshingly wired his campaign managers the simple message: 'Whatever you say, tell the truth': no alternative facts for Cleveland.

His instincts paid off handsomely. The more that came out about the Halpin affair, the better the light Cleveland appeared in. He himself had dutifully maintained an interest in the child's welfare and when Mrs Halpin began drinking heavily, he arranged for the boy to go to an orphanage while she was confined to a mental institution. When she escaped and kidnapped the child, Cleveland found a prominent New York family to adopt the boy, who grew up to become a respected doctor.

Meanwhile, the Democrats discovered that Blaine's first child had been born just three months after his marriage. When Cleveland was given the evidence, he tore it up, saying: 'The other side can have the monopoly on all the dirt in this campaign.'

The story leaked out anyway, but instead of coming clean, Blaine reached for alternative facts and brazenly lied that due to a mix-up involving the death of his father, there had been two marriage services. The first, he said, had occurred six months earlier. He produced no evidence to this effect and no one believed him. The contrast between the two candidates could scarcely have been more vividly drawn.

It was also discovered that Blaine had lied to a House committee investigating railroad contracts; and in a letter to a railroad executive, Blaine had solicited false testimony. The letter concluded with the incriminating line: 'Burn this letter.'

The campaign dissolved into a slanging match. Democratic mobs would chant: 'James G. Blaine, the continental liar from the state of Maine' and 'Burn this letter'. Republicans would yell: 'Ma, Ma, where's my pa?' That taunt the Democrats would counter with: 'Gone to the White House, ha, ha, ha.'

At an election meeting in Chicago, one voter eloquently summed up the position. 'We are told,' he said, 'that Mr Blaine has been delinquent in office but blameless in private life, while Mr Cleveland has been a model of official integrity, but culpable in his personal relations. We should therefore elect Mr Cleveland to the public office which he is so well qualified to fill, and remand Mr Blaine to the private station which he is admirably fitted to adorn.'

As the election drew closer, the race was neck and neck. Everything depended on the vote in New York, where Cleveland was unpopular. A week before the election, Blaine went to New York to woo the Irish Catholic vote. His mother was a Catholic and his sister was a mother superior. At a meeting of five hundred clergymen called to condemn Cleveland over his illegitimate child once again, the pastor of Murray Hill Presbyterian Church stood up and dubbed the Democrats the party of 'Rum, Romanism and Rebellion'.

New York Democrats seized on this anti-Catholic remark and swung the state. Cleveland won the election by 219 electoral votes to Blaine's 182, although he was ahead in the popular vote by just a sliver at 1,100.

In 1876, Cleveland's partner Oscar Folsom – probably the father of Mrs Halpin's baby – had been killed when he was thrown from a buggy. Cleveland was executor of Folsom's estate and looked after his widow and her eleven-year-old daughter Frances. For years, Cleveland saw a great deal of the two of them. No one suspected that his interest in his young charge was more than avuncular. Frances and her mother missed the inauguration, but they visited the White House that spring.

It was rumoured at this time that Cleveland was going to marry Mrs Folsom. In fact, Cleveland had often told friends who enquired why he was not married that he was waiting for his wife to grow up.

Soon after the visit, Cleveland wrote to Frances proposing marriage, and once she had graduated from Wells College, they became engaged.

On 2 June 1886, in the Blue Room in the White House, in front of fewer than forty guests, President Cleveland and Frances Folsom were married in a revised and shortened service. The word 'obey' was omitted. When the ceremony was over, a twenty-one-gun salute sounded from the navy yard and all the church bells in Washington peeled out.

At the reception and supper in the state dining room, Cleveland and his bride received a telegram of congratulations from Queen Victoria and one of the table decorations was a model of the full-rigged ship *Hymen* made out of pansies and pink roses.

There was, of course, intense public interest in the President's youthful bride. The story circulated that he had bought her first baby carriage. The press followed them on their honeymoon to Deer Park in Maryland, camping outside their honeymoon cottage and observing the newly-weds through telescopes. Cleveland commented that the reporters were 'doing their utmost to make American journalism contemptible'.

The President and his wife were an odd couple. She was twenty one, tall, graceful, dark-eyed, attractive. He was 260 pounds, bull-necked, physically unprepossessing and forty nine. In fact, newspapers wrote editorials warning the young bride of the physical dangers of intimate relations with a man of such weight and girth. Yet the marriage proved successful and they had five children.

In the 1888 election, Cleveland was sunk by his own side. Enemies in New York's Tammany Hall circulated a pamphlet that went way beyond anything Blaine had come up with and charged

Cleveland with bestial perversions during his Buffalo days as well as brutal treatment of his young wife. Although he won the popular vote, he lost the electoral vote by 168 to Benjamin Harrison's 233.

On leaving the White House on 4 March 1889, Mrs Cleveland said to the staff: 'Take good care of the furniture and ornaments in the house… for I want to find everything just as it is now when we come back again. We are coming back just four years from today.'

Frances Cleveland was not just the youngest First Lady, she was one of the most popular. Even while her husband was out of office, she never lost her place in the public's affection and the Clevelands indeed returned to the White House four years later as if she had been gone just a day, though she brought with her the first two of their five children.

In 1895, during his second term in office, Cleveland heard from Mrs Halpin again. She was now remarried and living in New Rochelle, New York. In a letter to the President, she demanded money and threatened to publish her side of the story. Nothing came of it.

Frances wept when she left the White House a second time, after William McKinley's inauguration. So did many of the staff. The couple moved to Princeton. Cleveland was happy there and she was at his side when he died in 1908. Four and a half years later, she married the Professor of Archaeology at Princeton. She survived until October 1947.

Until Cleveland married, the role of First Lady had been played by his unmarried sister Rose, a successful teacher, novelist and literary critic. In 1889, she began an intense friendship with Evangeline Simpson, a wealthy thirty year old. The two women exchanged a series of romantic letters. In one, Rose admitted: 'I tremble at the thought of you' and 'I dare not think of your arms'. Simpson replied, calling Miss Cleveland 'my Clevy, my Viking, my Everything'. After Simpson's husband died, the women moved to Italy in 1910 and lived together until Miss Cleveland died in 1918.

XXIII
Benjamin Harrison, #23

Benjamin Harrison was a stiff and formal man, nicknamed 'the human iceberg' – with echoes of Roy Cohn's accusation here. During his time at the White House, electric lights were installed, but he did not dare switch the light on in his bedroom, and he left the lights in the halls and living rooms on all night, fearing a shock if he touched the switch. The White House electrician had to turn them off when he reported for work in the morning.

Harrison did genuinely care for the plight of women. One of the few campaign promises his administration did fulfil was providing pensions for Civil War widows. However, this drained the treasury and put his administration into terminal decline.

Harrison's first wife, who was the first PresidentGeneral of the Daughters of the American Revolution, fell ill in 1892 and her widowed niece, Mrs Mary Scott Dimmick, took over as official hostess. Harrison was reluctant to leave his ailing wife to campaign for re-election. Ever the gentleman, his opponent Grover Cleveland refused to take advantage of the situation. This made for a lack-lustre campaign, the only excitement coming from the rise of a third party, the Populists. The result was a landslide to Cleveland.

In October 1892, before Harrison left office, his wife died of tuberculosis. After a service in the East Room of the White House, her body was returned to Indianapolis for burial.

Harrison returned to his law practice in Indianapolis and, in 1896, married Mary Scott Dimmick. This caused something of a scandal in the family and neither his son nor daughter from his first marriage attended the ceremony. The following year Harrison became a father again at the age of sixty three. He died of pneumonia in Indianapolis on 13 March 1901 and is buried in Crown Hill Cemetery, Indianapolis, alongside his two wives.

XXIV

Chester A. Arthur, #21

'My private life is nobody's damned business.'

The twenty-first President of the United States, Chester Arthur, burnt all his private papers the day before he died which has made it difficult for biographers to discover anything much about the private side of Arthur's life. However, it is safe to assume, particularly in this case, that if someone is hiding something then there is something to hide.

There were certainly plenty of things that Arthur did not want disclosed. For example, he may not have been eligible to be the U.S. President. He was not a 'natural born citizen' as the Constitution demanded, but was probably born in Canada, and therefore a British subject.

Arthur was close to New York's Republican boss, Senator Roscoe Conkling. Under Conkling's patronage, President Ulysses S. Grant appointed Arthur as Collector of the Customs House in New York harbour, well-known as a home of graft, theft and bribery. In 1877, the Jay Commission exposed the corruption in the authority and the newly elected President Rutherford Hayes demanded Arthur's resignation.

Arthur's wife, Ellen Herndon, was seven years his junior. Her father was in command of a mail packet sailing from New York, when she met 'Chet' Arthur, a young lawyer. Arthur fell for young 'Nell' and, when her father was lost in a storm off Cape Hatteras in 1859, they married. As part of Senator Roscoe Conkling's corrupt patronage, they became rich. But Ellen became distressed by the fact that her husband spent so much time away from home, ostensibly drinking and smoking with his political cronies. She felt lonely and neglected, and there was talk of separation.

In January 1880, he was away in Albany when she attended a

benefit concert in New York and caught a cold waiting for her carriage. When he heard the news of her illness, he jumped the milk train but by the time he arrived at her bedside she was unconscious. Two days later, she died.

Later that year, he was nominated Vice President and when James A. Garfield was shot Arthur became President. 'Honors to me now are not what they once were,' he wrote. In the White House, he kept a picture of his wife and put fresh flowers in front of it every day. He also presented a commemorative stained-glass window to St John's Church. It was on the south side, so he could see it from the White House at night.

No woman could replace his 'Nell' as First Lady, but Arthur persuaded his youngest sister, Mary McElroy, to spend several months each year as 'Mistress of the White House'.

While publicly, Arthur played the grieving widower, privately things were a little different. He left his daughter in New York with a governess and sent his son to Princeton, where he majored in girls, wild parties and expensive clothes.

President Arthur then threw himself into a round of state dinners and private suppers. Commentators said that he was 'almost seeming to act in a conscious effort to forget the death of his wife'. Guests were confronted with fourteen-course meals with eight different wines and the White House was full of women.

From the sidelines ex-president Hayes railed against 'liquor, snobbery and worse', but to most Washington socialites this was a refreshing change from the White House of Hayes' wife, the staunch temperance advocate 'Lemonade Lucy'. 'No President since the war has been so universally popular here,' wrote one Washington newspaper.

Arthur had always been a dandy. In the White House, it was rumoured that he would try on twenty pairs of trousers before settling on the ones he would wear. He wore tweeds during business hours, frock coats in the afternoon, and a dinner suit in the evening.

As President, Chester A. Arthur was the most eligible widower in the land. Mothers with marriageable daughters, widows eager to be consoled and hosts of romantic girls who saw President Arthur as a reincarnation of the legendary King Arthur flocked to his court. He paid a compliment to one, presented a posy of flowers to another and strolled in the White House gardens with a third. Gossips were constantly linking his name with eligible women.

He occasionally travelled with female companions, but he knew how to cover his tracks. When one nosy lady enquired a little too persistently into his love life, Arthur snapped: 'Madam, I may be President of the United States, but my private life is nobody's damned business.'

In fact, his very private, private life took up most of his time. His staff found it almost impossible to get him to give any of his attention to the affairs of state. It once took him a month to copy out a letter of condolence, which had already been drafted by the State Department and was destined for a European court. A White House clerk said later: 'President Arthur never did today what he could put off until tomorrow.'

After his first year of office, Arthur discovered he was dying of Bright's disease, a fatal kidney condition, and he seemed determined to enjoy what remained of his life.

How precisely he did that we shall never know. Whatever evidence there was went up in smoke on 16 November 1886, two days before he died when he ordered his papers, both private and official to be burnt.

XXV

James A. Garfield, #20

'Ripe for ruin and an active and willing servant of sin.'

James Garfield was the last of the 'log cabin' presidents. His father died when Garfield was two years old. He helped his mother work their small farm in Orange, Ohio, taking what schooling he could during the winter months. When he was seventeen, he worked driving the horses and mules that pulled flatboats along the Ohio canal.

Life on the canal was different from the stifling existence he had known in Orange. The young men were largely interested in one thing, and their trips took them down to Cleveland, a major port known for its abundance of brothels. Across the river in what was called Ohio City in 1849, it had been necessary to pass a law banning 'lewd and lascivious behaviour in any of the streets, lanes, alleys or public places'.

With the money he earned on the canals, Garfield enrolled in a local school run by the Disciples of Christ, a strict sect. He had a genuine conversion and became a preacher, working as a carpenter during the summer to put himself through Geauga Seminary in Chester, Ohio. Five years later, he repented of his life on the canal. 'Oh, at that time I was ripe for ruin and an active and willing servant of sin,' he wrote. 'How fearfully I was rushing with both soul and body to destruction.'

By that time, he had become excessively worried about masturbation. At the seminary, he pored over Henry Ward Beecher's *Seven Lectures to Young Men*, the Reverend John Todd's *The Young Man* and Orson S. Fowler's *Amativeness: Embracing the Evils and Remedies of Excessive and Perverted Sexuality, Including Warning and Advice to the Married and Single*, a tract utterly condemning masturbation. Garfield fervently wished that there were 'ten thousand copies... in every town in the United States'.

In his book, the Reverend Todd warned that nine out of ten boys indulged. It was okay for farmers and canal hands to waste their energies that way, but those, like Garfield, who were trying to rise in the world had to be self-sufficient and in control of their sexual desires. Masturbation was not just criminal and sinful. It doomed those who practised it to poverty and insanity.

Fowler warned of the 'pallid, bloodless countenance... hollow, sunken and half-ghastly eyes [and] half-wild, half vacant stare' of the masturbator. The signs were obvious for all to see: 'carrying of the hands frequently to the sexual organs by way of changing their position'; 'lascivious expression on observing females'; and 'unwillingness to look other people in the face'.

Garfield felt he suffered from all of these symptoms and struggled with the 'total abstinence' that Fowler recommended. Then a phrenologist examining his head noticed an over-developed 'bump of amativeness' at the base of the skull. This, it was believed, governed sexual desire, something Garfield plainly had too much of.

To cure himself, Garfield would take frequent cold showers – first publicly at one of the little dam mills on the Chagrin river when there were no women about. Later he built his own shower bath at Hiram College.

During this period, Garfield took an inordinate interest in homosexuality. He studied what the Bible had to say on the subject and, as a classical scholar, read Cicero, Virgil, Plutarch and Seneca. This may have been because many nineteenth-century writers associated the excessive masturbation that so plagued the young Garfield with homosexuality.

In fact, more than one writer has concluded that Garfield had a juvenile infatuation with a young man named Oliver B. Stone. Throughout his life, his diaries reveal a deep uncertainty Garfield felt about himself.

Garfield paid his way through the Hiram College by teaching English and ancient languages, for which he proved to have a singular gift. He was a passable poet and an accomplished classics scholar. He would astound friends by writing Greek with one hand and Latin with the other, simultaneously.

As a youth, Garfield had been deeply inhibited around young women and was frequently shocked by their forwardness. However, at the Eclectic College, he fell under the spell of Almeda A. Booth, one of the teachers whose early love affair had been ended prematurely by the death of her fiancé. The relationship remained purely platonic, but she helped knock the rough edges off the crude canal boy.

At the same time, Garfield fell in love with Mary Hubbell, one of his own students. He poured out his heart to her in poetry and love letters, and took her for walks in the moonlight. Garfield called the affair an 'adventure' and lapsed into coded Latin in his diary to describe the 'tender game' he played with Mary. She let her guard slip and they became close, perhaps even intimate, at Garfield's boarding house.

During this passionate affair, Mary and her family thought that the couple were engaged. When Garfield came down with a cold, they invited him into their house and put him through the standard treatment of the day. He was stripped, wrapped in a cold, wet sheet and laid in an unheated room for two hours. Then he was put to bed. Mary's parents went off to visit one of their other daughters and left Garfield alone in the house with Mary for a day. Mary nursed him, apparently attending to his every need – another coded note in Garfield's diary.

Suddenly Garfield's ardour cooled. It is often thought that Garfield's attitude changed as marriage grew closer. His mother's second marriage had been a disaster. After a year, she had simply packed her bags and moved back home. In the Cuyahoga Court of Common Pleas, she was found 'guilty of gross neglect of duty as a wife' and divorced, her reputation forever tainted.

Garfield began to look at other women. He had become more relaxed in their company. After he met another student at the college, Lucretia Rudolph, he announced that he and Mary were not going to marry and that they had never been engaged. Mary's family were outraged and threatened to make his love letters public. The ladies of Hiram blackballed him out of sympathy for their dishonoured sister and his name was dirt on campus thereafter.

Garfield himself was bitter. After all, he had never asked Mary to marry him. 'To the first view, life – the world and society – seem pleasant and alluring,' he wrote, 'but when their depths are penetrated, their secret paths trod, they are found hollow, soulless and insipid.'

From his humble beginnings, Garfield craved to become respectable. To this end he asked Lucretia 'Crete' Rudolph, the daughter of one of the founders of the Eclectic College, to marry him. She consented and he was allowed to visit her, unchaperoned, in the privacy of her bedroom.

Nevertheless, as the nuptials approached the thought of marriage gave him cold feet and sent him into a black depression. They had planned to marry in 1854 when Garfield graduated, but he managed to postpone the wedding for two years while he took a BA at Williams College in Williamstown, Massachusetts. Again he supported himself there by teaching.

Only once during his time at Williams did he return to Hiram to visit Lucretia, but he frequently found time to visit the Disciples of Christ at Poestenkill, New York. There he met Mrs Maria Learned, who was bored with her unfeeling husband and instead formed a deep attachment to Garfield.

When she learnt that he was to be married to Lucretia Rudolph in Ohio, she encouraged him to strike up a relationship with Rebecca Selleck, a frequent visitor to the Learned household. Sister Rebecca was much more passionate than the sedate Lucretia, and she and Garfield spent much time alone in a room they called the Prophet's Chamber. His letters make it clear that they made love there, with the collusion, if not the participation, of Maria Learned. The three of them began to refer to themselves as the 'holy trinity' and the 'triangle' in their letters.

After he graduated from Williams in 1856, Garfield returned to his teaching post at Hiram at a salary of $600 a year, but he wrote regularly to Rebecca who kept his desirous love letters in the cleavage between her breasts.

Rebecca came to visit Garfield in Hiram, but Lucretia suspected nothing. She even dismissed campus gossip about Garfield's divided affections as baseless lies.

Garfield then attempted to establish a new 'triangle' by encouraging Rebecca and Lucretia to become friends. They got together at Garfield's nightly Bible readings, but he found it difficult to explain the exact nature of what he was proposing to the prudish Lucretia.

After being back in Hiram for over a year, the question of marriage was pressing once again. Garfield knew that he could not dodge it this time. He took one last trip to Poestenkill, to the 'holy trinity' there. On his return, he confessed all to Lucretia. She forgave him, but could not find it in her heart to forgive the duplicity of Rebecca who she thought was her friend.

Lucretia offered to release Garfield from his engagement, so that he could marry Rebecca, but with marriage it was respectability he craved, not passion. He would go through with the wedding 'with all its necessities and hateful finalities'. What Garfield feared most was the 'narrow exclusiveness of marriage'. Lucretia was well aware of his indifference, but after their four-year engagement the marriage simply had to go ahead.

'I don't want much parade about our marriage,' wrote Garfield, dispassionately. 'Arrange that as you see fit.'

There was no honeymoon and both of them were soon deeply unhappy. Garfield confessed that the marriage had been 'a great mistake' and took frequent business trips alone. Then the Civil War came and he joined the Union Army.

After the Battle of Shiloh in 1862, his health began to deteriorate. He was sent home to convalesce. Lucretia nursed him and her tenderness during that period rekindled their romance. She worked out that, during the first four and three-quarter years of their marriage, they had been together less than twenty weeks. She vowed from then on that they would never be parted.

However, Garfield was not to be corralled. He found excuses to travel to New York on business and he dropped by on Rebecca Selleck. In the autumn of 1862 he had an affair with Mrs Lucia Calhoun, an eighteen-year-old reporter for *The New York Times*. The affair was brief and Garfield confessed to Lucretia. She forgave him, but in 1867, he went to visit Mrs Calhoun again, explaining that he had to collect indiscreet letters that he had written to her which might damage his political career. Lucretia feared that the affair might start all over again and prayed that 'the fire of such a lawless passion would burn itself out unfed and unnoticed'.

On that occasion, Garfield probably resisted, but it seems likely that at other times he could not contain his sexual passion. During the 1880 election, there were allegations that he had visited a prostitute in a New Orleans brothel.

Four months after being elected as President, Garfield was shot by a disgruntled office-seeker in the Baltimore and Potomac railroad depot in Washington, DC. He died on 19 September, 1881. Long after death, talk of his womanising continued while for the remaining thirty six years of her life, Lucretia Garfield lived in seclusion in Ohio, vehemently denying all rumours of her husband's infidelity.

XXVI
Rutherford B. Hayes, #19
'You are sister Fanny to me now.'

One night in 1852, when Rutherford Hayes was thirty, he said he found himself overwhelmed by physical desire. He was attending a lecture by Professor Agassiz at the Young Men's Mercantile Library Association in Cincinnati, when he saw a young woman in the audience and was deeply attracted to her.

After the lecture was over, he found himself compelled to follow her out into the street. In the pouring rain, he followed her down towards the river where she disappeared into a shabby house. It was only then that Hayes realized that the girl was a prostitute, and he knew that it was a matter of the greatest urgency that he get married. Up until then, the closest relationship he had had was with his sister Fanny. He doted on her and she reciprocated. 'I love you like my own life,' she told him once.

As a young lawyer, he became emotionally involved with one of his clients, a serving girl name Nancy Farrer. She had been accused of poisoning four people. He managed to save her from the gallows, but only by getting her committed to an insane asylum instead.

From a young age, Hayes was undoubtedly popular with women. At fifteen, he wrote to a friend: 'Tell me how A. Pickett flourishes with girls. Tell him I flourish like a green bay tree.'

At twenty two, he confided to Fanny: 'Between you and me, a little squad of girls have spent a great deal of time and pains in trying to get acquainted with me.' But he put them off by letting it be known that he was engaged to a girl in Columbus, Ohio – a figment of his imagination.

He started 'numerous courtships, smitten, but not in love' in

Lower Sandusky, now Fremont, Ohio, where he then lived. One evening, he climbed the fence of the Catholic convent for a tryst. The liaison ended as his sister Fanny heartily disapproved of this interest in village girls.

'Do not fall in love with any of the Sandusky beauties,' Fanny wrote. 'Perhaps I am prejudiced, but I wish you to take into consideration that you will not always live in Sandusky. So do not marry a wife you will blush for anywhere. Do forgive me, brother, if I am meddling; if you do not like such interference, say so, and I shall forbear in the future.'

Hayes decided that the woman he should marry must be the image of his sister Fanny. He rejected Julia Buttles of Columbus, Ohio, who, according to Fanny, 'turned sick at your name' when he would not court her.

He was slow off the mark in wooing the twenty-one-year-old blue-eyed niece of Judge Lane and found her surrounded by other suitors. Then he fell for the Lanes' house guest Fanny Perkins. In a long and heartfelt letter to his sister, he explained that this Fanny had all the attributes that his sister Fanny would have required in his wife. But Fanny Perkins rejected him, so he went awooing a 'Miss W – ', a Yankee girl in Columbus.

Hayes longed to get married. At twenty-one he had bet $25 that he would get married by the time he was twenty-five. With just a year to go, he lamented to Fanny: 'I have had no loves yet.'

He claimed to be 'one of the sunniest fellows in the world', but he confided that the reason why he really wanted a wife was 'to take charge of my correspondence with friends and relatives. Women of education and sense can always write good letters, but men are generally unable to fish up enough entertaining matter to fill half a sheet.' He was deadly serious. In 1850, he ended one flirtation with a Miss H – because she was too flirtatious.

In the end, it came to a straight choice between two girls – a friend of Fanny's called Helen Kelley and a straitlaced graduate of Cincinnati's Wesleyan Female College called Lucy Webb. Helen was 'a gay figure in the world of fashion'. She was sophisticated, coquettish and surrounded by a number of suitors with 'fast' reputations.

Plainly a passionate woman, she excited Hayes sexually, but she frightened him as much as she attracted him. Besides Helen's assertive personality sometimes clashed with Fanny's. The dour Lucy on the other hand soothed him. She was a strict Methodist and a safer bet. Hayes's indecision lasted eighteen months.

Helen was certainly Fanny's choice. Fanny thought that if they married, Helen would keep Hayes nearby in Columbus, but if he married Lucy she might take him away.

Meanwhile, Helen toyed with Hayes, first encouraging him, then distancing herself, professing her love for him, then seeing other suitors. Judging by his diaries, Hayes derived a certain masochistic pleasure from this.

Then in 1852, Hayes threw caution in the wind and married Lucy. Nevertheless, he remained almost unhealthily attached to his sister Fanny, despite the fact that she was now married with children. When Fanny died in childbirth, Hayes told Lucy: 'You are sister Fanny to me now.'

Lucy was a passionate opponent of slavery and convinced her husband to take an abolitionist position. She was also an early advocate of women's rights. When her husband was a Congressman, she accompanied him on official visits to schools, hospitals and prisons.

To the men of the 23rd Ohio Volunteer Infantry, her husband's Civil War regiment, Lucy was known as 'Mother Lucy' for her tireless efforts in ministering to the wounded and comforting the dying. In the White House, she became 'Lemonade Lucy' because she banned alcohol from the premises.

In office, Hayes had to confront problems with America's changing attitudes to sex. His own cousin John Humphrey Noyes founded a group of Bible Communists, called the Perfectionists, who practised 'complex marriage'. They were hounded out of Vermont as promiscuous adulterers and established the Oneida Community, dedicated to free love, in

New York.

The major political problem, however, was the Mormons who were still practising polygamy. Hayes took a tough line with them, arresting those who married more than once and excluding those who advocated polygamy from office.

Anti-pornography campaigner Anthony Comstock pushed through a federal law banning obscene material from the mail in 1873. In June 1878, Ezra Hervy Heywood, founder of the New England Free Love League, was arrested for sending a pamphlet advocating the abolition of marriage through the posts.

'A man guilty of circulating, writing or publishing obscene books – books intended or calculated to corrupt the young – would find no favour with me,' Hayes said. But when Heywood was sent to jail, Hayes pardoned him on the grounds that his 'writings were objectionable but were not obscene, lascivious, lewd, or corrupting in the criminal sense'.

Despite her ban on alcohol, Lucy Hayes was a popular First Lady. Praise from prominent people filled six Morocco-bound volumes. Poems were penned by Henry Wadsworth Longfellow, Oliver Wendell Holmes, John Greenleaf Whittier. Mark Twain also made a wry contribution. 'Total abstinence is so excellent a thing,' he wrote, 'that it cannot be carried to too great an extreme. In my passion for it I even carry it so far as to totally abstain from Total Abstinence itself.'

XXVII
Ulysess S. Grant, #18
Whiskey

Born Hiram Ulysses Grant in 1822, he hated the idea of his name being abbreviated to HUG, so he abandoned the Hiram and added his mother's maiden name Simpson, making him U.S. – or 'Unconditional Surrender' – Grant.

Ulysses S. Grant was undoubtedly a great general, but he was useless as a president. Grant's administration was dogged by scandal and he admitted himself that accepting the presidency was the greatest mistake he made in his life. In fact, apart from generalship, Grant was useless at just about everything he turned his hand to in life due to his over-fondness for whiskey.

Julia Dent Grant, his wife, was one of the First Ladies who actually enjoyed her tenure of the White House. It was one of the few periods of her life that was not attended by deprivation and hardship. Brought up on a plantation near St Louis, Julia first met Ulysses S. Grant when her brother, his roommate, brought him home on vacation from West Point. She claimed the night before she met Grant that she had had a dream in which she met, fell in love with, and married an officer she did not know and had never seen.

Whatever the transcendent truth of this dream, on a pleasure trip they found themselves fording the swollen Gravois river in a light rig and she clung to him in fear of the water. This, Grant said, inspired him to ask for her hand in marriage. They became engaged and Julia wore his West Point ring thereafter. Her father opposed the match, saying that Grant was too poor. But Julia pointed out that as cash-starved slave-owners, they were no better off than he was.

The marriage was delayed until 1848 by Grant's service in the

Mexican war that added the state of Texas to the U.S. When he arrived back in his hometown of Bethel, Ohio, after the war with an attractive young woman, his family immediately took her to be Julia, the fiancée they had heard so much about. She was not – it was just someone he had picked up on the stagecoach.

After the war, Grant was stationed at Sackets Harbor, New York, where he eventually married Julia. Then the 4th Infantry was suddenly posted to Fort Vancouver in what would become Washington State. Grant left his wife and new-born son behind in the East, unwilling to risk their lives on the dangerous journey which would involve crossing the Isthmus of Panama,.

On the voyage, Grant struck up a friendship with Delia B. Sheffield. She claimed to be married but Grant did not believe her, saying she was too young. They reached the Isthmus of Panama on 13 July 1852, in the middle of the rainy season, and went by railroad as far as the Chagres river. From there, they travelled in flat-bottomed boats poled by 'stark naked' black 'natives' who apparently fascinated both Grant and Mrs Sheffield.

The posting was boring and the separation from his young family unsettled Grant. He tried his hand unsuccessfully at several business ventures, then sought solace in the bottle. In April 1854, he was found drunk in public and resigned his commission rather than face court-martial. Grant was reunited with Julia and his son, but hardship followed as Grant's business and farming ventures failed. The Civil War brought separation again when he returned to arms. Julia tried to join her husband as often as his duties allowed, but when she was not around, he missed her a lot and his heavy drinking 'seemed in part sexual', a contemporary said.

During his Presidential Candidacy in 1868, it was alleged that Grant had sired a child by a native-American woman in Vancouver. However, the alleged daughter was born less than nine months after Grant arrived there and her father was probably one Richard Grant. No one believed the allegation. Besides it was far more credible and defaming to play up the fact that he was a drunk.

Once in the White House, more allegations of sexual

impropriety were made against Grant. Typically, these came up as part of the notorious 'Whiskey Ring' scandal of 1875. Headed by General John McDonald, the ring skimmed millions of dollars of liquor taxes. Corruption was the deep state of the government. A telegram warning the ring of the investigation being conducted by the Internal Revenue Service was uncovered. It was signed 'Sylph'. One of the ring explained: '"Sylph" was a lewd woman with whom the President of the United States had been in intimate association, and... she had bothered and annoyed the President.' She continued to pester him even after he had broken off the affair. It was also said that she was 'unquestionably the handsomest woman in St. Louis. Her form was petite, and yet withal, a plumpness and development which made her a being whose tempting, luscious deliciousness was irresistible.' Again, everyone believed he was a drunk. But he was not like Donald Trump and no one believed that Grant was the sort of fellow who would consort with lewd women.

After the end of his torpid administration, Grant suffered a new business failure in 1884 and hardship returned for him and his wife. Before he died, he wrote his memoirs in which he claims never to have uttered a 'profane expletive', not even when in charge of a train of pack mules during the Mexican war, 'but I would have the charity to excuse those who may have done so'. The book became an instant bestseller.

Grant was helped by professional writer Adam Badeau. Gay, Badeau had joined Grant's staff during the Civil War in 1864 and the two men remained close for the rest of Grant's life. Badeau wrote several books about Grant but they lack a certain intimacy.

XXVIII

Andrew Johnson, #17

'Half dressed, dirty, shabby, with matted hair as though from mud.'

Abraham Lincoln was an impossible act to follow, and during his time in office Lincoln's successor Andrew Johnson got little credit for his lofty principles. He lacked the political skill to push through his conciliatory reconstruction plans after the Civil War and, for his pains, he was the first of the two U.S. Presidents ever impeached by Congress – in his case for replacing the Secretary of War.

Johnson was the only president never to have had a day's schooling in his life. He was born in an employee's shack at Casso's Inn, in Raleigh, North Carolina, where his father worked as an ostler and a janitor. He died of overexertion when Johnson was three after rescuing two friends from drowning. Johnson's mother married again and, when they were old enough, bound Andrew and his elder brother as apprentices to James Selby, a local tailor. They were to be fed and clothed in return for their work until they were twenty-one.

At sixteen, Johnson got into trouble for throwing stones at a woman's house in Raleigh and teasing her daughters. He also had fun flashing in front of the granddaughter of local aristocrat John Dereaux, streaking naked down the path outside her house. Threatened with arrest, Johnson grabbed his tailor's tools and fled first to Carthage and then to Laurens, South Carolina, where he set up as a journeyman tailor.

There, he fell in love with a beautiful girl named Mary Wood. She was eager and yielding to his amorous words, but her parents opposed the match of their beautiful daughter to a penniless illiterate.

When he returned to Raleigh, he found that there was a $10 reward on his head. His family sold up, loaded their possessions on to a cart and set out westwards across the Smokies. After a month's journey on the Daniel Boone trail, they stopped at Greeneville, Tennessee, where Johnson set up a tailor's shop.

As they arrived in town driving a blind pony hitched to a small cart carrying pots and pans, Johnson was spotted by Eliza McCardle. A friend remarked that he would make a fine husband for a Greeneville girl, once he had washed his face. Eliza said that she intended to be that girl. Within a year they were married. He was just eighteen and she seventeen.

Attractive with soft, wavy brown hair, hazel eyes and fine features, Eliza had a good basic education and she set about teaching Johnson to read and write. While he set about politicking in the back room of his tailor's shop, she raised five kids.

During the Civil War, Andrew Johnson was appointed military governor in Nashville. Eliza stayed in Greeneville to attend to business. When Jefferson Davis imposed martial law on East Tennessee and gave Unionists thirty six hours to leave, Eliza pleaded illness and was allowed to stay, but the Johnsons' property was impounded and she had to move in with relatives. Eventually she got permission to cross the lines and after an arduous journey joined her husband in Nashville. However, her health never recovered and she remained an invalid for the rest of her life.

She stayed in Nashville when her husband was sworn in as Vice President and feared for his safety after Lincoln's assassination. When she moved into the White House, she found the place had been wrecked by souvenir hunters. Congress appropriated $30,000 for renovations, but it was not nearly enough.

Eliza retired to a second-floor room and only twice came downstairs to appear in public – once when Hawaii's Queen Emma visited and once to attend the first children's ball held at the White House. Otherwise her eldest daughter Martha, the wife of Senator David T. Patterson, acted as hostess. Eliza died six months after her husband in 1875.

Throughout his career Johnson had trouble with his sons, Robert and Charles. Both became alcoholics and a constant source of embarrassment to him. In 1863, Charles died after falling from a horse, presumably drunk. Robert went on to become his father's private secretary, but the responsibility did not improve his behaviour.

'There is too much whiskey in the White House,' complained Johnson's envoy to Berlin Norman Judd, 'and harlots go into the private secretary's office unannounced in broad daylight. Mrs C. did that... while a friend of mine was waiting for an audience – and she came out leaning on the arm of the half-drunken son of the President.'

To add to his troubles, Johnson received letters from pardon-broker Jennie A. Perry, who attempted to blackmail him with tales about an illegitimate son, though apparently he never took her threats seriously.

President Johnson himself liked a drink. When he was sworn in as Lincoln's Vice President he was famously drunk and made a rambling incoherent speech. When the Chief Justice and Senator Foot went to tell him that Lincoln was dead and he was now the President, they found him 'half dressed, dirty, shabby, with matted hair as though from mud in the gutter, apparently trying to overcome a hangover'. After the oath of office had been administered, they went to inform Secretary of War Edwin Stanton. When they returned they found Johnson asleep again, so they dressed him as best they could and took him to the White House. There, they bathed him and called for a doctor, a barber and a tailor to fix him up. It was only in the late afternoon that they allowed visitors in to assure themselves that a new man had his hands firmly on the tiller of state.

Johnson and that other famous dipsomaniac General Ulysses S. Grant went on a whistle stop tour of the U.S. The crowds booed Johnson and demanded to see Grant. Sadly the great general was usually too inebriated to put in an appearance.

Robert Johnson eventually committed suicide in 1869.

XXIX

Abraham Lincoln, #16

'A strong, if not terrible, passion'

There are have been a number of attempts to prove that Abraham Lincoln was gay, largely based on the fact that he slept with other men in the same bed. On the other hand, William H. Herndale, Lincoln's partner in his law practice, said: 'Lincoln had a strong, if not terrible, passion for women. He could hardly keep his hands off a woman; and yet, much to his credit, he lived a pure and virtuous life. His idea was that a woman has as much right to violate the marriage vow as a man – no more, no less. His sense of right, his sense of justice, his honor, forbade his violating his marriage vow.' Furthermore, men often shared a bed in the nineteenth century simply to save money.

The young Abraham Lincoln seems to have been awkward in the company of women, perhaps due to his 'terrible passion'. He used to tell a story that shows he was interested in the opposite sex from an early age. In later life, he related an erotic fantasy from his time in Indiana when he must have been between the ages of seven and nine.

'When I was a little codger,' he wrote, 'one day a wagon with a lady and two girls and a man broke down near us, and while they were fixing up, they cooked in our kitchen. The woman had books and read us stories, and they were the first I had ever heard. I took a great fancy to one of the girls; and when they were gone I thought of her a great deal, and one day, when I was sitting out in the sun by the house, I wrote a story in my mind. I thought I took my father's horse and followed the wagon, and finally found it, and they were surprised to see me. I talked with the girl and persuaded her to elope with me; and that night I put her on my horse, and we started off across the prairie. After several hours we came to a camp; and when we rode up we found it was the one we had left a few hours before, and we went in. The next night we tried again, and the same thing happened – the horse came back to the same place. I stayed until I had persuaded her father to give her to me. I always meant to write the story out and publish it, and I began once, but I concluded that it was not much of a story. But I think it was the beginning of love in me.'

Lincoln probably believed that he was, like his mother Nancy, illegitimate. One traditional tale says that one-time Vice President and advocate of slavery John C. Calhoun was his father, after having a brief affair with his mother when she was a tavern maid. But there are several other versions and the truth has been lost in the mists of time.

Lincoln would certainly have been familiar with the physical side of love from an early age. He was brought up in a one-room log cabin with his mother, father Thomas Lincoln and sister. In 1818, when Lincoln was nine, his mother died of milk sickness, a poisoning caused by white snakeroot. When cows grazed on it, they passed its toxic quality on in their milk. The family fell into total squalor for almost a year until Thomas Lincoln returned to his hometown in Kentucky where he found a second wife, Sarah Bush Johnson, a widow, and brought her and her three children back to Indiana. Tradition has it that Thomas Lincoln had wooed Sarah before he had married Nancy. Learning that she was a widow when he was a widower, he seized the opportunity the second time around.

Lincoln doted on his stepmother, whom he described as his 'angel mother'. She encouraged him to read. His newly extended family now meant he was surrounded by girls. As well as his older sister Sarah, his stepmother brought with her two stepsisters, Betsy and Mathilda. The newly-weds, Lincoln and the girls were all crammed together in a single room and there can have been little chance for privacy.

During his brief schooling, Lincoln became attached to Katie Roby, but she married James Gentry, the son of Lincoln's employer, because his prospects seemed so much brighter.

Seventeen-year-old Caroline Meeker, niece of the local squire, fancied Lincoln whom she first saw defending himself in a Kentucky courtroom. Her uncle was also impressed and invited Lincoln to the house. Caroline waylaid him in the orchard and invited him to a cornhusking the following week.

The local custom was that, at a cornhusking, any man who found a red ear was allowed to kiss the girl of his choice. Lincoln did not find a red husk, but Caroline did. She hid it under her apron and, surreptitiously, slipped it to him. Then, in front of everyone, he kissed her. Later, he walked her home, but the penniless young Lincoln had no chance to take the affair any further. The aristocratic Caroline married a local landowner, but she never forgot her first, young choice.

When Lincoln was twenty one, his family moved to Illinois. He acted quite uninhibitedly with older married women, but in front of younger women he became shy and awkward. The matrons of New Salem took him under their wing and he formed close attachments to at least three married women.

Despite his shyness, Lincoln's name was also linked with several young women who went on to marry other men. One of them was Polly Warnick, the daughter of Major Warnick who employed Lincoln as a rail-splitter. She saw him when he made his first political speech and was impressed. But his lack of money and prospects stood in the way of the courtship yet again, and Lincoln was soon seen escorting other girls.

It was around that time he met Ann Rutledge, the daughter of the inn-owner John Rutledge who was a founder of New Salem. Ann, it is said, was the love of Lincoln's life. She was 'a gentle, amiable maiden without any of the airs of your city belles, but winsome and comely withal, a blonde in complexion with golden hair, cherry red lips and bonny blue eyes'.

There was a fly in the ointment, however. Ann was already engaged to the richest man in New Salem, John McNeil, although that romance had run into difficulty. It seems that McNeil's name was really John McNamar and he was living under a false name because he had swindled his parents out of everything they owned. Soon after his engagement to Ann, he headed back east to sort out some financial problems and never returned. By the time Lincoln met Ann, McNamar had been gone two years and she waited every day for a letter. She had received no formal release from her engagement.

Lincoln proposed to her, but he was not the only one in the field. His friend, Sam Hill, had also asked for her hand. He was rich while Lincoln, as ever, was penniless. Ann preferred the tall, awkward Lincoln, but her family were in dire financial straits, so marriage to Lincoln was out of the question.

In the summer of 1835, typhoid and malaria swept through the Mid-West. Ann died of 'brain fever' and, it is said, Lincoln's heart was buried with her.

Lincoln too had the symptoms of malaria, but he threw himself into his work to mend both his body and his broken heart. Whether Ann Rutledge ever loved Lincoln, we cannot know. It was said that she really died of a broken heart over John McNamar.

One of Lincoln's married lady friends was Mrs Bennett Abell. When the unmarried Mary Owens came to stay in her house, the twenty-five-year-old Lincoln was called in to keep her company. Mary had 'fair skin, deep blue eyes, with dark curly hair; height, five feet five inches, weighing about one hundred and fifty pounds'. She was handsome and well-educated. He proposed, but she refused him after some ungentlemanly behaviour on his part. They had been out riding with a number of other couples when they came to a ford. The other men helped their ladies across, but Lincoln rode on ahead.

'You are a nice fellow,' she chided when she caught up with him. 'I suppose you did not care whether my neck was broken or not.'

He replied simply that she was 'plenty smart to take care of herself'. This was not taken as a compliment.

They were forced to separate when he was elected to the Illinois state legislature at Springfield in 1837. There, he became enamoured of Mrs Orille H. Browning, a colleague's wife, though he continued writing to Mary Owens. Springfield was full of pretty women and as an up-and-coming young lawyer and politician, Lincoln was spoilt for choice. It was then that Lincoln 'began to discover the flaws' in Mary Owens's beauty. He decided that she was old and overweight, and 'rather too willing to marry'. However, being a mortal, if not morbid, man, he continued to press his suit. She, to his surprise, rejected him once again. To his relief he could return to Kentucky.

Free again, Lincoln began to play the local marriage field. He was perfectly placed to do so. Mrs Browning had two handsome and unmarried sisters who, between them, knew every eligible young woman in Springfield, if not the whole of Illinois.

Mary Todd was not quite twenty one when she met Lincoln. She was a celebrated beauty from Lexington, Kentucky, who had moved to Springfield after her mother died and her father married again. She was bright and vivacious. Her hair was chestnut, her eyes blue and her lips cherry-red and seductive. She was short and fiery – 'an alluring armful for a courageous man'.

They met at a ball given to mark the opening of the General Assembly of the State of Illinois. Every marriageable girl in Springfield was there. Mary wore a silk dress over seven or eight starched (or flounced) white petticoats but 'did not wear a great deal above her waist, for she knew she had an attractive neck and shoulders and she made the most of them'. That night, it was said, she dressed 'within an inch of her life. There was not a man there who did not turn and look after her, nor a woman who did not look after her without turning.'

Undoubtedly the belle of the ball, she spent most of the night dancing. But she noticed one tall man who did not dance with her. He stood around telling stories, so she commanded her cousin, Major John Todd Stuart, to bring him to her so they could be properly introduced. Lincoln was immediately captivated.

She chose him over all her suitors, she said later, because she knew he would be president – 'that was why I married him; for you know he is not handsome'. They became engaged, but she soon began complaining that he did not visit her as often as he should. He explained that he had a state election to fight.

When he was re-elected that excuse no longer held true. Lincoln became so exasperated by her demands on his time that he wrote her a letter breaking off the engagement, but a friend persuaded him to go and tell her in person. Mary wept copiously. It was ironic, she said, that she who had broken so many hearts was now being rejected. As he left, she demanded that he kiss her goodbye. The embrace was so warm and passionate, that Lincoln went home more engaged than ever.

At the same time, Mary Todd was flirting with another young politician, Stephen A. Douglas. They would go dancing whenever he was in town and the two of them were seen walking arm-in-arm in broad daylight. Worse, Lincoln did not reveal the slightest hint of jealousy.

At that time the young blonde Matilda Edwards, daughter of the governor of Illinois, had come to stay with Mary. The two girls shared the same bed – and the same suitor it seemed. Next time Mary went dancing with Douglas, she saw, over his shoulder, Matilda deep in conversation with Lincoln.

Matilda's parents saw the danger and lined up other eligible males for Matilda. Joshua Fry Speed, Lincoln's roommate, proposed and was refused. Thereupon Douglas then fell under Matilda's spell. He proposed and he too was rejected.

Mary became frantic. Whenever she flirted wildly with other men, Lincoln took no notice. She herself grew increasingly jealous of the growing attachment between Matilda and Lincoln. Her discomfort was all the greater because she and Matilda remained bedfellows.

Mary took the matter up with Lincoln, but he was unrepentant, even giving the impression that he loved Matilda more than he did Mary. Matilda, too, was brazen. If Mary could not keep hold of her lover, she said, she could not expect any help from other girls.

One night in bed Mary plucked up the courage to ask Matilda:

'Do you think Mr Lincoln really ever loved you?'

'Mercy, no!' said Matilda. 'He only thought he did.'

'Did he ever propose to you?' asked Mary

Matilda laughed. 'Propose to me? He never even paid me a compliment.'

Matilda Edwards went on, reputedly, to break more hearts – both men's and women's – than anyone in the history of Springfield, before marrying a man from out of town.

Mary could not escape the idea that Lincoln may love another and on 1 January, 1841 she broke off the engagement. In some versions of the story, the wedding was planned for that day and Lincoln simply did not show up. In others, Lincoln, half-crazy with passion, openly declared his love for Matilda Edwards. Meanwhile, Mary took up with a widower, but decided that she could not take on his children.

Whatever happened, Lincoln was so distraught that he had to spend several months away from Springfield, and he went to Louisville, Kentucky, with Joshua Fry Speed. As roommates Speed and Lincoln shared the same double bed and American gay activist groups have since claimed, on this evidence, that Lincoln was gay.

Even in his distress at losing Matilda and Mary, Lincoln did not shy away from other women. He had two tickets for *Babes in the Wood* and was determined not to let them go to waste. He took with him seventeen-year-old Sarah Richard, whom he had known since she was twelve. He later proposed to her, but she turned him down because of the difference in their ages. He was thirty three at the time. Nevertheless, their relationship was close and it lasted fifteen months.

Lincoln continued to be active in politics. He wrote an article for the *Sangamon Journal* ridiculing his political rival, Irishman James Shields. The article was signed 'Aunt Rebecca'. Mary Todd read it and liked it so much that she wrote a second article, continuing the satire and using the same penname.

Shields was annoyed by the first article and enraged by the second. He demanded to know who had written the two articles.

To protect Mary, the editor of the *Journal* told him that Lincoln had written both of them. Shields challenged Lincoln to a duel which ended without bloodshed when mutual friends intervened.

Slowly the truth of the matter came out in public and the names of Lincoln and Mary Todd were once again linked. Several secret meetings were arranged and on 4 November 1842, they were married. Recently unearthed evidence suggests that Mary was pregnant at the time and had trapped Lincoln into marriage.

The union was not a happy one. Mary Todd mixed extravagant flirtations with other men with jealous tantrums if he even so much as looked at another woman. But he was above reproach. Judge Davis told Lincoln's legal partner William Herndon in 1865: 'Mr Lincoln's honor saved many a woman.' Herndon agreed, saying: 'I have seen Lincoln tempted, and have seen him reject the approach of women.'

In 1846, Lincoln was elected to the U.S. Congress and Mary greatly enjoyed being part of Washington social life. They even took a little time off for a romantic cruise on the Great Lakes. However, his radical anti-slavery views found disfavour with the Illinois electorate. He was not reelected and Mary found her social aspirations dashed.

She set up home in Springfield and employed a number of maids. Many quit because they found Mary's tantrums intolerable and some expressed sympathy for Lincoln. All of them testified to her temper and that Lincoln, slow as he was, loved to hold her in his arms.

In 1858, Lincoln came to national prominence with a series of debates on slavery with Mary's former lover Stephen A. Douglas. Known as the 'Little Giant', Douglas was the Democratic incumbent in the Senate race. Lincoln was his opponent for the newly formed Republican party.

Lincoln lost the election, but his speeches were reproduced in newspapers across America. This was enough to win him the Republican nomination and then the Presidency in 1861. As First Lady, Mary was in her element. She spent lavishly money on fashionable clothes and her daring décolleté gowns were widely criticised.

'Mrs Lincoln had her bosom on exhibition,' wrote one visitor to the White House. Her extravagance during the Civil War was a continual political embarrassment – particularly as she was a Southerner and from a slave-owning family – and her gowns were so expensive that Lincoln worried about re-election, simply to continue his presidential salary.

Mary became so unpopular that she was charged with treason. Lincoln appeared before a Congressional hearing to quash the charges. Mary's sympathies were indeed with the South and Union soldiers sang ribald songs linking her sexually to the Confederate's president, Jefferson Davis.

Confederate propaganda also spread rumours about Mary and the men she was alleged to be planning to elope to a slave state with. These were without foundation. But it has to be said that, while in the White House, she continued to enjoy the attention of many men, particularly Charles Sumner who secured her a pension after the assassination of her husband.

During his time in office, Lincoln became far more comfortable around younger women and his wife felt she had to keep an eye on him constantly. He would tease her by listing the names of the women he fancied and those to whom he might talk. When Mary was out of town, Lincoln was in his element. He loved the racy dialogue of Shakespeare's comedies and would go to see dancing girls. One night at Ford's Theatre, he took a private box and carried on 'a hefty flirtation with the girls in the flies'. It was not unusual for Lincoln to receive pretty pictures or saucy notes from schoolgirls after the war. When he was shot, Laura Keene, star of *Our American Cousin* the play that was on that night, cradled his head in her lap.

After Lincoln died, William Herndon went about the country proclaiming that Lincoln had never loved his wife and had only married her after being nagged into matrimony. The love of Lincoln's life, Herndon said, was Ann Rutledge.

Mary Lincoln spent much of her time abroad after the death of her husband. Travelling back from France in 1880, on board the *Amérique*, she became friendly with the notorious actress Sarah Bernhardt. Slowly, Mary became mentally unstable. She died in 1882. On her finger was a ring that Lincoln had given her. In it were inscribed the words: 'Love is Eternal.'

XXX

James Buchanan, #15

'I have gone a wooing to several gentlemen.'

Another of the 'log-cabin' presidents, James Buchanan first saw the light of day at Stony Batter near Mercersburg, Pennsylvania. From an early age he was determined to make something of himself.

As a youth he moved to Lancaster, Pennsylvania. After graduating, he quit the company of the footloose young men he used to drink with in the backroom of taverns to spend evenings in the parlours of fashionable homes. His ploy was to make himself agreeable to wealthy families in the hope of ensnaring an unmarried daughter. As a rising young lawyer, he was himself an extremely eligible bachelor.

He became attached to Anne Coleman, the daughter of the ironmaster Robert Coleman, one of America's first millionaires. They became engaged in 1819, but Anne's father did not approve of James. He was a trustee of Dickson College, where Buchanan had come within a whisker of being dismissed for disorderly conduct. Buchanan's student friends had been a wild bunch and Buchanan himself had lost three tracts of land in a bet.

That year saw a financial panic and, at its peak, the old Federalist Party – the party of George Washington and John Adams – began falling apart. Buchanan was frantically busy trying to prevent the collapse of the Columbia Bridge Company and politicking for the party. He had little time for his fiancée and Lancaster society whispered that it was not Anne he was interested in but the Coleman fortune.

Returning from a business trip to Philadelphia, Buchanan dropped around to see Mrs William Jenkins. With her was staying the pretty and charming Miss Hubley. The gossip this visit inspired sent Anne into a fit of jealousy. She wrote to Buchanan breaking the engagement off and went to stay with her sister Margaret in Philadelphia. Before the couple could be reconciled, however, Anne had died in mysterious circumstances, possibly suicide. Buchanan wrote a note to Anne's father expressing his deep love for Anne and asking to be allowed to attend the funeral. The letter was returned unopened, further fuelling gossip that Anne had committed suicide when she believed her love to be unrequited.

What part Buchanan might have played in the death of Anne Coleman will never be known. Papers, which Buchanan intimated revealed all, were lodged in a New York bank during the Civil War to protect them from Confederate troops. But when Buchanan died, the sealed papers were destroyed without being opened, as he had stipulated in his will.

It has often been said that this incident prompted Buchanan to remain a bachelor for the rest of his life. However, in 1837, Buchanan wrote to Mrs Francis Preston Blair, saying: 'I would gladly join your party to the Hermitage next year... but long ere that time I expect to be married and have the cares of a family resting upon my shoulders.'

Senator William Rufus De Vane King of Alabama was also teasing Buchanan about suffering 'the anxieties of love' and neglecting his work. The woman in question was probably Mary Snyder, the young niece of Thomas Kittera. Kittera and his sister Ann brought up Mary after her mother died. They also raised Buchanan's niece Elizabeth Huston, after his sister Sarah died. So it is likely that a marriage of convenience was arranged to keep the money in the family. However, it is also possible that Buchanan intended to marry Ann Kittera, Thomas's sister, for the same reason. But subsequent wrangles over the inheritance scuppered his plans.

Later, Buchanan became seriously interested in Anna Payne, who lived with her famous aunt Dolley Madison in the grey house on Lafayette Square in Washington. At the time it was fashionable for young women to marry men old enough to be their grandfathers. The resulting unions were rarely satisfactory.

Buchanan let his better judgment overrule his heart and explained his decision to his intended in verse.

A match of age with youth can only bring
The farce of 'winter dancing with spring'.
Blooming nineteen can never well agree
With the dull age of half a century.

Until the end of his life, Buchanan still fondly harboured the idea that he would one day be married.

'I feel that it is not good for a man to be alone,' he wrote to his old friend Mrs James J. Roosevelt, 'and should not be astonished to find myself married to some old maid who can nurse me when I am sick, provide good dinners for me when I am well, and not expect from me any very ardent romantic affection.'

In fact, he already had a woman to do just that. He employed Ester Parker – or Miss Hetty as she was known – in 1834, when she was twenty eight, to be his housekeeper. She stayed with him until he died thirty-four years later.

Buchanan was sixty five when he became president, but it seemed to give him a new lease of life. On a trip through the South, the newspapers reported him to be 'gay and frisky as a young buck'. His companion on the journey, Secretary of the Interior Jacob Thompson, said that Buchanan 'kissed hundreds of pretty girls which made his mouth water'.

Mrs Kate Thompson was his favourite among the wives of his cabinet ministers. She was an 'easy and free-hearted woman' who loved to flirt. Buchanan was captivated by her passion and impetuous nature and would drop by to visit her when her husband was out of town.

He then became enamoured of Mrs Bass, a married woman with three young children. It was noted by the ladies of Washington society that the President would dress up in his finest clothes when he was to see her. Buchanan took her on a vacation, which was marred when an abolitionist ran off with her maid servant.

However, during Buchanan's lifetime, there were persistent rumours that he was gay. He had a twenty-three-year friendship with Senator William Rufus De Vane King. They were roommates in Washington and King's 'fastidious habits and conspicuous intimacy with bachelor Buchanan gave rise to some cruel jibes'.

Andrew Jackson called King 'Miss Nancy'. He was also known as Buchanan's 'better half', 'his wife' and 'Aunt Fancy'. And when King became Vice President under Buchanan's predecessor Franklin Pierce, he was known as 'Mrs Vice President'. Buchanan's own Postmaster Aaron V. Brown called King 'Mrs B' and made smirking references to 'Mr Buchanan and wife' and 'Aunt Fancy… rigged out in her best clothes'.

King himself penned long and intimate letters to Buchanan. When appointed ambassador to France, King wrote: 'I am selfish enough to hope you will not be able to procure an associate who will cause you to feel no regret at our separation.'

Knowledge of their relationship was not confined to Washington insiders. The contemporary press also speculated about Buchanan and King's relationship. When they died, their relatives destroyed their correspondence. But some survived. In one letter Buchanan wrote to King, after King left for France in 1844, he said: 'I am now solitary and alone, having no companion in the house with me. I have gone a wooing to several gentlemen, but have not succeeded with any one of them.'

King was the United States' only unmarried Vice President, and Buchanan the only unmarried President.

XXXI
Franklin Pierce, #14

From an early age, Franklin Pierce had believed that he was destined to go through life alone. Perhaps he should have. His marriage in 1834 to Jane Means Appleton, the shy, frail, tubercular daughter of his college principal was dogged with tragedy. Their first child, a son, died after three days. Their second, Frank, died of typhus at the age of four. Their third son Benny was healthy enough, but just two months before Pierce was sworn in as president, he was killed in a train crash near Andover, Massachusetts. His parents were on the train and escaped unscathed, but they watched the child die before their eyes. He was just eleven.

Mrs Pierce saw this tragedy as a sign from God and withdrew from public life. Pierce went on alone, gloomy and distracted. The loss of his son was a punishment for his own shortcomings, he thought. He refrained from taking the usual oath of office, simply affirming his loyalty to the Constitution instead.

Jane Pierce was too distraught to attend the inauguration and there was no inauguration ball. When Jane did arrive in Washington, the sombre mood deepened further with the death of Abigail Fillmore and, the following month, Vice-President Rufus King.

The loss of their third and final son pushed Jane Pierce over the brink of sanity and Franklin into heavy drinking.

Never strong, Jane's health declined in the White House. For years after, the Pierces travelled to the West Indies and across Europe in the hope that a change of climate and scenery would restore her health. Everywhere she went she carried her son's Bible and a box of hair from her 'precious dead' – her sons, her mother and her little sister. Nothing could shake her morbid affliction and the Pierces returned to New Hampshire where Jane died in 1863. She is buried near the grave of her son Benny.

Pierce was, by all accounts, a good-looking and active man. But finding a new partner seemed to be the last thing on his mind. He drank himself to death six years later.

XXXII
Millard Fillmore, #13

These days an affair between a pupil and schoolteacher would be fraught with issues, but the thirteenth President of the United States, Millard Fillmore, fell in love with his school-teacher as a school boy and married her – unlike the wife of President Macron of France, she was unmarried and did not yet have children.

Her name was Abigail Powers and she was born in Saratoga County, New York, in 1798. She was the daughter of a prominent Baptist preacher who died shortly after she was born. Her mother had moved westwards, thinking that her scant funds would stretch further in a more remote region and she educated her son and daughter herself, using her late husband's library.

At the age of twenty one, Abigail was teaching in New Hope, when nineteen-year-old Millard Fillmore joined her school as a pupil. He was the son of a dirt farmer, but his six-feet sturdy frame aroused her admiration and his dignified bearing, she thought, promised a bright future. He, in turn, fell for her large, dark eyes and her long black hair that was drawn tightly back across her head. It was the first time he had been around female company and during the bitterly cold winter months of 1819 they fell in love.

Abigail helped Fillmore in his struggle to become a lawyer and they married in February 1826, three years after he had been admitted to the bar. As they were still poor, Abigail continued working as a teacher.

Six years later, in 1832, when Fillmore was first elected to the House of Representatives, they had moved into a six-room house in Buffalo. Though she preferred books and cultivating her flower garden, she made an effort to enter society as the wife of a politician.

As a congressman, Fillmore was considered competent, if

colourless – an 'able and faithful public servant,' John Quincy
Adams complained. Always faultlessly groomed, he neither smoked
nor drank. He would seek out 'temperance hotels' to stay in when
he was away from home. He also had a horror of gambling and still
suffered agonies of guilt because he had won a turkey in a raffle
when he was fifteen.

'That was the beginning and the end of my gambling,' he said.
'I have never since gambled to the value of one cent.'

In the White House, Abigail presided over state dinners and
receptions, but ill health dogged her and she asked her daughter
Abby to take over her social duties.

With a grant from Congress, Abigail set about organising a
White House library in an upstairs room where Abby kept her
piano, guitar and harp. There was not so much as a bible in the
White House when she arrived. She also installed the first bathtub
in the Executive Mansion. The Fillmores always travelled in a
splendid wine-coloured carriage, with blue silk seats and silver-
mounted harnesses which had been presented to Abigail by the
women of New York. The coach cost $2,000, the horses $1,000
each. It was the Cadillac of its day.

At the inauguration of her husband's successor Franklin Pierce,
Abigail caught a severe chill and died a few weeks later in the
Willard Hotel, probably of bronchial pneumonia. Congress
adjourned as a mark of respect and her body was returned to
Buffalo for burial.

When their daughter Abby died of cholera the following year,
Fillmore took off on a trip to Europe. He met Pope Pius IX in
Rome; and in England, Queen Victoria, who said that he was the
most handsome man she had ever seen. Abroad he was also
frequently seen at the opera in the company of a number of
beautiful American women.

Back in America, he married Mrs Caroline C. McIntosh, a
wealthy widow. She was childless and had a tragic air about her
which caused some to compare her to the Mona Lisa grown old.
But the marriage brought him the largest mansion in Buffalo.

XXXIII
Zachary Taylor, #12

The thrusting Zachary Taylor, it seems, did not even marry his 'wife' Margaret Mackall Smith Taylor, the daughter of a well-to-do Maryland planter and a woman of genteel upbringing. Although a marriage licence was issued on 18 June 1810, there is no record of a ceremony being performed and no return was lodged with the marriage records of Jefferson County, Kentucky, where Taylor was stationed at the time. There are records, however, of their six children, all but one born in or around Louisville, Kentucky.

Old Rough and Ready, as Taylor was known in the army, was not much of a catch. At best, he was said to be 'an ordinary-looking man'. Others paint him as downright ugly – dumpy, thick-necked with a large head. He had a big nose, thick lips puckered in a permanent scowl and his bow legs were so short that his orderly had to help him into the saddle of his favourite war horse, 'Old Whitey'. A second lieutenant in his command wrote home: 'Taylor is short and very heavy, with pronounced face lines and grey hair, wears an old oil cloth, a dusty green coat, a frightful pair of trousers and on horseback looks like a toad.'

During the Mexican war, Taylor commanded the Indiana Volunteers. They were about to leave for the war when one of them accidentally tore the shirt from the breast of a companion, revealing his comrade-in-arms to be a woman. She explained that she had a father in Texas but did not have the money to get there. Taylor's men had a whip round and paid her fare.

Taylor himself was less charitable. He opposed the marriage of his second daughter, Knox, to a young lieutenant in his command. The lieutenant's name was Jefferson Davis, who went on to lead the Confederacy to defeat. Shortly after their wedding, Davis took his young bride home to Mississippi where she caught malaria and died. Taylor never forgave him.

When Margaret Taylor heard that the Whigs intended to nominate her husband for president in 1848, she decried it as 'a plot to deprive her of his society and shorten his life by unnecessary care and responsibility'.

She was right. Taylor died in office.

During his time in the White House, she took no part in the formal social functions. It is said, she preferred to spend her time in her room smoking a corn-cob pipe. Her twenty-two-year-old daughter Betty Knox Bliss acted as the 'Lady of the White House'. She organised stately dinners and lively dances, and was said by a visitor to combine 'the artlessness of a rustic belle and the grace of a duchess', Margaret herself remained upstairs, venturing out solely to go to church. Following the sudden death of her husband, she left Washington directly after the funeral and never spoke of the White House again.

XXXIV
James K. Polk, #11

Gloom descended over the White House when James Polk entered the White House. The First Lady was the forbidding Sarah Childress Polk. She was an educated woman, a rare thing in the nineteenth century. Her wealthy father had sent her to the Moravians' women's academy at Salem, North Carolina.

James K Polk – characterised by historian Carl R. Fish as 'the least conspicuous man who had ever been nominated for President' – and there was stiff nineteenth-century competition – had already begun his political career when they met and it is said that his political patron, Andrew Jackson, encouraged the romance. The couple married on 1 January 1824. She was twenty and he was twenty eight.

The marriage was childless and Sarah devoted herself to promoting his political career, helping him write speeches, dealing with his correspondence and giving him advice.

Sarah entertained with high style in the White House but, a devout woman, she prohibited dancing. Even at the inaugural ball, when the Polks arrived, the dancing ceased and resumed only after they had left. She would not go to the theatre or to horse races and discouraged visitors to the White House on a Sunday.

Polk died three months after leaving office, but Sarah survived another forty two years, turning their home Polk Place in Nashville into a shrine to her husband's memory.

XXXV
John Tyler, #10
'You spend so much time kissing.'

When President Harrison died in office, his Vice President John Tyler succeeded him and instantly brought scandal to the White House. Two years before he succeeded unexpectedly to the presidency, his wife Letitia had been crippled by a stroke. She moved into the White House with her husband, but lived in seclusion on the second floor, attending only one public function there – the wedding of their daughter Elizabeth.

They had married in 1813 and, although his letters talk of love, their marriage was really about uniting two sizeable fortunes. He was less than ardent. Three weeks before the wedding, Tyler confessed that he dare not even kiss her hand because she looked 'so perfectly reserved and modest'. Six days before the ceremony, Tyler wrote to a friend saying that he was approaching his nuptials like 'an old man'. However, by all accounts, Letitia was a great beauty. They remained happily married for twenty nine years and had seven children.

Letitia Tyler was the first president's wife to die in the White House. She passed away peacefully on 10 September 1842, with a damask rose in her hand. Four months later, in January 1843, Tyler met twenty-two-year-old Julia Gardiner. She was introduced to him at the White House by Congressman Fernando Wood.

Julia was renowned as the 'Rose of Long Island'. She was raven-haired with a radiant complexion, an hourglass waist and a full bust. President Tyler found her dark oval eyes animated and her full lips irresistible.

Julia was no stranger to love. During a European trip she had been courted by a Belgian nobleman and a War Office official in

England. And she had already made a number of conquests in Washington.

In fact she was a model. In 1839, she had posed for an advertisement for a department store alongside an older man dressed as a dandy. The handbill caused something of a scandal. Then, a few months later, a poem by one 'Romeo Ringdove' appeared on the front page of the *Brooklyn Daily News* singing the praises of the 'Rose of Long Island' with such immortal lines as:

> When gallants buzz like bees around
> Who sweets from flowers suck,
> Where shall the man so vain be found
> As hopes this rose to pluck.

For nineteenth-century America, this was pretty racy stuff.

At the White House reception where they met, Tyler was immediately smitten. So effusive were the 'thousand compliments' that he paid her that those nearby 'looked and listened in perfect amazement'. He had never been like this with his wife when she was still alive.

Julia was impressed too. She wrote: 'We could not help commenting, after we left the room, upon the silvery sweetness of his voice... the incomparable grace of his bearing, and the elegant ease of his conversation.'

Her sister Margaret, who was also there, was less enthusiastic and recalled later that the President was a rather jolly old man.

However, John Tyler had a rival for Julia's affections – his own son John Jr, who bombarded her with bad poetry. John Jr's unsuccessful attempts to divorce his wife Mattie Rochelle Tyler were common gossip around Washington. Margaret and Julia were also befriended by a second son, Robert Tyler, but found him 'not handsome'.

Meeting the President again at a whist drive at the White House, Julia was teased about her suitors. Tyler demanded to know how many she had 'in the name of the President of the United States'.

'He had quite a flirtation with Julia,' Margaret reported, 'and played several games of All Fours with her.'

Thomas Cooper, Robert Tyler's father-in-law, saw trouble coming. 'Do you see the President playing Old Sledge with Miss Gardiner,' he said. 'It will be in the *Globe* tomorrow.' The papers, however, did not pick up on this hand of cards. Nor did they pick up on the fact that, after the party, Margaret and Julia went upstairs to the presidential apartments.

When they made a move to leave 'what does he do but give me a kiss,' wrote Margaret excitedly. 'He proceeded to treat Julia in the same manner when she snatched away her hand and flew down the stairs with the President after her around the chairs and tables until at last he caught her. It was truly amusing.'

President Tyler and Julia conducted a whirlwind courtship amid a storm of rumour and vicious gossip as Tyler was still officially in mourning at the time. There was even some rivalry between Julia and her sister Margaret for the heart of the President.

'He was extremely affectionate,' Margaret recorded. 'Julia declared he was rather too tender, for he gave her three kisses while I received only two.'

Along with her sister and her father, Julia joined the President on the steam frigate *Princeton* for a cruise down the Potomac in February 1844. Tragedy struck when Julia's father was killed in a freak explosion. Tyler comforted her and they grew even closer.

Then at Washington's birthday in the White House on 22 February 1843, Tyler spotted Julia dancing with a young naval officer and could control himself no longer. As the young man's commander-in-chief, he cut in and led Julia away. Then he asked Julia straight out to marry him.

'I said, "No, no, no," she recalled later, "and shook my head with each word, which flung the tassel of my Greek cap into his face with every move. It was undignified, but it amused me very much to see his expression as he tried to make love to me and the tassel brushed his face".'

Tyler was not to be brushed off. He began writing love poems to Julia. He was so ardent that she was forced to inform her family of the President's proposal. They thought she should wait a few months to make sure of her feelings, especially as she was also being pursued by Judge John McLean. The fifty-seven-year-old McLean eventually stepped aside, telling a colleague that if he were twenty five years younger he'd have cut the President out.

Tyler's son Robert, meanwhile, was still writing letters wooing Julia, while Tyler's own love letters were read aloud by the whole of the Gardiner family and sent to their lawyers 'for perusal'.

Eventually Tyler wrote to Julia's mother making a formal request for her hand and guaranteeing, after the recent death of Julia's father, that he would maintain her financial and social status.

In March 1843, Tyler and his young love had come to a 'definite understanding', though no formal engagement was announced. Julia's mother Juliana was still against the match – after all, she herself was nine years younger than her prospective son-in-law – but in the end, she had no alternative but to accept it.

Even Tyler's friends thought he was making a fool of himself. In March 1844, while riding in his carriage, Tyler told Henry A. Wise, a Virginia politician, that he intended to marry a much younger woman.

'Have you really won her?' Wise asked in amazement.

'Yes,' said the President. 'And why should I not?'

'You are far too advanced in life to be imprudent in a love-scrape,' his friend said.

'How imprudent?' asked Tyler, pressing for an explanation.

'Easily,' said Wise. 'You are not only past middle age, but you are President of the United States, and that is a dazzling dignity which may charm a damsel more than the man she marries.'

'Pooh!' exclaimed the President. 'Why, my dear sir, I am just full in my prime!'

Wise was not convinced and told Tyler the story of a James River planter who had decided to marry a younger woman and asked his house slave, Toney, what he thought of the idea.

'Massa, you think you can stand that?' replied Toney.

'Yes, Toney, why not? I am yet strong and I can now, as well as ever I could, make her happy.'

'Yes, but Massa,' said Toney, 'you is now in your prime, that's true; but when she is in her prime, where then, Massa, will your prime be?'

Tyler laughed – but, at the age of fifty four, he went ahead and married twenty-four-year-old Julia Gardiner.

The wedding took place on 26 June 1844 in New York, just four months after the death of her father. The young bride wore a simple white dress of lisse 'with a gauze veil descending from a circlet of white flowers, wreathed in her hair'. Still in mourning, she wore no jewellery and was a picture of elegant simplicity.

The couple's age difference – some thirty years – attracted a great deal of public interest. Already known as 'Honest John', he now became 'Lucky Honest John'.

In fact, the news management of the story was brilliant. The story did not appear in the New York papers until the day after the marriage and it forced the sensational murder trial of Polly Bodine off the front pages for several days.

The *New York Herald* said: 'Miss Gardiner is an honour to her sex... the President has concluded a treaty of immediate annexation, which will be ratified without the aid of the Senate of the United States... Neither Polk nor Clay can bring to the White House such beauty, elegance, grace, and high accomplishments as does John Tyler, and meetings should be at once convened, committees appointed, and all proper measures taken to ensure the reign of so much loveliness for four years in the White House.'

But the Washington papers were taken completely by surprise. John Jones, the editor of the pro-Tyler *Madisonian*, had run a routine announcement the day before saying that the President had taken a temporary absence from his 'arduous duties' in the capital to take a few days 'repose'.

The *Herald* then mocked: 'John don't know what's going on. We rather think that the President's "arduous duties" are only beginning. "Repose", indeed!'

The ladies of New York were shocked and 'will not recover in some weeks', the papers said. Many were offended at having been left off the guest list while Tyler's socially unacceptable political cronies had been included.

Tyler's daughters were upset too. They had known nothing of their father's intentions. Just weeks before the wedding he had written to them saying he had 'nothing to write about which would be of interest to you'. When the deed was done, he wrote telling them that he had married 'the most beautiful woman of the age and at the same time the most accomplished' and begging for their understanding.

His oldest daughter Mary, who was five years older than his new bride, accepted the situation. But it was three months before his youngest daughter, twenty-one-year-old Elizabeth, could bring herself to write to 'My dear Mrs Tyler', explaining that 'even now it is with difficulty that I can convince myself that another fills the place which was once occupied by my beloved Mother.'

Tyler's second daughter Letitia never accepted Julia at all and the feud lasted for the rest of their years. His sons, though, accepted their new stepmother gladly.

The honeymoon turned into a triumphant procession. The wedding night was in Philadelphia. There was a brief stopover in Baltimore, then on to Washington. Julia was thrilled by the public's reaction.

'Wherever we stopped, wherever we went, crowds of people outstripping one another, came to gaze on the President's bride,' she said. 'The secrecy of the affair is on the tongue and admiration of everyone. Everyone says it was the best managed thing they ever heard of.'

On Friday 28 June, there was a formal reception in the Blue Room of the White House.

'I have commenced my auspicious reign,' Julia told her mother, 'and am in quiet possession of the Presidential Mansion.'

However, the happy couple soon fell out. Tyler complained that his wife had trouble getting out of bed in the morning and that she constantly demanded his attention rather than letting him get on with his work.

Despite the triumph of his marriage, Tyler was still unpopular and had a difficult election to face.

Julia's sister Margaret even complained: 'You spend so much time kissing, things of more importance are left undone.' Julia's mother urged her: 'Let your husband work during all business hours. Business should take the precedence of caressing – reserve your caressing for private leisure and be sure you let no one see it unless you wish to be laughed at.'

Despite the forthcoming election, on 1 July, the newlyweds set off by boat to Old Point Comfort, where they stayed in what Julia described as a 'true love cottage'. Tyler had put Colonel Gustavus A. De Russy, commanding officer of Fort Monroe, in charge of bedroom arrangements. He provided 'a richly covered high post bedstead hung with white lace curtains looped up with blue ribbon, and the cover at the top of the bedstead lined also with blue – new matting which emitted its sweet fragrance, two handsome mahogany dressing tables, writing table and sofa'.

The President should have been preparing himself for the 1844 election. Instead, he stayed on at his honeymoon cottage, spending his time writing love poetry to his new wife. One of his poems – 'Sweet Lady, Awake! – A Serenade Dedicated to Miss Julia Gardiner' – was set to music by Julia herself. I can't imagine that The Donald has much time for poetry, but Julia was thrilled and completely happy.

'The P. bids me tell you the honeymoon is likely to last

forever,' she told her mother, 'for he finds himself falling in love with me every day.'

Her mother was sceptical. 'You must not believe all the President says about the honeymoon lasting always,' she told her daughter. 'He has found out that you in common with the rest of Eve's daughters are fond of flattery.'

On 6 July, Tyler took her up to Sherwood Forest, the plantation he had bought as his retirement home. He assembled his sixty slaves to greet their new mistress. They, naturally, were embarrassed. So Tyler called out to one of the older men: 'Well, how do you like her looks?' He said: 'She is mighty handsome – just like a doll-baby.' Julia took this as 'the quintessence of a negro compliment'.

Back in the White House, the new Mrs Tyler greeted guests with ostrich plumes in her hair and surrounded herself with maids of honour dressed in white. But her reign was short – just eight months. When Tyler returned from his honeymoon, he decided that there was more to life than being President and stood aside after one term.

Tyler and his wife attended inauguration of the next president James K. Polk, then they retired to Sherwood Forest and started having babies. After the birth of their first child, the papers began running stories of their separation and possible divorce. The problem was their May-to-December marriage, it was said. But the Tylers confounded their critics, stayed together and produced seven children.

When Tyler's old friend Henry A. Wise, who had counselled against marriage, returned to the U.S. in the autumn of 1847, after a spell as ambassador to Brazil, and bumped into the Tylers on a riverboat. Among the expresident's baggage, he spotted a double-seater wicker baby carriage.

'It has come to this, has it?' said Wise, shaking his head.

'You see how right I was,' said Tyler. 'It was not vain boast when I told you I was in my prime. I have a houseful of goodly babies budding around me.'

In Tyler's correspondence, there is no indication that he ever worried about the thirty-year age gap between him and his wife. Indeed, their seventh and last child was born when he was seventy. Nor did Julia worry about the long widowhood she knew she would face. On his sixty-second birthday she wrote:

Then listen, dearest, to my strain –
And never doubt its truth –
Thy ripen'd charms are all to me,
Wit I prefer to youth!

Tyler and Julia were buried together at Hollywood Cemetery, Virginia. His first wife, Letitia, lies alongside her parents at Cedar Grove, where she was born.

XXXVI
William Henry Harrison, #9

William Henry Harrison hardly counts as a president. He rode to his inauguration on horseback through a rainstorm. Hatless and coatless, he was sworn in on the East Portico of the Capitol, then insisted on giving an 8,441-word speech which took an hour and forty minutes to read. After attending three inaugural balls, he took to his bed with a chill. This turned into full-blown pneumonia and he died a month to the day after taking office.

Ironically, his wife, who was too ill to accompany him to Washington for his inauguration, outlived him by twenty-three years.

As a youth, Harrison had joined the army and gained a considerable reputation as a fighter in the battles with the native Americans. The only women he saw were the officers' wives whom he escorted to remote posts and the Indian women who gleefully scalped dead soldiers and tortured the wounded to death.

One day in 1797, Harrison rode up to the Short mansion in Lexington were Anna Turthill Symmes was staying. The moment she saw the gallant young captain on horseback, she fell in love with him. Her father Judge Symmes, former chief justice of the New Jersey Supreme Court, disapproved of the rough fighter. When he asked how Harrison intended to support his daughter, Harrison replied: 'By my sword and by my right hand.'

This may not have impressed the judge, but it certainly impressed the romantic twenty-year-old Anna. She secretly married Harrison, her father grudgingly giving his approval four weeks later. The marriage produced ten children and Harrison seems to have mainly slaughtered native Americans before his political career took off and fizzled out.

XXXVII
Martin Van Buren, #8
'Wedded to Mr King.'

Hannah Hoes Van Buren was the First Lady who never was. Not only did she die eighteen years before her husband entered the White House, he omitted her from his autobiography on the grounds that a gentleman would not bandy around the name of a lady in public.

Martin Van Buren and Hannah Hoes had been childhood sweethearts in the close-knit Dutch-American community in Kinderhook, New York. They married in 1807 and had five sons, one of whom died in childhood.

The Van Burens spoke Dutch at home and Martin called his wife by her Dutch name Jannetje. In 1817, the family moved to Albany where Martin became state attorney. He built his reputation on a number of high-profile rape and murder cases.

The winter of 1818 was particularly severe and Hannah developed tuberculosis. She died on 5 February 1819 at the age of thirty-six. Little is known of her beyond her obituary which described her as 'an ornament of the Christian faith'. Her niece Maria later recalled Hannah's 'perfect composure' on her deathbed. She also asked for her money to be given to the poor.

Van Buren's feelings about his wife are unknown. He rarely mentioned her in his correspondence. The inscription on her gravestone, which was presumably written by him, refers to her only as a 'tender mother and a most affectionate wife'.

Hannah's sister Christina stepped in to help bring up the children. Van Buren liked female company and he soon began escorting a number of eligible women to parties and was positively promiscuous in his correspondence with female friends.

Elected to the Senate, Van Buren would have had ample

opportunity as a single and powerful man in Washington. He was widely known for his polite dalliances with a variety of women. His close friend and political ally, Congressman Louis McLane of Delaware, suspected him of 'licentious' conduct and filled his letters home with stories of Van Buren's affairs. As both men were fond of good food and good wines and frequently ate together, McLane was in a position to know what Van Buren confided to friends about his private life.

New York politician De Witt Clinton, from Van Buren's home state, also said that Van Buren had several sexual affairs. He certainly enjoyed the company of women, especially those of wit and intellect. He was positively gallant in the Peggy Eaton affair – about the wife of one President Jackson's Cabinet members who was ostracised by the other wives – though his gallantry also led to his political advancement.

Van Buren's name was publicly linked with those of a series of eligible young ladies. Thomas Jefferson's granddaughter was often seen in his company. Once, at a ball, she asked the band to play 'The Yellow-haired Laddie'. As Van Buren was known for his golden locks and tongues began to wag and when he went to Virginia, gossips had him married off to her or one of her sisters.

A 'Mrs O.L.' was also mentioned as a prospective wife for Van Buren by Washington insider Churchill C. Cambreleng. Van Buren's response to this assertion was to call Cambreleng a rogue, while admitting that the rumour had put him in a 'peck of trouble'. When President Andrew Jackson made Van Buren Secretary of State it was predicted by all that he would divide his time evenly between 'international law and the ladies'.

Washington grande dame Harriet Butler accused Van Buren of being promiscuous with his affections. While flirting in Washington, apparently, he was sending amorous messages to a woman in Albany, while allowing another to wear 'an emblematic color' for him. Mrs Butler also offered to tell a certain 'Elvira the Fair' that there was no chance for her. Van Buren's response to Harriet's interest in his love life was to court her too.

'Nothing serves so well to season the perpetual dissipation of this Sodom as an occasional letter from a kindhearted and sensible female friend,' he said.

To another woman he wrote: 'Your letter has been to me a green shoot in the midst of a desert of political cares.' To a third he said he hoped he deserved 'half the compliments' that she had given him. To Lucy Evans, wife of political ally David E. Evans, he sent a small present – a twig from a cedar growing next to Washington's tomb at Mount Vernon.

Some husbands objected to his amorous letters. His friend Louis McLane eventually got jealous of the steady stream of missives between his wife and Van Buren and accused Van Buren of being 'morally licentious'. His correspondence with a Mrs Taylor ended when 'her little husband interdicted it'. But usually Van Buren managed to smooth things over with the husbands and carried right on writing love letters.

Maybe the husbands did not really have anything to worry about. Van Buren himself admitted that he merely liked 'to hear the gossip of the female world… for those concerns [are] among the real comforts of life'. Within weeks of arriving in Washington, he had moved out of the downtown Strother's Hotel on Pennsylvania Avenue, which was inhabited by the other New York congressmen, and into Peck's Hotel in Georgetown where Senator Rufus DeVane King lived. Indeed, they were so close that it was rumoured that Van Buren was 'wedded to Mr King'.

Van Buren was extravagant in his praise of other men. Secretary of War John C. Calhoun was a 'fascinating man'. Congressman John Randolph was 'an extraordinary man' and they often went riding together. Van Buren liked to befriend young politicians new in town.

From the beginning of his political career, Van Buren had an extraordinary reputation for exuberant clothing. This is how journalist Henry B. Stanton described how Van Buren's 'exquisite personal appearance' dazzled the congregation at the First Presbyterian Church in Rochester, New York, one Sunday morning: 'His complexion was a bright blond and he dressed accordingly. On this occasion he wore an elegant snuff-coloured broadcloth coat, with velvet collar to match; his cravat was orange tinted silk with modest lace tips; his vest was of pearl hue; his trousers were white duck; his silk hose corresponded to his vest, his shoes were Morocco; his nicely fitting gloves were yellow kid; his hat, a long-furred beaver, with broad brim, was of Quaker colour.' And this was in the middle of a long political tour during a hot New York summer.

On another occasion Stanton described him wearing a 'snuff-coloured' coat with an orange cravat, white duck trouser and yellow gloves, gossiping with married women and exchanging jokes with younger men. He was also known for his green dress coats, his white-topped boots and, always, his extravagant use of lace. He was vain enough to have his portrait painted twice while he was secretary of state.

If one were of a mind, it is possible to conclude that Van Buren was sexually attracted to men. This would explain why, when he had such ample opportunity with willing women, he did not marry again. Certainly having a woman around the house would have been invaluable to a busy politician bringing up four growing boys.

Washington's tongues had something else to wag about than prying into Martin Van Buren's amorous adventures while in office. His tracks were overshadowed by the sex scandals surrounding his Vice President, Richard Johnson. A Kentucky senator, the married Johnson had taken as his mistress Julia Chinn, an 'octoroon' (one eights' slave ancestry, 7 eights' white) and slave whom he had inherited from his father but had not freed. He was open about his relationship with Chinn, whom he could not legally marry as she remained a slave, and he acknowledged her two daughters as his children. They bore his surname and he raised them as free women (after his death, they nonetheless did not inherit under Kentucky law). This cost him his seat in the Senate in 1829, though his district returned him to the House the following year.

When Julia died of cholera in 1833, he took another of the

family's slaves as his mistress. And when she ran off with an Indian, he had her captured and sold. Her empty place in his bed was then filled by Julia's younger sister.

Johnson's lewd private life was constantly discussed in the press, on the hustings and even in Congress, where mention was made of 'the Vice President's swarthy wife and dingy children'. There was speculation that, should Van Buren die, Johnson would move his 'coloured family' into the White House. Such a thing, of course, could never happen. On 22 August 1839, U.S. Postmaster Amos Kendall wrote to Van Buren, protesting that the Vice President was living with his third African-American mistress and Johnson was not nominated for a second term as Vice President.

XXXVIII
Andrew Jackson, #7
'The most mischievous of the youngsters'

Known as 'Old Hickory' by his men in War of 1812, Andrew Jackson was the first president to be born in a log cabin and the first to come from West of the Appalachians. Nevertheless he sought to emulate the Eastern patricians who had preceded him, playing fast and loose with the slave women. One woman from a nearby plantation recalled years later that the young Jackson was the 'most mischievous of the youngsters thereabouts'.

Jackson's father died before he was born and the rest of his family were wiped out during the War of Independence. One grandfather left him nearly £400 when Jackson was fifteen and he headed off to Charleston where he spent it on clothes and gambling. There he sowed his wild oats and lived a life of almost complete dissipation.

At eighteen, he moved to Salisbury, North Carolina, where he was renowned as 'the most roaring, rollicking, game-cocking, horse-racing, card-playing, mischievous fellow, that ever lived in Salisbury... the head of the rowdies hereabouts'.

'Why he was such a rake that my husband would not let him in the house,' one village matron recalled.

He cut quite a swathe with the young ladies and there were rumours of mixed-race mistresses. While still a poor man with no income and very few resources, he found $300 (£60) to buy a 'negro woman named Nancy, about eighteen or twenty years of age'. It is hard to imagine what a young bachelor would need a domestic servant for. On the other hand it is not difficult to imagine what a young bachelor would need a young female domestic servant for.

'We all knew he was wild and was by no means a Christian man,' said one young female admirer. 'Still his ways and manners were most captivating.'

He was tall and athletic with red hair, steel blue eyes and a marked Northern Irish accent. He was 'quite a beau in town' and was often away on 'parties of pleasure'. He wooed and won a number of young ladies in the vicinity, but their parents objected to marriage because they 'thought he would get killed before he was many years older'.

He liked practical jokes. One Christmas, Jackson succeeded in outraging the whole town by sending invitations to the Christmas ball to the town's two most notorious prostitutes, Molly Wood and her fun-loving daughter. It was just 'a piece of fun', Jackson maintained. The respected pillars of the community did not see it that way, and when Molly and her daughter turned up in their finery, they were escorted from the ballroom.

Jackson went on to become known for fighting the Indians. It is said that he fought the Creek with such fervour, and conspicuous lack of mercy, because he suspected that they indulged in 'infernal orgies'.

When Jackson moved to Nashville, he stayed at the boarding house of Mrs John Donelson and fell in love with her daughter Rachel. An extremely pious woman, Rachel had been married at seventeen to Kentucky land owner Lewis Robards, but his jealousy sent her running back to her mother's boarding house to live separated from her husband.

When Robards heard rumours about a liaison between his wife and Jackson, he turned up at the boarding house and there was a fight. To protect Rachel, Jackson took her to Natchez, now in Mississippi but then in Spanish territory.

As was the custom on the frontier at the time, Rachel began calling herself Mrs Jackson. Hearing of their 'elopement', Robards filed for divorce on the grounds of his wife's desertion. Jackson and Rachel seized the opportunity to get married in 1791.

Jackson was a lawyer by then and should have known better. Robards had only filed for divorce. It had not been granted and

Jackson did not check. Two years later he discovered that Robards still had not obtained a divorce. Rachel was a bigamist – a shock from which she never entirely recovered – and he himself was an adulterer. Robards eventually obtained a divorce on the grounds of adultery and, in 1794, the Jacksons got married again – this time legally.

Jackson tried to keep this honest mistake quiet and, throughout his wife's lifetime, was quick to defend his wife's honour against any slight. He even fought a duel over it and only escaped with his life because the bullet lodged in the thick coat he was wearing. His opponent, who had accused Rachel of adultery, died in the exchange of fire.

In the bitter, muck-raking 1828 election that brought him to power, the old accusations surfaced again. The *Cincinnati Gazette* asked: 'Ought a convicted adulteress and her paramour husband be placed in the highest offices of this free and Christian land?'

And one anti-Jackson pamphlet read: 'Anyone approving of Andrew Jackson must therefore declare in favor of the philosophy that any man wanting anyone else's pretty wife has nothing to do but take his pistol in one hand and a horsewhip in the other and possess her.'

Even Jackson's mother was considered fair game. As she had given birth shortly after his father had died, she was branded a 'common prostitute'.

Somehow Jackson managed to keep these accusations from his wife. But after he was elected, she came across some election literature defending her and realised that the whole world knew her secret. The White House ceased to hold any attraction for her. A deeply religious woman, she said: 'I would rather be a door-keeper in the house of God than live in that palace in Washington.'

She quite simply died of shame just days after the election. Jackson blamed his opponent John Quincy Adams for Rachel's death and never forgave him. She was buried in the gown that she had bought for the inauguration. Her epitaph reads: 'A being so gentle and so virtuous slander might wound, but could not dishonor.'

They had no children. A young niece named Emily Donelson took over the duties of first lady, which would not have passed without comment these days. When she died in 1836, the role was taken by Sarah Yorke Jackson, the wife of Andrew Jackson Jr, a nephew the Jacksons had adopted.

Jackson took office, grieving for his wife. Nonetheless, his administration soon had its very own sex scandal. No one thought Jackson would last his term and rivalries broke out in cabinet over who would be his successor. The two contenders were Vice-President James C. Calhoun from South Carolina and Secretary of State Martin Van Buren. It was not a political issue they fought over, but Peggy O'Neal Eaton, the wife of the Secretary of War.

Peggy O'Neal was a green-eyed brunette, the daughter of a Washington tavern keeper, who was happy to bounce on customers' knees and dance with them. Indeed, the distribution of her favours was the talk of Washington. However, when a young congressman from Tennessee, who had a lovely young wife at home, tried it on with her she hit him with the fire tongs. She preferred marriage to dancing, despite appearances to the contrary.

At the age of fifteen, Peggy tried to elope with an army officer who was staying at the tavern, but her father caught them and ended the match. Later she married a purser in the U.S. Navy, John Bowie Timberlake, and had three children, one of whom died in infancy. However, while he was at sea, she began an affair with Jackson's old friend and campaign manager Senator John Henry Eaton. When her husband died – some said he drank himself to death over the affair – Eaton turned to Jackson for advice.

'Sir, I want to marry Peggy O'Neal,' Eaton said. 'Do you think I should? You know what people are saying.'

Indeed, Jackson did. He had been present one night when the politician Henry Clay had made a Shakespearean wisecrack at Peggy's expense. 'Age cannot wither nor custom stale her infinite virginity,' Clay had quipped. However, Clay was a long-time political opponent, and Jackson blamed the death of his wife on this sort of gossip. He also knew Peggy and had stayed at her father's inn when he had first come to Washington.

Jackson advised Eaton to marry Peggy. The couple were wed and Eaton joined the cabinet as Secretary of War. Other Washington wives, however, snubbed her. Leading the anti-Peggy campaign was John Calhoun's wife Floride, who refused to invite her to dinner parties where other cabinet members and their wives would be present. The infighting became so intense that it was almost impossible for the government to conduct its regular business. But Jackson stood firm.

'I did not come here to make a cabinet for the ladies of this place, but for the nation,' he responded.

Jackson also learnt that Calhoun had secretly opposed his invasion of Florida and had taken up the issue of Peggy to crush his administration. Jackson publicly compared the treatment of Peggy Eaton to the slanders that had destroyed his wife Rachel and declared, in cabinet, that Peggy was as 'chaste as a virgin'. At a formal cabinet dinner, he seated her next to him. Peggy wore a gown with a plunging neckline that further outraged the Washington wives, who walked out when she took to the dance floor.

Martin Van Buren led the pro-Peggy faction. He threw a party in her honour and persuaded his bachelor friends to do the same. Cabinet members, congressmen, even foreign diplomats had to take sides in the 'petticoat war'. Soon the administration was a laughing stock over the Peggy Eaton affair. Van Buren proposed a cure of the 'Eaton malaria'. He and Eaton would resign. Then Jackson would ask for the resignation of Calhoun and the rest of the anti-Peggyites. The entire cabinet would be dissolved, leaving Jackson free to pick new men.

All this makes Donald Trump's White House seem almost orderly by comparison. Van Buren was rewarded for this gesture by being picked as Jackson's running mate in 1832. Jackson even introduced the two-thirds rule in the nominating convention to give no other contender a chance. The two-thirds rule stayed in place until 1936.

Peggy's life of scandal did not end there. When Eaton died, he left her a small fortune. At sixty one she married twenty-one year old Antonio Buchignani, her granddaughter's dancing teacher. Less than a year later he eloped to Italy with all her money and her granddaughter. Peggy had to take work as a dressmaker to support herself. She died in 1879 and is buried in Oak Hill Cemetery next John Eaton. At her funeral a large bouquet of white roses sent by President and Mrs Rutherford B. Hayes was placed on her grave.

Despite the heated sexual atmosphere surrounding the Peggy Eaton scandal, Jackson never looked at another woman after the loss of his wife. He had a miniature of her on a strong black cord around his neck. One night when his private secretary disturbed him on some pressing presidential business, he found Jackson holding his wife's prayer book. A larger miniature of her was propped against some books in front of him.

Jackson kept a large portrait of her in his bedroom, opposite his bed. Each morning he would kneel before it and thank God that he had been spared so that he could look once more on her face. When he did die, he died staring at her portrait on the wall opposite.

XXXIX

John Quincy Adams Jr, #6

The Crackbrain Club

The sixth president of the United States, John Quincy Adams was the eldest son of President John Adams, he was also a self-proclaimed dedicated puritan. He deliberately denied himself pleasure and welcomed adversity as a method of improving his character. He enjoyed nude swimming in the Potomac – his wife Louisa thought he swam too often. Nonetheless, the milk of Christian charity didn't flow but trickle from him. He held grudges and kept a neat list of his enemies.

While president, he was caught out skinny dipping by Anne Royall, an enterprising journalist to whom he had refused an interview. She had heard of his habit and followed him one morning. She watched from a safe distance while the President undressed. Then, when he had waded into the water, she sat down on his clothes. An embarrassed Adams said he would grant her an interview back at the White House, but Royall would have none of it. She refused to move until the naked President had answered all her questions there and then.

John Quincy Adams maintained that there were three rules to live by – regularity, regularity, regularity. But in his youth he had enjoyed drinking, dancing and the company of women. On 21 January 1788, he noted in his diaries that he 'danced with the oldest Miss Frazier, with Miss Fletcher and with Miss Coates'. He noted Miss Fletcher's 'genteel shape'. Miss Coates was also 'agreeable'. She was an only child and 'her father has money'. But it was Miss Frazier he was interested in. They had met a week before at her home where they played 'pawns', a kissing game.

'Ah! What kissing!' John Quincy Adams wrote. ''tis a profanation of one of the most endearing demonstrations of love.'

The problem was that Mary Frazier was only fourteen – even then not yet a marriageable age.

His ardour thwarted, John Quincy Adams found himself in low spirits. 'Not even dissipation has been able to support me,' he wrote. He had trouble sleeping, and when he finally dozed off he was disturbed by 'extravagant dreams'.

He became ill, but found a cure in writing love poetry to Mary. Some of it was published in *Massachusetts Magazine* and other Boston journals. Gradually picnics and long walks with Mary restored his health and his ambition to possess her made him finish his law studies which had been flagging since his discovery of cider. He confided to a friend: All my hopes of future happiness in this life, centre on the possession of that girl.'

However, he could not get his law firm set up quickly enough to marry her. His family was poor and could not support them. His father was then existing on the meagre salary of Vice President. His older sister had married a man who was not prepared to work and had recently produced her third child by him.

His mother urged him to marry a rich woman, if he was to marry at all. Eventually, his parents forced him to give up his love, leaving him crushed. It was a blow he never fully got over. He stopped writing poetry and dedicated himself with puritanical zeal to duty.

Mary too was devastated. It was only years later, after she heard that John Quincy Adams had married someone else, that she married Daniel Sargent Jr, one of his friends. She died of consumption in 1804.

In 1864, a local paper, the *Newburyport Herald*, carried an account of the love affair. In it, John Quincy Adams was quoted at the age of seventy, recalling Mary's beauty, intellect and purity, rating her above any woman in Europe or America, and saying that he loved her then and loved her still.

However, his loss of Mary did not leave him quite as upset as it might. In 1791, on his way home from Philadelphia by boat, he spent several hours admiring 'the prettiest Quaker girl' he had ever seen. Back in Boston, he quickly returned to his life of drinking and dancing in Boston's inns. During the Revolution, his father said that bastards and legislators were born in the taverns of Boston.

Adams joined the 'Crackbrain Club', full of like-minded young men, and danced until well after midnight. One night, he admitted, he made 'an intentionally offensive reply' to a young woman and found himself 'heavy and dissipated'. He began to visit prostitutes. His diaries recount meetings with unknown persons in strange places, late at night. Boston was teeming with prostitutes at the time. Benjamin Franklin, no stranger to the trade, noted women 'who by throwing their heads to the right or the left of everyone who passed by them, I concluded came out with no other design than to revive the spirit of love in disappointed bachelors and expose themselves to sale at the highest bidder'. Indeed, the innocently named Mount Vernon in Boston was then known as Mount Whoredom.

John Quincy Adams was freed from the grip of vice by a letter from George Washington appointing him U.S. Minister to the Netherlands. On the way there, he stopped in London where he noted: 'There is something so fascinating in the women I meet in this country that it is not well for me. I am obliged immediately to leave it.' However, after just two months in The Hague, John Quincy Adams was ordered back to London where he met Louisa Johnson.

Louisa Adams, as she became, was born in England and never felt at home in her husband's country, especially not in the White House. She thought of it as a prison. Her father had been born in Maryland, but had moved to England in 1771. He married an Englishwoman and Louisa was born in London in 1775. Her father had remained loyal to his American origins and, during the War of Independence, moved to France. After 1790, he became a U.S. consul.

At school, Louisa had a crush on her teacher, Miss Young,

who wore men's clothing. Louisa was extremely pretty and, according to one observer, had 'the most bewitching smile'. This could have been because she kept her lips closed when she smiled. Her fondness for sweets meant she began losing her teeth at an early age.

Nevertheless, she did not find any trouble in attracting young marriageable men, especially in the countryside where she could put away the wire stays and cork bustles that were all the rage in the city. She fell in love repeatedly. One man asked for her hand only to be 'lured to destruction' by the wiles of married women during a trip to America, Louisa noted. However, she mended her broken heart with a round of other brief affairs.

In 1794, Louisa met the young, ambitious American ambassador just returned from the Netherlands, John Quincy Adams. He had just received a letter from his younger brother Charles who was about to marry one Sarah Smith. Adams was furious when he heard the news. Charles had no profession, no income and was younger than John Quincy Adams had been when he was forced to give up Mary Frazier.

John Quincy Adams wrote to his parents remonstrating. They were unsympathetic. He decided that he must marry as a matter of urgency and get on with his life. He had only one requirement – that the woman be short. Otherwise he feared she would appear superior to him.

At first he wooed Nancy Johnson, Louisa's older sister, but Louisa seized his attention by issuing him a challenge. If he really was a poet, as he claimed, he would have to prove it by writing a poem to her. He did and handed it to her one evening over the dinner table. It was a love poem. Louisa took it and began to read it aloud, much to everyone's great embarrassment. The situation was saved by Louisa's governess who stopped her mid-flow with the admonition that it was rude to read at table. But the cat was out of the bag. Nancy went into a sulk and Louisa completed her conquest at her twenty-first birthday ball, by spending the night dancing with her sister's former lover.

Still, Louisa was not entirely sure that John Quincy Adams was really the man for her. 'An American minister was to me a very small personage,' she wrote.

Her parents were keen. He was the first man they ever allowed her to be alone with. He was the first man she kissed, and the first who ever held her in a passionate embrace. 'I can swear before the living God that I came pure and virtuous to his arms,' she wrote.

The engagement was a stormy one. They rowed constantly, usually over his sloppy manner of dressing. When John Quincy Adams's parents got wind of the affair, they wrote disapprovingly. They thought 'the siren' was too English – anti-British feelings were still running high in the U.S. His parents' disapproval made the match all the more appealing to Adams.

The match made sense too. She was twenty two; he was thirty. They had both been disappointed in early loves and were now at an age when they must marry. He concluded that marriage was better than celibacy. She, on the other hand, compared it to hanging.

They married at All Hallows Church on Tower Hill in London in 1797. The custom of the time in England was for the wedding guests to carry the bride and groom to their wedding chamber, making lewd and suggestive comments on the way. Once they were alone, the bride was supposed to scramble into bed naked except for a pair of long white gloves. These her husband would symbolically remove before they proceeded to consummate the marriage.

But the wedding of John Quincy Adams and Louisa Johnson, typically, was an altogether more sober affair. Even on their honeymoon, a tour of England by carriage, the newly-weds were accompanied by chaperones. Within days of their marriage, her father was ruined by the loss of a ship in the Indian Ocean. Then it transpired that he had been swindled by his partner in Maryland. He could not pay the huge dowry he had promised and fled his creditors, who sought recompense from Adams.

When Adams could not pay, he considered himself disgraced and Louisa carried the shame to her death. She wrote later that, at that moment, she had lost all her husband's esteem.

It was an inauspicious beginning. Worse was to come. John Quincy Adams and his penniless new wife were totally incompatible. She was a free spirit, used to the uninhibited ways of Europe. Much of her childhood had been spent in France. He was a hidebound New Englander.

'Though Boston is the land of learning,' she wrote later, 'I never found it the land of wit.'

Adams was appointed U.S. ambassador to Prussia where they spent four years. While he went soberly about his business, Louisa became the toast of Berlin society, accompanied everywhere by Adams' brother Thomas who many regarded as her surrogate husband. She had frequent arguments with the irascible Adams, usually over rouge. The Queen of Prussia had given her some, but he disapproved and forbade her to use it. Eventually, Louisa stood up to her husband and wore make-up when she chose to.

In between they must have managed to make up occasionally. In Berlin, she gave birth to a son and then had the first of many miscarriages. In the first thirteen years of their marriage, she was pregnant eleven times. Her twelfth and final pregnancy happened in 1817, when she was forty two. She was terrified each time, but Adams on the other hand considered the pain and danger of pregnancy 'the pleasing punishment that women bear'.

Louisa was much more astute than her husband. While John Quincy Adams considered Prussia to be nothing more than a nation of soldiery and the king a model of propriety, Louisa had 'a peep behind the scenery' care of her friend Countess Neale, maid of honour to the Queen. Louisa's journal is full of stories of the beautiful Princess Lucia, who became pregnant by the king and was shipped off to a frontier town with her husband, and 'a very beautiful cousin… who had twins supposed to be his majesty's and married off to an officer of the army who was promoted suddenly for the occasion'. Slow on the uptake, John Quincy Adams only gradually became aware of what he later condemned as this 'sea of dissipation'.

In 1801, Louisa made her first visit to America. She spent two months with her parents who then lived outside Washington, DC, before joining her husband in Quincy, Massachusetts. She disliked austere Massachusetts society and clashed with her mother-in-law. She got on well with John Adams though and learned to love him.

She was delighted when John Quincy Adams's election to the Senate meant she could leave Massachusetts for Washington, DC. In the summer recess, her husband would travel home alone, leaving her in the capital.

Voted out of office after just one term, John Quincy Adams was appointed ambassador to Russia. Leaving her two oldest sons at school in Massachusetts, she travelled with her husband to St Petersburg. Life at the Tsar's court was exhausting and the winters intolerably cold. She bore a daughter there in 1811, but the child died the following year.

John Quincy Adams went to Belgium to negotiate the Treaty of Ghent in 1814, ending the war with the British. He sent word for Louisa to join him in Paris. The forty-day coach-trip across war-torn Europe in winter filled her with 'unspeakable terror'. Her reward was a two-year sojourn in London, where at least she felt at home.

Then in 1817, John Quincy Adams was appointed Secretary of State and Louisa returned to Washington with him. They received Joseph Bonaparte, Napoleon's brother and exiled king of Spain, when he visited the U.S. His wife had refused to accompany him so he kept his mistress Annette Savage at Bow Hill – renamed Beau Hill – in Trenton.

Around that time Louisa suffered from haemorrhoids – not a condition to have in the days before anaesthetics and sterile surgery. After an horrendous operation, during which she had to be strapped down, the haemorrhoids were wired and fell off. She made a complete recovery. The treatment cost $100.

Louisa went on to become a notable hostess and her drawing room became a hub of political and diplomatic activity in the run up to the presidential election of 1825. The move to the White House did not suit her though.

'There is something about the great unsocial house,' she wrote, 'which depresses my spirit beyond expression and makes it impossible for me to feel at home or to fancy that I have a home anywhere.'

However, life in the White House had its moments. Senator Mills dropped round for dinner one evening, where he 'found Mrs A and her two nieces, and had a supper of roast oysters in the shell, opening them, which of course was not a very pleasant or cleanly process; but with whiskey and water with supper and a little hot punch after it, we had quite a frolic'.

Louisa's health gradually suffered, though she managed to provide the elegant hospitality her position called for. However, her husband became increasingly unpopular and his English wife was an easy target for his political opponents. When he was voted out of office, she was relieved, though she feared permanent retirement in Massachusetts.

Fortunately, in 1831, he began a new political career in the House of Representatives. After years of stormy marriage, they gradually grew together, campaigning together against slavery and for women's rights.

She took up the case of an Irish serving girl who had been seduced by her master. This was not an uncommon occurrence, even in the Adams family. The maid had lived in hope that her master would marry her, but when he married a younger, prettier maid, she drank mercury and died in agony.

In Congress, John Quincy Adams championed the antislavery cause. Pro-slavery factions argued that the women's petitions Adams brought to the House came from 'mulattos and infamous prostitutes'.

John Quincy Adams answered: 'I am inclined to believe it is

the case, that in the South there existed great resemblances between the progeny of the coloured people and the white men who claim possession of them. Thus, perhaps, the charge of infamous might be retorted to those who made it, as originating from themselves.' At this, there was, the Congressional record shows, 'great agitation in the House'.

On another occasion in the House, Adams openly accused slave-owners of sexual misconduct. The life of a slaveowner, he said, 'is but one of unbridled lust, of filthy amalgamation'.

However, although he opposed slavery and thought that miscegenation was the only solution to America's race problem, he said he was 'disgusted' by Desdemona pursuing a 'nigger' in Shakespeare's *Othello*.

The Quincy Adams children did not turn out too well. One son, Charles, visited prostitutes and kept a mistress while he was a student. Widespread knowledge of his liaison caused problems when he tried to marry nineteen-year-old socialite Abigail Brooks.

Another son, George, was turned down by a number of eligible young ladies in Boston. He took to the bottle and his law office became known as a centre for drunkenness and fornication. He committed suicide by jumping off a boat and drowned somewhere off Long Island.

Their third son Thomas, who became an alcoholic, married a woman everyone considered beneath him.

XXXX

James Monroe, #5

Madison's successor James Monroe – of the Monroe Doctrine (the end of European influence in the Americas) – was a bit more of a lad. During the War of Independence he fell in love with Christine Wynkoop, the daughter of a Dutchman who had rallied to the American cause. But she was already engaged and turned him down when he proposed marriage.

Monroe was stationed in New Jersey where he enjoyed convivial evenings at the governor's mansion 'Liberty Hall'. He fell in love with Catherine, the daughter of Lord Stirling – or, at least, she fell in love with him.

Complaining to Mrs Prevost, the future wife of Vice President Aaron Burr, Monroe wrote: 'A young lady who either is, or pretends to be, in love, is, you know, my dear Mrs Prevost, the most unreasonable creature in existence. If she looks a smile or a frown, which does not immediately give or deprive you of happiness (at least to appearance), your company soon becomes very insipid. Each feature has its beauty, and each attitude the graces, or you have no judgment. But if you are so stupidly insensible of her charms as to deprive your tongue and eyes of every expression of admiration, and not only to be silent respecting her, but to devote them to an absent object, she cannot receive a higher insult; nor would she, if not restrained by politeness, refrain from open resentment.'

Catherine was exceedingly jealous and even resented Monroe's correspondence with Mrs Prevost. However, the relationship progressed almost to the point of a formal engagement. But when it became clear that the attachment was standing in the way of his political ambitions, he rather awkwardly broke it off.

Instead he married Elizabeth Kortright, a High Tory and, perhaps, a strange choice of wife for a Jeffersonian Republican. She was expected to have done better. However she soon found that she was the wife of a U.S. Senator, and went on to become the toast of Paris – when he was the U.S. ambassador to France – before becoming First Lady.

Elizabeth was born in 1768 in New York City. Her father had made his fortune as a British privateer during the French and Indian War. He was hurt, financially, by the Revolution but with aristocratic hauteur his daughter Elizabeth was determined to get on under the new order.

Not yet eighteen, she married James Monroe in 1786, attracted perhaps by his political ambitions. She was known as 'the most beautiful woman in the United States', while he was considered a 'not very attractive Virginia congressman'. They had two daughters and a son who died in infancy.

The Monroes spent nearly ten years abroad. She disliked London, where the envoy from the United States was looked down on, but in Paris she was celebrated as *'la belle Americaine'*. At the theatre, they would be cheered and the orchestra would strike up 'Yankee Doodle' in their honour.

In France, Elizabeth Monroe was celebrated as much for her courage as for her beauty. When Lafayette's wife was arrested by a Revolutionary tribunal and sentenced to death, Elizabeth visited her in prison and announced loudly that she would visit her again the following day, after the time she was supposed to have gone to the guillotine. Fearing diplomatic protests from America, the Revolutionary authorities thought better of executing her and released Madame Lafayette instead.

In 1811, Monroe was appointed Secretary of State and Elizabeth accompanied him to Washington. She became an accomplished hostess but, when Monroe became President in 1817, her health faltered. She did not have the strength to visit the wives of foreign ambassadors and other dignitaries all over Washington, struggling along unpaved streets as Dolley Madison had. Consequently, she was considered cold and distant, and her White House entertaining thought formal and European in style.

Elizabeth Monroe died on 4 July 1830, aged sixty-three, five years after her husband left the White House. John Quincy Adams gave the eulogy but it was clear that he knew as little about her as did the rest of Washington.

XXXXI

James Madison, #4

Drinking and brothels

The fourth president James Madison was another straitlaced puritan and a confirmed bachelor when, at the age of forty three, he met a vivacious young widow named Dolley Payne Todd. Not only did Dolley transform the life of the dour Madison, she presided over the role of 'First Lady' for nearly fifty years. 'Queen Dolley' was described as the 'leader of everything fashionable in Washington' – quite an achievement for a woman who spent the first twenty four years of her life as a Quaker.

Born in May 1768 in Piedmont, North Carolina, Dolley Payne was the daughter of two settlers from Virginia. She was brought up in the strict discipline of the Society of Friends, but her maternal grandmother was an Anglican who taught her about fine food and fabrics. She secretly wore her grandmother's gold brooch beneath her plain Quaker dress and later spoke of her grandmother as the greatest influence in her life.

In 1783, the family moved to Philadelphia, where her father went into business. Dolley married a young lawyer, John Todd Jr, in 1790, but he died in the epidemic of yellow fever that hit Philadelphia three years later, leaving Dolley with a young son.

By this time, the Payne family had fallen on hard times. Dolley's father's business had failed and he had been disowned by the Quakers for falling into debt. Dolley's mother opened a boarding house, catering for delegates to the Continental Congress. There the beautiful young widow attracted the amorous attentions of the accomplished womaniser Aaron Burr. When she rejected his advances because he was married, he introduced her to the forty-three-year-old delegate from Virginia, James Madison.

Dolley wrote to a friend: 'Thou must come to me. Aaron Burr says that the great little Madison has asked to be brought to see me this evening.' Determined to impress, Madison wore his new 'round beaver', a hat bought from Quaker merchant Isaac Parrish.

Seventeen years her senior, Madison was such a confirmed bachelor that the mothers of Philadelphia had decided he was a hopeless prospect for their daughters. But as soon as he met Dolley, he was smitten. He bombarded her with a series of rather plain love letters and implored her to marry him. Dolley was sceptical but her sister Anna, half in love with Madison herself, forced the pace. She suggested that Dolley spend the summer in Virginia though the heat there would be even more intense than in Philadelphia. Madison rented a coach, absented himself from Congress and accompanied her.

Despite Madison's reputation for dullness, there was a wild man inside, trapped. As a youth, he wrote doggerel about drinking and brothels. Tradition has it that he met his first love, Mary Freneau, sister of the poet Philip Freneau, while he was a student at Princeton. Then at the age of twenty, he had fallen for a 'pretty Philadelphian' named Catherine 'Kitty' Floyd. She was just fifteen and boyish in appearance. There was great rivalry for her among the delegates to the Continental Congress. She accepted Madison's offer of his heart and his hand. He carried her picture, painted on ivory, in a heavy locket and she carried his. But at the end of his first term, she dropped him.

Instead of being the father of Kitty's children, Madison went on to become one of the fathers of the Constitution. He was still trying to get it ratified by Congress when he absented himself with Dolley Payne. News of the affair spread quickly throughout Philadelphia. The difference in their ages caused much comment and people were scandalized that Dolley should be enjoying male company so soon after the death of her husband.

Madison and Dolley married in September 1794. The honeymoon was far from satisfactory as young John Payne,

Dolley's son, slept with his mother and continued to do so. But Madison so relished the 'joys perpetual' of married life that he was soon talking of retiring from Congress.

Madison and Dolley produced no children of their own. They had separate bedrooms, but Dolley always kept the door between them open. Madison reconciled himself to being childless from early on. Why that was is a matter for speculation. Just eighteen months after the wedding, Aaron Burr remarked to James Monroe: 'Madison is still childless, and I fear likely to continue so.'

Dolley, disowned by the Quakers for marrying outside the faith, took the opportunity to put aside the Society's dull garb and to dress in the finest fashions. She championed the French style, created by Napoleon's Josephine, with its plunging necklines. First Lady Abigail Adams attacked Dolley's décolleté dress as 'an outrage upon all decency'.

'Most ladies wear their clothes too scant upon the body and too full upon the bosom for my fancy,' Abigail clucked. 'Not content with the show which nature bestows, they borrow from air, and literally look like nursing mothers.'

When James Madison had become president in 1809, Abigail maintained the fashion reflected on him. She sourly said: 'Since Dolley Madison and her sisters adopted the new fashions and seemed in every way delighted with the Frenchinfluenced manners of Philadelphia society, we may assume ex-bachelor Madison enjoyed fully the "luxuriant" feminine displays for which the Republican Court of the 1790s was famous – or infamous.'

In the French court during the 'age of undress' women were practically topless.

Dolley attended elegant balls and presided over fashionable dinner parties in Philadelphia and at Madison's plantation in Montpelier, Virginia. These chic gatherings made Dolley the country's leading hostess. Men flocked to her and vied for the right to escort her to dinner. Even Washington fell for her, declaring her to be 'the sprightliest partner I've ever had'. When Jefferson became president he invited Dolley to organize formal functions and, briefly, their names were coupled romantically. She also became a close friend of Andrew Jackson and Alexander Hamilton.

When the British set fire to the Presidential Mansion in 1812, Dolley saved what she could, including a famous portrait of George Washington. She returned to Washington, DC, before her husband, to the cheers of crowds lining the streets. While the marks of the British flames on the Presidential Mansion were being covered with a coat of white paint – making it the White House – she continued her elegant entertaining from the Octagon.

When Madison left office in 1817, Dolley simply moved the centre of fashionable society to Montpelier. When the Marquis de Lafayette visited in 1824, he wrote: 'Nowhere have I encountered a lady who is lovelier or more steadfast.'

Dolley acted as her husband's secretary and took down *My Advice to My Country* which Madison dictated shortly before his death in 1836. The following year Dolley returned to Washington where she played hostess to numerous presidents.

Martin Van Buren said: 'Mrs Madison is the most brilliant hostess in the country.' And Daniel Webster described her as the only permanent power in Washington.

Her son John Payne Todd remained a source of scandal. He served briefly as Madison's secretary then, in 1813, was sent to Russia with the Peace Commission. In St Petersburg, as stepson of the U.S. President, he was treated as an American prince. He began drinking heavily. He fell in love with a Countess Olga. They got engaged, but her father abducted her to prevent the marriage going ahead. She was never heard of again.

Todd then headed for Paris, where he was overwhelmed by the beauty of the women and began his dissipation in earnest. Back in America, his name was linked romantically with a series of women, before he became a 'puffed and reckless libertine' and, though his stepfather tried to pay off his creditors, he ended up in jail for debt on two occasions.

When Dolley's son's financial mismanagement and gambling debts forced her to sell the Montpelier estate, Congress helped her out by buying her husband's papers. At the age of eighty, she was still dispensing advice to Sarah Polk, when her husband became president. When Dolley Madison died in 1849, at the age of eighty one, the then president, Zachary Taylor, eulogised: 'She will never be forgotten because she was truly our First Lady for a half-century.'

XXXXIV
Thomas Jefferson, #3
Sally Hemmings

'Mad Tom' Jefferson was the author of the Declaration of Independence and probably the most intelligent man ever to be president. When President Kennedy held a reception in the White House honouring a number of Nobel laureates in 1962, he remarked that they comprised 'the most extraordinary collection of talent, of human knowledge, that has ever been gathered at the White House, with the possible exception of when Thomas Jefferson dined alone.' (In a similar situation, Donald Trump might refer to himself with such a quip.)

As a young man, Thomas Jefferson had a close friendship with Dabney Carr, the son of a wealthy Virginia planter. On one of their long rambles in the hills around Shadwell, Jefferson's birthplace, they came across a huge oak tree which Jefferson named Monticello. Later he built a house there. Romantically, the two young men swore to be buried there. In 1773, shortly after Jefferson's marriage, Carr died and Jefferson interred him there in a small private plot. Over half a century later, Jefferson joined him.

As a youth, Jefferson liked to keep company with his own sex. He believed in the strict segregation of men and women. Even when he was seventy three, he was warning that the promiscuous mixing of men and women would produce 'deprivation of morals and ambiguity of issue' – that is, bastard children.

However, at nineteen, Jefferson briefly courted a girl he called 'Belinda', the sixteen-year-old Rebecca Burwell. Usually he fought shy of virgins. As a young man, he courted a married woman and, later, married a widow.

The married woman was Betsy Walker, the wife of John

Walker, one of his classmates at William and Mary College. In 1769, while Walker was away, he wrote notes to her suggesting that there was no harm in occasional promiscuity among friends.

Apparently, he tried to slip these notes into Betsy's dress. Betsy complained that Jefferson laid siege to her for over ten years – longer than the siege of Troy. Even in 1779, seven years after Jefferson married, he was still to be seen loitering near to her bedroom with amorous intent. On one occasion, she said he entered her bedroom with the intention of taking her by force, but she fought him off with a pair of scissors. For Jefferson, it seems no was not no.

Jefferson met Martha Wayles Skelton – the woman who was to become his wife – when he was twenty nine. She was twenty two, but she was already a widow and the mother of a son who died in early childhood. With hazel eyes and auburn hair, she was a famous beauty. They were brought together by a love of music. The first thing that Jefferson bought for her at the home he was building at Monticello was a piano.

They married on 1 January 1772 at her plantation home, then travelled to Monticello. On the way, they were caught in a snowstorm and had to abandon their carriage and proceed on horseback. They arrived at Monticello late at night to find the house dark and deserted, but Jefferson managed to find half a bottle of wine on a shelf behind some books to celebrate their homecoming.

Martha bore him six children. Only two – Martha, known as 'Patsy', and Mary, known as 'Polly' – survived infancy. Her own health was further weakened when she narrowly escaped capture twice as British forces overran Virginia. In 1781, she became pregnant again and Jefferson retired briefly from public life to nurse her. She gave birth in May 1782, but never regained her strength. As she lay dying, he promised her that he would never marry again.

Jefferson devoted himself to his daughters, taking Patsy with him to Paris when he was sent there as ambassador. He sent for

Polly later. Jefferson eventually gave up his post in Paris, fearful that his daughters would marry louche Europeans. He was outraged by the 'depravity' he saw there, claiming that fidelity between lovers never lasted more than a year.

Ironically, Jefferson's own loose behaviour in Paris led to a scandal after he became President in 1801. The man who broke the story was Scottish journalist James Callender. He had first come to Jefferson's attention with the publication of *The Political Progress of Britain*, which predicted the imminent downfall of the British Empire (a century and a half too soon). The two men met and Jefferson, by then Vice President in the administration of John Adams, promised his help with Callender's next publication. This was *The History of the United States for the Year 1796*, which exposed Secretary of the Treasury and Jefferson's political rival Alexander Hamilton's illicit affair with Mrs James Reynolds – an affair that Hamilton was forced to admit publicly.

Twenty-three-year-old Maria approached the thirty-four-year-old Hamilton, who was also married, asking for the fare back to New York after her husband James had abandoned her. Hamilton consented and delivered the money in person to Maria later that night. As Hamilton himself later confessed: 'I took the bill out of my pocket and gave it to her. Some conversation ensued from which it was quickly apparent that other than pecuniary consolation would be acceptable.' They began an illicit affair that would last over three years. When James Reynolds discovered this, he took a practical turn and charged Hamilton more than $1,000 to allow him to continue sleeping with his wife. A scandal ensued and in response, Alexander Hamilton accused Jefferson of being a 'concealed voluptuary… in the plain garb of Quaker simplicity'.

Although himself a man of high morals, Jefferson liked the fact that Callender was a scruffy drunk, who stooped to Steve Bannon-like scandalmongering. Callender accused George Washington of profiting from the privations of his troops at Valley Forge, John Jay of being a traitor and John Adams of being a British spy. But he took care to espouse all of Jefferson's political ideas – to the point where he was accused of being a 'hireling'. Indeed, Jefferson was Callender's patron, but claimed the money he gave Callender was 'charity'.

Callender's accusations eventually led to his conviction under the Sedition Act. He was sent to prison for nine months and fined $200. When Jefferson became President in 1801, however, he pardoned Callender and ordered that the fine imposed on him be reimbursed. The local marshal in Richmond, where Callender had been sentenced, defied the order and claimed that the fine could not legally be refunded and Callender thought that Jefferson was trying to hold out on him.

To prove his good faith, Jefferson had a fund established to refund the money and donated $50 himself. Callender accepted this as 'hush-money' but warned that he could not be bought off so cheaply, expecting to be made Postmaster of Richmond as a reward.

Jefferson braced himself for the onslaught. He thought that Callender would accuse him of aiding in the publication of the tracts that had later been judged libellous in Federal Court. Instead, Callender wrote an article for the *Richmond Recorder*, a Federalist and rabidly anti-Jeffersonian paper, that accused Jefferson of lewd behaviour with women. He regurgitated the story of Betsy Walker and Betsy's husband demanded a public apology from the President. In response, Jefferson's supporters smeared Callender, saying that he had abandoned his wife while she was dying of venereal disease. Privately, Jefferson admitted that 'when young and single I offered to love a handsome lady. I acknowledge its incorrectness.' John Walker accepted this and the scandal ebbed away.

A second allegation proved much more damaging. Callender said that Jefferson had a relationship with a young slave girl named Sally Hemings who bore him several children, subsequently kept as slaves at Monticello. Not only that, Sally was the half-sister of his dead wife. Callender painted the picture of Jefferson, under the agonised gaze of his innocent daughters, sending out to the kitchen 'or perhaps to the pigsty, for his mahogany-coloured charmer'. Callender said that Jefferson regularly enjoyed the favours of his 'black Venus' and could be seen frolicking with his 'black wench and her mulatto litter'. In fact, another slave described her as 'mighty near white... very handsome, long straight hair down her back' and Jefferson's grandson called her 'light coloured and decidedly good looking'.

Callender went on to warn that if the eighty thousand white men in Virginia followed their President's example, there would soon be four hundred thousand additional slaves in the Commonwealth and the race war which Jefferson so earnestly sought to avoid would be inevitable.

As the story of Jefferson and his slave girl seized the American public's imagination, Callender upped the ante and accused Jefferson of maintaining a 'Congo harem' in the Executive Mansion itself. Then he claimed to have identified a slave named 'Yellow Tom', a lightskinned man at Monticello who bore a striking resemblance to the President.

Mrs Francis Trollope – mother of novelist Anthony – picked up the theme in her 1832-bestseller *The Democratic Manners of the Americans*. She said that Jefferson was the progenitor of 'unnumbered generations of slaves'. She also said that Jefferson had forced Harriet Hemings, Sally's sister, into a life of prostitution in Baltimore. Federalist poet William Cullen Bryant wrote:

Go wretch, resign the presidential chair,
Go scan, Philosophist, thy Sally's charms,
And sink supinely in her sable arms,
But quit to abler hands the helm of state.

Even John Quincy Adams was moved to versify, anonymously, bewailing Jefferson's words about freedom even as he enjoyed the favours of his slave concubines. And the English poet Tom Moore wrote:

> The patriot, fresh from freedom's council come,
> Now pleas 'd, retires to lash his slaves at home;
> Or woo some black Aspasia's charms
> And dreams of freedom in his bondsmaid's arms.

(Aspasia was a courtesan who became the mistress, then wife, of the Greek statesman Pericles.)

Although still leader of the Federalist Party, Alexander Hamilton was in no position to take advantage of the situation, given his own sex scandal and admission. Nevertheless Tom Paine leapt to Jefferson's defence, only to be accused of seducing the 'African Venus' himself and cuckolding his friend.

The controversy surrounding Jefferson's affair with a slave woman continues to this day. Many historians still deny that it happened. 'Dusky Sally' was a 'quadroon' and her quarter-part African heritage barely showed. Her mother was Betty Hemings, the daughter of an African slave and an English sea captain.

Betty Heming and her children came into Jefferson's possession in 1773, when Jefferson's father-in-law, wealthy Virginia planter John Wayles, died. The children's father was probably Wayles himself. He had been a long-time widower and used the slave women in his possession. It was certainly not unusual for slave-owners in eighteenth-century Virginia to take their slave women as concubines. Peter and Samuel Carr, sons of Jefferson's childhood friend Dabney Carr, certainly made free with the slave women. Ellen Randolph Coolidge, Jefferson's granddaughter, called Samuel Carr 'the most notorious good-natured Turk that ever was master of a black seraglio kept at other men's expense'.

Sadly, few slave-owners acknowledged their offspring from these illicit unions, but they were so common that many slaves were practically white in appearance, like Sally Hemmings. The Comte de Volney, who visited Monticello in 1796, remarked that there were a number of slaves, 'who, neither in point of colour nor features, showed the least trace of their original descent'.

Sally Hemings (probably Jefferson's wife's half-sister) and her family were accorded some special treatment at Monticello. They were not put to work in the fields, but given highly desirable household jobs or taught spinning or carpentry.

Jefferson's racial attitudes – especially towards people of mixed race – underwent a profound change after the Hemingses arrived at Monticello. Previously, he had believed that miscegenation – the mixing of the races – was one of the reasons that the institution of slavery must be preserved, at least until all those of African descent could be returned to Africa. The privileges given to the Hemings family, however, were soon extended to other light-skinned slaves born at Monticello. There were a lot of them. The workload of mixed-race slaves was lightened and they were not sold or hired out. The only child of Betty Hemings to be sold was Thenia, who became the property of James Monroe, fifth President of the United States.

It had all started with Paris. Betty Hemings and her young daughter Sally helped in Mrs Jefferson's sick-room during her final illness. Sally remained at Monticello doing light housework until 1787 when she was picked to accompany Jefferson's daughter Mary to Paris. Her brother James Hemings was already in Paris with Jefferson. He had been taken there to learn to cook.

Jefferson was not expecting Sally. He had written instructing that Mary be accompanied by a gentleman and 'a careful negro woman, Isabel, for instance, if she has had the smallpox'. However, fourteen-year-old Sally was despatched instead.

When Mary Jefferson arrived in England en route to Paris, Abigail Adams took charge and wrote to Jefferson that Sally was much too young and inexperienced for the job, needing 'more care than the child' – Mary herself.

When Mary and the teenage Sally arrived in Paris, Jefferson was already coming round to the French way of doing things. Initially, he had been shocked by the sexual mores of the French.

In the manner of the time, he was required to pay court to women, but he tried to avoid sexual encounters. Those who received his attentions were largely young enough to be his daughter, or old enough to be his mother. But then he was introduced to Maria Cosway, the wife of a celebrated English miniaturist, and he was electrified.

Born in Italy, she was an artist in her own right. She was intelligent, beautiful and surrounded by a court of admirers. In London, it was said that the Prince of Wales had a tunnel dug between his house and hers.

Maria's husband, Richard Cosway, was much older than her and she plainly did not love him. She had only married out of financial necessity, having even considered entering a nunnery to escape poverty before her marriage. Cosway had settled £2,800 on her and supported her penniless mother.

Maria confided to Jefferson that she despised her husband. His only use for women was as models – she was his favourite. He used his models to pose for the erotic scenes he painted on pornographic snuffboxes which he produced as a lucrative sideline. Maria believed that her husband was habitually unfaithful to her, probably with young men. He kept her with him because her beauty attracted profitable commissions.

Maria quickly turned Jefferson from a stuffy puritan into a man about town, and he admitted that, for the first time since the death of his wife, he was happy. At the time, his thoughts were certainly on sexual love. He raved over the nude statue of Venus Pudique he found in the niche of an English garden, which was 'turned half round as if inviting you with her into the recess'. Maria, he recorded, provoked in him a 'generous spasm of the heart'. In an adolescent attempt to show off in front of her, he leapt over a fence and broke his wrist.

Then suddenly in 1786, Maria Cosway and her husband left Paris. In what must be one of the most eloquent love letters of all time, Jefferson poured out his feelings in what he called *A Dialogue Between Head and Heart*. The head spoke for reason, the heart for emotion. His heart claimed to be 'the most wretched of all earthly beings' and 'overwhelmed with grief at her departure'. He said he was also 'overwhelmed with more and greater misfortunes than have befallen a descendant of Adam for three thousand years... and perhaps, after excepting Job, since the creation of the world'.

'When heaven has taken some object of our love,' he wrote, 'how sweet is it to have a bosom whereon to recline our heads, and into which we may pour the torrent of our tears.'

Later, he wrote to Maria again, begging for her love. Her letters too became passionate. He wanted to know when she was coming back to him, promised to have breakfast with her every day and 'forget that we are ever to part again'.

In August 1787, she returned to Paris, without her husband, and threw herself into Jefferson's arms. In December, though, she had to return to London. She skipped their farewell breakfast, writing later that she could not bear this second parting. In response, he said that the affair had left him 'more dead than alive'.

This seems a little disingenuous as the affair seems to have rekindled his amorous instincts. Later that month, he took up with Mrs Angelica Schuyler Church, Alexander Hamilton's sister-in-law. When she left Paris a few months later, she left her daughter in his care. The letters between Angelica and Jefferson became steamy. 'I esteem you infinitely,' she wrote. 'I am with you always in spirit; be you with me sometimes?'

Maria Cosway knew Angelica Church and got wind of the relationship. 'If I did not love her so much I would fear her rivalry,' Maria wrote to Jefferson, 'but no I give you free permission to love her with all your heart, and I shall feel happy if I think you keep me in a little corner of it, when you admit her even to reigning Queen.' Later Maria upbraided Jefferson for not writing to her as frequently as he had done before.

In 1789, Jefferson suggested that Maria join him and Angelica at Le Havre and travel with them to the United States. Maria declined this offer sharply. She wanted to be alone with him, not the third comer of a ménage á trois.

The affair with Angelica Church did not last either. Much later, Jefferson wrote to Maria Cosway from Monticello, saying that he feared he was destined to lose everything he loved. But Maria had long realised that no one could truly take the place of his dead wife Martha in Jefferson's heart. In February 1787, she asked him bluntly: 'Are you to be painted in future ages sitting solitary and sad, on the beautiful Monticello, tormented by the shadow of a woman?'

Plainly, he wasn't. Behind the scenes Jefferson had taken up with Sally Hemings, but sleeping with a slave girl was not something an upright Virginian could admit to openly, even in the relaxed atmosphere of Paris. However, it was noted that Sally would frequently accompany her master on shopping trips and return with expensive clothes.

In 1790, when he returned to Virginia, she went with him. Back at Monticello, Sally became, officially, his chambermaid. As his mistress, she bore him five children.

Two of them were allowed to leave Monticello. Harriet was given $50 and put on the stagecoach for Philadelphia and her brother Beverly was allowed to 'run away' to Pennsylvania, a free state. Both were light enough to pass for Caucasian, married white people and passed into the white community. The remaining members of the Hemings family were freed by Jefferson in his will. Their son, Eston Hemings, married a white woman and passed into the white community. Madison Hemings, who was said to resemble Jefferson, claimed he was named by Dolley Madison, during a visit to Monticello. He married a black woman and moved to Pike County, Ohio.

Sally herself was freed by Jefferson's daughter Martha and spent her last years living with Madison. She died in 1835. In 1873, Madison Hemings told the editor of the *Pike County Republican* that, before she had died, his mother had told him that he, his brothers and his sisters were indeed the children of

Thomas Jefferson. She had said that her first child had been conceived in 1789, while Jefferson was still Minister to France. When he was recalled to America, she decided to return with him rather than stay in France with her brother James and be free, because she was pregnant. That child had died in infancy, but Sally had continued to be Jefferson's lover at Monticello on the condition that her children would eventually be set free. This was confirmed by Israel Jefferson, a former slave from Monticello and a long-time friend of Sally's.

The political scandal surrounding the Sally Hemings affair did little damage to Jefferson in the long run. He made the Louisiana Purchase, founded the University of Virginia and was elected for a second term of office.

In 1998, the University of Leicester did DNA tests on the descendants of former slave Eston Hemings, which proved that Thomas Jefferson had had children with one of his slaves. America was once again scandalised.

John Adams Sr, #2

'Wholesome as the sweetly blowing spices of Arabia.'

John Adams (father of the later President John Quincy Adams) was one of the signatories to the Declaration of Independence, principal author of the U.S. Constitution and Vice President under George Washington before becoming President himself. He was serious about love.

His first romance was with one Hannah Quincy. When she broke it off, he was relieved, believing that he had been saved from a marriage that 'might have depressed me to absolute poverty and obscurity to the end of my life'.

Instead he found himself admiring the 'wit' of seventeen-year-old Mary and fourteen-year-old Abigail Smith, the daughters of the Reverend William Smith of Weymouth. Soon he was writing to 'Miss Adorable' – Abigail – complaining that, for the two or three million kisses that he had given her, he had received only one in return.

'Of consequence, the account between us is immensely in favour of yours,' he wrote, and called for her to settle up. Still, he teased that 'Miss Aurora' – Abigail's sister Mary – was a 'sweet girl' whose 'breath is wholesome as the sweetly blowing spices of Arabia'.

Marriage plans were soon under way with Abigail and Adams's ardour reached fever-pitch. 'Itches, aches, agues and repentance might be the consequence of a contact at present,' Adams warned Abigail. Then he turned up on her doorstep with a letter demanding that she give the bearer 'as many kisses and as many hours of your company after nine o'clock as he shall please to demand and charge them to my account'.

They married in 1764 and they remained passionately in love

throughout their lives, though they were frequently parted by affairs of state. During their long separations they wrote uninhibited letters to each other. Early in their relationship they addressed each other in their correspondence as 'Lysander' and 'Diana'. Lysander was a Spartan military leader, while Diana was the goddess of fertility. Later she became 'Portia', after the Roman matron renowned for her virtue and the learned female jurist in *The Merchant of Venice*. This probably suited her better. Although 'Diana' bore five children between 1765 and 1772, the Continental Congresses became birth control between them the more he was away.

Adams was not a sensualist. At the Constitutional Convention in Philadelphia in 1776, Adams suggested as symbol for the Great Seal of the new nation a favourite classical image of his – Hercules choosing between the 'rugged mountain' of virtue and the 'flowery path' of pleasure. Hercules – and Adams – naturally chose the rugged mountain.

Abigail Adams's face was very masculine and commanding, and he was short and fat. Commonly called 'His Rotundity' during his period as president, he was a little boring judging by dull state papers and turgid treatises by his hand.

Posted to Paris as assistant to Benjamin Franklin, Adams took little advantage of the opportunities for pleasure that France offered. He was, in fact, greatly shocked by the behaviour of French women as other Americans were. The first day he arrived in France, he noted, 'one of the most elegant ladies at table, young and handsome, though married to a gentleman of the company, was pleased to address her discourse to me.'

She said: 'Mr Adams, by your name I conclude you are descended from the first man and woman, and probably in your family may be preserved the tradition which may resolve a difficulty which I could never explain. I never could understand how the first couple found out about the art of lying together?'

Adams was taken aback. He blushed, but was determined not to be disconcerted. 'I thought it would be as well for one to set a brazen face against a brazen face and answer a fool according to her folly,' he confided in his autobiography.

Adams went on to explain to the woman that 'the subject is fully understood by us, whether by tradition I could not tell: I rather thought it was by instinct, for there is a physical quality in us resembling the power of electricity.' The lady said quipped she knew nothing of electricity, except that sex 'is a very happy shock'.

'This is a decent story in comparison with many heard in Bordeaux, in the short time I remained there, concerning married ladies of fashion and reputation,' Adams lamented.

In a letter to his wife, he warns his countrymen against the 'plague of Europe' – sexual promiscuity.

But slowly, like all American visitors, he was seduced by Paris.

'To tell you the truth, I admire the ladies here,' he later wrote to his 'dearest friend' – Abigail, his wife. 'Don't be jealous. They are handsome and very well educated. Their accomplishments are exceedingly brilliant. And their knowledge of letters and arts exceeds that of the English ladies much, I believe.' Nevertheless, he still professed to be scandalised by the 'profligate females' he saw in France.

He also had 'as great a terror of learned ladies, as you have. I have such a consciousness of inferiority, as mortifies and humiliates my self-love, to such a degree that I can scarcely speak in their presence. Very few of these ladies have ever had the condescension to allow me to talk. And when it has so happened, I have always come off mortified at the discovery of my inferiority.'

Adams's behaviour was in stark contrast to that of his boss Benjamin Franklin. Franklin cut a dash by appearing in the French court dressed in the plain garb of the American farmer. His straight, unpowdered hair, round hat and brown cloth coat stood out against the laced and embroidered coats and powdered and perfumed heads of the courtiers of Versailles. It also turned the heads of French women. His reputation as the most skilled of natural philosophers, his patriotism and his fame as an apostle of liberty all added to the effect. Elegant entertainments were laid on in his honour. At one, the most beautiful woman was picked out of the three hundred present to place a crown of laurels upon his head and kiss him twice upon each cheek. Afterwards the other women smothered him with kisses too.

'My venerable colleague enjoys a privilege here that is much to be envied,' Adams wrote. 'Being seventy years of age, the ladies not only allow him to embrace them as often as he pleases, but they are perpetually embracing him.'

However, Adams complained, jealously perhaps: 'The life of Dr Franklin's is a scene of continual dissipation.' But then Franklin has quite a track record. At the age of twenty four, Franklin had an illegitimate son with a 'low woman'. He was raised by Franklin's common-law wife – they could not marry as she was already wed. This was, of course, twice scandalous at the time.

At the age of thirty nine, Franklin wrote to a young male friend, recommending taking an older mistress rather than a younger one. The list of practical advantages included: 'when women cease to be handsome, they study to be good'; 'there is no hazard of children'; 'they are more prudent and discreet'; they 'prevent his ruining his health and fortune with mercenary prostitutes'; 'the pleasure of corporal enjoyment... is at least equal, and frequently superior, every knack being by practice capable of improvement'; 'the sin is less [than] debauching a virgin'; 'the compunction is less... having made a young girl miserable may give you bitter reflections, none of which can attend the making an old woman happy'; 'and lastly they are so grateful'. After all, Franklin observed, 'in the dark all cats are grey'.

In England, Franklin had been a friend of Sir Francis Dashwood, founder of the Hell Fire Club. He attended its meetings where prostitutes, local girls in search of excitement and even society ladies seeking titillation indulged in group sex.

They began the evening, at least, dressed as nuns. Dashwood was also thought to have the largest collection of pornography in England and Franklin was a known bibliophile. He was one of the first Americans to own a copy of John Cleland's *Fanny Hill; or the Memoirs of a Woman of Pleasure* and, as a bookseller, carried such titles as *The Arraignment of Lewd Women* and *The Garden of Love*.

In eighteenth-century Paris, Franklin was in his element and Abigail feared that he would a bad influence on her husband. According to Adams, he could never get to see Franklin before breakfast to read the diplomatic correspondence. Then rest of Franklin's morning was taken up with visitors 'some philosophers, academics, economists, but by far the greater part were women'.

Then, in the afternoon, 'Madam Helvétius, Madam Chaumont, Madam Le Roy etc., and others I never knew and never enquired for who were complaisant enough to depart from the custom of France as to make tea for him'.

The evenings too, Adams complained, were spent 'in hearing the ladies sing and play upon their piano fortes'.

Franklin actually spent most evenings in the company of the Brillon family, who lived nearby. Monsieur Brillon, 'a rough kind of country squire', was usually accompanied by his lover, who lived with the family and posed as a companion of Madam Brillon. Madam Brillon had a lover of her own – apart from Franklin – who also attended these dinners.

Adams was deeply shocked.

'I was astonished that these people could live together in such apparent friendship and indeed without cutting each other's throats,' he wrote. 'But I do not know the world. I soon saw and heard so much of these things in other families and among almost all the great people of the kingdom that I found it was the natural course of things. It was universally understood and nobody lost any reputation by it.'

Adams was also shocked by Franklin's behaviour at the

Auteuil household, where Franklin simultaneously tried to seduce the lady of the house and her two daughters. Then there was Madam Le Roy, the tiny wife of one of Franklin's scientific collaborators, who Franklin called his 'pocket wife'. A Madame Filleul would have him picked up by her carriage and sent notes saying how she 'looked forward to kissing him'.

Adams tried not to criticise his colleague and the elder statesman too harshly in his autobiography, noting simply: 'Mr Franklin, who at the age of seventy odd, has neither lost his love of beauty nor his taste for it.' He mentions that Mademoiselle de Passy, the beautiful young daughter of the noble lord of the village outside Paris where Franklin lived, was 'his favourite and his flame and his love and his mistress, which flattered the family and did not displease the young lady'.

During Adams's time in France, his wife reproached him for neglecting her. She wrote that 'the tears have flowed faster than ink' and that she might 'assume the signature of Penelope' – the faithful wife who rejected other suitors while her husband Odysseus was away having fun. But, as Adams reminded his wife, 'my voyages and journeys are not for my private information, instruction, improvement, entertainment or pleasure, but laborious and hazardous enterprises of business'.

When in 1784 Abigail Adams joined her husband in France, she too, in turn, was taken aback by the behaviour of French women – especially Franklin's lover Madame Helvétius.

'This lady dined with at Dr Franklin's,' she wrote, 'she entered the room with a careless, jaunty air; upon seeing ladies who were strangers to her, she bawled out, 'Ah! mon Dieu, where is Franklin? Why did you not tell me there were ladies here?' You must suppose her speaking all this in French. 'How I look!' she said, taking hold of a chemise made of tiffany, which she had on over a blue lute-string. She was once a handsome woman; her hair was frizzled; over it, she had a small straw hat, with a dirty gauze half-handkerchief round it, and a bit of dirtier gauze, that ever my maids wore, was bowed on behind.

'She had a black gauze scarf thrown over her shoulders. She ran out of the room; when she returned, the Doctor entered at one door, she at the other; upon which she ran forward to him, caught him by the hand, 'Hélas Franklin'; then she gave him a double kiss, one upon each cheek, and another upon his forehead. When we went into the room to dine, she was placed between the Doctor and Mr Adams. During dinner, she frequently locking her hand into the Doctor's sometimes spreading her arms upon the backs of both gentlemen's chairs, then throwing her arm carelessly upon the Doctor's neck.

'I should have been greatly astonished at this conduct, if the good Doctor had not told me that in this lady I should see a genuine French woman, wholly free from affectation of stiffness of behaviour, and one of the best women in the world. For this I must take the Doctor's word; but I should have set her down for a very bad one, although sixty years of age, and a widow. I own I was highly disgusted, and never wish for an acquaintance with any ladies of this cast. After dinner she threw herself upon a settee, where she showed more than her feet. She had a little lapdog, who was, next to the Doctor, her favorite. This she kissed, and when he wet the floor, she wiped it up with her chemise. This is one of the Doctor's most intimate friends, with whom he dines once every week, and she with him.'

Adams's daughter Abby wrote of the same event in her journal: 'Dined at Dr Franklin's invitation, a number of gentlemen, and Mme Helvétius, a French lady, sixty years of age. Odious indeed do our sex appear when divested of those ornaments, with which modesty and delicacy adorn them.'

Although she was no longer a great beauty, Madame Helvétius was still sexually attractive, and a witty, liberated woman. Seeing her in a daringly low-cut dress, the writer Bernard Le Bovier de Fontenelle, then in his nineties, sighed: 'Oh, to be seventy again.'

Franklin used to say that the purest and most useful friend a man could possibly procure was a Frenchwoman of a certain age. 'They are,' he said, 'so ready to do you a service and, from their knowledge of the world, know so well how to serve you wisely.'

After Paris, John and Abigail Adams were posted to London, where he became the U.S. ambassador to the Court of St James. After that, they returned to America where Adams became Washington's Vice President.

Abigail Adams, an educated woman, had a huge influence on the early presidency. Unlike Martha Washington, who had never travelled overseas, she had observed European courts first-hand and, both as the wife of the first Vice President and as First Lady, she helped bring European style to state occasions. Mrs President, as she was often called, was the first First Lady to entertain in the new Presidential Mansion in Washington, DC, which was built during Adams's term of office. She held state dinners and receptions despite the primitive conditions she found there.

'We had not the least fence, yard or other conveniences without,' Abigail wrote, 'and the great unfinished audience room, I made a drying room of.'

The Adamses only had to suffer the privations of Washington for a short while though. John Adams was voted out of office after one term. Abigail was disappointed, but took consolation in the fact that for the next seventeen years, living in retirement in Quincy, Massachusetts, they were rarely separated.

Their sexual passion for each other continued into later life. In one of her letters, the long-suffering Abigail wrote: 'No man, even if he is sixty, ought to live more than three months at a time away from his family.' He replied irately: 'How dare you hint or lisp a word about 'sixty years of age'. If I were near, I would soon convince you that I am not above forty.'

At other times, Adams bemoaned the fact that his 'sauciness' continued into later life. He wrote 'when a man's vivacity increases with years it becomes frenzy at last'. Towards the end of his life he complained in his notebooks of being 'coaxed by a fascinating woman into a subscription' for a book he did not really want.

When Abigail came down with typhoid fever in 1818, Adams wrote to Jefferson: 'The dear partner of my life for fifty four years and for many years more as a lover, now lies *in extremis*, forbidden to speak or be spoken to.' When she died the following week, Adams stood next to her bed and said simply: 'I wish I could lay down beside her and die too.'

Adams's daughter-in-law Louise Catherine replaced his wife in his affections. They began a long and intimate correspondence. Even in old age his spark had not left him. At eighty nine, he greeted a lady he had known in his youth with the line: 'Madam, shall we not go walk in Cupid's Grove together?'

She was mortified by this remark, but after an embarrassed pause, she admitted: 'It would not be the first time we walked together.'

In 1820, John Quincy Adams' wife Louise wrote to John Adams saying she had just learned that the orphan asylum would need more space because 'the fathers of the nation had left forty cases to be provided for by the public'.

Forty pregnant women left behind by the 16th Congress – and there were only 232 members. Furious, asylum trustee Louisa Adams huffed: 'I recommended a petition to Congress next session for that great and moral body to establish a foundling institution' and use the $2-a-day pay increase they had voted themselves to fund it. Of course, that never happened.

XXXXIV
George Washington, #1
Feel the sap rising

'The love of my country will be the ruling influence of my conduct,' wrote George Washington. But his love of women was stronger and it is amazing that he found the time to fight the British or found a nation.

Washington's interest in sex began on a trip to survey the Shenandoah Valley when he was sixteen years old. He was already infatuated with Frances Alexander of Fredericksburg, to whom he addressed some rather embarrassing adolescent love poetry. He bemoaned his 'poor restless heart, wounded by Cupid's dart', but he could not bring himself to tell her of his feelings. 'Ah, woe is me, that I should love and conceal; Long have I wished and never dare reveal,' he wrote excruciatingly.

However in Shenandoah, he took up with another 'Low Land Beauty' with more success. There is speculation that she was a Miss Grimes, who later married a man named Henry Lee. Her son, General Henry Lee – known during the War of Independence as Light Horse Harry – was a favourite of Washington's.

That December, after returning from Shenandoah, Washington met the love of his life. She was the wife of his best friend George William Fairfax, whose father, Lord Fairfax, was Washington's patron. George Fairfax had been brought up in England where his family had made his life miserable by spreading rumours that he was a mixed race. When he came out to the colonies, a marriage was arranged with Sarah 'Sally' Cary, the eighteen-yearold daughter of a planter. Fairfax found her an acceptable wife, but Washington found her irresistible. Washington would often visit Belvoir, the Fairfax's estate. He was sixteen at the time and, as Lord Fairfax observed, was 'beginning to feel the sap rising'.

At first, when he stayed at Belvoir with the Fairfaxes, Washington tried not to think about sex. He wrote to a friend 'was my heart disengaged [I might] pass my time very pleasantly, as there's a very agreeable young lady lives in the same house… but as that's only adding fuel to the fire, it makes me the more uneasy for, by often and unavoidably being in the company with her, revives my former passion for your Low Land Beauty, whereas was I to live more retired from young women, I might in some measure alleviate my sorrows by burying that chaste and troublesome passion in the grave of oblivion or eternal forgetfulness.'

The 'agreeable young lady' Washington mentioned here was Mary Cary, Sally Fairfax's sister, but it was Sally who eventually stole his heart.

Sally was two years older than Washington, attractive, vivacious and the most fascinating woman he ever met. He was totally smitten by her and throughout his life he could not think of her without being choked with emotion.

He found relief from his infatuation in fox-hunting, English-style. Thomas Jefferson said later that he was 'the best horseman of his age and the most graceful figure that could be seen on horseback'.

Washington also took time out to compose his famous '110 Rules of Civility and Decent Behavior'. These included: 'When in company, put not your hands to any part of the body not usually discovered' and 'Put not off your clothes in the presence of others, nor go out of your chamber half dressed.' He was against spitting in the fire, killing fleas, lice and ticks in the presence of others, picking your teeth and talking with your mouth full. But the most important rules were: 'Let your recreations be manful not sinful' and 'Labour to keep alive in your breast that little spark of celestial fire called conscience.'

A tall, impressive man, Washington had light, grey-blue eyes, auburn hair and – according to several contemporaries – the largest hands and feet they had seen. Two local women would have been able to confirm this. In the summer of 1751, Washington went swimming in the Rappahannock near his mother's home, when the two women stole his clothes. The women were arrested and one of them turned state's evidence. The other, Mary McDaniel, was convicted of 'robbing the clothes of Mr George Washington when he was washing in the river' and received fifteen lashes on her naked back.

Washington was not there to see the punishment carried out. He had sailed for Barbados in September 1751, possibly to escape from an affair with the wife of a neighbour, Captain John Posey, who was heavily in debt to Washington. Mrs Posey's first son was, like Washington, inordinately tall. Washington also paid for his education and he rose through the ranks of the Continental Army with unusual speed.

In the Caribbean, he met 'an agreeable young lady' named Miss Roberts. They went to see the fireworks on Guy Fawkes night. He found the women there 'generally agreeable but by ill custom'.

In 1752, Washington courted fifteen-year-old Betsy Fauntleroy, the daughter of a wealthy Richmond planter. Her father did not think that Washington was rich enough to maintain her in the manner to which she had become accustomed and she turned him down. Washington wrote to her begging her for a 'revocation of her former cruel sentence', but she married a prosperous planter's son and died a wealthy woman. Washington consoled himself with one of the less sophisticated women in the valley. Nevertheless his infatuation with Sally Fairfax continued.

In 1753, Washington indulged his lifelong passion for uniforms and joined the Virginia militia. Sally Fairfax was there to see him march off with General Braddock on a campaign to retake Fort Duquesne, in what is now Pittsburgh, from the French. She was a terrible coquette and could not resist flirting with Braddock.

Within twenty four hours of leaving, Washington had fired off a letter to Sally. Two more letters followed in the next six weeks. When Sally failed to reply, Washington wrote to her brother and sister, asking them to persuade her to write, but it was George Fairfax's sister, having found out what was going on, who wrote to Washington, reproaching him.

Washington was not to be put off. When Braddock sent him on an errand to Williamsburg, he stopped off at Belvoir to see Sally. She rebuked him and told him to stop writing to her. He did not. If she would only send him a letter, he begged in his next missive, it would 'make me happier than the day is long'.

As it happens, his thoughts were not solely on Sally during the expedition. In a letter a fellow officer mentions a 'Mrs Neil', saying: 'I imagine you by this time plunged in the midst of delight heaven can afford and enchanted by charms even stranger to the Ciprian dame.' The 'Ciprian dame' means Venus who was said to have risen from the water near Cyprus where her cult of temple prostitution later flourished.

There was only one thing on the minds of these young officers. George Mercer, then a captain in the Virginia Regiment, later Washington's aide-de-camp, wrote to him from Charleston lamenting the quality of the women there: 'A great imperfection here too is the bad shape of the ladies, many of them are crooked and have a very bad air, and not the enticing heaving throbbing alluring… exciting breasts come with our Northern belles.' Another talks of his brother officer softening 'his austerity in the arms of some fair nymph – could he reconcile the toying, trifling, billing sports of love to the solemnity and gravity of his deportment – amusements and joys unbecoming of his philosophic temper'.

Washington also wooed Native Americans. He noted that to ingratiate himself Queen Aliquippa he gave her 'a match-coat and a bottle of rum'. Encamped at Wills' Creek, the soldiers came across some Delaware Indians. The young Indian women liked the British – as Washington then was – and hung around Braddock's camp. It was reported that 'they were not destitute of attractions; for the young squaws resemble the gypsies, having seductive forms, small hands and feet, and soft voices'. One particular girl caught Washington's attention – 'one who no doubt passed for an Indian Princess'. Her name was Bright Lightning. She was the daughter of Chief White Thunder. And it is clear that the intercourse between the Indian women and the soldiers was not entirely chaste. The secretary of the expedition wrote to governor Morris, later one of authors of the Constitution and no strange to the 'Ciprian mystery' with his French mistress: 'The squaws bring in money aplenty; the officers are scandalously fond of them.'

Eventually, the Delaware warriors got jealous and Bright Lightning and the other Indian women had to be banned from the British camp. But this did not stop them from meeting elsewhere. Eventually, for the sake of peace, Bright Lightning and the other Native American women were sent home to Aughquick.

As Braddock progressed towards Fort Duquesne, his mission turned into a disaster. The column was ambushed by hostile Indians and Braddock died in the ensuing battle. Washington discharged himself bravely. Two horses were shot out from under him and four bullets tore through his clothes, miraculously, without hurting him. Already a full colonel, the twenty three-year-old Washington assumed command of all Virginia's troops. He returned home to Mount Vernon a hero and found a letter from Sally waiting for him there. In it, Sally expressed her joy that he had returned home safely and she begged him to come to Belvoir the next day, if he was fit. If he was not, she would come to Mount Vernon, but she would not be alone. A second note was also signed by Ann Spearing and Elizabeth Dent. And a letter from a leading Virginian named Archibald Cary said that 'Mrs Cary and Miss Randolph join in wishing you that sort of glory which will most endear you to the fair sex'.

To avoid a double, or even triple date, Washington rode to the Fairfax mansion the next day. Suddenly, Washington found that his feelings for Sally were, to some extent, reciprocated and he and Sally began an intense correspondence – though Sally repeatedly urged him to observe certain proprieties. She insisted, for example, that he did not write to her directly, rather he should communicate via a third party. The ardent young Washington took no notice and, though Sally chided him, she continued to write to him. In a brief note to her from Fort Cumberland, he wrote of his joy 'at the happy occasion of renewing a correspondence which I feared was disrelished on your part'. She even began performing wifely tasks for him, like having his shirts made.

Washington gradually began to accept the fact that he could never possess his true love, so he was constantly looking around for other marriageable women. On a visit to New York in 1756, he met Mary Eliza Philipse, who was known as 'the agreeable Miss Polly'. This was not least because of her social connections and the size of her inheritance. She was statuesque with a full, sensuous mouth and she was very wealthy. Her father owned 51,000 acres of prime New York real estate. Washington took her dancing and to a mechanical exhibition called 'The Microcosm, or World in Miniature'. Passion flared in his breast and his accounts show that he spent sundry pounds 'for treating ladies'.

However, the main purpose of the trip to New York was not love, but military matters. The *Virginia Gazette* had accused Washington and his officers of 'all manner of debauchery, vice and idleness'. This was unfair. Washington was a stern disciplinarian, if anything he was rather too fond of the lash. He meted out brutal floggings of up to five hundred strokes.

In New York, Governor Shirley grilled Washington for several days on the conditions on the frontier and Polly grew impatient. Her affections turned elsewhere. Eventually she married Captain Roger Morris, who had been with Washington on the Braddock expedition. During the War of Independence, Morris remained loyal to the British crown. Washington confiscated his house to use as his headquarters. He met Polly there again and there are indications that they had an affair. She was attractive: 'Although slim, Polly was also statuesque; her delicate features were somehow expressive of cool strength; her full mouth was both sensuous and firm.'

After his trip to New York, Washington returned to Virginia and, during the winter of 1757-58 he fell ill. The doctor put him on a diet of 'jellies and such kinds of foods', but among the fourteen slaves he had inherited and the six – including a woman and her child – he had bought, there was no one at Mount Vernon capable of preparing such things, he complained. Sally came to his rescue.

Following the death of his father, George Fairfax had gone to England to sort out the estate. Sally had been left behind, alone, at Belvoir and she rode over to see Washington frequently. She prepared jellies for him, hyson tea and a special wine that was mixed with gum arabic. When Washington rose from his sickbed, he was more in love with her than ever.

Their letters of that period are full of veiled suggestions and innuendo, but their conduct was always restrained and discreet. Even among their small circle of friends there was not a whiff of scandal. He urged her to destroy his letters as the 'world had not business' knowing their feelings for one another. Those that survive are loaded with innuendo. In one, he said he felt 'the force of her amiable beauties in the recollection of a thousand tender passages'. He admits to being a 'votary to love' and that he wishes to obliterate his feelings for her 'till I am bid to revive them – but experience alas! sadly reminds me how impossible this is'.

Undoubtedly this was the high point of their affair. Soon after Washington was well again, George Fairfax returned from England and Washington set about finding himself a wife in earnest. As his heart was already taken, he decided to marry instead for money and started wooing Martha Custis, a widow and the richest woman in Virginia.

Martha Custis had been born Martha Dandridge on 2 June 1731 on a plantation near Williamsburg. The oldest daughter of plantation owners John and Frances Dandridge, her education was limited to social and domestic skills. She displayed a natural ability as a horsewoman and as a young woman had horrified her aunt and stepmother when she rode her horse Fatima up and down the stairs of her uncle's house.

At the age of eighteen, she married wealthy planter Daniel Parke Custis, twenty years her senior, and took up residence in the Custis family home, which was called, ironically, the White House. She had four children by him, two of whom died in infancy. Her husband died in 1757, after seven years of marriage. The following year, the twenty-six-year-old Washington paid his first visit to her. He was eight months her junior. They sat in the parlour and talked. He stayed the night. A little more than a week later, he visited her again. This time he promised to marry her. She was not Sally Fairfax. Martha was plump, dowdy and rather shy. She once described herself as 'an old-fashioned housekeeper'. But Washington was sincere; after all, she was who he was looking for. He ordered from London 'as much of the best superfine blue cotton velvet as will make a coat, a waistcoat and breeches for a tall man, with a fine silk button to suit it… six pairs of the very latest shoes… [and] six pairs of gloves'. At the same time, Martha sent out to have her nightgown dyed a more fashionable colour.

When Sally got wind of Washington's impending engagement, she wrote congratulating him. Although he was pleased to hear from her, he had hoped that she would have taken this last opportunity to spell out her feelings towards him. He felt he had nothing to lose and wrote back declaring his love for her – but also his resolve to go ahead with his marriage if she did not reciprocate.

'If you allow that any honour can be derived from my opposition to our present system of management, you destroy the merit of it entirely in me by attributing my anxiety to the animated prospect of possessing Mrs Custis,' he wrote. 'When – I need not name it – guess yourself. Should not my own honour and country's welfare be the excitement? 'tis true, I profess myself a votary of love. I acknowledge that a lady is in the case, and further I confess that this lady is known to you. Yes, Madam, as well as she is to one who is too sensible of her charms to deny the power whose influence he feels and must ever submit to. I feel the force of her amiable beauties in recollection of a thousand tender passages that I could wish to obliterate. You have drawn me, dear Madam, or rather I have drawn myself, into an honest confession of a simple fact. Misconstrue not my meaning; doubt it not, nor expose it. The world has no business to know the object of my love, declared in this manner to you, when I want to conceal it. One thing, above all things in this world I wish to know, and only one person of your acquaintance can solve that, or guess my meaning. But adieu to this, till happier times, if I ever shall see them.' By comparison, Washington's letters to Martha are pedestrian.

Sally's reply has never been found. She did respond because, on 25 September 1758, Washington wrote again, still desperate for some declaration of love from Sally: 'Dear Madam, Do we still misunderstand the true meaning of each other's letters? I think it must appear so, though I would feign hope the contrary as I cannot speak plainer with. But I'll say no more and leave you to guess the rest…'

He went on to make an allusion to Juba, an African prince, who loves Cato's daughter Marcia, in the play Cato, by Joseph Addison, which spawned some of the American Revolution's most memorable quotes, such as 'Give me liberty or give me death' and 'I only regret that I have but one life to lose for my country.'

He says that he would be 'doubly happy in being Juba to such a Marcia as you must make'. In the play Marcia is asked why she hides her love for Juba? She replies: 'While Cato lives, his daughter has no right to love or hate, but as his choice directs.'

This letter caused a scandal when it was published by the *New York Herald* in 1877. It was dated 12 September 1758, four months after Washington had become engaged to Martha Dandridge Custis, the richest widow in Virginia.

Washington already knew their love was doomed. The situation was impossible. George Fairfax had returned from England. In 1758, there was no way that Sally could have divorced her husband and married Washington. It would have caused an immense scandal, leaving them both social outcasts. Continuing a clandestine affair would easily have had the same result. Either way, Washington exposed himself to a ruinous lawsuit from her aggrieved husband. Both he and Sally would have remembered when George Washington's half-brother Lawrence had prosecuted a neighbour for allegedly raping his wife, Sally's sister-in-law Anne Fairfax, before her marriage. The court proceedings were reported in salacious detail in newspapers in Virginia, Maryland and

Pennsylvania. Before it was over, everyone wished that Lawrence had kept quiet.

Washington set about trying to make Martha happy. He sent to Philadelphia for a ring and at 1pm on 6 January 1759, after what would have been considered a whirlwind romance, they married in front of forty guests. The ceremony was brief; the reception formal.

They honeymooned at the Custis White House, while renovations were being completed at Mount Vernon. When they were completed, Washington moved his ready-made family there. Martha was a popular addition to the household. Later a slave at Mount Vernon would say: 'The General was only a man, but Mrs Washington was perfect.'

Within a year, Washington was writing to a friend: 'I am now I believe fixed at this seat with an agreeable consort for life and hope to find more happiness in retirement than I ever experienced amidst the wide and bustling world.'

In later life, he compared unfavourably 'the giddy round of promiscuous pleasure' he enjoyed in his youth with the 'domestic felicity' he found in marriage. He summed up his attitude to marriage in a letter to his stepdaughter. He advised her not to 'look for perfect felicity before you consent to wed. Nor conceived, from the fine tales the poets and lovers of old have told us of the transports of mutual love, that heaven has taken its abode on earth. Nor do not deceive yourself in supposing that the only means by which these are to be obtained is to drink deep of the cup and revel in an ocean of love. Love is a mighty pretty thing, but, like all other delicious things, it is cloying; and when the first transports of the passion begin to subside, which it assuredly will do, and yield, oftentimes too late, to more sober reflections, it serves to evince that love is too dainty a food to live on alone, and ought not to be considered further than as a necessary ingredient for that matrimonial happiness which results from a combination of causes: none of which are of greater importance than that the object on whom it is placed should possess good sense, a good disposition, and the means of supporting you in the way you have been brought up. Such qualifications cannot fail to attract (after marriage) your esteem and regard into which or into disgust, sooner or later love naturally resolves itself.... Be assured, and experience will convince you that there is no truth more certain than that all our enjoyments fall short of our expectations, and to none does it apply with more force than to the gratification of the passions.'

Later still he wrote to his granddaughter telling her that 'men and women feel the same inclinations to each other now that they always have done, may find, perhaps, that the passions of your sex are easier raised than allayed... there is no truth more certain than that all our enjoyments fall short of our expectations; and to none does it apply with more force than the gratifications of the passions.'

He warned: 'In the composition of the human frame there is a good deal of inflammable matter, however dormant it may lie. When the torch is put to it, that which is within you may burst into a blaze.' But in marriage, he said, 'the madness ceases and all is quiet again. Why? not because there is any diminution in the charms of the lady, but because there is an end of hope.'

For Washington, though, this was not the whole story. The inflammable material would burst back into a blaze with the war, but for those first years of marriage the madness had ceased and for the moment, he devoted himself to the management of their joint estate and the rearing of Martha's children.

Martha had brought to the marriage livestock and goods worth almost £20,000, along with three hundred slaves. Washington was as brutal to the slaves as he was to his troops. Men were forced to work even when ill. Runaways were hunted down and severely flogged. Children were left without clothes or blankets. One died of the mange. He was no better with the female slaves. In his diaries, Washington refers quite dispassionately to this or that slave woman as 'a wench of mine'. He often had the women flogged too.

During his presidency, one female slave ran away from Washington's house in Philadelphia. He wanted her hunted down and punished for her 'ingratitude'. Such things may be quite all right in Virginia, he was told, but in Pennsylvania – a free state – the result would be a riot.

Washington was particularly harsh on 'nightwalking' – that is, slaves visiting each other's huts after dark – because, he complained, it left his servants and field hands 'unfit for the duties of the day'. He knew what was going on because there is every indication that, like many Virginia planters, he visited women in the slave quarters at night himself.

After Washington's marriage, he still saw Sally. In fact, Sally and George Fairfax were regular visitors at Mount Vernon. Mrs Fairfax even attended Mrs Washington on her sickbed when Martha had the measles. Behind the backs of their respective spouses, Sally and Washington kept up a clandestine correspondence.

Then in September 1774, Sally Fairfax fell ill. The medical attention she required could only be found in Europe, so she and her husband sailed for England. Washington was heartbroken to see his love go. To console himself he bought £169-worth of her possessions, including the bolster and pillows from her bed. The Fairfaxes were Tories who supported the king and could not return after the Revolution.

Even though they slept together, George and Martha Washington never had children of their own. There has been a great deal of speculation about the reason for this. Martha had given birth to four children in her previous marriage, so she was certainly fertile. Washington's biographer James T. Flexner concludes that Washington was sterile. Certainly, there is nothing in his behaviour to suggest that he was impotent. He was fond of women, enjoyed their company and had a passion for dancing. He and Martha shared a bedroom at Mount Vernon, and he shared the eighteenth-century fear of bathing even in the hot Virginia summers.

A proud man and a natural athlete, Washington never reconciled himself to the fact that he may not have children. He only seems to have become sterile after catching smallpox in Barbados. In his later years, he came to believe that, if Martha died and he were to remarry a 'girl', he might yet father an heir nonetheless.

Washington tried to be a good father to Martha's children. Her son Jack was a constant worry to him. Washington engaged a live-in tutor and kept a constant eye on the boy's studies. When that did not work out, Jack was sent to a school run by the Reverend Jonathan Boucher. Soon his schoolmasters were complaining of Jack's laziness and Boucher wrote that never had he known a lad 'so exceedingly indolent, or so surprisingly voluptuous'.

Boucher also complained that Jack had 'a propensity to the female sex, which I am at a loss how to judge, much more how to describe. One would suppose nature had intended him for some Asiatic prince.'

Jack quit school without his parents' permission and enrolled at King's College, which later became Columbia University. There, without even consulting his parents, he got engaged to Nelly Calvert, the daughter of an illegitimate son of the fifth Lord Baltimore, former governor of Maryland.

Washington intervened. He wrote to Mr Calvert saying that Jack must finish his education before he got married and hurried the boy off to New York. There he cut a swathe, living up to the reputation of an 'Asiatic prince'. He finally married, not to Nelly, at nineteen and was known generally as a wealthy idler. However, when the War of Independence came, he served as an aide to his stepfather. He died of 'camp fever' – typhus – shortly after in the battle of Yorktown. Meanwhile, Washington's surviving brother shared his overactive libido and married five times.

According to Marvin Kitman, author of *The Making of the President 1789*, Washington was an accomplished womaniser. His A-list of possible lovers include a Lucy Flucker Knox, who abandoned her Tory family to rally to the Revolutionaries; Mrs Clement Biddle, wife of the leader of the 'Quaker Blues'; Mrs George Olny, who when Washington grabbed her in public told him to mind his hands; Theodosia Provost Burr, wife of Aaron Burr who was knocking of their maid at the time, siring two illegitimate kids by her; Lady Kitty Alexander Duer, New York party girl; Lady Stirling, Lady Kitty's mother who was often seen in Washington's arms on the dance floor; Elizabeth Gates, who often wore men's clothing and was called 'a daemoness' by General Charles Lee; Phoebe Fraunces, serving wench at the tavern owned by her father Black Sam Fraunces and Washington's only nod to egalitarianism, in his love life at least; Elizabeth Willing Powel, the young widow of the mayor of Philadelphia and notorious political groupie; society hostess Mrs William Bingham, another of the Willing clan; Mrs Perez Morton, poetess known in literary circles as 'The American Sappho'; and the ubiquitous Kitty Greene, 'a younger version of Sally Fairfax,' an intimate remarked.

Colonel Freeman said of the twenty-two-year-old Kitty: 'She enlivened many a black night in the revolutionary headquarters.' An orphan, she was bewitchingly pretty and grew up to be the beauty of Providence, Rhode Island. In 1774, she married General Nathaniel Greene, but remained a notorious flirt. With the outbreak of war, she rushed to the front, while other generals' wives were being packed off home. At Valley Forge she became the mistress of General Lafayette, the French marquis who rallied to the revolutionaries' cause. She said so herself, remarking in a letter to Colonel Wadsworth that she was 'sleeping with the Marquis'. Lafayette even wrote to his wife, telling her how fond of Kitty he was.

She also slept with her husband's business partner, Colonel Kósciuszko and General 'Mad' Anthony Wayne. It was soldiers she loved most of all. In a letter to a friend in March 1779, General Greene complained that Washington had danced with his wife non-stop for three hours, a gross breach of etiquette. Washington himself remarked in a letter home to Martha how fond he was of Kitty. Add the off-the-record statement of an anonymous coach-driver and their relationship would have been enough to be bought up by the *National Enquirer*.

On Kitman's B-list are the two daughters of a Mrs Watkins of Passaic, New Jersey, who had an affair with Washington before he visited the then widowed Theodosia Provost; Mrs Bache, Benjamin Franklin's goddaughter who danced the night away with Washington at his twentieth wedding anniversary; Mary Gibbons who Washington meet during the war and reportedly 'maintained genteelly in Hoboken, New Jersey'; and unemployed seamstress – and 'beautiful young widow' – Betsy Ross, who is credited with making the first American flag.

Washington was also approached by the renowned poetess, Annie Boundinot Stockton, then an attractive widow. She sent him a poem and begged his absolution for writing it. He wrote back saying that if she would dine with him 'and go through the proper course of penitence, which shall be prescribed, I will strive hard to assist you in expiating these poetical trespasses on this side of purgatory'.

If his intentions were not clear enough, he continued: 'You see, Madam, when once the woman has tempted use and we have tasted the forbidden fruit, there is no such thing as checking our appetites, whatever the consequences may be.'

The Continental Congresses in Philadelphia and the War of Independence certainly gave Washington the opportunity to spend a lot of time for affairs away from Martha. He was away from Mount Vernon for eight years during the war. Martha paid a conjugal visit to the front on an average of one week a year.

Washington's predilection for young women led to a scandal known as the 'Washerwoman Kate Affair'. It seems that a Congressman Harrison acted as Washington's procurer in Philadelphia while Washington was at the front. In a letter to Washington, Harrison wrote: 'As I was in the pleasing task of writing to you a little noise occasioned to turn my head around, and who should appear but pretty little Kate, the washerwoman's daughter, over the way, clean, trim, and rosy as the morning. I snatched the golden glorious opportunity, and but for that cursed antidote to love, Sukey [his wife, Mrs Harrison], I had fitted her for my General against his return. We were obliged to part, but not till we had contrived to meet again; if she keeps the appointment I shall relish a week's longer stay – I give you now and then some of these adventures to amuse you and unbend your mind from the cares of war.'

The letter was intercepted, found its way into the hands of the *Boston Weekly News-Letter* and was picked up by the *Gentleman's Magazine* in London. The story then became the nub of a play which opened on Broadway with the rather unwieldy title of *The Battle of Brooklyn: A Farce of Two Acts: As It Was Performed on Long Island, on Tuesday the 27th day of 1776, by the Representatives of Americans, Assembled at Philadelphia.*

Throughout the War of Independence, the British used sexual propaganda against Washington. Rumours were spread that he had mistresses – both black and white – throughout the colonies. It was also argued that Washington was a woman dressed in men's clothing, which explained why he had fathered no children by Martha.

In the play, Lady Gates, wife of General Horatio Gates, a retired British general fighting for the revolutionaries, cross-questions her maid Betty about her relations with Benjamin Harrison who, it seems, had bought her services for fifty 'hard' dollars, only to hand her over to Washington. But Betty was not unhappy with the arrangement. She tells Lady Gates that she could not stand Harrison even for half a night. George Washington, by contrast, was the 'sweetest, meekest, melancholy sighing gentleman; and then he is such a warrior – oh, mam, I shall always love the General'. Washington then gave her a thirty-dollar bill – 'he assured me that it would have been more, but that he was obliged to repay Harrison the fifty hard dollars.'

In fact, the British propaganda was not wholly off the mark. During the war, Washington billeted himself at various well-appointed mansions and enjoyed the attentions of the pretty daughters of the house. He would get them to sing for him and he would enjoy watching his aides flirt with them.

He also enjoyed the banter of women himself. During one absence, Annie Boudinot Stockton, a handsome widow, sent him a poem with a request for him to give her absolution for writing poetry. Washington wrote back, saying if she would dine with him 'and go through the proper course of penitence, which shall be prescribed, I will strive hard to assist you in expiating these poetical trespasses on this side of purgatory'.

Then he got downright direct. 'You see, Madam,' he wrote, 'when once the woman has tempted us and we have tasted the forbidden fruit, there is no such thing as checking our appetites, whatever the consequences may be.'

Washington frequently chose this line of forthright attack – even with the wife of a brother officer. At a dinner party given by Colonel Clement Biddle, the Revolutionary Army's Foragemaster General, the ladies withdrew to leave the men to their wine. George Olney, a civilian commissary, made it plain that he did not approve of the soldiers' drinking, so Washington and his cohorts attempted to get him drunk. He fled to be with the ladies and Washington led the assault on the drawing room to get him back.

The officers advanced 'with great formality to the adjoining room, and sent in a summons which the ladies refused. Such a scuffle then ensued as any good-natured person might suppose.'

The increasingly bullying confrontation of Mr Olnay suddenly culminated when Mrs Olney shouted at Washington 'in a violent rage'. If he did not let go of her hand, she said, 'I will tear out your eyes and the hair from your head.' She also told Washington that he thought he was a general, but he was just a man.

Even at Valley Forge, the Revolutionary forces did not go without sex. General Charles Lee was caught smuggling local girls into the camp. On one occasion, Washington was apparently besieged by the beautiful actress Margaret 'Peggy' Shippen, wife of Benedict Arnold. She began running about his headquarters practically naked, shouting that there was 'a hot iron on her head, and no one but General Washington could take it off'. When he went to comfort her, she appeared topless in a dressing gown. According to another account, she was in bed when he went to comfort her and the distraught woman pulled back the bedclothes, 'revealing her charms'.

Washington did not hide his intentions from his wife. A French officer at Morristown observed with surprise that Washington 'admires pretty women… notices their gowns and how their hair is dressed. He does it quite openly, and before his wife, who does not seem to mind at all.'

The wife of a Virginia colonel wrote to a female confidante: 'Now let me speak of our noble and agreeable commander, for he commands both sexes, one by his excellent skill in military matters, the other by his ability, politeness and attention… from dinner till night he is free for all company. His worthy lady seems to be in perfect felicity when she is by the side of her Old Man as she calls him. We often make parties on horseback.'

But when Martha was not around, the woman notes, Washington 'throws off the hero and takes on the chatty, agreeable companion. He can be downright impudent sometimes – such impudence, Fanny, as you and I like.'

Washington tried to keep Martha at home, but when the British marched into Virginia and threatened Mount Vernon, it was the perfect excuse for her to join him permanently. She spent the war tending wounded soldiers, mending clothes, knitting socks and doing what she could to boost morale. 'Whilst our husbands and brothers are examples of patriotism,' she told American women, 'we must be patterns of industry.'

At the end of the war, Washington and Martha returned to Mount Vernon. In 1789, when he became the United States's first President, Martha reluctantly followed her husband first to New York, then to Philadelphia as the first Lady, a role she hated.

'I cannot blame him for having acted according to his ideas of duty in obeying the voice of his country,' she wrote. But she took little satisfaction in the formal functions and ceremonies that aimed to put the revolutionary court on a par with those in Europe.

Washington himself, however, greatly enjoyed being President. He had always revelled in the admiration of women. He must have thought he was in heaven on 21 April 1789 when he passed through Trenton, New Jersey – the site of his first victory during the War of Independence – on his way to New York for his inauguration. The people there had built an archway with thirteen pillars, one for each of the states. On it was the inscription: 'The defender of the mothers will be the protector of the daughters.' Thirteen young women, dressed in simple white gowns, scattered flowers in his path. They sang:

> Welcome, mighty Chief! Once more
> Welcome to this grateful shore!
> Now no mercenary foe
> Aims again the fatal blow –
> Aims at thee the fatal blow.
> Virgins fair, and matrons grave,
> Those thy conquering arms did save,
> Build for thee triumphal blowers,
> Strew our hero's way with flowers.

Then the ladies of the town gave him a reception. The following morning one of Washington's aides sent a note to James F. Armstrong, governor of New Jersey. It read: 'General Washington cannot leave this place without expressing his acknowledgements to the matrons and young ladies who received him in so novel and grateful a manner at the triumphal arch in Trenton, for the exquisite sensation he experienced in that affecting moment.'

Martha found herself increasingly trapped. 'I think I am more like a state prisoner than anything else, there is certain bounds set for me which I must not depart,' she wrote. The position of First Lady, she wrote, would suit 'many younger and gayer women'. Washington seized every opportunity to meet ladies at the afternoon tea parties the First Lady gave.

In April 1791, Washington made a tour of the southern states. He was much impressed with the women he saw there, recording in his diary that there were 'about seventy' in Newbern, 'sixty-two' in Wilmington and in Charleston 'at least four hundred ladies, the number and appearance of which exceeded anything of the kind I have ever seen'. He later sent his 'grateful respect' to the 'fair compatriots' of Charleston who had so 'flattered him.

During his presidency, Washington had a notably close relationship with a number of women, one of whom was the handsome Henrietta Liston, the Scottish-born wife of Robert Liston, the British ambassador to the United States. She was considerably younger than both her husband and Washington. With her, he opened up as he did with few others.

Another was Elizabeth Willing Powel, the wife of Samuel Powel, the last pre-revolutionary mayor of Philadelphia. They met when he attended the First Continental Congress in 1774. He wrote to her throughout the war and visited her regularly, even though she and her husband were widely suspected of harbouring proBritish sympathies.

She was a striking brunette, attractive, playful and coquettish – a quality Washington loved in women. She fulfilled his craving for approval. He loved to be looked up to by attractive women. She even persuaded him to run for a second term of office, when he had decided to quit. In her letters to him, she teased him about his 'continence to the ladies'. In response, he implied that he would be unconcerned at being caught in adultery. What would worry him more, he said, would be having 'betrayed the confidence of a lady'.

When an epidemic of yellow fever hit Philadelphia in August 1793, Washington urged Eliza Powel and her husband to flee with him to Mount Vernon. When they refused, Washington abandoned his plan and stayed behind too. Samuel Powel came down with the disease and died.

When Washington stepped down in 1797 after two terms as President, he left Philadelphia after a flurry of deeply affectionate letters to Eliza Powel. She addressed him as 'My very dear sir', while he signed himself 'your sincere affectionate friend'.

On moving back to his small house at Mount Vernon, Washington and Martha found themselves with too much furniture. Some of it was put up for sale and Eliza Powel bought a desk. In a drawer, she found a large bundle of what she described as 'love letters to a lady' – though she claimed not to have read them. When she returned them to Washington, he denied that they were letters professing 'enamoured love'. If they had been, he said, they would have been consigned to the flames.

The Washingtons quit public life and 'settled down to the pleasant duties' at Mount Vernon where Martha found herself as 'steady as a clock, busy as a bee, and cheerful as a cricket'. A local landowner asked the retired President: 'What would you have been, if you hadn't married the widow Custis?'

In 1798, a year and a half before his death and twenty-five years after they last met, George Washington wrote to his enduring love Sally Fairfax. Neither the War of Independence nor his Presidency seemed to have done anything to quench his ardour for her. 'None of these events, however, nor all of them together, have been able to eradicate from my mind, the recollection of those happy moments, the happiest in my life, which I have enjoyed in your company,' he wrote. He begged her to return to Virginia now that she was a widow, but the wide Atlantic Ocean stayed between them.

The year after George Fairfax died in 1787, she had written to her sister-in-law, saying: 'I know now that the worthy man is to be preferred to the high-born who has not merit to recommend him...when we enquire into the family of these mighty men we find them the very lowest of people.' And Washington confessed again in a letter to Sally in later life that she was the passion of his youth. She died in 1811. Among her possessions was found Washington's letter regretting the fact that he was going to marry Martha.

Later Washington warned his step-granddaughter: 'In the composition of the human frame there is a great deal of inflammable matter, however dormant it may lie. When the torch is put to it, that which is within you may burst into blaze.' But in marriage, he said, 'the madness ceases and all is quiet again. Why? Not because there is any diminution in the charms of the lady, but because there is an end of hope.'

Meanwhile, he continued his correspondence with Eliza Powel. Eighteen months after retiring, Washington left Martha at Mount Vernon and returned to Philadelphia for a month-long visit. During that period Eliza Powel did not entertain any of her other friends. She took long walks with Washington, including one on a chilly, rainy Sunday. He visited her house on several afternoons and, she let slip in a letter, he breakfasted with her at her house one morning.

Six months on, in 1799, Washington died of a chill. The official story is that he caught cold riding his horse while it was snowing. According to Harvard historian Karal Ann Marling, Washington actually caught his chill jumping out of a back window with his trousers in his hand 'after an assignation with an overseer's wife in the Mount Vernon gardens on a cold afternoon'. While distinguished British historian Arnold Toynbee said Washington contracted his chill 'visiting a slave on his estate.

Washington was buried at Mount Vernon. Martha had the bedroom that they had shared closed off. Then she burnt his letters, including those from Sally Fairfax and Kitty Greene, and prepared to follow him to the grave. But the young United States of America had one more sacrifice to ask of her. In the new Capitol building, a crypt had been constructed where the body of George Washington was to be laid. At the request of Congress, Martha agreed to let his body be moved there, noting: 'I cannot say what a sacrifice of individual feeling I make of a sense of public duty.'

Before he could be shifted, Martha died of a 'severe fever' on 22 May 1802 and the executors of Washington's will refused to let the body be moved. So the crypt in the Capitol lies empty and George and Martha lie side by side at their beloved Mount Vernon.

Although Martha did a thorough job destroying Washington's letters, some emerged in the nineteenth century. According to author Dixon Wechter, the secretary librarian to the financier J.P. Morgan came across a number of 'smutty' letters written by Washington, which he burnt, denying future generations a clear insight into the erotic nature of the founder of the nation.